CHURCH DOGMATICS

For further resources, including the forewords to the original 14-volume edition of the *Church Dogmatics*, log on to our website and sign up for the resources webpage: http://www.continuumbooks.com/dogmatics/

KARL BARTH

CHURCH DOGMATICS

VOLUME I

THE DOCTRINE
OF THE WORD OF GOD

§ 8–12

THE REVELATION OF GOD: THE TRIUNE GOD

EDITED BY
G. W. BROMILEY
T. F. TORRANCE

t & t clark

Published by T&T Clark
A Continuum Imprint
The Tower Building, 11 York Road, London, SE1 7NX
80 Maiden Lane, Suite 704, New York, NY 10038

www.continuumbooks.com

Translated by G. W. Bromiley, G. T. Thomson, Harold Knight

British Library Cataloguing-in-Publication Data
A catalogue record for this book is available from the British Library

ISBN13: 978-0-567-61027-0

Typeset by Interactive Sciences Ltd, Gloucester, and Newgen Imaging Systems Pvt Ltd, Chennai
Printed and bound in Great Britain by CPI Antony Rowe, Chippenham, Wiltshire

PUBLISHER'S PREFACE TO
THE STUDY EDITION

Since the publication of the first English translation of *Church Dogmatics I.1* by Professor Thomson in 1936, T&T Clark has been closely linked with Karl Barth. An authorised translation of the whole of the *Kirchliche Dogmatik* was begun in the 1950s under the editorship of G. W. Bromiley and T. F. Torrance, a work which eventually replaced Professor Thomson's initial translation of *CD I.1*.

T&T Clark is now happy to present to the academic community this new *Study Edition* of the *Church Dogmatics*. Its aim is mainly to make this major work available to a generation of students and scholars with less familiarity with Latin, Greek, and French. For the first time this edition therefore presents the classic text of the translation edited by G. W. Bromiley and T. F. Torrance incorporating translations of the foreign language passages in Editorial Notes on each page.

The main body of the text remains unchanged. Only minor corrections with regard to grammar or spelling have been introduced. The text is presented in a new reader friendly format. We hope that the breakdown of the *Church Dogmatics* into 31 shorter fascicles will make this edition easier to use than its predecessors.

Completely new indexes of names, subjects and scriptural indexes have been created for the individual volumes of the *Study Edition*.

The publishers would like to thank the Center for Barth Studies at Princeton Theological Seminary for supplying a digital edition of the text of the *Church Dogmatics* and translations of the Greek and Latin quotations in the original T&T Clark edition made by Simon Gathercole and Ian McFarland.

London, April 2010

HOW TO USE THIS
STUDY EDITION

The *Study Edition* follows Barth's original volume structure. Individual paragraphs and sections should be easy to locate. A synopsis of the old and new edition can be found on the back cover of each fascicle.

All secondary literature on the *Church Dogmatics* currently refers to the classic 14-volume set (e.g. II.2 p. 520). In order to avoid confusion, we recommend that this practice should be kept for references to this *Study Edition*. The page numbers of the old edition can be found in the margins of this edition.

CONTENTS

§ 8–12

GOD IN HIS REVELATION

God's Word is God Himself in His revelation. For God reveals Himself as the Lord and according to Scripture this signifies for the concept of revelation that God Himself in unimpaired unity yet also in unimpaired distinction is Revealer, Revelation, and Revealedness.

1. THE PLACE OF THE DOCTRINE OF THE TRINITY IN DOGMATICS

If in order to clarify how Church proclamation is to be measured by Holy Scripture we first enquire into the prior concept of revelation, already in this enquiry itself we must keep to Holy Scripture as the witness of revelation. Perhaps more important than anything dogmatics can say with reference to the pre-eminent place of Scripture in the Church and over against the Church is the example which dogmatics itself must give in its own fundamental statements. It must try to do what is undoubtedly required of the Church in general, namely, to pay heed to Scripture, not to allow itself to take its problems from anything else but Scripture. The basic problem with which Scripture faces us in respect of revelation is that the revelation attested in it refuses to be understood as any sort of revelation alongside which there are or may be others. It insists absolutely on being understood in its uniqueness. But this means that it insists absolutely on being understood in terms of its object, God. It is the revelation of Him who is called Yahweh in the Old Testament and θεός EN1 or, concretely, κύριος EN2 in the New Testament. The question of the self-revealing God which thus forces itself upon us as the first question cannot, if we follow the witness of Scripture, be separated in any way from the second [296] question: How does it come about, how is it actual, that this God reveals Himself? Nor can it be separated from the third question: What is the result? What does this event do to the man to whom it happens? Conversely the second and third questions cannot possibly be separated from the first. So impossible is any separation here that the answer to any one of the questions, for all the autonomy and distinctiveness it has and must continue to have as the answer to a particular question, is essentially identical with the answer to the other two. *God* reveals Himself. He reveals Himself *through Himself*. He reveals *Himself*. If we really want to understand revelation in terms of its subject, i.e., God, then

---

EN1 God
EN2 Lord

1

the first thing we have to realise is that this subject, God, the Revealer, is identical with His act in revelation and also identical with its effect. It is from this fact, which in the first instance we are merely indicating, that we learn we must begin the doctrine of revelation with the doctrine of the triune God.

In the first edition of this book (p. 127) I referred to these three questions and then continued with the words: "Logically they are quite simply questions about the subject, predicate and object of the short statement: 'God speaks,' *Deus dixit.*'" On various sides these words have been taken amiss. The serious or mocking charge has been brought against me that here is a grammatical and rationalistic proof of the Trinity, so that I am doing the very thing I attack elsewhere, namely, deriving the mysteries of revelation from the data of a generally discernible truth. Along these lines a doctrine of the Trinity might equally well be constructed on the utterance of the revelation of any other god or supposed god, or even on the statement: "I show myself" (so T. Siegfried, *Das Wort und die Existenz*, 1928, 52). That is to say, words which I can still repeat to-day in due form were then in fact used unguardedly and ambiguously. Attentive and sympathetic readers could see even then, of course, how they were intended. The words were obviously not meant to be a proof themselves. They were simply meant to reduce a completed proof provisionally to a suitable formula which would be as perspicuous as possible. Naturally it was not my thought then, nor is it now, that the truth of the dogma of the Trinity can be derived from the general truth of such a formula. Rather, it is from the truth of the dogma of the Trinity that the truth of such a formula can perhaps be derived in this specific application, namely, to the dogma of the Trinity. We must say "perhaps," for the truth of the dogma of the Trinity does not stand or fall with such a formula. I still fail to see why as a formula it is not a right one for the questions demanded by the matter itself. All dogmatic formulations are rational, and every dogmatic procedure is rational to the degree that in it use is made of general concepts, i.e., of the human *ratio*. It can be called rationalistic, however, only when we can show that the use is not controlled by the question of dogma, i.e., by subordination to Scripture, but by something else, most probably by the principles of some philosophy. If it is clearly understood that dogmatics generally and necessarily involves rational formulation, a rational formulation which is, of course, related to a completed proof and which takes account of Scripture, then no objection can be taken to logical and grammatical formulae as such, for we fail to see why these should be especially suspect any more than certain legal formulae. The only thing is that we must ask whether in a given case they are appropriate to the matter or not, which means, concretely, whether it is an arbitrary anticipation, simplification or even complication to say that what Holy Scripture tells us about the revelation that it attests constrains us to enquire into the subject, predicate and object of the short statement in question, or to say that our attention is drawn to the doctrine of the Trinity by these three questions or the answer to them that we find in Scripture, or to say that in these three questions there is opened up a way, not to prove, but certainly to understand the doctrine of the Trinity. Whether a doctrine of the Trinity might be derived from the statement "I show myself" is something we need not investigate here. But it might be asked especially whether this can be regarded as obligatory and meaningful in the same way as the biblical statement that "God speaks."

[297]

In practice the nature of the biblical answer to the question: Who is God in His revelation? is such as to answer at once the two other questions: What is He doing? and: What does He effect? and to answer them, not just incidentally, not just in such sort that what we hear can be erased the next time these other questions are put, but in such a way that in receiving the answer to the first question we are bound to hear the answer to the others too, so that the first answer is properly heard only when it is heard as given in the other answers. Is this true in regard to other records of revelation too? Possibly so, possibly not; that is not our concern here. It is certainly true in the Holy Scriptures of the Christian Church. The first question that must be answered is: Who is it that reveals Himself here? Who is God here? and then we must ask what He does and thirdly what He effects, accomplishes, creates and gives in His revelation. But if the first question is intelligently put, when it is answered the second and third questions will be answered as well, and only when answers to the second and third questions are received is an answer to the first question really received.

1. The Bible certainly tells us who the God is whom it attests as self-revealing.

It names and describes Him as Elohim (perhaps Him that is to be feared), Yahweh (we shall have to come back specifically to this most important name), El Shaddai (perhaps the All-sufficient), the Lord and Protector of Israel, the Creator of heaven and earth, the Ruler of the world and its history, the Holy and the Merciful and in the New Testament as the Lord of the coming kingdom, the Father in heaven, the Father of Jesus Christ, the Redeemer, the Spirit, love, etc.

2. But does anyone really hear and understand here without also hearing and understanding what is said further about the That and the How of the revelation of this God? That this revelation happened and how it happened is no accident in face of the fact that we are referring specifically to the revelation of this God. In the That and the How of this revelation He also and specifically shows Himself to be this God. Indeed, this God will and can make Himself manifest in no other way than in the That and the How of this revelation. He is completely Himself in this That and How.

This is already true in the Old Testament in view of the fact that here it is on the figures of [298] Moses and the prophets that the reported process of revelation concentrates (they are really not just instruments in God's hand but as such His representatives too, not just witnesses of revealed truth but delegates of the self-revealing God). But already in the Old Testament we must also point to the remarkable figure of the angel of Yahweh who in some places is identical with Yahweh in His acts. The same applies to an even greater extent in the New Testament, where revelation coincides with the manifestation of Jesus Christ. Thus it is in the event of revelation itself that we are now to seek and discern the Revealer.

3. But according to the direction of the whole Bible the question who God is in His revelation is to be answered thirdly with a reference to the men who receive the revelation, with a reference to what the Revealer wills and does with them, to what His revelation achieves in them, to what His being revealed thus signifies for them.

In the Bible revelation is always a history between God and certain men. Here one man is separated and led out into a foreign country like Abraham. There another is called and anointed to be a prophet, a priest, or a king. Here a whole nation is chosen, led, ruled, blessed, disciplined, rejected and adopted again. There faith and obedience are aroused, or

3

there is complete hardening. There a Church is gathered in the light of this whole occurrence, and the kerygma and sacraments are instituted as signs of recollection and expectation, because man is now "in Christ," a future has been won, and along with it a present between the times.

All this, this revealedness of God attested in Scripture, is not just the effect of the Revealer and His revelation, an effect which is simply to be differentiated from these, as indeed it is. It is also the answer to the question: Who reveals Himself? and to the second question: How does He reveal Himself? Thus the man who asks about the God who reveals Himself according to the witness of the Bible must also pay heed to the self-revealing as such and to the men to whom this self-revealing applies.

The fact that in putting the first question we are led on at once to a second and a third is what first brings us close to the problem of the doctrine of the Trinity. Close, for we could not say that these considerations summon us to develop the doctrine of the Trinity. The one thing we now know is that the God who reveals Himself in the Bible must also be known in His revealing and His being revealed if He is to be known. These considerations become significant and indeed decisive in this context only when we go on to make the two statements that follow.

4. The question: Who is the self-revealing God? always receives a full and unrestricted answer also in what we learn about God's self-revealing as such and about His being revealed among men. God Himself is not just Himself. He is also His self-revealing.

[299]   He comes as the angel to Abraham, He speaks through Moses and the prophets. He is in Christ. Revelation in the Bible is not a minus; it is not another over against God. It is the same, the repetition of God. Revelation is indeed God's predicate, but in such a way that this predicate is in every way identical with God Himself.

Again He Himself is not just Himself but also what He creates and achieves in men.

For this reason the Word that the men of the Bible hear and pass on can be called the Word of God even though it is heard by their ears and shaped by their mouths and is indubitably their word. All gifts and graces and also all punishments and judgments in the Bible are significant not for what they are in themselves apart from revelation and apart from Him who reveals Himself but because they are His work on man, and in them He is either near men or far from them, either friend or foe.

Thus it is God Himself, it is the same God in unimpaired unity, who according to the biblical understanding of revelation is the revealing God and the event of revelation and its effect on man.

5. It does not seem possible, nor is any attempt made in the Bible, to dissolve the unity of the self-revealing God, His revelation and His being revealed into a union in which the barriers that separate the above three forms of His divine being in revelation are removed and they are reduced to a synthetic fourth and true reality.

Nowhere in the Bible are we left in any doubt about the fact that without prejudice to His revelation God as God is invisible, i.e., inaccessible to man as such, since in distinction from man He is and continues to be eternal and holy. If this God reveals Himself—and without prejudice to His invisibility He does reveal Himself, He does make Himself accessible to man—He is in revelation after a manner with which His first being can be identified indirectly but not directly, not simply, not by removal of the distinction. The angel of Yahweh in the Old Testament is obviously both identical and not identical with Yahweh Himself. It is quite impossible that the non-identity, too, should not be and remain visible. In the New Testament the names of Father and Son are similarly inexchangeable. But the same applies to the revealedness of God attested in the Bible. If God gives Himself to man, He is still someone other as Giver and as gift. So the names Christ and Spirit or Word and Spirit are inexchangeable.

Thus to the same God who in unimpaired unity is the Revealer, the revelation and the revealedness, there is also ascribed in unimpaired differentiation within Himself this threefold mode of being.

It is only—but very truly—by observing the unity and the differentiation of God in His biblically attested revelation that we are set before the problem of the doctrine of the Trinity.

So once again, and perhaps understandably as the subsequent formulation of something presented by the Bible, it may be said that we stand before the problem that in the statement that God speaks—not in the general statement but in that taken from the Bible—the subject, predicate and object are to be both equated and also differentiated. It is cheap to say that this can also be formulated of the equivalent general statement or of similar statements about some other god or even of the statement: "I show myself." We *can* do all kinds of things. But it is obviously not unimportant here that while we can do many things only theoretically we do not actually do them because there is neither cause nor need to do so. If any one wants to assert that even outside the biblical witness to revelation we are actually and not just potentially brought up against the problem of the doctrine of the Trinity, then if he is to present a substantial objection he must show—by taking it upon himself actually to develop the other doctrine of the Trinity in another dogmatics in another church—that there is cause and need to do what perhaps we only *can* do in relation to these other statements. [300]

If, then, in understanding the concept of revelation it is right to ask first who God is, and if guided by the Bible we have to ask this in the way we have just done briefly, then, in accordance with the question thus disclosed, we have to pursue the answer already disclosed. That is to say, we must first address ourselves, naturally following again the answer just disclosed, i.e., Holy Scripture, to a development of the doctrine of the triune God.

In putting the doctrine of the Trinity at the head of all dogmatics we are adopting a very isolated position from the standpoint of dogmatic history.

Yet not wholly isolated, for in the Middle Ages Peter Lombard in his *Sentences* and Bonaventura in his *Breviloquium* took the same position.

Otherwise it neither has been nor is the custom to give this place to the doctrine of the Trinity. The reason for this strange circumstance can be sought only in the fact that with overwhelming unanimity it has obviously been

5

thought that a certain formally very natural and illuminating scheme of questioning should be followed in which one can and should speak first of Holy Scripture (or in Roman Catholic dogmatics the authority of the teaching office, or in Modernist dogmatics the reality and truth of religion) as the *principium cognoscendi*[EN3] (apart from the actual content of faith), and then that even in the doctrine of God itself one can and should deal first with God's existence, nature and attributes (again apart from the concrete givenness of what Christians call "God").

Even Melanchthon and Calvin, and after them Protestant orthodoxy in both confessions, followed this pattern in a way that was strangely uncritical, and similarly none of the later movements in Roman Catholic and Protestant theology has led to the taking of a different path at this point.

The reason why we diverge from this custom is this. It is hard to see how in relation to Holy Scripture we can say what is distinctive for the holiness of this Scripture if first we do not make it clear (naturally from Holy Scripture itself) who the God is whose revelation makes Scripture holy. It is also hard to see

[301] how what is distinctive for this God can be made clear if, as has constantly happened in Roman Catholic and Protestant dogmatics both old and new, the question who God is, which it is the business of the doctrine of the Trinity to answer, is held in reserve, and the first question to be treated is that of the That and the What of God, as though these could be defined otherwise than on the presupposition of the Who.

At this juncture Calvin himself might be quoted against the procedure adopted by him: *Quomodo enim immensam Dei essentiam ad suum modulum mens humana definiat …? Imo vero, quomodo proprio ductu ad Dei usque substantiam excutiendam penetret …? Quare Deo libenter permittamus sui cognitionem. Ipse enim demum unus, ut inquit Hilarius, idoneus sibi testis est, qui nisi per se cognitus non est. Permittemus autem si et talem concipiemus ipsum qualem se nobis patefacit: nec de ipso aliunde sciscitabimur quam ex eius verbo*[EN4] (*Instit.* I. 13, 21).

There is in fact a serious risk, in the doctrine of Scripture as well as the doctrine of God, that we may lose ourselves in considerations and be driven to conclusions which have nothing whatever to do with the supposed concrete theme of the two doctrines, if we begin by discarding the concreteness as it is manifest in the trinitarian form of the Christian doctrine of God. And the doctrine of the Trinity itself is threatened by the same danger, the danger of irrelevant speculation, if we state it only at a later stage and do not give it the first word as that which gives us information on the concrete and decisive question: Who is God?

[EN3] principle of knowing
[EN4] For how could the human intellect according to its little measure define the immense essence of God? … Even more, how could it by its own leading penetrate to an examination of God's substance? … Therefore we should willingly leave to God the knowing of himself. For in the end he is, as Hilary says, the only fitting witness to himself, who is not known except through himself. And we will leave it to him if we conceive him such as he has disclosed himself to us, and do not inquire about him anywhere else than from his word

1. The Place of the Doctrine of the Trinity in Dogmatics

The common idea that one must follow the far too obvious and illuminating scheme: How do we know God? Does God exist? What is God? and only last of all: Who is our God? is in direct contradiction to the very important declarations that no one can then avoid making, about the actual and comprehensive significance of the doctrine of the Trinity. What we are trying to bring to practical recognition by putting it first is something which has not been concealed in the history of dogmatics and which has often enough been stated very strongly, namely, that this is the point where the basic decision is made whether what is in every respect the very important term "God" is used in Church proclamation in a manner appropriate to the object which is also its norm. The doctrine of the Trinity is what basically distinguishes the Christian doctrine of God as Christian, and therefore what already distinguishes the Christian concept of revelation as Christian, in contrast to all other possible doctrines of God or concepts of revelation. Certainly the decision is repeated at every stage. But it is from this point that it is repeated. This is where it gains its momentum. It is on this basis that it becomes so serious, so simple and at the same time so complicated, as in the last resort it always actually is.

If we do not know God in the way in which He reveals Himself as the One, namely, *distincte in tribus personis*[EN5], the inevitable result is that *nudum et inane duntaxat Dei nomen sine vero Deo in cerebro nostro volitat*[EN6] (Calvin, *Instit.* I, 13, 2). *Quia de Deo sentiendum est sicut se patefecit: Credimus, agnoscimus, confitemur et invocamus tres personas, Patrem, Filium et Spiritum sanctum .... De re summa et excellentissima cum modestia et timore agendum est et attentissimis ac devotis auribus audiendum, ubi quaeritur unitas trinitatis, Patris, Filii et Spiritus sancti. Quia nec periculosius alicubi erratur, nec laborosius quaeritur, nec fructuosius invenitur*[EN7] (M. Chemnitz, *Loci*, 1591, I, 31). *Ignorato vel negato Trinitatis mysterio tota salutis* οἰκονομία *ignoratur vel negatur*[EN8] (J. Gerhard, *Loci*, 1610, III, 1, 7). *Deus Deus esse non potest nisi tres habeat distinctos existendi modos sive personas*[EN9] (B. Keckermann, *Systema S. S. Theol.*, 1611, 20, cited according to H. Heppe, *Dogm. d. ev.-ref. Kirche*, 1861, 86). *Qui non addunt mentionem trium personarum in descriptione Dei, eam nequaquam genuinam aut completam sistunt, quum sine iisdem nondum constet, quisnam sit verus Deus*[EN10] (A. Calov, *Systema loc. theol.*, 1655 f., II, 182, cited according to H. Schmid, *Dogm. d. ev.-luth. Kirche*, 4th edn., 1858, 78). "So long as theism only distinguishes God and the world and never God from God, it is always caught in a relapse or transition to the pantheistic or some other denial of absolute being. There can be full protection against

[302]

[EN5] distinctly in three persons

[EN6] only the bare and empty name of God as far as it applies, [but] without the true God, flutters in our brains

[EN7] Because God is to be thought of as he has revealed himself, [therefore] we believe, acknowledge, confess and invoke three persons, Father, Son, and Holy Spirit ... When the unity of the Trinity, Father, Son, and Holy Spirit, is inquired after, one must treat [this] highest and most excellent subject with modesty and awe, and listen with the most attentive and devout ears. For there is no place where straying is more dangerous, inquiring more laborious, nor finding more fruitful

[EN8] If the mystery of the Trinity is unknown or denied, the whole economy of salvation is unknown or denied

[EN9] God would not be God without having three distinct persons or modes of existing

[EN10] Those who do not include mention of the three persons in a description of God stop at a description that is neither genuine nor complete, since without these, it is not yet clear who the true God is

7

atheism, polytheism, pantheism or dualism only with the doctrine of the Trinity .... Faith in
the eternal, holy love which God is can be achieved in both theory and practice only by
knowledge of the perfect, eternal object of the divine self-knowledge and love, i.e., by the
thought of the Father's love for the only-begotten Son. Finally the full quickening nature
and impartation of God, which is neither a diminution nor a limitation of His being, can be
safeguarded only by the trinitarian doctrine of the Spirit" (C. J. Nitzsch, *System d. christl.
Lehre*, 6th edn., 1851, 188). "With the confession of God's triunity stands or falls the whole
of Christianity, the whole of special revelation. This is the kernel of the Christian faith, the
root of all dogmas, the substance of the new covenant. From this religious, Christian concern the development of the Church's doctrine of the Trinity has sprung. What was really at
issue was not a metaphysical theorem or philosophical speculation but the very heart and
essence of the Christian religion itself. So strongly was this felt that all who still set store by
the name of Christian acknowledge and honour a positive Trinity. In every Christian confession and dogmatics the deepest question is this, how can God be one and yet also three. And
precisely in proportion as this question is answered does Christian truth come either less or
more into its own in all parts of Christian doctrine. In the doctrine of the Trinity beats the
heart of the whole revelation of God for the redemption of mankind" (H. Bavinck,
Gereformeede Dogmatiek, Vol. II, 4th edn., 1918, 346 f.). "The trinitarian name of God
expresses the specifically Christian consciousness of God, and since the consciousness of
God is the basis and content of all faith the trinitarian name of God is the Christian Gospel.
For this reason baptism is in this name" (A. Schlatter, *Das. chr. Dogma*, 2nd edn., 1923, 354).
Even Troeltsch found in the trinitarian formula, naturally according to his own understanding of it, "a brief expression of Christianity as the revelation of God given in Christ and
effective in the Spirit ... the abiding classical formula of Christianity in which the whole
doctrine of the faith can be summed up" (*Glaubenslehre*, 1925, 124). Cf. also Joseph Braun,
S.J., *Handlexikon der kathol. Dogmatik*, 1926, 55: "The doctrine of the Holy Trinity is the basic
dogma of Christianity."

If this or something similar must be said, it is hard to see why it should not
find expression in the external and especially the internal position of the doctrine of the Trinity in dogmatics.

[303]   There is a group of modern dogmaticians who have met this need at least externally by
constructing what they call special dogmatics according to the threefold division of Father,
Son, and Holy Spirit: P. K. Marheineke, *Grundlehren der christl. Dogm. als Wiss.*, 1827; A.
Schweizer, *Glaubenslehre d. ev.-ref. Kirche*, 1844 f. and *Christl. Glaubenslehre nach prot.
Grundsätzen*, 2nd edn., 1877; H. Martensen, *Die chr. Dogm.*, 1856; T. Haering, *Der christl.
Glaube*, 1906; M. Rade, *Glaubenslehre*, 1924 f. Now it is true that the need for this emphasis,
and therefore the constitutive significance of the doctrine of the Trinity, is mostly not very
clear from what the authors say about it in itself and as such. Thus in A. Schweizer it is
obscured by the broadly developed natural theology in Part I, which is put in by force first.
Nor do I know any among those mentioned in whose development of the doctrine, even
though it serves as a framework for the whole, there is any evidence of a material decision
that is significant for this whole. Nevertheless, the choice of this order, irrespective of the
reasons for it, is unmistakably a factual confirmation of the presence and urgency of at least
the problem of the Trinity. The same naturally applies to Schleiermacher too, who could put
the doctrine of the Trinity outside the series of other dogmatic *Loci*[EN11] and use it as a
solemn conclusion to his whole dogmatics. Of course, the fact that Schleiermacher can use

[EN11] topics

his doctrine of the Trinity only as the conclusion to his dogmatics and not equally well as its beginning shows that it does not have constitutive significance for him either, so that here again the fact is more important than the intention or the manner.

In giving this doctrine a place of prominence our concern cannot be merely that it have this place externally but rather that its content be decisive and controlling for the whole of dogmatics. The problem of the Trinity has met us in the question put to the Bible about revelation. When we ask: Who is the self-revealing God? the Bible answers in such a way that we have to reflect on the triunity of God. The two other questions: What does this God do and what does He effect? are also answered primarily, as we have seen, by new answers to the first question: Who is He? The problem of the three answers to these questions—answers which are like and yet different, different and yet like—is the problem of the doctrine of the Trinity. In the first instance the problem of revelation stands or falls with this problem.

Apart from the indicated way by which we have reached it, two mutually related historical facts strengthen us in this conviction that discussion of the doctrine of the Trinity belongs directly to the context of discussion of revelation. The older Protestant orthodox, whether or not they knew what they were saying, could not emphasise enough the character of the Trinity as a mystery or indeed as *the* mystery of the faith. *Mysterium trinitatis neque lumine naturae inveniri, neque lumine gratiae, neque lumine gloriae potest comprehendi ab ulla creatura*[EN12] (H. Alsted, *Theol. scholast.*, 1618, cited according to Heppe, *op. cit.*, p. 86 f.). *Sublimitas tanta est, ut ὑπὲρ νοῦν, ὑπὲρ λόγον καὶ ὑπὲρ πᾶσαν κατάληψιν: Quare ex ratione nec oppugnari nec expugnari, nec demonstrari, sive a priori, sive a posteriori potest aut debet*[EN13] (J. F. König, *Theol. pos. acroam.*, 1664, I, § 78). For this reason, in harmony with the fathers and the mediaeval Schoolmen, they never spoke so impressively as here about the need for revelation as the only source of the knowledge of this mystery that governs all mysteries. And this fits in exactly with the aversion that Modernist Protestantism has had for this very doctrine from the days of Servetus and other anti-Trinitarians of the age of the Reformation. As Schleier- [304] macher very rightly saw and stated, it is distinguished from all other Christian doctrines by the fact that it cannot be made comprehensible as the immediate utterance of Christian self-consciousness. "Or who would assert that the impression made by the divine element in Christ obliges us to think of such an eternal distinction (in the supreme being) as the basis of it (namely, the impression)?" (*Der. chr. Glaube*, § 170, 2). The fact that this theology declares it has no access to the matter from the standpoint of what it understands by revelation we take to be a sign that this matter must be noted and discussed first when it is a question of real revelation.

2. THE ROOT OF THE DOCTRINE OF THE TRINITY

Thus far we have merely established the fact that in enquiring into what Holy Scripture attests as revelation we come up against the doctrine of the

---

[EN12] The mystery of the Trinity cannot be discovered by the light of nature, nor, by the light of grace or the light of glory, can it be comprehended by any creature

[EN13] The loftiness is so great that it is beyond mind, beyond reason, and beyond all comprehension. Therefore it neither can nor should be assailed nor captured nor demonstrated by reason, whether by arguing from first principles or on the basis of experience

Trinity and thus have good reason to turn our attention to this first. We need to examine it at this stage in order to make it clear that the Christian concept of revelation already includes within it the problem of the doctrine of the Trinity, that we cannot analyse the concept without attempting as our first step to bring the doctrine of the Trinity to expression.

According to Scripture God's revelation is God's own direct speech which is not to be distinguished from the act of speaking and therefore is not to be distinguished from God Himself, from the divine I which confronts man in this act in which it says Thou to him. Revelation is *Dei loquentis persona*[EN14].

From the standpoint of the comprehensive concept of God's Word it must be said that here in God's revelation God's Word is identical with God Himself. Among the three forms of the Word of God this can be said unconditionally and with strictest propriety only of revelation. It can be said of Holy Scripture and Church proclamation as well, but not so unconditionally and directly. For if the same can and must be said of them too, we must certainly add that their identity with God is an indirect one. Without wanting to deny or even limit their character as God's Word we must bear in mind that the Word of God is mediated here, first through the human persons of the prophets and apostles who receive it and pass it on, and then through the human persons of its expositors and preachers, so that Holy Scripture and proclamation must always become God's Word in order to be it. If the Word of God is God Himself even in Holy Scripture and Church proclamation, it is because this is so in the revelation to which they bear witness. In understanding God's Word as the Word preached and written, we certainly do not understand it as God's Word to a lesser degree. But we understand the same Word of God in its relation to revelation. On the other hand, when we understand it as revealed, we under-

[305] stand it apart from such relations, or rather as the basis of the relations in which it is also the Word of God. We thus understand it as indistinguishable from the event in virtue of which it is the one Word of God in those relations, and therefore as indistinguishable from God's direct speech and hence from God Himself. It is this that—we do not say distinguishes, since there is no question of higher rank or value—but rather characterises revelation in comparison with Holy Scripture and Church proclamation (cf, on this § 4, 3 and 4).

According to Holy Scripture God's revelation is a ground which has no higher or deeper ground above or below it but is an absolute ground in itself, and therefore for man a court from which there can be no possible appeal to a higher court. Its reality and its truth do not rest on a superior reality and truth. They do not have to be actualised or validated as reality from this or any other point. They are not measured by the reality and truth found at this other point. They are not to be compared with any such nor judged and understood as reality and truth by reference to such. On the contrary, God's revelation has its reality and truth wholly and in every respect—both ontically and

---

[EN14] the person of God speaking

noetically—within itself. Only if one denies it can one ascribe to it another higher or deeper ground or try to understand and accept or reject it from the standpoint of this higher or deeper ground. Obviously even the acceptance of revelation from the standpoint of this different and supposedly higher ground, e.g., an acceptance of revelation in which man first sets his own conscience over it as judge, can only entail the denial of revelation. Revelation is not made real and true by anything else, whether in itself or for us. Both in itself and for us it is real and true through itself. This differentiates it even from the witness which the prophets and apostles and the witness which the expositors and preachers of Scripture bear to it, at any rate to the extent that this witness is considered *per se*. If we can also say that the witness both in itself and for us is grounded through itself, this is in virtue of the fact that this witness does not merely seek to relate itself to revelation but does actually relate itself to it, because revelation has become an event in it. This can happen. And it must happen if Scripture and proclamation are to be God's Word. They must become it. Revelation does not have to become it. The fulness of the original self-existent being of God's Word reposes and lives in it.

For this whole context cf. Eduard Thurneysen, "*Offenbarung in Religionsgeschichte und Bibel*," *Z.d.Z.*, 1928, 453 f. The Old and New Testaments are fully at one in the view that the divine oracles as they went forth to men according to their witness constitute a self-contained *novum*[EN15] over against everything men can say to themselves or to one another. One can either obey or disobey, either believe or not believe, what is called revelation in the Bible—both are possible—but from no other standpoint can one get into a position to see whether it has really happened and its content is true. One cannot produce it oneself, as the priests of Baal wanted to do on Carmel in 1 K. 18. Nor can one control revelation, as was [306] vainly attempted when Jesus was asked for signs. One can only stand within its self-closed circle, or rather one can only move within it or stay and move outside it—the enigmatic yet always uncannily close possibility of the *mysterium iniquitatis*[EN16], "concluded under unbelief" (Rom. 11^{32}). Jesus speaks ὡς ἐξουσίαν ἔχων[EN17], Mt. 7^{29}. What does this mean? The verse goes on, Not as their scribes, i.e., obviously not like those who at best must refer to the higher court of a witness to revelation already present. This is why it is so important for the apostle Paul to have seen and heard the Lord Jesus Himself and not just to be acquainted with Him through the tradition. His apostolate stands or falls with this immediacy to revelation, i.e., with this immediacy of revelation itself. Equally self-grounded and ultimate in authority is what the New Testament especially introduces as the Spirit with His decisions in matters both great and small (down to the route of the apostles' journeys). The man who according to the Bible came to share God's revelation and became obedient to it had no motives or grounds for this, he was not instructed or persuaded, he followed neither his own reason or conscience nor the reason or conscience of other men—all this might also happen, but the Bible has little to say about it and it is not the important thing in this matter. He was simply confronted with this ἐξουσία[EN18] and he bowed to it and not to anyone or anything else. He obeyed a command.

[EN15] new thing
[EN16] mystery of iniquity
[EN17] as one having authority
[EN18] authority

§ 8. *God in His Revelation*

We may sum all this up in the statement that God reveals Himself as the Lord. This statement is to be regarded as an analytical judgment. The distinction between form and content cannot be applied to the biblical concept of revelation. When revelation is an event according to the Bible, there is no second question as to what its content might be. Nor could its content be equally well manifested in another event than this. Although, in keeping with God's riches, revelation is never the same but always new, nevertheless as such it is always in all circumstances the promulgation of the $\beta\alpha\sigma\iota\lambda\epsilon\acute{\iota}\alpha\ \tauο\hat{υ}\ θ\epsilon ο\hat{υ}$, of the lordship of God. And how can the promulgation of this $\beta\alpha\sigma\iota\lambda\epsilon\acute{\iota}\alpha$[EN19] be made except through what we call revelation here? To be Lord means being what God is in His revelation to man. To act as Lord means to act as God in His revelation acts on man. To acquire a Lord is to acquire what man does in God when he receives His revelation—revelation always understood here in the unconditional sense in which it encounters us in the witness of Scripture. All else we know as lordship can only be a copy, and is in reality a sad caricature of this lordship. Without revelation man does not know that there is a Lord, that he, man, has a Lord, and that God is this Lord. Through revelation he does know it. Revelation is the revelation of lordship and therewith it is the revelation of God. For the Godhead of God, what man does not know and God must reveal to him, and according to the witness of Scripture does reveal to him, is lordship. Lordship is present in revelation because its reality and truth are so fully self-grounded, because it does not need any other actualisation or validation than that of its actual occurrence, because it is revelation through itself and not in relation to something else, because it is that self-contained *novum*. Lordship means freedom.

[307] The biblical concept of $\dot{\epsilon}\xi ο\upsilon\sigma\acute{\iota}\alpha$ which we have emphasised above obviously includes both.

Godhead in the Bible means freedom, ontic and noetic autonomy. In the decisions taken in this freedom of God the divinely good becomes event, and truth, righteousness, holiness, and mercy deserve to be called what their names declare because they are real in the freedom of God. It is thus, as One who is free, as the only One who is free, that God has lordship in the Bible. It is thus that He also reveals it. The self-sufficiency or immediacy so characteristic of the biblical revelation is the very thing that characterises it as God's revelation on the one side and as the revelation of lordship on the other. But all this becomes fully characteristic only when we note that what we have here is not an abstract revelation of lordship but a concrete revelation of the Lord, not Godhead (even Godhead understood as freedom) but God Himself, who in this freedom speaks as an I and addresses by a Thou. That this happens is revelation in the Bible and it is thus the revelation of His lordship. By the fact that He speaks as an I and addresses by a Thou God announces His kingdom

---

[EN19] lordship

12

and differentiates this intimation from all speculations about freedom, lordship, or Godhead such as man might perhaps engage in even without revelation. As freedom, lordship and Godhead are real and true in God Himself and only in God Himself, being inaccessible and unknown if God Himself, this I, does not speak and address by a Thou, so, in God Himself, they are the meaning of the event that the Bible calls revelation. That God reveals Himself as the Lord means that He reveals what only He can reveal, Himself. And so, as Himself, He has and exercises His freedom and lordship, He is God, He is the ground without grounds, with whose word and will man can only begin without asking Why, so that in and with this he may receive everything that deserves to be called true and good. It becomes and is true and good through the fact that we receive it from Him, that God, as Himself, is with us, with us as a man who says I and addresses us as Thou is with others, but with us as the One He is, as the Lord, as He who is free. According to the Bible God's being with us is the event of revelation.

The statement, understood thus, that God reveals Himself as the Lord, or what this statement is meant to describe, and therefore revelation itself as attested by Scripture, we call the root of the doctrine of the Trinity.

Generally and provisionally we mean by the doctrine of the Trinity the proposition that He whom the Christian Church calls God and proclaims as God, the God who has revealed Himself according to the witness of Scripture, is the same in unimpaired unity and yet also the same thrice in different ways in unimpaired distinction. Or, in the phraseology of the Church's dogma of the [308] Trinity, the Father, the Son and the Holy Spirit in the biblical witness to revelation are the one God in the unity of their essence, and the one God in the biblical witness to revelation is the Father, the Son and the Holy Spirit in the distinction of His persons.

When we call the statement that God reveals Himself as the Lord, or the revelation denoted by this statement and attested by Scripture, the root of the doctrine of the Trinity, this implies two things.

First, and negatively, the statement or statements about God's Trinity cannot claim to be directly identical with the statement about revelation or with revelation itself. The doctrine of the Trinity is an analysis of this statement, i.e., of what it denotes. The doctrine of the Trinity is a work of the Church, a record of its understanding of the statement or of its object, a record of its knowledge of God or of its battle against error and on behalf of the objectivity of its proclamation, a record of its theology and to that degree of its faith, and only to that extent, only indirectly, a record of revelation. The text of the doctrine of the Trinity, whether we have in view one of its dogmatic formulations by the Church, or our own or some other theologico-dogmatic explication of the Church dogma, is not, then, identical with one part of the text of the biblical witness to revelation. The text of the doctrine of the Trinity is at every point related to texts in the biblical witness to revelation. It also contains certain concepts taken from this text. But it does this in the way an interpretation

13

does. That is to say, it translates and exegetes the text. And this means, e.g., that it makes use of other concepts besides those in the original. The result is that it does not just repeat what is there. To explain what is there it sets something new over against what is there. We have in view this difference from revelation and Scripture, which the Church and theology must be aware of in their own work, when we call our statement about revelation—and already it, too, can be regarded only as an interpretation—merely the root of the doctrine of the Trinity.

Already in the early Church the doctrine of the Trinity was attacked on the ground that it is not biblical, that in the form in which it was formulated by the Church's theology it cannot be read anywhere in the Bible. This is especially true of the crucial terms "essence" and "person" which theology used. But it is also true of the word "Trinity" itself. Now this objection can be raised against every dogma and against theology in general and as such. It would also have to be raised against proclamation, which does not stop at the mere reading of Scripture but goes on to explain it too. Now explanation means repeating in different words what has been said already. The fathers of the Church and the councils, and much later the Reformers in their battle against the new anti-Trinitarians, were naturally well aware that the doctrine of the Trinity is not in the Bible. But they rightly rejected the view that in relation to

[309] the legitimacy. i.e., the biblical Character of a church dogma or theology what counts is *ipsa etiam verba* (i.e., the words of Holy Scripture) *totidem syllabis et literis exprimere*[EN20] (M. Chemnitz, *Loci*, 1591, I, 34). This would be an *iniqua lex*[EN21] for the Church, an arresting of all biblical exposition, whose very essence is *explicare quod Scripturis testatum consignatumque est*[EN22] (Calvin, *Instit.* I, 13, 3). *Si oporteret de Deo dici solum illa secundum vocem quae sacra scriptura de Deo tradit, sequeretur quod nunquam in alia lingua posset aliquis loqui de Deo, nisi in illa in qua prima tradita est scriptura veteris vel novi testamenti. Ad inveniendum autem nova nomina antiquam fidem de Deo significantia coegit necessitas disputandi cum haereticis*[EN23] (Thomas Aquinas, *S. th.* I, *qu.* 29, *art.* 3). Inaccurate explanations of the Bible, made in the speech of a later period, had to be countered in the speech of the same period. There thus arose in every age the task of dogma and dogmatics. This is what gives dogma and dogmatics their own special character as distinct from the Bible. But they are not necessarily on this account unbiblical or contrary to the Bible. As we must admit at once, they find themselves in the same dangerous sphere as the errors which they must repel. But this is no other sphere than that of the *ecclesia militans*[EN24] which seeks to listen to the prophets and apostles but seeks to understand their word in the language of later periods, to understand it aright even at the risk of misunderstanding. *Nec enim Deus frustra donum prophetiae dedit ecclesiae ad interpretandas scripturas, quod inutile sane foret, si rem scripturis traditam nefas esset aliis vocabulis exprimere*[EN25] (F. Turrettini, *Instit. Theol. elenct.*, 1679, I, *L.* 3, *qu.* 23, 23). But even if this objection is to be

---

[EN20] to express even the words themselves in all of their syllables and letters

[EN21] perverse law

[EN22] to explicate what has been witnessed and recorded in the scriptures

[EN23] If it were permitted to speak of God only in accordance with the words which holy scripture provides, it would follow that it would never be possible for anyone to speak of God in a language other that that in which the writings of the Old and New Testaments were handed down. But the necessity of arguing with heretics demands that we find new ways of communicating our ancient faith in God

[EN24] church militant

[EN25] For it was not without purpose that God gave the gift of prophecy to the church for the interpretation of the scriptures, which would in fact be useless if it were not permitted to express the subject matter handed down in the scriptures in other terms

resisted, we should take from it not merely this reminder of the risk of all theology but also with Calvin the insight that in doctrine as such we are always dealing with *impropria loquutio*[EN26] as regards the object, that the explanation as such, in so far as it is different from the text, in so far as it must work with concepts alien to the text, might be gladly "buried" if a right understanding of the text could be assured in some other way. (*Utinam quidem sepulta essent, constaret modo haec inter omnes fides, Patrem et Filium et Spiritum esse unum Deum: nec tamen aut Filium esse Patrem, aut Spiritum Filium …* [EN27] *ib.*, 5.) In contrast it is a confusion of categories as well as a wresting of the facts to think one can achieve this assurance: *Trinitatis dogma non est ecclesiae traditio tantum, sed doctrina in sacris literis expressa*[EN28] (J. Wollebius, *Christ. Theol. Comp.*, 1626, *L.* I, *cap.* 2, *can.* 2, 1).

Secondly, and positively, to call revelation the root of the doctrine of the Trinity is also to say that the statement or statements about the Trinity of God purport to be indirectly, though not directly, identical with the statement about revelation. The newness or otherness with which they stand alongside the first statement (or its content) cannot mean that a first age, which we may call biblical, had faith without revelation or knowledge of the Triune God, that what it meant by the contrast and unity between Yahweh and the angel of Yahweh, between the Father, the Son and the Spirit, was in reality an imperfectly clarified monotheism, a greatly disrupted polytheism or the like, and then there came a second age, let us say that of the early Church, which for various reasons thought it should give to the same faith a trinitarian formulation in the sense of the dogma, and that we now stand in a third age, the modern period, for which the Bible and the dogma are both records of the faith of past ages in face of which we are free to express our own faith either in the same way or not. No, we regard the dogma—with what right and in what sense has still to be shown of course—as a necessary and relevant analysis of revelation, and we thus think that revelation itself is correctly interpreted by the dogma. The Bible can no more contain the dogma of the Trinity explicitly than it can contain other dogmas explicitly. For its witness, which was given in a specific historical situation or in many such, does indeed confront erring humanity generally as the witness to revelation, but it does not confront the specific errors of Church history as such. Its witness as the witness to revelation is not just the record of the faith of a given time. Even as it is this, it is also the authority by which faith must always let itself be measured, and can be measured, irrespective of the difference of times. [310]

There is thus no meaningful way in which one could or can refute Arius or Pelagius, Tridentine Roman Catholicism or Servetus, Schleiermacher or Tillich, directly out of the Bible, as though their errors were already answered there *totidem syllabis et literis*[EN29], chapter

---

[EN26] unsuitable speech

[EN27] Indeed, would that they were buried, if only this faith were established among all, that Father and Son and Spirit are one God, but that nevertheless the Son is not the Father, nor the Spirit the Son …

[EN28] The dogma of the Trinity is not only a tradition of the church, but a doctrine expressed in the holy scriptures

[EN29] in their every syllable and letter

and verse, as though the Word of God had there pronounced on all the specific concerns of different ages and had only to be looked up to produce the proper decision. For dogmatic decision in the specific concerns of different ages one can and must argue from a basis of Scripture that has to be discovered each time afresh if one is not to argue as arbitrarily and untheologically as the adversary would seem to do.

It thus follows that we cannot prove the truth of the dogma that is not as such in the Bible merely from the fact that it is a dogma, but rather from the fact that we can and must regard it as a good interpretation of the Bible. Later we shall have to show why it is that dogmas must be approached with some prejudgment in favour of their truth, with some very real respect for their relative, though not absolute, authority. But this includes rather than excludes the fact that dogmatics has to prove dogma, i.e., to indicate its basis, its root in revelation or in the biblical witness to revelation. If dogma had no such root, if it could be shown that its rise was mostly due to eisegesis rather than exegesis, if, then, it could not be understood as an analysis of revelation, it could not be recognised as dogma.

In this sense we cannot recognise as dogma a whole series of Roman Catholic dogmas, e.g., that of justification coincident with sanctification, or that of Mary, or that of purgatory, or that of the seven sacraments, or that of papal infallibility. As little, naturally, can we recognise as dogma the specific dogmas of Protestant Modernism such as that of the historical development of revelation or that of the continuity between God and man in religions experience. We fail to detect the "root" that these teachings would have to have in revelation or its biblical attestation to be able to be dogmas.

In calling revelation the root of the doctrine of the Trinity we are thus indicating that we do not confuse or equate the biblical witness to God in His revelation with the doctrine of the Trinity, but we do see an authentic and well-established connexion between the two. This obviously means that the doctrine of the Trinity has a wholly actual and not just a historical significance for us and for the dogmatics of our age, even though this is a very different age from that of Arius and Athanasius. In other words, it means that the criticism and correction of Church proclamation must be done to-day, as it was then, in the form of developing the doctrine of the Trinity. It means that the text of the doctrine of the Trinity—naturally in our own exposition, for to abandon exposition would be to abandon the text too—must become for us a commentary that we have to make use of in expounding the Bible and therefore in employing the dogmatic criterion.

[311]

But let us come to the point: The basis or root of the doctrine of the Trinity, if it has one and is thus legitimate dogma—and it does have one and is thus legitimate dogma—lies in revelation.

Qu. 25 of the *Heidelberg Catechism* runs as follows: "Since there is but one divine Being, why namest thou three, Father, Son and Holy Ghost?" The question is taken almost word for word from the *Geneva Catechism* of 1545, where Calvin himself answers it as follows: *Quoniam*

16

2. *The Root of the Doctrine of the Trinity*

in una Dei essentia Patrem intueri nos convenit ... deinde Filium ... postremo Spiritum sanctum[EN30] (K. Müller, *Bekenntnisschr. d. ref. Kirche*, 1903, 118, 25). What is meant by *Quoniam nos convenit*[EN31]? Calvin gives a clearer answer in the *Institutio* (I, 13, 2): *nam ita se praedicat unicum esse, ut distincte in tribus personis considerandum proponat*[EN32]. And the *Heidelberg* formulates its answer accordingly: "Because that God hath thus revealed Himself in His Word, that these three distinct persons are the one true eternal God." Therefore for this reason and to this extent *convenit*[EN33]. We might object at this point that in appealing to revelation Calvin and his followers meant only that like much else the triunity of God is attested in Scripture. But the fact that the introduction of this particular doctrine is established in this singular way would still be very striking. And we may recall at this point the words already quoted from Calvin and others to the effect that for the older Protestants the doctrine of the Trinity was not just one article of faith among others but was the basic answer to the question: Who is God? to which all the other articles are related. In answering this question with the doctrine of revelation as such, we are technically doing something that was not done in this way four hundred years ago. But materially we are not diverging from the intention of that age when we point out that revelation as such, namely, the revelation attested in the Bible, is the basis of the doctrine of the Trinity, or that the doctrine of the Trinity is the appropriate interpretation of this revelation as such.

We are not saying that the doctrine of the Trinity is merely the interpretation of revelation and not also an interpretation of the God who reveals Himself in revelation. This would be nonsensical, for revelation is the self-interpretation of this God. If we are dealing with His revelation, we are dealing with God Himself and not, as Modalists in all ages have thought, with an entity distinct from Him. And it is as an answer to the question of the God who reveals Himself in revelation that the doctrine of the Trinity interests us. This means that it is a constituent part, the decisive part, of the doctrine of God, which is not yet under discussion at this stage. We now anticipate the discussion of this part of the doctrine of God and will later construct whatever else must be developed in this connexion on this presupposition of God's triunity. In a dogmatics of the Christian Church we cannot speak correctly of God's nature and attributes unless it is presupposed that our reference is to God the Father, the Son, and the Holy Spirit. But the fact that the doctrine of the Trinity is the basic presupposition of the doctrine of God too is no obstacle to regarding it already as also and precisely the interpretation of revelation as such. Not as an exhaustive interpretation; to give that we should have to speak not only of the God who reveals Himself but also of the way He does it and the man to whom He does it, and we should thus stand in need of further anticipations from the area of specific doctrines; there are certain parts of christology and pneumatology that we should have to consider. What we do in fact gather from the doctrine of the Trinity is who the God is who reveals

[312]

[EN30] Because it is appropriate for us to see in the one essence of God the Father ... then the Son ... and finally the Holy Spirit

[EN31] Because it is appropriate for us

[EN32] for He proclaims Himself to be one in this way: that He gives Himself to be perceived in three distinct persons

[EN33] it is appropriate

§ 8. *God in His Revelation*

Himself, and this is why we present the doctrine here as an interpretation of revelation. We are not saying, then, that revelation is the basis of the Trinity, as though God were the triune God only in His revelation and only for the sake of His revelation. What we are saying is that revelation is the basis of the doctrine of the Trinity; the doctrine of the Trinity has no other basis apart from this. We arrive at the doctrine of the Trinity by no other way than that of an analysis of the concept of revelation. Conversely, if revelation is to be interpreted aright, it must be interpreted as the basis of the doctrine of the Trinity. The crucial question for the concept of revelation, that of the God who reveals Himself, cannot be answered apart from the answer to this question given in the doctrine of the Trinity. The doctrine of the Trinity is itself the answer that must be given here. When we say, then, that the doctrine of the Trinity is the interpretation of revelation or that revelation is the basis of the doctrine of the Trinity, we find revelation itself attested in Holy Scripture in such a way that in relation to this witness our understanding of revelation, or of the God who reveals Himself, must be the doctrine of the Trinity.

We do not have in view only those passages which in view of their wording one can or should with a high degree of probability regard as explicit references to the doctrine of the Trinity as this rightly arises and is already presented in revelation or in the biblical witness to it. We do not have in view, then, only the passages in which there is plain reference to a unity in trinity or trinity in unity of the self-revealing God.

[313]   In the Old Testament Is. $61^{1f.}$ might be adduced as one such explicit reference. This speaks in one breath both of the Lord Yahweh and also of a bearer of the message of salvation who is anointed by this Lord and on whom the Spirit of this Lord rests. In the New Testament we are naturally thinking in the first instance of the baptismal command in Mt. 28^{19}. Here, no matter to what stratum of the tradition it may belong, the Father, Son and Holy Ghost are not just mentioned expressly and in distinction and even in what became later the classical order, but they are also comprehended in the concept of the divine "name" into which (or into the divine reality denoted by this name) the "nations" are to be baptised. Alongside this verse one might also place Rom. 1^{1-4}, where according to the author the Gospel is εὐαγγέλιον θεοῦ EN34 and according to content it treats of the υἱὸς θεοῦ EN35, while the πνεῦμα ἁγιωσύνης EN36 is mentioned as the factor by which this Son of God was marked off as such in His resurrection and to that extent was instituted (ὁρισθείς) as such (for those to whom He is manifested and who believe in Him). At the climax of the same Epistle we then find (11^{36}) the well-known saying: ἐξ αὐτοῦ καὶ δι᾽ αὐτοῦ καὶ εἰς αὐτὸν τὰ πάντα EN37, on which one should not put the many and serious exegetical and systematic stresses that Wobbermin does (esp. *Systemat. Theol.* III, 1925, 392) since it is definitely not so much a statement about God as rather about the world and its relation to God. But for this reason the saying is the more illuminating for the connexions in which the divine αὐτός EN38

EN34 the gospel of God
EN35 Son of God
EN36 Spirit of holiness
EN37 from him and through him and to him are all things
EN38 self

18

may be seen as three times the same and three times the same in different ways. Nor can the way in which the terms $\theta\epsilon\acute{o}s$, $\kappa\acute{v}\rho\iota os$, $\pi\nu\epsilon\hat{v}\mu a$ [EN39] occur and are used in 2 Thess. 2^{13} be purely fortuitous. (On the other hand the passage 1 Jn. $5^{7F.}$, which was still highly valued in the age of orthodoxy, is in the original form of Spirit, water and blood an interesting testimony to the unity and distinction between Christ and the Spirit, but in the later form of Father, Son and Spirit, in which it enjoyed some publicity and renown, it cannot be used to ascertain New Testament teaching as such.) Alongside these four references we may then set a series of others in which the three appear more or less clearly in the same specific functions but in much varied sequence. Thus according to 1 Pet. 1^2 the election of the saints is grounded in the $\pi\rho\acute{o}\gamma\nu\omega\sigma\iota s$ $\theta\epsilon o\hat{v}$ $\pi a\tau\rho\acute{o}s$ [EN40], worked out in the $\acute{a}\gamma\iota a\sigma\mu\grave{o}s$ $\pi\nu\epsilon\acute{v}\mu a\tau os$ [EN41] and directed $\epsilon\acute{\iota}s$ $\acute{v}\pi a\kappa o\grave{\eta}\nu$ $\kappa a\grave{\iota}$ $\rho a\nu\tau\iota\sigma\mu\grave{o}\nu$ $a\acute{\iota}\mu a\tau os$ $^{\prime}I\eta\sigma o\hat{v}$ $X\rho\iota\sigma\tau o\hat{v}$ [EN42]. Rev. 1^4 tells us that the grace and peace wished for the seven churches come $\acute{a}\pi\grave{o}$ $\acute{o}$ $\grave{\omega}\nu$ $\kappa a\grave{\iota}$ $\acute{o}$ $\grave{\eta}\nu$ $\kappa a\grave{\iota}$ $\acute{o}$ $\acute{\epsilon}\rho\chi\acute{o}\mu\epsilon\nu os$ [EN43] (note how the first and basic concept is here again paradoxically broken into a significant trinity) $\kappa a\grave{\iota}$ $\acute{a}\pi\grave{o}$ $\tau\hat{\omega}\nu$ $\acute{\epsilon}\pi\tau\grave{a}$ $\pi\nu\epsilon\upsilon\mu\acute{a}\tau\omega\nu$ $\grave{a}$ $\acute{\epsilon}\nu\acute{\omega}\pi\iota o\nu$ $\tau o\hat{v}$ $\theta\rho\acute{o}\nu ov$ $a\grave{v}\tau o\hat{v}$ [EN44] (the one Spirit is here obviously meant to be called too the specific Spirit of each of the seven churches) $\kappa a\grave{\iota}$ $\acute{a}\pi\grave{o}$ $^{\prime}I\eta\sigma o\hat{v}$ $X\rho\iota\sigma\tau o\hat{v}$ [EN45] the faithful witness, etc. If in two instances Christ, though certainly important, stands in the third place, in two others He is first. This is so in 2 Cor. 13^{13}, where the so-called apostolic blessing ascribes grace to Jesus Christ, love to the Father and $\kappa o\iota\nu\omega\nu\acute{\iota}a$ [EN46] to the Holy Ghost, and then in Mk. $1^{9F.}$, where it is on Jesus as the main subject of the baptism story that the Holy Spirit descends, whereupon a voice from heaven confirms His divine sonship. (Cf. on this F. Turrettini, *Instit. Theol. elenct.*, 1679, I, *Loc. 3, Qu. 25, 7: Alius auditur, sed nec videtur, nec descendit. Alius non auditur, sed visibili specie descendit. Alius descendit et ascendit e flumine baptizatus in conspectu omnium* [EN47].) Again there are passages in which the Holy Spirit is named as the first and in the context the most notable member of the Trinity. Thus in Jud. 20–21 the Father and the $\kappa\acute{v}\rho\iota os$ $^{\prime}I\eta\sigma o\hat{v}s$ $X\rho\iota\sigma\tau\acute{o}s$ [EN48] follow the Holy Spirit and in 1 Cor. $12^{4F.}$ and Eph. $4^{4F.}$ the classical order of Father, Son, and Holy Ghost is reversed, and another special feature in these two passages is the stress on unity in the $a\grave{v}\tau\acute{o}s$ or $\epsilon\acute{\iota}s$ [EN49] with which the three terms are introduced.

We have agreed that we need not expect to find the doctrine of the Trinity [314] expressly in the Old Testament or the New. But in view of the presence of these explicit references we cannot deny that the problems that developed later in the doctrine of the Trinity are not alien to the Bible but are at least prefigured in it. And the explicit indication of the doctrine is given added weight by the fact that it is enveloped in a whole net of implicit references and especially by the fact that the whole theme of God's revelation as it is treated in the Old and

---

[EN39] God, Lord, Spirit
[EN40] foreknowledge of God the Father
[EN41] sanctification of the Spirit
[EN42] to obedience and sprinkling of the blood of Jesus Christ
[EN43] from him who is and who was and who is to come
[EN44] and from the seven spirits which are before his throne
[EN45] and from Jesus Christ
[EN46] communion
[EN47] One is heard, but is not seen and does not descend. Another is not heard, but descends in visible form. Another descends and ascends from the river baptised in the sight of all
[EN48] Lord Jesus Christ
[EN49] he or one

New Testaments, with its focus on the New, cannot be discussed, let alone grasped, without encountering the prefiguration of these problems. This is what we have now to show.

God reveals Himself as the Lord; in this statement we have summed up our understanding of the form and content of the biblical revelation. The question now is whether we must take this statement in a threefold sense without infringing the unity of its content or whether we must take it in its unified content without infringing its threefold sense. If this statement demands this understanding, not in any general signification but in relation to what the Bible calls revelation, then we see something that can only be conjectured as highly probable on the basis of the passages adduced, namely, that this statement is in fact the "root" of the doctrine of the Trinity, that the problems of the doctrine of the Trinity are in fact prefigured in revelation as it is attested in the Bible. And now we are no longer following the schema of subject, predicate, object (revealer, revelation, revealing), which was only designed to show to what extent we are in fact led by revelation itself to the problem of triunity. Or rather, we now dissolve this scheme—which still has and retains its significance—in the manner suited to the concrete form of revelation on the one side and the doctrine of the Trinity on the other. The question of revealer, revelation and being revealed corresponds to the logical and material order both of biblical revelation and also of the doctrine of the Trinity. We shall thus return to this order when the latter is developed. But we must now follow another order if we are to see how biblical revelation and the doctrine of the Trinity are interconnected, how the second could and did proceed out of the first. This is a historical question which has as such its own special form. But it is governed by the fact that biblical revelation has on the one side a specific historical centre and the doctrine of the Trinity has on the other side a specific historical occasion in biblical revelation. Historically considered and stated the three questions answered in the Bible, that of revealer, revelation and being revealed, do not have the same importance. The true theme of the biblical witness is the second of the concepts, God's action in His revelation, reve-

[315] lation in answer to the question what God does, and therefore the predicate in our statement. Within this theme the two other questions, materially no less important, are answered. Similarly the doctrine of the Trinity, when considered historically in its origin and development, is not equally interested in the Father, the Son and the Holy Ghost. Here too the theme is primarily the second person of the Trinity, God the Son, the deity of Christ.

In dogmatic history this is the insight which Harnack (*Lehrb. d. Dogmengesch.*, 4th edn., 1909, Vol. I, 90) formulated in the sentence: "Confession of the Father, the Son and the Spirit ... is a development of the belief that Jesus is the Christ." O. Scheel (*RGG*[2] Art. "*Dreieinigkeit*," III) is in material agreement : "The history of the doctrine of the Trinity is primarily a history of the Logos concept in Christianity." This is the same insight as that which Irenaeus already developed in relation to the name of Christ and with appeal to Is.

2. *The Root of the Doctrine of the Trinity*

61[1]: *In Christi enim nomine subauditur qui unxit et ipse qui unctus est et ipsa unctio in qua unctus est. Et unxit quidem Pater, unctus vero est Filius in Spiritu qui est unctio*[EN50] (*C. o. h.* III, 18, 3).

Within this framework of the question of Christ's deity, but claiming equal weight both logically and materially, the other two questions then arose in the first instance as a necessary counterpart to the question of the Son, namely, the question of the Father on the one side and that of the Spirit of the Father and the Son on the other.

If this was so necessary and right, we should have to say that in the order in 2 Cor. 13[13], that of Christ, God, and Spirit, we have the most authentic form of the biblical witness in this matter. At any rate, the historical development of the doctrine of the Trinity out of the witness to revelation followed this route, and this is the route we must now take.

1. Revelation in the Bible means the self-unveiling, imparted to men, of the God who by nature cannot be unveiled to men. The element of self-unveiling in this definition may be described as the historical if not the logical or material centre of the biblical revelation. When the Bible speaks of revelation, it does so in the form of the record of a history or a series of histories. The content of this history or of each of these histories, however, is that self-unveiling of God. But as the record is given, our experience also is, of course, that the One who thus unveils Himself is the God who by nature cannot be unveiled to men, and that this self-unveiling is to specific men. Logically and materially this is just as important as the recorded self-unveiling. Historically the latter constitutes the centre. But what does self-unveiling mean here? Since the One who unveils Himself is the God who by nature cannot be unveiled to men, self-unveiling means that God does what men themselves cannot do in any sense or in any way: He makes Himself present, known and significant to them as God. In the historical life of men He takes up a place, and a very specific place at that, and makes Himself the object of human contemplation, human experience, human thought and human speech. He makes Himself an authority and factor, a concrete authority and historical factor, a significant and effective element of human life in time and in historical relations. He Himself, as God, exists for men exactly as other things or persons exist for them, as Esau did for Jacob, Mount Horeb or the ark of the covenant for Israel, John for Peter or Paul for his churches. He naturally does so in His own special form which cannot be mistaken for any other. But He does so truly and concretely, so that the men concerned can say without any speculation or metaphor: Immanuel, God with us! so that without any fiction or self-deception they can say Thou to Him and pray to Him. This is what self-revelation is. This is what man cannot provide for himself, what only God can give him, what He does give him in His revelation. The concept of form is the concept we must

[316]

EN50 For in the name of Christ there may be understood to be included the one who anointed and the one who was himself anointed and the unguent with which he was anointed. Now the Father anointed and the Son was anointed in the Spirit, who is the unguent

single out from what has been said as the decisive one. No matter who or what else the self-revealing God may be, it is beyond dispute that in His revelation according to the biblical witness He takes form, and this taking form is His self-unveiling. It is not impossible nor is it too petty a thing for Him to be His own *alter ego* in His revelation. His *alter ego* to the extent that His self-unveiling, His taking form, obviously cannot be taken for granted but is an event, and an event that cannot be explained by or derived from either the will or act of man or the course of the world at large; to the extent that He Himself must take a step towards this event; to the extent that this step obviously means something new in God, a self-distinction of God from Himself, a being of God in a mode of being that is different from though not subordinate to His first and hidden mode of being as God, in a mode of being, of course, in which He can also exist for us. The God who reveals Himself here can reveal Himself. The very fact of revelation tells us that it is proper to Him to distinguish Himself from Himself, i.e., to be God in Himself and in concealment, and yet at the same time to be God a second time in a very different way, namely, in manifestation, i.e., in the form of something He Himself is not.

To be God a second time in a very different way—this may be seen in the Old Testament primarily in the fact that almost all the attributes that characterise the Yahweh of Israel, His righteousness with which He watches over His covenant with Israel, His goodness and faithfulness to His own, His glory and also His Word and Spirit, the wisdom of the later Old Testament, and the countenance which is anthropomorphically—or should we say not at all anthropomorphically—ascribed to Him, His arm, His hand, His right hand, all these are sometimes referred to as though they were not just in or of Yahweh but were Yahweh Himself a second time in another way. Revelation means that all these human, all too human concepts are not just that, are not just descriptions and representations of the reality of Yahweh; they are themselves the reality of Yahweh. In these concepts, and therefore in the sphere, physical as well as intellectual, of men who are truly different from Himself, Yahweh has what [317] we have called form. In them all Yahweh Himself is there; He subsists; He has objectivity for those to whom He is manifest. Religious science usually defines concepts used in this way as hypostases, i.e., realities of the one God which are both distinguishable and yet also indistinguishable from Him. And why should we not accept this definition? Religious science for its part has obviously borrowed it from the history of Christian dogma. Now the fact is that in this series of hypostases there is one that stands out in a significant and, if appearances do not deceive, a comprehensive way as the epitome of what God is a second time in another way in His self-unveiling. This is the concept of the name of God. Knowledge, love, fear, trust, hope, praise, preaching, invocation are all related continually to this apparent sub-centre alongside Yahweh and yet even so they are unmistakably connected to Yahweh Himself. The righteous man thinks, speaks and acts in this name when he stands before Yahweh, under His protection and blessing. To this name of Yahweh, not to the One who dwells in Sinai or according to the later view in heaven, a house or temple is built in Jerusalem. Conversely this name is the court for whose sake Yahweh forgives and is gracious and guides and does not forsake Israel; His name dwells indeed, as Yahweh chose, in Jerusalem. But the angel of Yahweh, who is frequently mentioned, also stands in the closest connexion to the name of Yahweh. What makes Him the angel of Yahweh according to Ex. 23[21], and what gives Him authority as such, is that "my name is in him." In His name is concentrated everything He is in His relation to His people, to the righteous, and from His name proceeds in some way everything that the people or the righteous can expect from Him as they stand in this relation. What does all this mean? Not for the old Testament alone but for ancient thought generally, and perhaps for what is called primitive thought (though it is not really primitive), a man's name is not something that comes to him from without, something accidental and non-essential, a mere *nomen* in the sense of the mediaeval debates. At this point, and perhaps only at this point in distinction from the attributes mentioned earlier, the name is a being, belonging of course to another being, identical with it in a way one cannot explain, yet still a separate being, so that statements about the name and him who bears it can be differentiated from and yet can also replace one another "Where the name is, there is the bearer of the name; where the name works, the bearer of it works" (Hans Schmidt, *RGG²*, Art. "*Namensglaube*," I). When the Old Testament applies this realistic view of the name to Yahweh, this means on the one side that it distinguishes between Yahweh who dwells on Sinai or in heaven and Yahweh who dwells in Canaan, Shiloh, and later Jerusalem, between Yahweh in His hiddenness and Yahweh in His historical form in which, as the fact that His name is given shows, He is known in Israel and has dealings with Israel. "God's name is an expression for His personal essence as present in the sanctuary and people" (O. Procksch in G. Kittel, *TWNT*, Vol. I, Art. ἅγιος, p. 90 (*TDNT*, 91)). But it also means on the other side that the Old Testament does not pretend to knowledge of two or many gods. It knows only one God. The hidden Yahweh Himself is present in His name and all the predicates of the name are those of the hidden Yahweh Himself. Nevertheless, it knows the one God a first time and then a second time in a very different way. And for Israel or the righteous everything depends on knowing Him thus, this second time in a very different way. For the Yahweh who exists this second time in a very different way, the name of Yahweh, is the form in which Yahweh comes to Israel, has dealings with it, is manifest to it. Therefore the decisive act of revelation by which Israel is chosen as Israel and becomes the people of this God is the revelation of the name of God. It is significant enough that this revelation of the name (Ex. 3[13f.]) is in fact, in content, the refusal to give a name, for "I am that I am" can hardly mean more than that "I am He whose true name no one can utter." By its very wording the revealed name is intended to recall the hiddenness even of the revealed God. But under this name, which in itself and as such pronounces His mystery, God does reveal Himself to His people, i.e., He begins, as Ex. 3 instructively shows, to have dealings with Israel through the announcing by Moses of its deliverance out of Egypt. From this standpoint one must add to the concept of the name of God that of the covenant, which belongs to a very different plane, if one is to see fully what the form of God, and to that degree His being in concealment, signifies in the Old Testament. In covenant with this people—"I will be their God and they shall be my people" (Jer. 31[33])—the name of God is actualised. i.e., in the covenant with its divine promise and claim, with its record deposited in the Law, everything takes place that does take place through the name of Yahweh. In the language of our historians, "the thought of the covenant is the form in which is clothed Israel's consciousness of the relation with this God made in history and also of that which is divinely willed in this relation" (J. Hempel, *RGG²*, Art. "*Bund*," II, A). To have knowledge of the name of Yahweh, and to that degree knowledge of Yahweh Himself, and to participate in His revelation, is to be a partner in the covenant made by Him. Yahweh is thus God a second time in a very different way in the fact that He elects a people, makes it His people and rules it as His people.

[318]

It is now relatively simple to see the fundamental concern in the New Testament. God a second time in a different way is obviously the point here too, but in a manner incomparably more direct, unequivocal and palpable. It is so much more direct that even the hypostases of the Old Testament are weak in comparison; to use the well-known metaphor of Hebrews, they appear only as shadows. It is so much the more direct that especially the notable position and significance of the name of Yahweh may be regarded quite simply and yet at the same time quite meaningfully, as the Church has always maintained against Judaism even if only from this standpoint, as a prophecy of the fulfilment present here. Into the place, not of Yahweh on Sinai or in heaven, but of the name of the Lord which finally dwells very really in a house of stone in Jerusalem, there now comes the existence of the man Jesus of Nazareth. At one of the high points of the New Testament message He is called" my Lord and my God" (Jn. 20^{28}). The remote but ever near and actual background is here again the God who has no historical form, the "Father in heaven." But the Jesus of the New Testament calls precisely this God not merely the Father who has sent Him but very emphatically my Father alongside whom He may place Himself, or knows that He is placed, as He lives as man among men, as He does the Father's will, i.e., as He reveals Him, the Father, from whom He is separated not by anything essential but simply by this form of His as man, i.e., by the possibility of being God in this form. Inalienably important as this background is, little as it can be thought away even for a single moment, the picture which the New Testament itself sets before us is that of the self-disclosure of this Father in which He is not the Father but the Son, the historical figure of this Man on His way from Bethlehem to Golgotha, the "name" of Jesus. Again, the concreteness and actuality of the self-unveiling of God for man, and the enigma of the self-distinction in God Himself which makes this self-unveiling possible, has not just increased quantitatively here in comparison with the Old Testament. Is not perhaps every purely speculative or figurative or fictitious understanding of the real objectification of God in His revelation ruled out for the first time here? Is not the question of faith in revelation, of acceptance of the God with us, put for the first time here in such a way that it demands decision—here where in place of the invisible form of the name of the revealed God, which is real only in the sphere of human conception, there has now entered the unique, contin-

[319] gent, somatic, human existence of Jesus? Has not the rejection of Jesus by the Jews made it shatteringly clear that it was possible to accept the God of the Old Testament in what seemed to be the most profound reverence and the most zealous faith and yet in fact to deny Him to the extent that His form, now become quite concrete, became an offence to the righteous? Or what other objection could Israel bring against Jesus apart from the divine self-unveiling which now, not for the first time, but for the first time quite unequivocally, encountered it, making, as it were, bodily contact with it? In thinking that it has to defend against Jesus as against a blasphemer the name of God dwelling in the house of stone in Jerusalem, it denies this very name, and thus separates itself from it and from its own Holy Scripture, which is one long witness to this name as God's real presence and action in the human sphere. This presence and action of God Israel declines. Why is it that the Lord's Prayer in the New Testament begins in the style of the Old Testament: "Hallowed by thy name!"? How else could it begin? one might almost reply. This is the whole point with Jesus. His concern is not with something new but with that which is first and primal, with the God who wills to be God and to be known as God a second time in a different way, the God of Abraham, Isaac and Jacob, the God who wills to be revealed in His name and hallowed in His name. This is why, in explanation of the first petition, the Lord's Prayer continues at once: "Thy kingdom come! Thy will be done, as in heaven, so (N.B.) on earth!" This καὶ ἐπὶ γῆς [EN51] was the self-unveiling, the form of God which Israel found attested in its Holy Scripture on every page and which now, when it stood fulfilled before it, it denied again just as the fathers in the desert had murmured against Moses and later the prophets had been stoned, not out of irreligion, but in the protest of the most refined and most ponderable religion against revelation, which will not leave even or especially the righteous man alone but literally confronts him with God. Thus the revelation in Jesus ends with His crucifixion by the most pious men of their time, who even though they had Immanuel daily on their lips and in their hearts did

---

[EN51] so on earth

not want this Immanuel in its unconditionally enacted fulfilment. But just because Immanuel had been unconditionally fulfilled in Jesus the crucifixion of Jesus was bound to mean something different from the stoning of even the greatest prophets, namely, the end of the history of Israel as the special people of revelation, the destruction of the house of stone as the dwelling of the name of the Lord, the free proclamation, not of a new Gospel but of the one ancient Gospel to both Jews and Gentiles. As the Word became Flesh: λόγος συντελῶν EN52, bringing fully to light what revelation in the Old Testament had always brought to light only in the form of a pointer, it had also to become λόγος συντέμνων EN53, the dissolution of this revelation and its written testimony, not their contradiction, abolition, or destruction, but their dissolution into itself, just as the early light of dawn disappears in the brightness of the rising sun itself (Rom. 9²⁸): Christ the τέλος EN54 of the Law (Rom. 10⁴). We see here the theme of the great battle which Paul above all others fought at the rise of the Church. It was not a battle against the Old Testament, but like the battle of Jesus Christ Himself, to whom he simply wished to testify, it was a battle for the Old Testament, i.e., for the one eternal covenant of God with men sealed in time, for acknowledgment of the perfect self-unveiling of God.

That God is capable of what the Bible ascribes to Him in its accounts of what happened from the patriarchs by way of Moses and the prophets to Golgotha and on to Easter and Pentecost; that God can be made manifest to men in the strictly real sense, as one may finally see in the revelation in Jesus, i.e., that God can become unlike Himself in such a way that He is not tied to His secret eternity and eternal secrecy but can and will and does in fact take temporal form as well; the fact that God can and will and actually does do this we now understand as a confirmation of our first statement that God reveals Himself as the Lord. To all talk of other revelations apart from that attested in the Bible our primary question must be whether the reference there too is to an authentic assumption of form by the Godhead over against man, and not perhaps to mere appearances for which identity with the Godhead cannot be seriously claimed but only a certain participation in it. A second question must then be whether the lordship which is perhaps ascribed to the Godhead there too is also seen there in this intrinsic freedom of God, i.e., the freedom to be unlike Himself. When these questions cannot be answered in the affirmative, or to the extent that they cannot be answered thus with certainty, one should at least exercise great caution in inserting the biblical revelation into the series of other revelations. But be that as it may, the lordship discernible in the biblical revelation consists in the freedom of God to differentiate Himself from Himself, to become unlike Himself and yet to remain the same, to be indeed the one God like Himself and to exist as the one sole God in the fact that in this way that is so inconceivably profound He differentiates Himself from Himself, being not only God the Father but also—in this direction this is the comprehensive meaning of the whole of the biblical witness—God the Son. That He

[320]

EN52 word that brings to completion
EN53 word that cuts off
EN54 end

reveals Himself as the Son is what is primarily meant when we say that He reveals Himself as the Lord. This Sonship is God's lordship in His revelation.

2. Revelation in the Bible means the self-unveiling, imparted to men, of the God who by nature cannot be unveiled to men. We now emphasise the second part of the saying and in so doing we return to the subject of revelation. The revelation attested in the Bible is the revelation of the God who by nature cannot be unveiled to men. There are other things and even other gods that are inscrutable to man. That is, man does not in fact have any experience or concept of them. Yet he might very well have some experience or concept of them, so that their inscrutability is only factual. Some day it might be set aside by another fact, since it is not grounded in the nature of the matter or the god in question. But inscrutability, hiddenness, is of the very essence of Him who is called God in the Bible. As Creator, this God is different from the world, i.e., as the One He is, He does not belong to the sphere of what man as a creature can know directly. Nor can He be unveilable for man indirectly in the created world, for He is the Holy One to see whom, even indirectly, other eyes are needed than these eyes of ours which are corrupted by sin. And finally this God by His grace, i.e., by His self-unveiling, says to everyone to whom it is [321] imparted that of himself he could not do what is there done to him and for him. It is thus of the very nature of this God to be inscrutable to man. In saying this we naturally mean that in His revealed nature He is thus inscrutable. It is the *Deus revelatus*[EN55] who is the *Deus absconditus*[EN56], the God to whom there is no path nor bridge, concerning whom we could not say nor have to say a single word if He did not of His own initiative meet us as the *Deus revelatus*. Only when we have grasped this as the meaning of the Bible do we see the full range of its statement that God reveals Himself, i.e., that He has assumed form for our sake. We cannot withdraw one iota from our previous interpretation of revelation, namely, that it consists in God having assumed form. To deny that is to deny revelation itself. But the fact that it is the God who by nature cannot be unveiled to man that reveals Himself there has distinct significance for our understanding of His self-unveiling. It necessarily means that even in the form He assumes when He reveals Himself God is free to reveal Himself or not to reveal Himself. In other words, we can regard His self-unveiling in every instance only as His act in which He reveals Himself to a man who is unable to unveil Him, showing Himself indeed in a specific form, but still unveiling Himself. Revelation always means revealing even in the form or means of revelation. The form as such, the means, does not take God's place. It is not the form, but God in the form, that reveals, speaks, comforts, works and aids. The fact that God takes form does not give rise to a medium, a third thing between God and man, a reality distinct from God that is as such the subject of revelation. This would imply that God would be unveilable for men, that God Him-

---

EN55 revealed God
EN56 hidden God

self would no longer need His revelation, or rather that God would be given up into the hands of man, who, God's form being given him, could more or less control God as he does other realities. The fact that God takes form means that God Himself controls not only man but also the form in which He encounters man. God's presence is always God's decision to be present. The divine Word is the divine speaking. The divine gift is the divine giving. God's self-unveiling remains an act of sovereign divine freedom. To one man it can be what the Word says and to another true divine concealment. To the same man it may be the former to-day and the latter to-morrow. In it God cannot be grasped by man or confiscated or put to work. To count on it is to count on God's free loving-kindness, not on a credit granted once and for all, not on an axiom to which one may have recourse once and for all, not on an experience one has had once and for all. If this were so, the revelation in question would not be that of the God who by nature cannot be unveiled to man. We should simply have one of those mysteries that one day unveil themselves to us and are mysteries no more. The mysteries of the world are of such a kind that some day they can cease to be mysteries. God is always a mystery. Revelation is always [322] revelation in the full sense of the word or it is not revelation, or at any rate not what is called revelation in the Bible.

We have already noted the remarkable circumstance that the great revelation of the name in Ex. 3 according to the most likely interpretation of the text consists precisely in the refusal to give a name. "Wherefore askest thou after my name, seeing it is wonderful?" is also the answer of the angel of the Lord to Manoah in Jud. 13[18], cf. Gen. 32[30]. In revelation there is no delivering up of God to man such as a knowledge of His true name would imply. Revelation itself is to be understood, and to continue to be understood, as the revelation of the free loving-kindness of God. This reserve of Yahweh, His concealment even in His revelation, is also indicated by the urgent warning in Ex. 3: "Draw not nigh hither; put off they shoes from off thy feet, for the place whereon thou standest is holy ground." Similarly and more generally the concept of God's holiness in the Old Testament bears no relation to speculation about the transcendent God but belongs strictly to His immanence, i.e., to His revelation. His name. In the Old Testament everything is holy that is connected with what we call the form of God in His revelation, with what in this connexion and because of it demands another attitude from man than the profane world in whose sphere and environment it may be seen and heard as the form of God, a discerning, reserved and utterly reverent attitude, an attitude in which man has to set aside all self-assertion or clumsy interference—one has only to think of the unfortunate experiences that could be had by meddling with the ark of the covenant. Everything the Old Testament says about God's self-unveiling stands *eo ipso* under what seems to be the very opposite sign as well: "Am I a God at hand, saith the Lord, and not (also) a God afar off?" (Jer. 23[23]). In Mal. 3[1] the angel of the covenant is Himself expressly called the Lord, though this does not prevent Him from also being sent by the Lord. In Is. 6 the manifest God whose mere train fills the temple is holy, while He Himself sits on a high and lofty throne, incomprehensible to the prophet and the people, even as He turns to them with His revelation. God is holy, and what is connected with Him is holy, because and in so far as God, even in disclosing and imparting Himself, also draws and establishes the boundary which separates man from Him and which man, therefore, may not cross. Holiness is the separation in which God is God and in which, as God, He goes His own way even and precisely as He is "God with us." It is the reserving of His gracious or non-gracious decision with which one must always reckon in relation to Him and in virtue of which He must always be sought afresh and always with the same humility. Holiness also has unquestionably the meaning of strange; God comes to men, but not to be at home with them. This God is not only a God of action, as the founding of the Sabbath tells us with special beauty. He can not only work; He can also rest from all His works. Even as He enters the sphere of our existence, He still inhabits and asserts the sphere which is proper to Him and to Him alone. In relation to this God, as one may gather from the attitude of the prophets and especially the psalmists, we are always dealing with the totality, and the history of His acts is a history of ever renewed beginnings. Of course there is and ought to be a tradition of revelation, an institutional cultus, but over against it in the sharpest dialectic stands prophetism, always ready and armed thoroughly to unsettle afresh everything that wants to settle down, and to set afresh before the mystery of Yahweh everything that wants to clarify itself in human, in only too human fashion. From this standpoint the sharpness of the prohibition of images is to be seen as a ban not so much on the enjoyment of the senses as on the pious obtrusiveness and cocksureness of the religion of Canaan. One cannot stress enough that

[323]

this concealment of God in the Old Testament is never a matter of esoteric metaphysics, that it rather is and always continues to be supremely practical, because it is the concealment of the revealed and active God. But the very fact that this God can be seen and heard only as the active God, and never (or only *per nefas*[EN57]) as comprised and enveloped in a medium, is guaranteed by His concealment, by His incomprehensibility.

This relation is not altered in the New Testament either. On the contrary, it is now supremely true that God conceals Himself in revealing Himself, that even and precisely in assuming form He remains free to become manifest or not to become manifest in this form. The form here is that of the *humanitas Christi*[EN58]. And this brings us up against one of the hardest problems of Christology that will claim our attention more than once: Can the incarnation of the Word according to the biblical witnesses mean that the existence of the man Jesus of Nazareth was as it were in itself, in its own power and continuity, the revealing Word of God? Is the *humanitas Christi* as such the revelation? Does the divine sonship of Jesus Christ mean that God's revealing has now been transmitted as it were to the existence of the man Jesus of Nazareth, that this has thus become identical with it? At this stage we can only reply that when this view has really been held, there has always been more of less clearly discernible the very thing which, as we have seen, the Old Testament tried to avoid with its concept of the holiness of the revealed God, namely, the possibility of having God disclose Himself through man, of allowing man to set himself on the same platform as God, to grasp Him there and thus to become His master. The "fairest Lord Jesus" of mysticism, the "Saviour" of Pietism, Jesus the teacher of wisdom and friend of man in the Enlightenment, Jesus the quintessence of enhanced humanity in Schleiermacher, Jesus the embodiment of the idea of religion in Hegel and his school, Jesus a religious personality according to Carlyle's picture in the theology of the end of the 19th century—all this looks at least very dubiously like a profane and sacrilegious intrusion in the Old Testament sense in which it is thought possible to come to terms, as it were, with the presence of God in Christ and to take control of it with the help of certain conceptions deriving from the humanity. From the fact that such attempts at secularisation were not made in the New Testament we may see that here even Christ's humanity stands under the caveat of God's holiness, i.e., that the power and continuity in which the man Jesus of Nazareth was in fact the revealed Word according to the witness of the Evangelists and apostles consisted here too in the power and continuity of the divine action in this form and not in the continuity of this form as such. As a matter of

---

[EN57] wrongly
[EN58] humanity of Christ

28

fact even Jesus did not become revelation to all who met Him but only to a few. Even these few could also deny and leave Him and one of them could be His betrayer. Revealing could obviously not be ascribed to His existence as such. His existence as such is indeed given up to death, and it is in this way, from death, from this frontier, since the Crucified was raised again, that He is manifested as the Son of God. Nor is His resurrection described as an operation proper to the *humanitas Christi* but rather as something done to it, as a being raised from the dead by God (frequently, cf. Gal. 1¹; Rom. 6⁴; Eph. 1²⁰ expressly by God the Father). To use the language of a later age, the Godhead is not so immanent in Christ's humanity that it does not also remain transcendent to it, that its immanence ceases to be an event in the Old Testament sense, always a new thing, something that God actually brings into being in specific circumstances. In the comprehensive formula of Paul in 2 Cor. 5¹⁹: θεὸς ἦν ἐν Χριστῷ κόσμον καταλλάσσων ἑαυτῷ EN59, one should not lay such stress on ἦν EN60 that its connexion with the verb καταλλάττειν EN61 is overlooked. This reconciling action of God is the *being* of God in Christ, but it is this reconciling *action* that is the being. The Son "glorifies" the Father, yet not without the Father glorifying Him, the Son (Jn. 17¹). It is not any son that speaks here, but the Son of this Father, who even as the Father of this Son remains the Father in heaven, the Father who sends the Son, to conclude with this Johannine description of the divine action.

[324]

And now we repeat that the God of the biblical revelation can also do what is ascribed to Him in this respect by the biblical witnesses. His revelation does not mean in the slightest a loss of His mystery. He assumes a form, yet not in such a way that any form will compass Him. Even as He gives Himself He remains free to give Himself afresh or to refuse Himself. This His new self-giving remains man's only hope. His "second time in a different way" does not really prevent Him from remaining the same. In all this we hear confirmation a second time, though obviously in a very different way from the first, that God reveals Himself as the Lord. And again we have also to ask whether in other instances in which men think they can speak of revelation the abiding mystery of the self-revealing God really belongs also to the concept of revelation, whether the lordship there ascribed to "God" can really exist in this freedom of God with regard to His own utterances, or whether in these cases revelation does not always consist in a secularisation of God and therefore in an empowering of man, so that "God" does not remain free at all but at best must become a partner and at worst a tool of the religious man. Even there one may also speak of "revelation," but it would be as well, we repeat, not to be in too big a hurry at least to link biblical revelation with the other variety. But that is merely by the way. What is beyond dispute is that the lordship of God discernible in the biblical revelation consists in this freedom of His, in His permanent freedom to unveil Himself or to veil Himself. God reveals Himself as the Father, that is to say, as the Father of the Son in whom He takes form for our sake. God the Father is God who always, even in taking form in the Son, does not take form, God as the free ground and the free power of His being God in

---

EN59 in Christ God was reconciling the world to himself
EN60 was
EN61 to reconcile [in the present tense]

the Son. It would not be revelation within the bounds of the biblical witness if God did not also reveal Himself thus, as the Father. That He does this is the other thing—really other, the same, yet not to be brought under a single denominator as the first—that is meant when we say that He reveals Himself as the Lord. God's fatherhood, too, is God's lordship in His revelation.

3. Revelation in the Bible means the self-unveiling, imparted to men, of the God who by nature cannot be unveiled. Our stress is now on the words "imparted to men." We have asked: Where does revelation come from? We now ask: Where does it go to? The revelation attested in the Bible does not just take place in the sphere of man, as might also be said of the theogonies and cosmogonies which are the theme of the witness in the records of, e.g., Babylonian religion. It is also aimed at man, not just mythical man, man in general, but always a specific man occupying a very specific place, a specific historical place. Part of the concept of the biblically attested revelation is that it is a historical event. Historical does not mean historically demonstrable or historically demonstrated. Hence it does not mean what is usually called "historical" (*historisch*). We should be discarding again all that we have said earlier about the mystery in revelation if we were now to describe any of the events of revelation attested in the Bible as "historical" (*historisch*); i.e., apprehensible by a neutral observer or apprehended by such an observer. What a neutral observer could apprehend or may have apprehended of these events was the form of revelation which he did not and could not understand as such. It was an event that took place in the human sphere with all the possibilities of interpretation corresponding to this sphere. In no case was it revelation as such.

[325]

Millions in the ancient Orient may have heard the name of Yahweh or seen His temple on some occasion. But this "historical" element was not revelation. Thousands may have seen and heard the Rabbi of Nazareth. But this "historical" element was not revelation. The "historical" element in the resurrection of Christ, the empty tomb as an aspect of the event that might be established, was not revelation. This "historical" element, like all else that is "historical" on this level, is admittedly open to very trivial interpretations too.

As regards the question of the "historical" certainty of the revelation attested in the Bible we can only say that it is ignored in the Bible itself in a way that one can understand only on the premiss that this question is completely alien to it, i.e., obviously and utterly inappropriate to the object of its witness. The neutral observer who understood the events recorded in it as revelation would cease thereby to be a neutral observer. And for the non-neutral, for the man who hears and sees, for the believer, there is and always will be in the form of revelation its mystery too. That is, he has to realise that what can be established here "historically" (*historisch*) is very little or nothing at all or something quite different which is of no importance for the event of revelation. This cannot be what we have in view, then, when we say that the biblical revelation is by definition a historical event. What we mean by this is rather that the Bible always understands what it calls revelation as a concrete relation to concrete men. God in His incomprehensibility and God in the act of His revelation is not the formula of an abstract metaphysics of God, the world, or religion which is supposed to obtain at all times and in all places. It is rather the record of an event that has taken place once and for all, i.e., in a more or less exact and specific time and place. If the time and place are largely obscure for us "historically," if the individual data the Bible offers concerning them are subject to "historical" criticism, this is not surprising in the documents of a time and culture that had no knowledge at all of a "historical" question in our sense, quite apart from the fact that "historical" interest even in the sense that was possible in that age and culture could play no serious role in the composition of these documents, which were meant to be records of revelation. Nevertheless this does not alter the fact that the Bible by what it calls revelation always means a specific event at a specific time and place. Thus, even if according to the standards of modern historiography it does in certain instances, having no interest in this regard, commit "errors" in what it says about the time and place, the important thing is not the more or less "correct" content but the very fact of these statements. This fact that the Bible in both the Old Testament and the New does continually and with notable emphasis make chronological and topographical statements, that it thus wishes in each instance to ascribe a set place in time and space to the divine revelation which it records, that the recorded processes in which revelation comes to men are put in the setting of other events at the same time and in the same place, that ancient Egypt, Assyria and Babylon come into view on the horizon of the experiences of the people of Israel, that Cyrenius the governor of Syria cannot be left out of the Christmas story and Pontius Pilate has an authentic place in the Creed— all this signifies that when the Bible gives an account of revelation it means to narrate history, i.e., not to tell of a relation between God and man that exists generally in every time and place and that is always in process, but to tell of an event that takes place there and only there, then and only then, between God and certain very specific men. The divine self-unveiling which it records, with the holiness which it ascribes to God in this act, is not imparted to man but to such and such men in very definite situations. It is a very specific event and as such it is incomparable and cannot be repeated. To hear the Bible as the witness to God's revelation is in all cases to hear about this history through the Bible.

[326]

Hearing history such as that which is an event in the revelation attested in the Bible obviously cannot mean regarding such an event as possible, probable, or even actual on the basis of a general concept of historical (*geschichtlich*) truth. Even histories enacted between God and man do, of course, come under this general concept of history on their human side and therefore in relation to the statements on its temporal form which are so assiduously emphasised in the Bible. But they do not fall under this general concept on their divine side. Hence the "historical" (*historisch*) judgment which presupposes this general concept can in principle relate only to the temporal side. It can neither claim nor deny that at this point or that God has acted on men. To be able to claim or deny this it would have to abandon its presupposition, that general concept, and become a confession of faith or unbelief *vis-à-vis* the biblical witness. No genuinely "historical" verdict can be passed on the singular historicity of the history recorded in the biblical witness. But again—and this is less obvious—hearing a history such as that enacted in the revelation attested in the Bible cannot be dependent on the "historical" assessment of its temporal form. The judgment in virtue of which a biblical story may be regarded with some probability as history in the sense of the general concept of historical truth is not necessarily the judgment of faith *vis-à-vis* the biblical witness. For the judgment may be passed without any understanding of the story in its particularity, i.e., as history between God and man. Again, the opposite judgment need not be that of unbelief, for it may involve an understanding of the story in its particularity, i.e., as history between God and man. The question which decides hearing or non-hearing of the biblical history cannot be the question of its general historicity; it can only be that of its special historicity.

[327]

Thus the judgment that a biblical story is to be regarded either as a whole or in part as saga or legend does not have to be an attack on the substance of the biblical witness. All that might be said is that according to the standards by which "historical" truth is usually measured elsewhere or generally, this story is one that to some degree eludes any sure declaration that it happened as the narrative says. Saga or legend can only denote the more or less intrusive part of the story-teller or story-tellers in the story told. There is no story in which we do not have to reckon with this aspect, and therefore with elements of saga or legend according to the general concept of "historical" truth. This applies also to the stories told in the Bible. Otherwise they would have to be without temporal form. Yet this fundamental uncertainty in general historicity, and therefore the positive judgment that here and there saga or legend is actually present, does not have to be an attack on the substance of the biblical testimony. For (1) this judgment can in any case concern and contest only the general historicity of a biblical record, (2) even in the clearest instance it is by nature only a judgment of probability, and (3) even saga or legend is in any case meant to be history and can thus be heard as a communication of history irrespective of the "historical" judgment. So long as this is so, the question of the particular historicity of the story at issue is at least not answered negatively.

The situation changes when the category of myth is introduced. The verdict that a biblical story is to be understood as a myth is necessarily an attack on the substance of the biblical witness. This is because "myth" does not intend to be history but only pretends to be such. Myth uses narrative form to expound what purports to be always and everywhere true. It is an exposition of certain basic relationships of human existence, found in every time and place, in their connexions to their own origins and conditions in the natural and historical cosmos, or in the deity. These are given narrative form on the assumption that man knows all these things and can present them thus or thus, that he controls them, that in the last resort they are his things. Myth (cf. for what follows Eduard Thurneysen, "*Christus und die Kirche,*" *Z.d.Z.*, 1930, esp. 189 f.) does not impute any exclusive character to the event narrated by it—in other words: "What myth narrates as a fact may happen in any time or place. It is not a unique event but one that can be repeated .... But what can be repeated and can happen over and over again, even though it may be surprising, is a general possibility akin to natural occurrence. What happens in this way rests on nothing other than the assumption that the man to whom the revelation narrated in myth is imparted stands ultimately in an original and natural relation and connexion, hidden, of course, but present potentially at least everywhere, to the final ground of his existence, to his God. In the events narrated in myth this latent possibility becomes, so to speak, active. In ever new theophanies man experiences the ground of the world as present and himself as connected to it. But this means that there is here an ultimate identity between God and man. There is no thought of a profound and final distinction. What myth, then, recounts as a unique happening is not unique at all; it is the unchanging, final, basic relation which, evoked by all kinds of wizardry and magic, is again lived through and experienced and will be continually lived through and experienced."

> Joyous was it years ago— [328]
> So eagerly the spirit strives
> To seek and come to know
> How nature, in creating, lives.
> And 'tis the eternally One
> That is manifold revealed.
> Small the great and great the small,
> Each according to its kind;
> Ever changing, standing fast,
> Near and far and far and near,
> Forming thus and then transforming—
> To marvel am I here.
>
> (Goethe, *Parabase*, Jub. Edn., Vol. II, 246).

This is the birth of myth. (The only distinction between myth and speculation proper is that in speculation the narrative is stripped off again like a garment that has become too tight, so that what is presented as fact in myth is now elevated to the sphere of pure idea or concept, and the present and acknowledged wealth of the origins and relations of human existence is thus expressed in its "in and for itself." Myth is the preparatory form of speculation and speculation is the revealed essence of myth.) To be sure, one cannot prevent a historian from applying the category of myth to some of the events recorded in the Bible. One might ask, of course, whether the supposed myths have really been found in the text of the Bible and not somewhere behind the text, whether the context in which the passage concerned finds its point has not been dissolved, whether what it says in the context has not been ignored on the assumption that so-called "sources" of a special character and independent content underlie the biblical text, and whether certain parts of the biblical text have not been combined with parts of non-biblical texts which might perhaps be claimed as mythical. In a word, one might ask whether the verdict "myth" as applied to the biblical texts is not even from the purely "historical" standpoint a mistaken verdict because it can perhaps be made only when there is a failure to hear what the real biblical texts are trying to say and do say if we read them as we actually have them, in their narrower and broader context, as biblical texts. But even if this objection does not seem to make sense, the historian who resolves on this verdict must realise at least that if this verdict is possible for him he has as it were read the Bible outside the Christian Church, that he is not asking about revelation but about something else, perhaps myth or speculation, that perhaps he himself is quite unaware or forgetful of the fact that there is such a thing as revelation, that perhaps he himself is aware, or at this moment aware, of no more than man's general ability to control the origins and relations of his existence by fable or thought or some other means, because these are in fact his own things. It is really quite natural that an age whose thought, feeling and action are so highly mythical as the so-called modern period that culminates in the Enlightenment (including Idealism and Romanticism) should seek myth in the Bible too— and find it. Historicism is "the self-understanding of the spirit in so far as its own achievements in history are concerned" (E. Troeltsch, *Ges. Schriften*, Vol. III, 1922, 104). Good! For the person who does not ask about revelation there is nothing left, of course, but to ask about myth, and the man who asks about myth because he must, because myth is his own last word, will not be restrained by the objection that even a historian might feel from seeking myth in the Bible too, and really finding it there, and perhaps, strictly speaking, finding a little of it in every part of the Bible. We can only declare that the interpretation of the Bible

[329]   as the witness to revelation and the interpretation of the Bible as the witness to myth are mutually exclusive. The category of saga, the questioning of the general historicity of the biblical narratives, is not an attack on the substance of the Bible as witness, but the category of myth is, for myth does not just question but fundamentally denies the history as such, and therefore the special historicity of the biblical records, and revelation regarded as myth would not be a historical event but a supposed non-spatial and timeless truth, i.e., a creation of man.

The Bible lays such extraordinary stress on the historicity of the revelation recorded by it because by revelation it does not mean a creation of man. It says so emphatically that revelation was imparted to these men in these situations because it is describing it thereby as an impartation to men. This is what the use of the concept of myth rather than saga in relation to the Bible overlooks or denies. The revelations attested in the Bible do not purport to be manifestations of a universal or an idea which are special by nature but which can then be comfortably compared with the idea and understood and evaluated in their particularity.

Because this is not the case, the philosophy of religion of the Enlightenment from Lessing by way of Kant and Herder to Fichte and Hegel, with its intolerable distinction between the eternal content and the historical "vehicle," can only be described as the nadir of the modern misunderstanding of the Bible.

The revelation attested in the Bible purports to be a historical event. In this regard, if we bring in the concept of history in explanation, our only possible *tertium comparationis*[EN62] can be the fact that in revelation as in history the reference is to a definite event which is different from every other event and which is thus incomparable and cannot be repeated. If with the Enlightenment we were to regard the event as again the mere exponent of some general occurrence, a special case under a rule, or the realisation of a general possibility; if history were to be understood as a framework within which there might also be something like revelation, then at this point we should have to reject the concept of historicity no less emphatically than that of myth. In relation to revelation the term historical can only denote event as a fact over which there is no court by reference to which it may be regarded as a fact, as this particular fact. It is thus that revelation is imparted to man according to the Bible, and this is why the Bible lays such stress on chronology, topography and contemporary world history, i.e., on the contingency and uniqueness of the revelations recorded by it. In doing this it is simply saying that revelation comes vertically from heaven. It befalls man with the same contingency with which, living in this specific place at this specific time and in these specific circumstances he is this specific man at this specific stage of his inner and outer life, the only difference being that this historical contingency of his can still be

---

[EN62] basis of comparison

surveyed and explained in all possible dimensions. The statement: *Individuum* [330]
est ineffabile^{EN63}, can indeed be made but characteristically it cannot be proved,
whereas revelation is the *ineffabile*^{EN64} which encounters and reaches man and
proves itself to be such. From this standpoint, then, we finally achieve full clarity regarding what was said in 1. and 2. about the unveiling and veiling of God
in His revelation. These two relationships in which the Bible regards God as
existing cannot be interpreted as the elements of a present and known truth
and reality that must be established by a general necessity of thought. Otherwise, even if we were not ready to admit it, we should still be regarding the
biblical revelation as a myth. The fact that the *Deus revelatus* is also the *Deus
absconditus* and the *Deus absconditus* the *Deus revelatus*, that the Father glorifies
the Son and the Son the Father, is not self-evident, i.e., intelligible *per se*, as the
immanent dialectic of this or that sphere of human life, or perhaps a dialectic
like the Hegelian In itself and For itself, is intelligible *per se*, i.e., resolvable into
a third. If the goodness and holiness of God are neither experiences we can
manufacture nor concepts we can form for ourselves but divine modes of
being to which human experiences and concepts can at least respond, then
their conjunction, their dialectic, in which both are only what they are, is certainly not a dialectic which we can know, i.e., achieve for ourselves, but one
which we can only ascertain and acknowledge as actually taking place. And this
actual occurrence, this being ascertained and acknowledged, is the historicity
of revelation. By this concept we mean that in the Bible revelation is a matter
of impartation, of God's being revealed, by which the existence of specific
men in specific situations has been singled out in the sense that their experiences and concepts, even though they cannot grasp God in His unveiling and
God in His veiling and God in the dialectic of unveiling and veiling, can at least
follow Him and respond to Him.

The thing to note at this third point is the element of vocation in the biblical concept of
revelation. We again find agreement between the Old Testament and the New in their view
that man can in no wise produce revelation for himself. We have referred already to the
priests of Baal on Carmel who in their attempts to invoke God show precisely how man has
no access to Yahweh. The so-called false prophets of the Old Testament are obviously viewed
in the same way as proclaimers of a self-snatched revelation which for that very reason is no
revelation at all. Similarly in the New Testament (e.g., Mk. 10^{17f.}; Lk.9^{57f.}) those who want to
win life or follow Jesus in their own strength are shown to be the very people who are unable
to do it. On the other hand the promise given to Abraham is in the first instance for Abraham himself as well as Sarah (Gen. 17¹⁷) a matter of mirth, while Jacob-Israel (quite apart
from other traits that are found objectionable to-day) is in Gen. 32^{22f.} a fighter, and indeed a
victorious fighter, against God, and the resistance to calling seen in a Moses, Isaiah, Jeremiah
or Jonah seems to be of the very essence of the genuine prophet. The great New Testament
example of this is naturally the calling of Saul to be Paul. And even in relation to Peter the
view of the tradition is perhaps that his true calling is by the Risen Lord, i.e., after his denial

---

^{EN63} The individual is ineffable
^{EN64} ineffable

[331]   of Jesus. To him in particular it is most emphatically said that flesh and blood have not revealed it (the divine sonship of Christ) to him. It would naturally be foolish to see in all this a kind of negative disposition of the men concerned towards revelation. In many callings this resistance is not especially stressed, though neither is there in any instance a preparation for the call. What the Bible is trying to say here is obviously that there is no disposition in man at all. Calling is a non-derivative fact, or derivative only from election. The prophets and apostles are not portrayed as heroes. They stand there in their utter humanity. Yet for all that they have as it were come from heaven as prophets and apostles. They are no less astonishing to themselves than to those around them. They are set in an office which cannot be explained by their existence and they bear a "burden" which they have not taken up themselves but which has been laid on their shoulders. In the New Testament the puzzle or the solution of the puzzle of this inconceivably factual presence of real men at God's revelation is expressed by the concept of $\pi\nu\epsilon\hat{\upsilon}\mu\alpha$ [EN65]. As by unveiling we ultimately say no other than Easter, and as by veiling, with an unavoidable backward glance at the source of revelation, we say no other than Good Friday, so now, looking forward to the man to whom and for whom the revelation becomes event, to the threshold over which revelation crosses into history, we say no other than Pentecost, the outpouring of the Holy Ghost. The $\pi\nu\epsilon\hat{\upsilon}\mu\alpha$ is the miracle of the presence of real men at God's revelation. At Pentecost we are not dealing with anything other than the event of Good Friday and Easter. But here it is for real men, for such human men as the apostles according to the way they are depicted in the New Testament. The event of Good Friday and Easter can and does concern them, come home to them, call them. Not just Jesus Christ is there, but Jesus Christ in the Church of Jesus Christ, in faith in Jesus Christ. This is the specific feature of Pentecost and the Spirit in the New Testament. We had Pentecost in view when we called revelation an event that from man's standpoint has dropped down vertically from heaven. How else can we put it if we are to keep close to this text and perhaps to all the New Testament texts bearing on the "Spirit of God" or the "Spirit of Christ." The miracle that we cannot stress too strongly corresponds simply on the one side to the mystery of God from which revelation comes forth and by which it is always invested and then on the other side to the paradox that in revelation God really does come forth out of His mystery. This is how it is with God's being revealed.

Without God's being historically revealed in this way, revelation would not be revelation. God's being revealed makes it a link between God and man, an effective encounter between God and man. But it is God's own being revealed that makes it this. In this respect too, with reference to the goal, our statement that God reveals Himself as the Lord is confirmed. The fact that God can do what the biblical witnesses ascribe to him, namely, not just take form and not just remain free in this form, but also in this form and freedom of His become God to specific men, eternity in a moment, this is the third meaning of His lordship in His revelation. There is talk of revelation outside the Bible too, and we have no reason to say that this is absolutely impossible. But there is every reason to put the third question whether the concept of revelation presupposed in such talk takes into account this element of God's being revealed as an act of God Himself, this understanding of the appropriation of revelation as

[332]   an absolute assignment irrespective of any disposition, or whether in these other places where people think they should accept the attestation of reve-

[EN65] Spirit

lation the decisively important role is not played rather by perhaps the positive or perhaps (as in Buddhism) the negative disposition of man, whether what is called revelation here would not better be described as myth because the decisive point is really man's debate with himself. But we are not stressing these side-issues. Our positive concern is that in the biblical witness the lordship of God in this third sense is one of the decisive marks of revelation. God reveals Himself as the Spirit, not as any spirit, not as the basis of man's spiritual life which we can discover and awaken, but as the Spirit of the Father and the Son, and therefore the same one God, but the same one God in this way too, namely, in this unity, indeed, this self-disclosing unity, disclosing itself to men, of the Father and the Son. The fact that He does this; this third thing which does not follow self-evidently from the first and the second, just as there is nothing at all self-evident in their being and being together either; the fact that there is this being revealed of the Father and the Son, this is what we have in mind when we say that He reveals Himself as the Lord. The fact that according to Jn. 4^{24} God is Spirit is also God's lordship in His revelation.

We look back and draw to a close. We have been asking about the root of the doctrine of the Trinity, its root in revelation, not in any revelation, not in a general concept of revelation, but in the concept of revelation taken from the Bible. We have been asking whether revelation must be understood as the ground of the doctrine of the Trinity, whether the doctrine of the Trinity must be understood as having grown out of this soil. And after a side-glance at the passages in the biblical witness which directly reflect the doctrine of the Trinity, we have enquired what revelation means in the Bible, asking, but asking concretely with reference to the biblical texts, whether the statement that God reveals Himself as the Lord really has a threefold meaning and yet a simple content in these texts. If we have been right to emphasise in the biblical witness to revelation the three elements of unveiling, veiling and impartation, or form, freedom and historicity, or Easter, Good Friday and Pentecost, or Son, Father and Spirit; if we have rightly characterised these elements in detail; if we have set them in a right relation to one another; if our threefold conclusion that God reveals Himself as the Lord is not, then, an illicit move but a genuine finding; if in this statement we have really said the same thing three times in three indissolubly different ways, then we may now conclude that revelation must indeed be understood as the root or ground of the doctrine of the Trinity. As its root or ground, we say. The doctrine of the Trinity has not yet encountered us directly. Even in the verses which sound trinitarian the characteristic elements of the doctrine itself are missing. Our concepts of unimpaired unity and unimpaired distinction, the concept of the one essence of God and of the three persons or modes of being (*Seinswesen*) to be distinguished in this essence, and finally the polemical assertion, which we touched on only briefly, that God's triunity is to be found not merely in His revelation but, because in His revelation, in God Himself and in Himself too, so that the Trinity is to be understood as "immanent" and not just "economic"—none of

[333]

37

this is directly biblical, i.e., explicitly stated in the Bible; it is Church doctrine. We have established no more than that the biblical doctrine of revelation is implicitly, and in some passages explicitly, a pointer to the doctrine of the Trinity. In its basic outline it must be interpreted as also an outline of the doctrine of the Trinity. If the doctrine of the Trinity can be established and developed as such, we have to say that in respect of revelation there is a genuine and necessary connexion with the doctrine of the Trinity. The doctrine of the Trinity with its implications, distinctions and synopses is concerned with a problem that is really and very centrally posed by the biblical witness to revelation. It is in fact exegesis of this text. It is not, as we may now say already, an arbitrarily contrived speculation whose object lies elsewhere than in the Bible. Any child knows that it uses some of the philosophoumena of declining pagan antiquity. But according to our findings this cannot mean that it is a non-Church construct, i.e., one which was not necessary as such in the Church, one which did not arise in its day on the basis of Scripture, of the faith in God's revelation to which Scripture gave rise, a doctrine dealing merely with a theme of pagan antiquity. On the contrary, its statements may be regarded as indirectly, though not directly, identical with those of the biblical witness to revelation. It is Church exegesis, i.e., it exegetes this text, the witness to revelation which is accepted as such in the Church. When we come to expound it in detail as Church exegesis of this text, we must never cease to refer back to this biblical text itself with the question whether and how far we are on the right track in our treatment. The fact that it is Church exegesis, that the theses of the doctrine of the Trinity stand in relation to biblical revelation as directly as only an answer can stand in relation to a question, should be provisionally guaranteed by the proof which we have already offered.

3. VESTIGIUM TRINITATIS

[334] Before we turn to the actual development of the doctrine of the Trinity in the final section, a critical discussion is required in respect of the findings we have reached thus far. We have asked about the root of the doctrine of the Trinity. In trying to analyse the biblical concept of revelation, we have arrived at the thesis that this analysis reduced to its simplest form, the threefold yet single lordship of God as Father, Son and Spirit, is the root of the doctrine of the Trinity. In other words the biblical concept of revelation is itself the root of the doctrine of the Trinity. The doctrine of the Trinity is simply a development of the knowledge that Jesus is the Christ or the Lord. When we say that the doctrine of the Trinity grows from this root we are saying critically and polemically that it does not stem from any other root. It is the fact that it does not stem from any other root which we must now consider specifically. The problem of the *vestigium trinitatis*[EN66] which is posed by the history of the doctrine

---

[EN66] trace of the Trinity

38

of the Trinity gives us cause to do this. This expression seems to come from Augustine and it means an analogue of the Trinity, of the trinitarian God of Christian revelation, in some creaturely reality distinct from Him, a creaturely reality which is not a form assumed by God in His revelation, but which quite apart from God's revelation manifests in its own structure by creation a certain similarity to the structure of the trinitarian concept of God, so that it may be regarded as an image of the trinitarian God Himself.

Augustine deals with the subject in, e.g., *Conf.* XIII, 11, 12; *De civ. Dei* XI, 24 f., and especially *De trin.* IX–XI. Instructive for a general understanding of the problem as the fathers and School-men saw it is *De trin.* VI, 10: *Oportet igitur, ut creatorem per ea quae facta sunt intellectum conspicientes, trinitatem intelligamus, cuius in creatura, quomodo dignum est, apparet vestigium. In illa enim trinitate summa origo est rerum omnium et perfectissima pulchritudo et beatissima delectatio .... Qui videt hoc vel ex parte, vel per speculum et in aenigmate, gaudeat cognoscens Deum et sicut Deum honoret et gratias agat: qui autem non videt, tendat per pietatem ad videndum* [EN67].

It must be sharply stressed that our concern here is (unfortunately) not with the distinction imparted to a creaturely reality in revelation, in virtue of which a man, an angel, a natural or historical event, human words or actions, and supremely, finally, yet also as the epitome of all the creatures thus distinguished, the *humanitas Christi* [EN68], becomes a divine organ or instrument or medium. We might, of course, call this, and we can certainly call the form that God assumes in His unveiling as the Son or Word, the *vestigium trinitatis*. But this is not what was meant in the development and use of the concept. The concern here was with an essential trinitarian disposition supposedly immanent in some created realities quite apart from their possible conscription by God's revelation. It was with a genuine *analogia entis* [EN69], with traces of the trinitarian Creator God in being as such, in its pure createdness. If it be acknowledged that there are *vestigia trinitatis* [EN70] in this second sense then the question obviously arises—and this is why we must discuss the matter in the present context—whether we do not have to assume a second root of the doctrine of the Trinity alongside the one we have indicated in the previous subsection. The *vestigium trinitatis* would patently have to be considered as a second root of this kind if there is such a thing in the second sense of the term. We should then have to ask whether the development of the doctrine of the Trinity must not also, at least, be traced back to the insight into these traces of the Trinity that are present and perceptible in the created world quite apart

[335]

[EN67] Therefore, in regarding the Creator, who is known through the things which have been created, we should recognise the Trinity, of which a trace appears in the creature to the extent that is merited. For in this Trinity is the supreme origin of all things and the most perfect beauty and the most blessed delight ... Whoever sees this, whether in part or whether through a glass and darkly, should rejoice in knowing God, honor him as God and give thanks; but whoever does not see it should strive through piety toward seeing

[EN68] humanity of Christ

[EN69] analogy of being

[EN70] traces of the Trinity

from the biblical revelation. And if this question be admitted, then the further question can hardly be avoided: Which of the two roots of the doctrine of the Trinity that both call for consideration is the true and primary root, and which is a secondary "runner"? But then we should also have to allow the question whether the derivation of the doctrine of the Trinity from the biblical revelation is not just the later confirmation of a knowledge of God which can be won from His revelation in creation quite apart from the biblical revelation. And then it is difficult to omit the final question whether these *vestigia*[EN71] on which the doctrine of the Trinity is really based are in fact to be regarded as the *vestigia* of a Creator God transcending the world and not as determinations of the cosmos which must be viewed as strictly immanent and, because the cosmos is man's cosmos, as determinations of man's existence; whether we should not then erase the concept of natural revelation as well as biblical revelation and adjudge the doctrine of the Trinity to be a bold attempt on man's part to understand the world and ultimately himself, i.e., adjudge it to be a myth. The problem which is posed when the presence and knowability of these *vestigia trinitatis* are asserted is actually, then, of the greatest importance, not only for the question of the root of the doctrine of the Trinity, but also for that of revelation, of the grounding of theology in revelation alone, and finally even for that of the meaning and possibility of theology as distinct from mere cosmology or anthropology.

The question is whether these *vestigia trinitatis*, in virtue of the conclusions that are to be drawn from their acknowledgment even if only in the form of the list of questions mentioned, do not compel us to pass over first to the easy double track of "revelation" and "primal revelation" (P. Althaus) and then very quickly from this half-measure to the genuine Roman Catholic theology of the *analogia entis*. And then would they not bring to our attention at the right moment the fact that theology would do well to desist from the impossible attempt to understand itself as theology and to acquiesce in being the only thing it can be at root, namely, part of man's understanding of the world and himself, in the development of which the concept "God," like a superfluous x in the numerator and denominator, should now be cancelled out to simplify the counting on both sides, since with or without the concept the only real concern is man, or, in this case, man's own triunity. But the question can, of course, be put in a very different way: Do we not have in this idea of the *vestigium trinitatis* an ancient Trojan horse which one day (for the sake of *pulchritudo*[EN72] and *delectatio*[EN73], to echo Augustine) was unsuspectingly allowed entry into the theological Ilium, and in whose belly—so much more alert have certain experiences made us since Augustine's day—we can hear a threatening clank, so that we have every cause to execute a defensive movement—perhaps there is no more we can do here—by declaring, perhaps only very naively, that we do not want to have anything to do with it?

[336]

To acquaint ourselves first with the *quaestio facti*[EN74], the question what can be and has been in mind concretely when there is reference to *vestigia trinitatis*,

---

[EN71] traces
[EN72] beauty
[EN73] delight
[EN74] question of fact

let us subdivide into phenomena from nature, from culture, from history, from religion, and from the life of the soul.

Since there can be no possibility of any kind of systematic completeness, we may give some typical examples from each of the five spheres. (For what follows cf. H. Bavinck, *Geref. Dogmatick*, 1918, Vol. 2, 332 f.)

1. Nature. Anselm of Canterbury compares Father, Son and Spirit in the Trinity to the existence and mutual relation of spring, stream and lake, which as a united whole might be called the Nile. Not just the united whole, however, but the spring, stream and lake individually are also the Nile. Yet the spring is not the stream, the stream is not the lake, and the lake is not the spring, while on the other hand there are not three Niles but only one. The one whole Nile is spring, stream, and lake. It is just as difficult or impossible as in the case of the persons of the Trinity to say what the common concept is under which all three fall. But it is equally clear in this case that the spring does not derive from the stream or the lake, that the stream does not derive from the lake but the spring, and the lake derives from both the spring and the stream (*Ep. de incarn. verbi, c.* 13). Luther, in his Table Talk at least, seems to be fond of the principle that *in omnibus creaturis licet invenire et cernere trinitatem istam esse expressam*[EN75], and he illustrates it by examples from the sun, water, the stars, plants, etc. A concise account of one of these illustrations from natural phenomena is to the effect that "in all creatures there is and may be seen an intimation of the Holy Trinity. First their nature signifies the omnipotence of God the Father, then their figure and form signifies the wisdom of the Son and thirdly their usefulness and power is a sign of the Holy Ghost, and therefore that God is present in all creatures, even in the tiniest little leaf and poppy seedlet" (*W.A., Ti.* 1, 395 f.). Let it suffice us to mention by way of example that weight, number and measure, or the solid, fluid and gaseous states, or the three dimensions of solids, or the primary colours of yellow, red and blue, or the harmony of the key-note, third and fifth, have all been brought into connexion with the Trinity.

2. Culture. Teachers, soldiers and producers in society, epic, lyric and drama in poetry, and the three basic disciplines of mediaeval scholarship are all supposed to be *vestigia trinitatis* in this sphere. Luther is again our spokesman: "The Father in divine things is *Grammatica*[EN76], for He giveth the Word and is the fountain-head from which, if one may so speak, floweth good, excellent, pure speech. The Son is *Dialectica*[EN77]; for He giveth the arrangement whereby a thing should be set in good order of succession so that conclusion and consecution be certain. But the Holy Ghost is *Rhetorica*[EN78], the orator, for He excellently sustaineth, bloweth, and impelleth, maketh quick and powerful, so that an impression is made and hearts are taken" (*W.A., Ti.* 1, 564).

3. History. To this sphere belongs a doctrine which constantly recurs in Church history, that of the three kingdoms which are supposed to be seen in the Old Testament age, the New Testament age, and the age of the Christian Church, or, with an eschatological thrust and in combination with the three great apostolic figures, (1) the Petrine age, the past, which is the kingdom of fear, i.e., of the Father, (2) the Pauline age, the present, which is the kingdom of truth, i.e., of the Son, and (3) the Johannine age, the future, which is the kingdom of love, i.e., of the Spirit. In this connexion the Holy Spirit became the special catchword of all the so-called fanatical, or, better, the chiliastic parties in the Church; one might almost say He became the specifically non-Church or anti-Church God, so that it could even happen that, e.g., Luther, meeting this one-sided appeal, sometimes felt he had to be equally

[337]

[EN75] in all creatures one can find and discern the Trinity itself being expressed
[EN76] Grammar
[EN77] Dialectic
[EN78] Rhetoric

41

one-sided in His appeal to the Word, and "spiritualistic" came to be a term specifically used in criticism of everything fanatical. Moeller van den Bruck (*Das dritte Reich*, 2nd edn., 1926, 13) has called the idea of the third kingdom "a cosmological concept" which "reaches beyond reality." "It is no accident that the ideas which arise already with the concept, being ideologically unmasked from the very outset ... with the name of the third kingdom, are strangely nebulous, sentimental and vague, and completely other-worldly." Moeller v. d. Bruck, as is well-known, wanted "to rescue (the concept) from the world of illusion and relate it entirely to the political sphere." But even in this secularisation he retained something of the feeling of the early and mediaeval philosophy of the historical *vestigium trinitatis* as it lived on—to mention only a single name—in Joachim of Fiore.

4. Religion. The Middle Ages had already referred in this connexion to the subjective religious consciousness: *cogitatio, meditatio, contemplatio*[EN79], or *fides, ratio, contemplatio*[EN80], or the *via purgativa, illuminativa* and *intuitiva*[EN81] of mysticism influenced by the Areopagite, whose nature and order reflected the Trinity. Alongside this one may set the statement of Wobbermin that Christian trinitarian monotheism brings the basic conviction of all religious belief to fruition in so far as the latter always includes three motifs that come to expression in the sense of religious dependence, the sense of religious security and the sense of religious longing (*Wesen und Wahrheit des Christentums*, 1925, 432). Yet it was not the modern age with its interest in the history of religion but rather the older theology, as is clear from J. Gerhard, *Loci*, 1610, *L.* 3, 30, which was the first to note that the number three, especially in the Godhead, played an outstanding role in the objective phenomena of religion too, including non-Christian religion. We single out the fact that the ancient Babylonians had two triads of gods, a cosmic: Anu, Enlil and Ea (the gods of heaven, earth and water) and then a superior and sidereal triad: Shamash, Sin and Ishtar (sun, moon and the planet Venus). The ancient Egyptians also had the divine family of Osiris with his spouse Isis and their son Horus, and in a similar relationship the ancient Cananites, Syrians and Carthaginians knew a supreme God, then the *magna mater*[EN82] later worshipped also under the name Cybele, and the Son of God known, e.g., as Attis or Adonis, while again, presumably in a similar relationship, ancient Etruscan Rome had the so-called Capitoline triad, *Jupiter optimus maximus*[EN83], *Juno regina*[EN84] and *Minerva*. Later Brahmanism has the so-called Trimurti: the mystical unity of Brahma, who brings forth the world, Vishnu, who upholds it, and Siva (or Rudra), who destroys it. To this day the confession of a convert to Buddhism runs: "I take my refuge in Buddha, I take my refuge in Dhamma, I take my refuge in Sangha" (the "three jewels"), Buddha denoting personality, Dhamma teaching and Sangha the community of the founder of the religion.

5. The Human Soul. The reference here according to Augustine is to the three powers of the soul, *mens*[EN85] the power of inward apprehension, *notitia*[EN86] the power of outward apprehension, and *amor*[EN87] the power to relate the one to the other and thus to complete apprehension. But the reference might also be to the three corresponding elements in the actual process of consciousness, *memoria*[EN88], i.e., the underlying act of subjective and object-

---

[EN79] cognitation, meditation, contemplation
[EN80] faith, reason, contemplation
[EN81] the purgative, illuminative [and] intuitive way
[EN82] Great Mother
[EN83] Jupiter Best and Greatest
[EN84] Queen Juno
[EN85] intellect
[EN86] cognizance
[EN87] love
[EN88] memory

iveness consciousness generally and intrinsically as pure form, *intellectus*[EN89], i.e., the consummation in thought of a subjective or objective conception in a definite image, and [338] *voluntas*[EN90], i.e., the affirmation of this image and also the return of the image to pure consciousness. Thus it is the same *vestigium* in different words and not another one when Augustine makes the distinction: *amans, id quod amatur, amor*[EN91]. Let us hear Augustine himself in a particularly pregnant formulation of his thought: *sine ulla phantasiarum vel phantasmatum imaginatione ludificatoria mihi esse me, idque nosse et amare certissimum est. ... Quid si falleris? Si enim fallor, sum. Nam qui non est, utique nec falli potest. ... Consequens est autem, ut etiam in eo quod me novi nosse, non fallor. Eaque duo cum amo ... quiddam tertium ... eis ... adiungo*[EN92] (*De civ. Dei*, XI, 26). What Augustine thought he saw in this structure of human consciousness was more the *imago Dei* or *trinitatis*[EN93] than a mere *vestigium*. But this theory of the *vestigium* above all others made an impression and formed a school throughout the centuries. We find it in all sorts of modifications, e.g., in Anselm (*Monol.* 67 and *passim*), Peter Lombard (*Sent.* I, *dist.*, 3), Thomas Aquinas (*S. theol.* I, *qu.* 45, *art.* 7), Bonaventura (*Breviloq.* II, *c.* 12), in the Reformation period Melanchthon (*Enarr. Symb. Nic.*, 1550, *C.R.* 23, 235; *Loci*, 1559, *C.R.* 21, 615, etc.), among the Reformed B. Keckermann (*Syst. S. S. Theol.*, 1611, 20 f.), in the Enlightenment Lessing's *Education of the Human Race*, § 73, in the 19th century A. Twesten (*Dogm. d. ev.-luth. Kirche*, Vol. 2, 1837, 194 f.), more recently none other than A. Schlatter: "Since we are in possession of our image, there constantly arises in us a kind of triunity; to the person who knows there comes the one known, yet not in such a way that the two stand over against one another, but there appears at once the third, the person who knows himself in the one known" (*Das chr. Dogma*, 2nd edn., 1923, 24). Equally trinitarian for him is the order of our volition: "We have a direct volition, an elective volition, and the union of the two, the volition elected by us, which has within it the power to act" (*op. cit.*, p. 148). We need only refer to the relation which results from this to Schelling's triad of subject, object and subject-object and to Hegel's "in itself" of the subjective spirit as thesis. "for itself" of the objective spirit as antithesis, and "in and for itself" of the absolute spirit as synthesis. We may quietly state that these very climaxes of Idealist philosophy would be quite unthinkable except against the background of Christian dogmatics even if they were not just new variations on Augustine's proof of the Trinity. It is clear that the logico-grammatical scheme of subject, object and predicate would also belong to this context if it were our real key to the doctrine of the Trinity. And it is equally clear that the mediaeval construct of the religious consciousness, and that of Wobbermin too, must also be seen in this context as a variation on the general Augustinian argument from consciousness.

What are we to say to all this material? What are we to make of it? The first step is naturally to try to think of it in the sense in which it was originally intended, namely, as an interesting, edifying, instructive and helpful hint towards understanding the Christian doctrine, not to be overrated, not to be used as a proof in the strict sense, because we need to know and believe the Trinity already if we are really to perceive its *vestigia* as such in the microcosm

---

[EN89] understanding
[EN90] will
[EN91] that which loves, that which is loved, love
[EN92] without any deceptive imagining of ideas or images, it is absolutely certain to me that I am, and that I both know and love that I am. What if you are deceived? Well, if I am deceived, I am. For if someone is not, neither can he be deceived .... And it follows that I am not deceived, either, in my knowing that I know. And when I love these two facts ... I add ... to them ... a certain third thing
[EN93] image of God [or] of the Trinity

and the macrocosm, but still to be valued as supplementary and non-obligatory illustrations of the Christian Credo which are to be received with gratitude.

[339]   Irenaeus already sounded the warning that we have not to understand *Deum ex factis, sed ea quae facta sunt, ex Deo*[EN94] (*C. o. h.* II, 25, 1). Augustine himself expressly added to his exhortation that man should learn to see the Trinity in himself the further admonition: *cum invenerit in his aliquid et dixerit, non iam se putet invenisse illud, quod supra ista est incommutabile*[EN95] (*Conf.* XIII, 11). Peter Lombard, too, obviously draws back: *Non enim per creaturarum contemplationem sufficiens notitia trinitatis potest haberi vel potuit sine doctrinae vel interioris inspirationis revelatione .... Adiuvamur tamen in fide invisibilium per ea quae facta sunt*[EN96] (*Sent.* I, *dist.* 3 F), and he refers expressly to the *dissimilitudines*[EN97] which are to be found even in the Augustinian *similitudo*[EN98]. *Trinitate posita, congruunt hujusmodi rationes; non tamen ita, quod per has rationes sufficienter probetur trinitas personarum*[EN99] (Thomas Aquinas, *S. th.* I, *qu.* 32 *art.* 1). Similarly Luther's statements on the matter are certainly not to be regarded as a theological basis but simply as theological table-talk.

We need not regard the achievements of the older theology at this point as just an idle game, no matter how trifling much of what is adduced may undoubtedly seem to be.

The other impression we undeniably get from the whole material is that in varying degrees there must be "something in" the connexion between the Trinity and all the "trinities" to which reference is made here. Why should there not be something in it? The only question is what. Theology and the Church, and even the Bible itself, speak no other language than that of this world which is shaped in form and content by the creaturely nature of the world and also conditioned by the limitations of humanity: the language in which man as he is, as sinful and corrupt man, wrestles with the world as it encounters him and as he sees and tries to understand it. The Bible, the Church and theology undoubtedly speak this language on the presupposition that there might be something in it, namely, that in this language God's revelation might be referred to, witness might be given, God's Word might be proclaimed, dogma might be formulated and declared. The only question is whether this possibility is to be understood as that of the language and consequently of the world or man, or whether it is to be regarded as a venture which is, as it were, ascribed to the language, and consequently to the world or man, from without, so that it is not really the possibility of the language, the world,

---

[EN94] God from things created, but created things from God
[EN95] when he finds and reports anything in these things, he should not think that he has found that which is unchangeable above them
[EN96] For adequate cognizance of the Trinity cannot and never has been able to be obtained through the contemplation of creatures apart from the revelation of doctrine or inner inspiration ... But we are aided in our belief in invisible things by those things which have been created
[EN97] unlikenesses
[EN98] likeness
[EN99] If the Trinity is given, then statements of this sort are appropriate; but it is not the case that such statements are sufficient to prove a Trinity of persons

or man, but the possibility of revelation, if in the form of concepts and ideas that exist elsewhere and independently, in correspondence with the created world and the capacity of man as he attempts an understanding of this world, we really come to speak of revelation and therefore of the Trinity, of the remission of sins and eternal life, i.e., of things for which man's speech as such has no aptitude whatever. Now it cannot be said that the discoverers of *vestigia trinitatis* have made this distinction. As we make it, we are brought back to a realisation that the true *vestigium trinitatis* is the form assumed by God in revelation. So far as I can see, this was not the view of the fathers and Schoolmen when they spoke of the *vestigium trinitatis*.

But with the help of this distinction one can understand how they came on the one hand to affirm the idea of the apprehensibility of the *vestigium trinitatis* and on the other hand to bracket it again at once with the declaration that there can be true apprehension of it only on the presupposition of revelation, *trinitate posita*[EN100]. They might actually have meant something very different from what they seemed to be saying. They were in search of language for the mystery of God which was known to them by revelation, which, as they constantly repeated, was known to them only by revelation, and which could be made known to all men only by revelation. In this search for language, the first materials they encountered apart from those offered by the Bible consisted, as is known, in a number of applicable abstract categories from the philosophy of the day. [340]

Strictly speaking the term *trinitas*[EN101] as such would have to be regarded as a *vestigium trinitatis* found in the field of logic. And F. Diekamp, *Kathol. Dogm.*, Vol. I, 6th edn., 1930, 260, rightly points out that the analogies adduced by the fathers are in the long run only further expositions and multiplications of the biblical terms Father, Son, and Spirit, which are already analogical.

The dogma was then formulated in this biblico-philosophical language. But the mystery of revelation which still lived on in the formulated dogma made a further and even more urgent demand for language now that a correct understanding had been decided. And it was now found for the first time, not that the language could grasp the revelation, but that revelation, the very revelation correctly and normatively understood in the formulated dogma, could grasp the language, i.e., that on the basis of revelation enough elements could be found in the familiar language used by all to be able to speak about revelation, not exhaustively or appropriately or correctly, but still to some extent intelligibly and perspicuously, elements which could be employed with some prospect of success to denote certain factors and relations in what can be said about revelation. When men wanted to talk about the Father, Son, and Spirit,

[EN100] if the Trinity is given
[EN101] Trinity

45

or *unitas in trinitate*[EN102] and *trinitas in unitate*[EN103], they opened their eyes and ears and found they could and should venture to refer, with this end in view, to spring, stream and lake, or weight, number and measure, or *mens, notitia* and *amor*[EN104], not because these things were in and of themselves suitable for the purpose but because they were adapted to be appropriated or, as it were, commandeered as images of the Trinity, as ways of speaking about the Trinity, because men who knew God's revelation in Scripture thought they might be given the power to say what in and of themselves they naturally do not say and cannot say. There is "nothing in it" if we try to say that source, stream and lake or *esse, nosse* and *velle*[EN105] are related to one another in the same way as Father,

[341] Son and Spirit. But there is "something in it" if we say that Father, Son and Spirit are related in the same way as source, stream and lake. Men were sure of the Trinity but they were not sure of the language of the world in relation to the Trinity. Nevertheless, they had to speak about the Trinity in this language. They thus had to claim it for the Trinity, namely, for witness to the Trinity. What happened, then, was not that they tried to explain the Trinity by the world but on the contrary that they tried to explain the world by the Trinity in order to be able to speak about the Trinity in this world. It was not a matter of apologetics but of polemics, not of demonstrating the possibility of revelation in the world of human reason but of establishing the actual possibilities of the world of human reason as the scene of revelation. *Vestigia trinitatis in creatura*[EN106], they said, but perhaps what they really had in mind was *vestigia creaturae in trinitate*[EN107]—naturally in the Trinity of self-revelation, in the Trinity inasmuch as it takes creaturely form. They did not believe that the Trinity is immanent in things and that things have the capability of reflecting the Trinity. On this side everything is admittedly incomplete and questionable and dependent on preceding revelation. But they did have confidence that the Trinity can reflect itself in things, and all the more or less felicitous discoveries of *vestigia* were an expression of this confidence, not of confidence in the capacity of reason for revelation but of confidence in the power of revelation over reason. In this sense one may say that the problem at issue is that of theological language, which even though it can only be the language of the world, must still believe at root, cost what it will, that contrary to the natural capabilities of this language it can and should speak of God's revelation in this language as theological language. Understood in this radical way—in so far as it may be understood thus—the doctrine of the *vestigia* is no playing with words.

But why does it so commonly, and, as we continually feel, so necessarily and legitimately make this impression on us, the impression that it is all table-talk

---

[EN102] unity in Trinity
[EN103] Trinity in unity
[EN104] intellect, cognizance [and] love
[EN105] being, knowing [and] willing
[EN106] Traces of the Trinity in the creature
[EN107] traces of the creature in the Trinity

which is not to be taken too seriously, and that fundamentally it is in some ways a dangerous profanation of holy things? We can only answer that this is so because we can never be so clear about the purpose which may lawfully be pursued here that there is not at every moment the possibility of a reversal of the whole order just developed, polemics becoming apologetics, the attempt to fashion theological language becoming a surrender of theological language in favour of some alien speech, the assumed and asserted intelligibility of revelation becoming an original commensurability of reason with revelation, the synthetic "God into the world" becoming an analytic "God in the world," the claiming of the world by revelation becoming a claiming of revelation by the world, and the discovered intimation becoming a self-conceived proof. When there was no guarantee against this reversal—and to a large extent there was not—the idea of a second root of the doctrine of the Trinity was bound to take hold. It could now be believed that fundamentally the root and basis of the Trinity may be just as well found in human consciousness or other created orders as in Holy Scripture, and this was bound to give rise to the danger already indicated that interest would increasingly focus on the trinities in the world that are so much closer to men, and it would be increasingly supposed that the divine Trinity is to be found in them as such. Was it really found? Was the Triune God who was supposedly to be found in the world first and then independently, really the One whom Holy Scripture calls God? Or was He just an epitome, a supreme principle of the world and ultimately of man? Though the proof given proved something, did it not fail to prove what it was meant to prove, and if this was not perceived, did it not really lead away from what it was meant to prove? Was not the proof of the Trinity along these lines bound to lead logically to a denial of the trinitarian God of Holy Scripture because it proved and put in His place a God constituted *totaliter aliter*[EN108]?

[342]

Let us suppose that someone seriously wanted to prove the truth of the divine Trinity from its attestation in the history of religion. What would he or could he prove? The two Babylonian triads and the Brahman Trimurti can be demonstrated only as formulations of a triply membered world principle. In the Egyptian, Canaanite and Etruscan triads it is no less plain that what is really intended and worshipped is the basic relation of the family. In the three jewels of Buddhism, the personality, teaching and community of Buddha, we obviously have, in so far as there is any reference to a divine Trinity, the deified historical process of the founding of religion. If all that is found here by way of a triadic Godhead deserves to be called God, then the history of religion offers a confirmation of the Christian Trinity; but not otherwise. For what is left over when one deducts the question as to the nature which is described here as God's nature is really only the number three. And the reasons the history of religion provides for the divinity of this number ("it is perhaps sacred because primitive man was not yet acquainted with any higher number," *RGG*², Art. "*Dreieinigkeit*," I) can hardly be described as particularly illuminating. J. Gerhard (*op. cit.*) really said all that can be said on the value of the history of religion for this problem: *In verbis nobiscum consentiunt, in*

[EN108] wholly other

47

verborum istorum explicatione ac sensu dissentiunt[EN109]. We only step into the void if we try to plant our feet here.

Let us further suppose that someone wanted to base faith in the Triune God secondarily on the philosophy of history. It could easily be shown that the three-beat rhythm of history which is continually advanced is just the rhythm of wrestling with past, present and future in which active man always finds himself as he reflects on his action. One can certainly count on it that the third element which is decisive in every philosophy of history always denotes the precise point where the relevant philosopher himself stands or which he is striving to reach, the two not being so very different. If the dream he dreams from this standpoint is the wisdom of God, then this philosophy of history is a proof of the doctrine of the Trinity, but certainly not otherwise, for if it is not, the philosopher of history has proved nothing at all apart from his own vision and his own will.

[343]   Luther already drew attention to the threat in the Augustinian argument from consciousness. We have seen how cheerfully he engaged in all other possible arguments of this kind. The more admirable, then, is the instinct which stopped him using this one, in contrast to Melanchthon. He declared that the fatal *disputatio de libro arbitrio*[EN110] must follow from the Augustinian doctrine, from the *imago dei*[EN111] in man present in *memoria, intellectus* and *voluntas.*[EN112] *Ita enim dicunt: Deus est liber, ergo cum homo ad imaginem Dei sit conditus, habet etiam liberam memoriam, mentem et voluntatem .... Ita nata est hinc periculosa sententia, qua pronuntiant Deum ita gubernare homines, ut eos proprio motu sinat agere*[EN113] (*Comm. on Gen.* 1²⁶, W.A. 42, 45, 25). The development of anthropological speculation by way of Descartes and Kant to Schelling and Hegel and finally and logically Feuerbach has clearly justified him. Certainly Augustine thought he was remote from the possibility of a reversal of this kind. But when B. Keckermann (*op. cit.*) could venture to say: *quam est necessarium, hominem esse rationalem, ... tam est necessarium in Dei essentia tres esse personas*[EN114], the way was prepared for this reversal. Could it be avoided once this *quam ... tam*[EN115] was attempted? Unquestionably the image of God in consciousness is primarily and intrinsically and as such the image of free man. He who sees in this image as such the image of God is saying thereby that he knows free man as God. If this free man is really God, the proof is successful. But if God is not free man, if He confronts free man in sovereignty, then obviously this most natural and profound and historically influential proof has failed in a very distinctive way.

And so it is with the rest of the material once we consider it in itself with the question whether and how far *vestigia trinitatis in creatura* are really present in it. That there are *vestigia trinitatis* is undeniable of course; the only question is, of which trinity? If it is the divine Trinity that really meets us in the three dimensions of space, or the three notes of the simple harmony, or the three primary colours, or even the spring, stream and lake, then, as was seen in ancient Babylonia and India, God is the mysteriously threefold law or nature of the known world, the mystery of the cosmos whose traces meet us in this triplicity of all or at any

---

[EN109] In the form of their words they agree with us, but in the sense and meaning of those words they disagree

[EN110] debate over the freedom of the will

[EN111] image of God

[EN112] memory, understanding and will

[EN113] For they reason as follows: God is free, therefore since human beings were created in God's image, they have free memory, understanding and will ... And so there is born from this reasoning the dangerous proposition, from which they deduce that God so governs human beings, that he allows them to act by their own power

[EN114] just as it is necessary for human beings to be rational, ... so it is necessary for there to be three persons in God's essence

[EN115] just as ... so

rate many things, and which is obviously very intimately related to the mystery of man and the mystery of man's religion. If this is God—and it might be—why should not the plenitude of trinities in nature and culture really prove the trinity of this God? But only the trinity of this God. The question remains whether this God can really be claimed even as the Creator God and therefore whether he does not perhaps bear his name as "God" illegitimately.

Nor have we referred as yet to the profound incongruities, which even proponents of the doctrine have never denied, between the *vestigia* and the biblical and ecclesiastical doctrine of the Trinity. One will find that what are in fact the decisive theses in the doctrine, the indissoluble unity and the indestructible distinction of the three elements, cannot be sustained in relation to any of the *vestigia*. The proof which can be taken from them can never be more than the proof either of three divine beings alongside one another or of a single divine monad with no hypostatic self-differentiation, so that even if the presupposed divine being is worthy to be called God, the trinity of God in the sense of the Christian doctrine of God is the very thing that cannot be proved from these *vestigia*. Quenstedt is quite right: *nulla vera et plena similitudo trinitatis in creaturis reperitur*[EN116] (*Theol. did. pol.*, 1685, P. I, *c.* 6, *sect.* 2, *qu.* 3, *font. sol.* 5). Lombard was saying the same thing when he referred to the *dissimilitudines* in the *similitudo*, and finally, in spite of everything, Augustine could also have said the same. And so, as the possibility of the doctrine has been half conceded—it has seldom been contested outright—the objection has always been brought against it that it is much too easy, that the scorn of unbelievers has been evoked by it, and that it has led the simple into error (cf. Thomas Aquinas, *S. theol.* I, *qu.* 32, *art.* 1; Calvin, *Instit.* I, 13, 18; Quenstedt, *op. cit., font. sol.* 6), and in fact, in spite of Augustine's authority and in opposition to it, the problem is simply touched on by most of the older dogmaticians and then dropped again as useless and dangerous. What can this objection and this attitude of distrust mean in a matter that one neither can nor will deny altogether except that there has been a sense of the alien character of what was supposed to be demonstrated as "God" by means of the *vestigia*, and of the complete difference between this "God" and the God of Abraham, Isaac and Jacob, the New Testament Father, Son and Holy Ghost, who should be the theme of the doctrine of the Trinity.

[344]

This is the obvious reason for the impression of trifling and even frivolity one obviously gets when pondering this theologoumenon no matter how pleasing and credible it seems at first in the words of an Anselm or a Luther. The moment it is taken seriously it leads plainly and ineluctably into an ambivalent sphere in which in a trice, even with the best will in the world, we are no longer speaking of the God of whom we want to speak and whose traces we meant to find but of some principle of the world or humanity, of some alien God. The original intention was to speak of God's revelation. But what happened was talk about the world and man, and this talk, understood as talk about God's revelation, necessarily wound up by being talk against God's revelation. The conqueror was conquered. This game cannot yield serious results. Taken seriously it can be only a profanation of holy things. This explains the feeling of frivolity we can hardly avoid in its presence.

This does not mean, however, that the game can be forbidden in principle or that the admittedly distinguished theologians who have more or less seriously played it must be regarded out of hand as heretical in this matter. We

---

[EN116] no true and complete likeness of the Trinity is to be found in creatures have tried to show with what good intentions it might be played and we have also indicated its basis in the problem of theological language. But even in relation to these good intentions and the Linguistic problem there is a lesson to be learned here. There are obviously possibilities in language—and we seem to have one of these here—with whose development the Church and theology will be undertaking something which is not indeed forbidden in principle but which is certainly non-obligatory, outside the scope of its commission and very dangerous to the extent that the new translation, establishment and understanding of the theme which is the task here comes precariously close to the adoption of a totally different theme, to the extent that suddenly a μετάβασις εἰς ἄλλο γένος EN117 might take place. The finders of the *vestigia trinitatis* had no wish to postulate a second and different root of the doctrine of the Trinity side by side with revelation. Far less did they wish to represent this second root as the only true one or to deny the revelation of the trinitarian God. But their action is deeply overshadowed by the question whether this is not precisely what they did. We are plainly dealing with that non-obligatory, uncommissioned and dangerous possibility whenever theological language, as here, thinks it must not just be the interpretation of revelation but also its illustration. Interpretation means saying *the same thing* in other words. Illustration means saying the same thing *in other words.* Where the line is to be drawn between the two cannot be stated generally. But there is a line, for revelation will submit only to interpretation and not to illustration. If we illustrate it we set a second thing alongside it and focus our attention on this. We no longer trust revelation in respect of its self-evidential force. What we say about it must be buttressed and strengthened and confirmed by something other than itself. This other thing at least shares the interest. Its power to illustrate revelation, and who knows but what we should say at once its power to prove it, now becomes a circumstance important in itself, and the same obviously applies also to the being and nature of this other thing, which has already acquired such weight as the illustration of revelation that, because it lies much closer to man than revelation, because it is in the last resort his own being and nature, it inevitably becomes a threat to his attention to revelation, a limitation of the seriousness with which he takes it. Is not even the desire to illustrate revelation, let alone the claim that illustration is essential, let alone the assertion that this or that is an illustration of revelation, already to be regarded as tantamount to a desertion of revelation? Does it not imply that unbelief has already taken place? Does not the transition from interpretation to illustration already stand as such under the interdict: Thou shalt not make unto thee any likeness? Obviously this transition is one that should not take place in theological language. The point, then, is whether we do not perhaps have a typical example of it in the doctrine of the *vestigia,* an example which we are thus to reject as such. We may grant that no interpretation of revelation—not excepting the most care-

[345]

EN117 change of categories

ful dogmatics and even Church dogma itself—does not contain elements of illustration. We may grant that if, leaving the actual words of Scripture, we even open our mouths or take up our pens we shall depart from revelation in the direction of that non-obligatory, uncommissioned and dangerous possibility, i.e., in the present instance, in the direction of the *vestigia trinitatis*. Thus we have to realise that when in the previous subsection we sought to arrange the biblical concept of revelation under the aspects of veiling, unveiling and impartation we came remarkably close to the fatal Augustinian argument and in no sense safeguarded ourselves against the suspicion that we, too, might be using an illustration and playing a little game with a supposed *vestigium trinitatis* (that could perhaps be traced back to the little sentence "I show myself"). In [346] this respect did not we, too, let ourselves be buttressed, strengthened and confirmed by something other than revelation, namely, by a possibility of logical construction? In the last resort was it the Bible that spoke to us or only this possibility? Did we find the root of the doctrine of the Trinity in revelation or ultimately only this other root? We wanted to find the root of the doctrine in revelation, not another root. We did all kinds of things to make it clear that this and this alone was our concern. But if anyone were to bring against us the charge that the real issue for us too was the other root, we could never accuse him of malice, for even with the best will in the world we could not completely or unequivocally escape the appearance that this might be so. It is as well to be clear about all this. Here as elsewhere we are not as theologians to anticipate or to pronounce to ourselves the justification of our own acts. Nevertheless, this cannot alter in the least the validity of the command which is given to us as theologians on that boundary between interpretation and illustration which is always drawn for theological language if it is to be and to remain theological language. It does not alter in the least the need to take note of this boundary, the need to ask constantly where we are when we speak, on this side of it or on that. Decision regarding this is not really in our hands, just as it is not for us in the last analysis to decide whether the finders of *vestigia trinitatis* really crossed the boundary or not. But concern for this decision is certainly laid upon us and reflection and attentiveness are demanded. Theological language is not free to venture anything and everything. When we reflect on the crisis in which we always stand and which we can never escape, we will make distinctions in what we do. To derive the Trinity consciously and intentionally from the scheme of man's consciousness or from some other creaturely order instead of Scripture is not the same thing as to derive it from Scripture and at the same time to grasp at a scheme which admittedly bears no small resemblance to that of man's self-consciousness and other creaturely orders. True, there is only a relative difference. The difference does not justify us in doing the second and not the first. In the last resort, at the same risk as all the rest, including the finders of the ancient *vestigia trinitatis*, we can only try to point to the fact that the root of the doctrine of the Trinity lies in revelation, and that it can lie only in this if it is not to become at once the doctrine of another and alien god, of one of the gods, the man-gods, of this aeon, if it is not to be a myth. It is in the name of a pointer of this kind that we reject the doctrine of the *vestigia*. We cannot claim to be driving it from the field in the name and power of revelation. Revelation would not be revelation if any man were in a

[347] position to advance and to establish against others the claim that he specifically speaks of and from revelation. If we know what revelation is, even in deliberately speaking about it we shall be content to let revelation speak for itself. To show that this is what we are doing we shall finally confront the doctrine of the *vestigia* with a very simple and unassuming No, a No whose point is just that the boundary seems to us to be crossed in this doctrine, but a No whose power stands or falls with the fact that we relate it also and not least to ourselves, and in the last resort we delicately leave it unproved. Its only possible basis is that we are told no man can serve two masters. The master or lord who may be seen in the *vestigia* we can understand only as a different Lord from the one so called in the Bible.

There is of course, and with this we close, a true *vestigium trinitatis in creatura*[EN118], an illustration of revelation, but we have neither to discover it nor to bring it into force ourselves, As we have tried to understand it as the true and legitimate point of the *vestigia* doctrine, it consists in the form which God Himself in His revelation has assumed in our language, world, and humanity. What we hear when with our human ears and concepts we listen to God's revelation, what we perceive (and can perceive as men) in Scripture, what proclamation of the Word of God actually is in our lives—is the thrice single voice of the Father, the Son, and the Spirit. This is how God is present for us in His revelation. This is how He Himself obviously creates a *vestigium* of Himself and His triunity. We are not adding anything but simply saying the same thing when we point out that God is present for us in the threefold form of His Word, in His revelation, in Holy Scripture, and in proclamation.

In the light of this true *vestigium trinitatis*, if we are to apply what Luther said about *Grammatica, Dialectica* and *Rhetorica*[EN119] in his table-talk, we may say that the theological encyclopaedia will consist, as in § 1, 1, of exegetical, dogmatic and practical theology.

This *vestigium* is plain and reliable. It is the *vestigium* of the God who deserves to be called God. It is really the *vestigium* of the triune God in the sense of the Church doctrine of the Trinity. But this *vestigium* is better described as *vestigium creaturae in trinitate* as noted earlier. In adhering to this, we shall not be accepting a second root alongside the first but just the one root of the doctrine of the Trinity.

[EN118] trace of the Trinity in the creature
[EN119] Grammar, Dialectic and Rhetoric

§ 9 [348]

THE TRIUNITY OF GOD

The God who reveals Himself according to Scripture is One in three distinctive modes of being subsisting in their mutual relations : Father, Son, and Holy Spirit. It is thus that He is the Lord, i.e., the Thou who meets man's I and unites Himself to this I as the indissoluble Subject and thereby and therein reveals Himself to him as his God.

1. UNITY IN TRINITY

In order to achieve the necessary conceptual clarification of the question of the Subject of revelation we shall now address ourselves to the development of the Church doctrine of the Trinity.

The doctrine of the triunity of God, as this has been worked out and lightly maintained in the Church as an interpretation of biblical revelation regarding the question of the Subject of this revelation, does not entail—this above all must be emphasised and established—any abrogation or even questioning but rather the final and decisive confirmation of the insight that God is One.

The concept of the unity of God as such will claim our attention later in the doctrine of God. It concerns us here only in relation to the further insight that God's triunity does not imply any threat to but is rather the basis of the Christian concept of the unity of God.

In our demonstration of the root of the doctrine of the Trinity in the biblical revelation we began with and continually returned to the revealed name of *Yahweh-Kyrios* which embraces both the Old Testament and the New. The doctrine of the Trinity is not and does not seek to be anything but an explanatory confirmation of this name. This name is the name of a single being, of the one and only Willer and Doer whom the Bible calls God.

It is obvious that no difference can be or is made here by the distinction which is made in Holy Scripture itself between Yahweh dwelling on Sinai and Yahweh dwelling in Jerusalem, or in the New Testament the distinction between the Father and the Son, or the distinction manifested in the contrasts between Good Friday, Easter and Pentecost. The man who prays to the Father, who believes in the Son and who is moved by the Holy Ghost is a man whom the one Lord meets and unites to Himself. We quoted the Pauline passages 1 Cor. 12[4f.]; Eph. 4[4f.]; in these, however, one should note not only the distinction between $\theta\epsilon\delta s$, $\kappa\acute{v}\rho\iota os$, $\pi\nu\epsilon\hat{v}\mu\alpha$[EN1] but also the unity to which emphasis is given by the repetition of $a\mathring{v}\tau\delta s$[EN2] or [349]

EN1 God, Lord, Spirit
EN2 He

53

εἶς[EN3]. The Church doctrine of the Trinity, too, not only does not seek to obscure the εἶς θεός[EN4] but rather to set it in the light as such. From the very outset it opposes antitrinitarians as those who fail also and specifically to confess the one God. The presupposition and goal of the Church in this matter is the doctrine of the unity of God, of the divine μοναρχία[EN5], in which it sees τὸ σεμνότατον κήρυγμα τῆς ἐκκλησίας τοῦ θεοῦ[EN6] (Pope Dionysius, *Ep. c. Tritheistas et Sabellianos a.* 260, *Denz.* No. 48).

The trinitarian baptismal formula could not be more wrongly understood than by understanding it as a formula of baptism into three divine names.

Tertullian *Adv. Prax.,* 26 spoke of the *singula nomina*[EN7]. But the ὄνομα[EN8] of Father, Son and Holy Ghost in Mt. 28[19] is one and the same. *Ita huic sanctae trinitati unum naturale convenit nomen, ut in tribus personis non possit esse plurale*[EN9] (*Conc. Toled.* XI, *a.* 675, *Denz.* No. 287). Baptism is *in nomine*[EN10], not *in nominibus Patris, Filii et Spiritus sancti*[EN11], as is finely stressed in *Cat. Rom.* II, 2, 10.

The faith which is confessed in this formula, and similarly the faith of the great three-membered confessions of the ancient Church, is not, then, a faith which has three objects.

Non habes illic: credo in maiorem et minorem et ultimum; sed eadem vocis tuae cautione constringeris, ut similiter credas in Filium, sicut in Patrem credis, similiter in Spiritum sanctum credas, sicut credis in Filium[EN12] (Ambrose, *De myst.* 5. 28). *Quid sibi vult Christus, quum in nomine Patris et Filii et Spiritus sancti baptizari praecepit, nisi una fide in Patrem et Filium et Spiritum credendum esse? Id vero quid aliud est, quam clare testari Patrem, Filium et Spiritum unum esse Deum*[EN13] (Calvin, *Instit.* I, 13, 16).

Three objects of faith would mean three gods. But the so-called "persons" in God are in no sense three gods.

Deus Pater, Deus Filius, Deus Spiritus sanctus. Et tamen non tres dii sunt, sed unus est Deus. Ita Dominus Pater, Dominus Filius, Dominus Spiritus sanctus et tamen non tres domini sed unus est Dominus[EN14] (*Symb. Quicunque*).

EN 3 one

EN 4 one God

EN 5 rule of one

EN 6 the highest kerygma of the church of God

EN 7 individual names

EN 8 name

EN 9 Thus, one name naturally pertains to the holy Trinity, which, though in three persons, cannot be considered plural

EN10 in the name

EN11 in the names of the Father, the Son and the Holy Spirit

EN12 You do not have this formula: I believe in the greater and the lesser and the last; but rather, you are bound by the same token of your voice to believe in the Son just as you believe in the Father, to believe in the Holy Spirit just as you believe in the Son

EN13 What then did Christ mean when he commanded that people be baptised in the name of the Father, the Son and the Holy Spirit, except that it is necessary to believe in the Father, the Son and the Spirit with one faith? And what is that, except to bear explicit witness that the Father, the Son and the Spirit are one God?

EN14 The Father is God, the Son is God, the Holy Spirit is God. And yet there are not three gods, but God is one. In the same way, the Father is Lord, the Son is Lord, the Holy Spirit is Lord; and yet there are not three lords, but the Lord is one

1. *Unity in Trinity*

We may unhesitatingly equate the lordship of God, to which we found the whole of the biblical concept to be related, with what the vocabulary of the early Church calls the essence of God, the *deitas* or *divinitas*[EN15], the divine οὐσία, *essentia, natura,* or *substantia*[EN16]. The essence of God is the being of God as divine being. The essence of God is the Godhead of God.

The more explicit development of this concept must be reserved for the doctrine of God. At this point the definition of Quenstedt may suffice (*Theol. did.-pol.*, 1685, P. I, *c.* 6, *sect.* 1. *th.* 11). The essence of God is the *quidditas per quam Deus est, id quod est*[EN17]. From the biblical standpoint, it is that which makes *Yahweh-Kyrios*, or wherein *Yahweh-Kyrios* is, the One He describes Himself to be by this name, the name of the Lord.

It may be said of this essence of God that its unity is not only not abrogated by the threeness of the "persons" but rather that its unity consists in the three- ness of the "persons." Whatever else we may have to say about this threeness, in no case can it denote a threeness of essence. The triunity of God does not mean threefold deity either in the sense of a plurality of Gods or in the sense of the existence of a plurality of individuals or parts within the one Godhead.

[350]

The Church doctrine of the Trinity may be summed up in the equation *Deus est Trinitas*[EN18], but it is noted at once in relation to *Trinitas: non triplex sed trina*[EN19] (*Conc. Tolet.* IX, *Denz.* No. 278). *Quidquid est in Deo, est ipse Deus unus et solus*[EN20]; whatever one may have to say about the distinctions in God, they cannot denote a distinction of the divine being and existence (*essentia* and *esse*; Bonaventura, *Breviloq.* I, 4).

The name of Father, Son and Spirit means that God is the one God in three- fold repetition, and this in such a way that the repetition itself is grounded in His Godhead, so that it implies no alteration in His Godhead, and yet in such a way also that He is the one God only in this repetition, so that His one God- head stands or falls with the fact that He is God in this repetition, but for that very reason He is the one God in each repetition.

In relation to the name of Father, Son and Spirit we have to distinguish *alius—alius— alius*[EN21] but not *aliud—aliud—aliud*[EN22] as though we had here parts of a whole or individ- uals of a species (Fulgentius, *De fide ad Petrum, c.* 5). *Personas distinguimus, non deitatem separamus*[EN23] (*Conc. Tolet.* IX, *Denz.* No. 280). *Quibus est unum esse in deitatis natura, his est in personarum distinctione specialis proprietas*[EN24] (*Conc. Tolet.* XVI, *a.* 693, *Denz.* No. 296). The so-called "persons" are a *repetitio aeternitatis in aeternitate*[EN25], not then a threeness of eternity

---

[EN15] deity, divinity
[EN16] being, essence, nature, substance
[EN17] that something through which God is what he is
[EN18] God is Trinity
[EN19] Trinity: not triple, but threefold
[EN20] Whatever is in God is the one and only God himself
[EN21] one—another—another
[EN22] one thing—another thing—another thing
[EN23] We distinguish the persons, but we do not divide the deity
[EN24] Those who have one being in the nature of the deity have a special property in the distinction of persons
[EN25] repetition of eternity in eternity

extra se[EN26] but a threeness of eternity *in se*[EN27], so that *quotiescunque repetatur aeternitas in aeternitate, non est nisi una et eadem aeternitas*[EN28] (Anselm, *Ep. de incarn.* 15). *Simplicissimam Dei unitatem non impedit ista distinctio ...* for *in unaquaque hypostasi tota intelligitur natura*[EN29] (Calvin, *Instit.* I, 13, 19). *Ipsa etenim Dei essentia est maxime unita individua ac singularis, idemque de tribus personis tamquam species de individuo nullo modo dici potest*[EN30] (*Syn. pur. theol.*, Leiden, 1624, *Disp.* 7, 12).

The idea we are excluding is that of a mere unity of kind or a mere collective unity, and the truth we are emphasising is that of the numerical unity of the essence of the "persons," when in the first instance we employ the concept of repetition to denote the "persons." It is as well to note at this early stage that what we to-day call the "personality" of God belongs to the one unique essence of God which the doctrine of the Trinity does not seek to triple but rather to recognise in its simplicity.

[351]

This concept, too, will have to be dealt with explicitly in the doctrine of God. The concept—not what it designates but the designation, the explicit statement that God is a He and not an It—was just as foreign to the fathers as it was to the mediaeval and post-Reformation Scholastics. From our point of view, not theirs, they always spoke much too innocently and uncritically of the *deitas*[EN31], the *essentia divina*[EN32], etc. as though God were a neuter. The concept of the "personality" of God—which we are provisionally emphasising by defining God's essence as His lordship—is a product of the battle against modern naturalism and pantheism.

"Person" as used in the Church doctrine of the Trinity bears no direct relation to personality. The meaning of the doctrine is not, then, that there are three personalities in God. This would be the worst and most extreme expression of tritheism, against which we must be on guard at this stage. The doctrine of the personality of God is, of course, connected with that of the Trinity to the extent that, in a way yet to be shown, the trinitarian repetitions of the knowledge of the lordship of God radically prevent the divine He, or rather Thou, from becoming in any respect an It. But in it we are speaking not of three divine I's, but thrice of the one divine I. The concept of equality of essence or substance (ὁμοουσία, *consubstantialitas*) in the Father, Son and Spirit is thus at every point to be understood also and primarily in the sense of identity of substance. Identity of substance implies the equality of substance of "the persons."

The claim that the Church with its doctrine of the Trinity was defending the recognition of God's unity, and therefore monotheism, against the

---

[EN26] outside itself

[EN27] within itself

[EN28] however much eternity is repeated in eternity, there is but one and the same eternity

[EN29] This distinction does not stand in the way of the utterly simple unity of God ... for the whole nature is comprehended in each hypostasis

[EN30] Now the essence of God is absolutely one, undivided and singular, and thus in no way can the three persons be spoken of as a class, as if they were individual

[EN31] deity

[EN32] divine essence

antitrinitarians may well seem paradoxical at first, for the concern of antitrinitarians in every age has apparently been to establish the right relation between the unique significance and power of the revelation in Christ and His Spirit on the one side and the principle of monotheism on the other. It might be asked whether perhaps all one can say is that in spite of the doctrine of the Trinity the Church wanted to retain and has in fact retained the unity of God as well; that it has shaped the doctrine of the Trinity in such a way that it has attempted to do justice to Christian monotheism too, and succeeded in this attempt. But we must give an insistent No to this weaker understanding. Christian monotheism was and is also and precisely the point also and precisely in the Church doctrine of the Trinity as such. We have simply missed the point if we see here the competition between two different interests in the assertion of whose rights tensions and cleavages, etc., can easily arise. Certainly one can understand the antitrinitarian heresies from this standpoint. These all became heresies because they were answers to questions that had been wrongly put. In other words, they were attempts to reconcile falsely opposed concerns, i.e., to remove irrelevantly manufactured tensions. In contrast, the Church's line is already distinguished formally from the heretical line by the fact that what happens on it is intended and is to be understood from the very outset as responsibility to the one concern as well as the other, because in fact we do not have two concerns which are opposed to one another and then artificially reconciled. On this thin but steady line where the basic issue is not this or that principle but quite simply the interpretation of Scripture, the point from the very first and self-evidently is both the oneness of God and also the threeness of God, because our real concern is with revelation, in which the two are one. On the other hand all antitrinitarianism feels it must confess the threeness on the basis of Scripture and the oneness on the basis of reason, that it must then combine them, which it naturally cannot do because it is prevented already by the difference in the sources from which and the sense in which it speaks of the two. Inevitably—and we must see this if we are to understand the sharpness with which the Church has fought it—all antitrinitarianism is forced into the dilemma of denying either the revelation of God or the unity of God. To the degree that it maintains the unity of God it has to call revelation in question as the act of the real presence of the real God. The unity of God in which there are no distinct persons makes it impossible for it to take revelation seriously as God's authentic presence when it is so manifestly different from the invisible God who is Spirit. On the other hand—and this must be our primary concern here—to the degree that it is ready to maintain revelation but without acknowledging the substantial equality of the Son and the Spirit with the Father in heaven, the unity of God is called in question. In its concept of revelation it will not in fact be able to avoid interposing between God and man a third thing which is not God, a hypostasis which is not divine—it does not want that—but semi-divine; it cannot avoid making this the object of faith. In so far as it is not

[352]

57

a denial of revelation, antitrinitarianism in any form is a cruder or subtler deifying of revelation.

When Arius and his followers wanted to see and honour in Christ the first and highest and most glorious creature of the one God, of which it may be said that ἦν ποτε ὅτε οὐκ ἦν καὶ οὐκ ἦν πρὶν γένηται EN33, that it is created out of nothing like all other creatures, that as compared with the Father it is ἀλλότριος καὶ ἀνόμοιος EN34, that as υἱὸς τοῦ θεοῦ κτιστός EN35 it is called God without really being so—they obviously did violence to the divine unity by the very adoration they thought they should pay this creature, and the more so the more seriously the adoration was intended. If Christ is not very God, what else can faith in Him be but superstition? Similarly, when the Arian and non-Arian Pneumatomachi, e.g., Eunomius or Macedonius of Constantinople, regarded the Holy Spirit as a created and ministering spiritual power, was it not inevitable that all the earnest religious statements about this creaturely *pneuma* EN36 should represent it as a semi-divine authority alongside God and thus do very serious injury to the very monotheism this whole school was supposed to be serving? Christ and the Holy Spirit are simply "the vital forces by which God created the willing and achieving of good in men" (K. Holl, "*Urchr. u. Rel. Gesch.*," 1925, *Ges. Aufs. z. KGesch.*, Vol. II, 1928, 27). It was precisely against this talk of "vital forces" that the monotheistic spearhead of the Church dogma of the Trinity was directed. Subordinationist Christ-ology—we are thinking chiefly of Origen—will certainly let the Son and the Spirit share in

[353]

the essence of the Father, but in graduation; the idea of a hierarchy, a variable measure of divine substance, is introduced into the essence of God. One can only say that this solution, too, is incompatible with the unity of God. As for the Adoptionist Monarchians, an Artemon and then a Paul of Samosata, the same must be said in this respect of their human Christ, who is endowed with special divine power and finally exalted to divine dignity, as we have had to say about the Christ of Arius. And when we turn finally to the Modalist Monarchians, Noetus of Smyrna, Praxeas, especially Sabellius, and then Priscillian, in whose steps Schleier-macher and his school have walked in the modern period, we find that they did indeed assert the substantial equality of the trinitarian "persons" but only as manifestations behind which God's one true being is concealed as something other and higher, so that one may well ask whether revelation can be believed if in the background there is always the thought that we are not dealing with God as He is but only with a God as He appears to us. If the τρόπος ἀποκαλύψεως EN37 is really a different one from the τρόπος ὑπάρξεως EN38 and if the ὑπάρξις EN39 is the real being of God, then this means that God in His revelation is not really God. To take this unreal God seriously as God is diametrically opposed to monotheism even though it was and is the point of the distinction to protect this. The result is—and this gives rise to the questions we should put specifically to modern Sabellianism too—that belief in revelation necessarily becomes idolatry.

If revelation is to be taken seriously as God's presence, if there is to be a valid belief in revelation, then in no sense can Christ and the Spirit be subordinate hypostases. In the predicate and object of the concept revelation we must again have, and to no less a degree, the subject itself. Revelation and revealing

---

EN33 there was a 'once' when it was not and it was not before it came to be
EN34 of another type and essentially unlike
EN35 created son of God
EN36 spirit
EN37 mode of revelation
EN38 mode of existence
EN39 existence

must be equal to the revealer. Otherwise there is no room for them beside the revealer if this be the one God. The unity of God would render revelation and revealing impossible. Christ and the Spirit would not just be foreign to and totally unlike the Father, as Arius said in dangerous proximity to a denial of all revelation. They would have no more to do with Him than any other creatures. Only the substantial equality of Christ and the Spirit with the Father is compatible with monotheism.

In hac trinitate nihil prius aut posterius, nihil maius aut minus. Sed totae tres personae coaeternae sibi sunt et coaequales[EN40] (*Symb. Quicunque*). *Nullus alium aut praecedit aeternitate aut excedit magnitudine aut superat potestate*[EN41] (*Conc. Florent. a.* 1441, *Decr. pro Jacobitis, Denz.* No. 704).

2. TRINITY IN UNITY

As the doctrine of the *repetitio aeternitatis in aeternitate*[EN42] the doctrine of the Trinity confirms the knowledge of the unity of God, but not any knowledge of any unity of any God.

As we now know, a kind of monotheism is represented not only by Judaism and Islam but in some form, whether in the background or as the culminating superstructure of its pantheon or pandemonium, by almost every religion right back to the animisms of the so-called nature religions of Africa. A kind of monotheism—this cannot be sufficiently emphasised—had also permeated for a long time the philosophy, the teachings of syncretistic cults, and [354] especially the feeling for life of later antiquity in the West when Christianity arose and, e.g., Paul's Epistle reached the Rome of the time. One need not expect that the dogma and dogmatics of the Church will simply confirm any monotheism or let itself be measured by any monotheism. The antitrinitarian heresies arose and will continually arise on this false presupposition.

At issue here is the revealed knowledge of the revealed unity of the revealed God—revealed according to the witness of the Old and the New Testaments. The unity of God confirmed in the doctrine of the Trinity is not to be confused with singularity or isolation.

Sustulit singularitatis ac solitudinis intelligentiam professio consortii[EN43] (Hilary, *De trin.* 4).

Singularity and isolation are limitations necessarily connected with the concept of numerical unity in general. The numerical unity of the revealed God

---

[EN40] In this Trinity nothing is before or after, nothing is greater or less. But all three persons are co-eternal and co-equal with each other
[EN41] None precedes another in eternity or exceeds another in greatness or transcends another in might
[EN42] repetition of eternity in eternity
[EN43] The affirmation of communion has taken away the understanding of [the divine] singularity and solitariness

does not have these limitations. No logical necessity need prevent us from simply acknowledging and stating this.

It is true of numerical concepts in the doctrine of the Trinity generally that *haec sancta trinitas, quae unus et verus est Deus, nec recedit a numero, nec capitur numero*[EN44] (*Conc. Tolet.* XI, *Denz.* No. 229). *In divinis significant (termini numerales) illa de quibus dicuntur*[EN45], they are to be understood metaphorically, they do not posit quantity in God, and in the last resort they merely imply negations (Thomas Aquinas, *S. theol.* I, qu. 30, art. 3). *Quid ista ibi significent, ipso de quo loquimur aperiente, insinuare curemus*[EN46] (Peter Lombard, *Sent.* I, dist. 24 A). Thus the number 1 implies the negation of all plurality of or in God. All further deductions from the use of the concept of number are to be rejected as irrelevant. We must be quite clear that the use of concepts of number and rational concepts generally in the doctrine of the Trinity (and not only the doctrine of the Trinity) in the early Church stands under the sign of Hilary's statement (*De trin.* 4): *Intelligentia dictorum ex causis est assumenda dicendi, quia non sermoni res, sed rei sermo subjectus est*[EN47]. Without having this statement before us, we cannot understand the point here, and he who does not adopt this statement as his own methodological axiom is no theologian and never will be.

God is One, but not in such a way that as such He needs a Second and then a Third in order to be One, nor as though He were alone and had to do without a counterpart, and therefore again—this will be of decisive significance in the doctrine of creation and man and also in the doctrine of reconciliation—not as though He could not exist without the world and man, as though there were between Him and the world and man a necessary relation of reciprocity. In Himself these limits of what we otherwise regard as unity are already set aside. In Himself His unity is neither singularity nor isolation. Herewith, i.e., with the doctrine of the Trinity, we step on to the soil of Christian monotheism.

Μὴ συμπαραφέρου τοῖς Ἰουδαίοις πανούργως λέγουσι τὸ Εἷς θεὸς μόνος, ἀλλὰ μετὰ τοῦ εἰδέναι ὅτι εἷς θεὸς γίνωσκε ὅτι καὶ υἱός ἐστι τοῦ θεοῦ μονογενής[EN48] (Cyril of Jerusalem, *Cat.* 10, 2). *Confitemur: Non sic unum Deum, quasi solitarium*[EN49] (*Fides Damasi a.* 380?, *Denz.* No. 15).

[355] The concept of the revealed unity of the revealed God, then, does not exclude but rather includes a distinction (*distinctio* or *discretio*) or order (*dispositio* or *oeconomia*) in the essence of God. This distinction or order is the distinction or order of the three "persons," or, as we prefer to say, the three "modes (or ways) of being" in God.

[EN44] this holy Trinity, which is the one and true God, is neither devoid of number nor grasped by number

[EN45] In the divine, they (numerical terms) signify those things to which they refer

[EN46] We must take care to penetrate what those terms may mean there through the exposition of that itself of which we are speaking

[EN47] Our understanding of what is said must be governed by the causes which give rise to speech, because the subject matter is not subordinate to the language, but the language to the subject matter

[EN48] Do not follow the Jews, who say wickedly that God is single, but after knowing that God is one, know, too, that the Son is the only-begotten of God

[EN49] We confess that God is not one in the sense of being solitary

2. *Trinity in Unity*

At this point, not only we but without exception all who have studied this matter before us enter upon the most difficult section in the investigation. What is meant here by the commonly used word "person"? Or, more generally, what is meant by what is distinguished or ordered in God as Father, Son and Spirit? Under what common term are these three to be understood? What are these three—apart from the fact that all together as well as each individually they are the one true God? What is the common principle of their being, now as Father, now as Son, and now as Spirit?

We have avoided the term "person" in the thesis at the head of the present section. It was never adequately clarified when first introduced into the Church's vocabulary, nor did the interpretation which it was later given and which prevailed in mediaeval and post-Reformation Scholasticism as a whole really bring this clarification, nor has the injection of the modern concept of personality into the debate achieved anything but fresh confusion. The situation would be hopeless if it were our task here to say what is really meant by "person" in the doctrine of the Trinity. Fortunately this is not our task. Yet the difficulties in which we are involved in relation to this classical concept are only a symptom of the general difficulty of the question itself, to which some answer must now be given.

The word *persona*[EN50], πρόσωπον [EN51] like *trinitas*[EN52], which is supposed to have been used first by Tertullian, originates with the controversy against the Sabellian heresy and is thus designed to denote the being in and for themselves of Father, Son and Spirit respectively. But did not *persona*, πρόσωπον, also mean "mask"? Might not the term give new support to the Sabellian idea of three mere manifestations behind which stood a hidden fourth? In view of this the Greek Church largely preferred to translate *persona* by ὑπόστασις [EN53] rather than πρόσωπον. On the other hand ὑπόστασις necessarily suggested to the Westerners *substantia* in the sense of *natura* or *essentia*[EN54]. and so they saw themselves threatened here by the proximity of tritheistic ideas. Finally, if the West clung to *persona* and the East to ὑπόστασις neither party could be perfectly content with the other nor ultimately with itself.

It is something of a relief that a man of Augustine's standing openly declared (*De trin.* V, 9, VII, 4) that to call what is meant "person" is simply a *necessitas* or *consuetudo loquendi*[EN55]. A really suitable term for it just does not exist. The reference to the three divine persons certainly means something very different from a juxtaposition like that of three human persons, and for this reason, that a juxtaposition of human persons denotes a separateness of being (*diversitas essentiae*) which is completely excluded in God—in this way the possibility of the Greek objection to πρόσωπον is formally acknowledged. To the question: *quid tres?*[EN56] i.e., what is the *nomen generale*[EN57] or general concept for Father, Son and Spirit, no real answer can be given, *quia excedit supereminentia divinitatis usitati eloquii facultatem. Verius enim*   [356]

[EN50] person
[EN51] prosopon
[EN52] Trinity
[EN53] hypostasis
[EN54] substance, nature, essence
[EN55] necessity [or] habit of speaking
[EN56] three what?
[EN57] generic name

cogitatur Deus quam dicitur et verius est, quam cogitatur[EN58]. (The more the distinction of persons is regarded as taking place in and grounded in the divine essence itself, the more inconceivable in fact becomes the inconceivability of this distinction; this distinction participates in the inconceivability of the divine essence, which would not be the essence of the revealed God if it were conceivable, i.e., apprehensible in the categories of *usitatum eloquium*[EN59]. Hence neither *persona* nor any other term can perform the service of making this distinction really conceivable. There is place here only for more or less fruitful and clarifying designations of the incomprehensible reality of God.) If, thinks Augustine, one still uses the expression *tres personae*[EN60], this is done *non ut illud diceretur, sed ne taceretur omnino. Non enim rei ineffabilis eminentia hoc vocabulo explicari valet*[EN61]: not in order to say that the three in God are precisely *personae*[EN62] but in order to say with the help of the term *personae* that there are three in God—and even the number 3 here cannot express more than the negation that Father, Son and Spirit as such are not 1. Following Augustine, Anselm of Canterbury spoke of the *ineffabilis pluralitas*[EN63] (*Monol.* 38) of the *tres nescio quid: licet enim passim dicere trinitatem propter Patrem et Filium et utriusque Spiritum, qui sunt tres, non tamen possum proferre uno nomine propter quid tres*[EN64]. Anselm had against the term *persona* the soundly based objection that *omnes plures personae sic subsistunt separatim ab invicem, ut tot necesse sit esse substantias, quot sint personae*[EN65]. This is true of human persons but it is not true of the divine persons. Hence he, too, will speak of *personae* only *indigentia nominis proprie convenientis*[EN66] (*ib.*, p.79).

Under the influence of Aristotle the Middle Ages then tried to establish a special systematic content for the concept of person. The point of contact for the deliberations initiated here was constituted by the definition of Boethius (early 6th century, *C. Eutych. et Nest.* 3): *Persona est naturae rationabilis individua substantia*[EN67]. According to Thomas Aquinas (*S. theol.* I, qu. 29, art. 1–2) a *substantia individua*[EN68] (equivalent to *singulare in genere substantiae*[EN69] or *substantia prima*[EN70]) is an essence existing in and for itself, separate in its existence from others, unable to impart its existence to others, an individual essence. *Natura* denotes the general essence, the *essentia speciei*[EN71], the *substantia secunda*[EN72], to which such an individual essence belongs. *Natura rationabilis* or *rationalis* is thus rational nature (including God, angels and men on the mediaeval view) as opposed to *natura irrationalis*, irrational nature (including all other substances from animals downwards). *Persona*, then, is simply

---

[EN58] because the supreme excellence of the divinity exceeds the capacity of our customary speech. For God is more truly contemplated than spoken of, and exists more truly than he is contemplated

[EN59] customary speech

[EN60] three persons

[EN61] not because it has any value in itself, but simply so that we might not be altogether silent. For the excellence of an ineffable reality cannot be expressed properly by this phrase

[EN62] persons

[EN63] ineffable plurality

[EN64] three I know not what: for while it is permitted to say "Trinity" here and there because of the Father, and the Son, and the Spirit of both, who are three, nevertheless I cannot put forth in a single term on account of what [they are] three

[EN65] wherever persons are plural, they subsist separately from each other, so that it is necessary to posit as many substances as there are persons

[EN66] owing to the lack of any truly appropriate term

[EN67] A person is the individual substance of a rational nature

[EN68] individual substance

[EN69] singular in kind of substance

[EN70] a primary substance

[EN71] essence of the species

[EN72] secondary substance

substantia individua (which can also be called *res naturae, subsistentia*[EN73] or among the Greeks ὑπόστασις) to the degree that the individual essence in view belongs to rational nature. The definition of Boethius is thus to be translated in Thomas as follows: Person is the individual rational essence. Thomas argues that this concept can be applied to God (*ib., art.* 3) on the ground that *persona* carries with it the mark of a dignity, that it even denotes indeed the *perfectissimum in tota natura*[EN74]. This dignity or *perfectissimum*[EN75] must be attributed to God in an eminent sense, *excellentiori modo*. Unfortunately Thomas did not say in what, according to his view, this dignity contained in the concept of person, this *perfectissimum* of the *persona*, consists. Is it the superiority of the rational individual essence over the irrational? Is it the superiority of the individual rational essence over rational nature as such? Or is it both? Be that as it may, Thomas himself recognises the objection that the *principium individuationis*[EN76], which is also decisive for the concept of person, is a material that exists in individuation, a something with individual existence, a potentiality, even when the reference is to rational nature. But for Thomas too, and specifically, God is *immaterialis, actus purus*[EN77]. Thomas has to admit, therefore, that when the concept of person is applied to God all that remains of the element of *individua substantia* is the attribute of the *incommunicabilitas*, non- [357] communicability, of the existence of the essence concerned to others, so that all that remains of the concept of the individual essence is what makes it an *individual* essence, and the fact that it is an individual *essence* has been set aside (*ib., art.* 3, *ad.* 4). Thomas is also familiar, of course, with the even more important objection, raised already by Augustine and Anselm, that a plurality of persons necessarily involves a plurality of essences as well, and therefore, when applied to God, a plurality of divine essences, or at least a division of the one divine essence. He has thus to state, in a way which is materially correct but which is also a threat to his concept of person, that the *personae* of the Trinity are *res subsistentes*[EN78] in (i.e., in the one) *divina natura*[EN79]. Thomas cannot help conceding that the ὑπόστασις of the Greeks is in this respect nearer the facts than the Latin *persona* and that he avoids it only on account of the fatal translation *substantia*. But the *res subsistentes in divina natura*[EN80] are also, according to him, nothing but *relationes*[EN81], intradivine relations (*ib., qu.* 29, *art.* 4; *qu.* 30, *art.* 1). Glad as we are to follow him here, and glad as we are to agree with him methodologic- ally when he appeals here to the uniqueness of the concept in its relation to what is meant, i.e., to what is divinely revealed—*aliud est quaerere de significatione huius nominis "persona" in communi et aliud de significatione personae divinae*[EN82] (*ib., qu.* 29, *art.* 4c)—we can hardly feel convinced that even a comparative aptness—there can be no question of any other—in the use of the concept of person has been explained by Thomas in such a way that we are forced to abandon the reservations in relation to it for which appeal can always be made to August- ine and Anselm. If Thomas has provided a true explanation, within the bounds of the pos- sible, for what the three involve in triunity, he has done this, not in the form of an interpretation of the concept of person, but by means of the concept of relations.

[EN73] an instance of a nature, a subsisting thing
[EN74] the most perfect quality in the whole of nature
[EN75] most perfect quality
[EN76] principle [or source] of individuation
[EN77] immaterial, pure act
[EN78] subsistent entities
[EN79] divine nature
[EN80] subsistent entities in the divine nature
[EN81] relations
[EN82] it is one thing to inquire about the meaning of this term "person" in common usage, and another about the meaning of a divine person

§ 9. *The Triunity of God*

Quite in line with Augustine and Anselm (and materially not in contradiction to Thomas) Calvin could criticise the concept of person in the words: *Les anciens docteurs ont usé de ce mot de personne et ont dit, qu'en Dieu il y a trois personnes: Non point comme nous parlons en notre langage commun appelant trois hommes, trois personnes ou comme mesmes en la papauté ils prendront ceste audace de peindre trois marmousets* (mannikins) *et voilà la trinité. Mais*—is Calvin's further opinion—*ce mot de personnes en ceste matière est pour exprimer les propriétez lesquelles sont en l'essence de Dieu*[EN83] (*Congrégation de la divinité de Christ, C.R.* 47, 473). Later J. Gerhard (*Loci*, 1610, L. III, 62) also spoke of a *magnum imo infinitum discrimen*[EN84] between the divine persons and the human ones known to us.

What is called "personality" in the conceptual vocabulary of the 19th century is distinguished from the patristic and mediaeval *persona* by the addition of the attribute of self-consciousness. This really complicates the whole issue. One was and is obviously confronted by the choice of either trying to work out the doctrine of the Trinity on the presupposition of the concept of person as thus accentuated or of clinging to the older concept which since this accentuation in usage has become completely obsolete and is now unintelligible outside monastic and a few other studies. The first possibility was chosen in the teaching of the Roman Catholic theologian Anton Günther, who was condemned by Pope Pius IX in 1857. On his view the individual persons of the Trinity are individual substances, three independently thinking and willing subjects, proceeding from one another and related to one another, and thus coming together in the unity of the absolute personality. Along the same lines on the Protestant side Richard Grützmacher (*Der dreieinige Gott—unser Gott*, 1910) ascribed a separate I-centre with a separate consciousness and will and content to Creator, Son and Spirit respectively. As he saw it, each of the three is also absolute personality, one

[358] with the others in the fact that the essence of all three is love and holiness, so that they are always experienced as working side by side and together. One can only say that it is hard not to think here of the *trois marmousets*[EN85] rejected by Calvin and that it is thus hard not to describe this doctrine as tritheism. The definition offered by Melanchthon in more than one passage (e.g., *Exam. ordinand.*, 1559, *C.R.* 23, 2) and often quoted later: *Persona est subsistens vivum, individuum, intelligens, incommunicabile, non sustentatum ab alio*[EN86], has a suspicious sound in this regard, especially if one sets alongside it the fact that he could also say in the plural: *tres vere subsistentes ... distincti seu singulares intelligentes*[EN87] (*Loci*, 1559, *C.R.* 21, 613). *Vita*[EN88] and *intelligentia*[EN89] as features in the concept of person necessarily import at least an appearance of tritheism into the doctrine of the Trinity. And the attribute of individuality when it is related to Father, Son and Spirit as such instead of the one essence of God, the idea of a threefold individuality, is scarcely possible without tritheism. "In God, as there is one nature, so there is one knowledge, one self-consciousness" (F. Diekamp, *Kath. Dogmatik*[6], Vol. I, 1930, 271).

In face of the danger which threatened at this point almost all Neo-Protestant theology

---

[EN83] The ancient doctors used the word person and said that there are three persons in God: not at all in the way that we speak in our everyday language, when we call three people three persons, or in the way that under the papacy the have the audacity to paint three mannikins and call it the Trinity. But – is Calvin's further opinion – this word 'person' in this context is used to express properties which are intrinsic to the divine essence

[EN84] great even infinite difference

[EN85] three mannikins

[EN86] A person is a subsisting entity that is living, individual, intelligent, incommunicable, and not upheld by anything else

[EN87] three truly subsisting ... distinct or singular intelligences

[EN88] life

[EN89] intelligence

obviously thought it had to seek refuge in Sabellianism. It had on the one side a desire to apply the modern concept of personality to Father, Son and Spirit, but also a justifiable fear of doing this ontologically as Günther and Grützmacher had done. It thus limited itself to a purely phenomenological doctrine of the three persons, an economic Trinity of revelation, three persons in the sense that God Himself was still in the background as absolute personality. In relation to this view it has never been clear either in ancient or modern times how far the real reference was to a Quaternity rather than a Trinity, and the more seriously revelation is taken the greater is the risk of this. One can certainly see why Schleiermacher preferred to say nothing at all about the concept of the personality of God and why D. F. Strauss (*Die christl. Glaubenslehre*, Vol. I, 1840, § 33) and A. E. Biedermann (*Christl. Dogmatik*, 1869, §§ 618 and 715 f.) went to the length of eliminating it altogether, i.e., of banishing it from the realm of truth, in which God is nothing but absolute Spirit, and assigning it to the lower sphere of an inadequate religious idea. One may still ask, of course, whether the hypothesis of a threefold divine self-consciousness is not to be described also as polytheistic if the threefoldness is described "merely" as a matter of the economy of revelation or the religious idea. What does "merely" really mean here if man still lives in fact with God in the power of the economy of revelation or the religious idea, but at this very point the *trois marmousets* are nevertheless to be the final word?

The second possibility has been adopted by Roman Catholic theology, whose doctrine of the Trinity even to this day speaks of the "persons" as though the modern concept of personality did not exist, as though the definition of Boethius still continued to be relevant and intelligible, and above all as though the meaning of the definition had been so elucidated in the Middle Ages that it is possible with its help to speak profitably of the trinitarian three.

In view of the history of the term person in the doctrine of the Trinity one may well ask whether dogmatics is wise to continue using it in this connexion. It belongs to another locus, to the doctrine of God proper, and to this as a derivation from the doctrine of the Trinity. For it follows from the trinitarian understanding of the God revealed in Scripture that this one God is to be understood not just as impersonal lordship, i.e., as power, but as the Lord, not just as absolute Spirit but as person, i.e., as an I existing in and for itself with its own thought and will. This is how He meets us in His revelation. This is how [359] He is thrice God as Father, Son and Spirit. But is this really the concept which explains the threeness as such and which can thus be made the foundation of the doctrine of the Trinity as its hermeneutical principle? The man who wants to retain it consistently will find that in addition to ancient ecclesiastical and academic usage about the only valid argument for its venerable position is that he does not have any other or better concept with which to replace it. Yet we must always ask seriously whether the argument of piety on the one side or the technical one on the other is weighty enough to cause the dogmatician to add to the thought of the Trinity, which is difficult in any case, the extra burden of an auxiliary thought which is itself so difficult and which can be used only with so many reservations. We have no cause to want to outlaw the concept of person or to put it out of circulation. But we can apply it only in the sense of a practical abbreviation and as a reminder of the historical continuity of the problem.

The truly material determinations of the principle of threeness in the unity of God were derived neither by Augustine, Thomas nor our Protestant Fathers from an analysis of the concept of person, but from a very different source in the course of their much too laborious analyses of this concept. We prefer to let this other source rank as the primary one even externally, and therefore by preference we do not use the term "person" but rather "mode (or way) of being," our intention being to express by this term, not absolutely, but relatively better and more simply and clearly the same thing as is meant by "person." The fact that God is God in a special way as Father, as Son, and as Spirit, this aspect—not that of the participation of Father, Son and Spirit in the divine essence which is identical in all and which does not, therefore, describe Father, Son and Spirit as such, nor that of the "rational nature" of Father, Son and Spirit, which can hardly be called threefold without tritheism—is usually stressed in analysis as the first and decisive element even by those who think that they must analyse the concept of person at this point. Hence we are not introducing a new concept but simply putting in the centre an auxiliary concept which has been used from the very beginning and with great emphasis in the analysis of the concept of person. The statement that God is One in three ways of being, Father, Son and Holy Ghost, means, therefore, that the one God, i.e. the one Lord, the one personal God, is what He is not just in one mode but—we appeal in support simply to the result of our analysis of the biblical concept of revelation—in the mode of the Father, in the mode of the Son, and in the mode of the Holy Ghost.

[360]   "Mode (or way) of being" (*Seinsweise*) is the literal translation of the concept τρόπος ὑπάρξεως or *modus entitativus* as, e.g., Quenstedt (*Theol. did.-pol.*, 1685, P. 1, c. 9, sect. 1, th. 8) put it in Latin. But the word ὑπόστασις understood in the sense in which, after initial hesitation and in face of the permanent doubts of the West, the Eastern Church finally accepted it in place of πρόσωπον, means *subsistentia*[EN90] (not *substantia*), i.e., mode of existence or mode of being of an existent. It is perhaps in this sense that Heb. 1[3] already called the Son χαρακτὴρ τῆς ὑποστάσεως θεοῦ[EN91] i.e., in His mode of being an "impress" or countertype of the mode of being of God the "Father." We have seen already that Thomas defines the divine persons as *res subsistentes in natura divina*. The term *res*[EN92] would not be a happy one, for *res in natura*[EN93] does not sound too well. But the term *subsistere*[EN94] is one of the two serviceable elements in the older concept of "person." Similarly the main concept in Calvin's definition (*Instit.* I, 13, 6) is to the same effect: *subsistentia in Dei essentia*[EN95] (in the *Congrégation* quoted earlier he expressly declared that with the Greeks, and on account of the biblical basis in Heb. 1[3], he would regard the words *substance* or *hypostase* as *plus convenable*[EN96] in this matter). In the period that followed I. Wollebius (*Chr. Theol. comp.*,

---

[EN90] subsistence
[EN91] the express image of God's hypostasis
[EN92] entities
[EN93] entities in a nature
[EN94] to subsist
[EN95] subsistences in the essence of God
[EN96] more appropriate

1626, I, *c.* 2, *can.* 1, 4) said, e.g., that *persona* means *essentia Dei cum certo modo entis*[EN97], while *Syn. pur. Theol.*, Leiden, 1624, *Disp.*, 7, 10 speaks of *substantia divina peculiari quodam subsistendi modo*[EN98] and F. Burmann (*Syn. Theol.*, 1678, 1, *c.* 30, 13) of *essentia divina communis et modus subsistendi proprius*[EN99]. We may also appeal at this point to more recent Roman Catholic authors. M. J. Scheeben (*Handb. d. Kath. Dogmatik*, Vol. 1, 1874, new edn., 1925, 832) states expressly that the individuality of the divine persons is identical with the specific form in which each possesses the divine substance, being a modality of individuality that belongs essentially to the individuality of the divine substance itself. Again B. Bartmann (*Lehrb. d. Dogmatik*, 7th edn., Vol. I, 1928, 169) writes: "That whereby the three persons are distinguished from one another is not to be sought in the essentiality nor yet primarily in the person in itself, which is fully equal to the others and perfect and eternal, but in the different way of possessing the essentiality." It is what these theologians call *subsistentia, modus entis*[EN100], form or mode of possessing that we, by saying "mode (or way) of being" at the decisive point, are making the focus of attention, which in fact it has always been in the various analyses of the concept of person, although, as it seems to us, far too much obscured by the context.

What we have here are God's specific, different, and always very distinctive modes of being. This means that God's modes of being are not to be exchanged or confounded. In all three modes of being God is the one God both in Himself and in relation to the world and man. But this one God is God three times in different ways, so different that it is only in this threefold difference that He is God, so different that this difference, this being in these three modes of being, is absolutely essential to Him, so different, then, that this difference is irremovable. Nor can there be any possibility that one of the modes of being might just as well be the other, e.g., that the Father might just as well be the Son or the Son the Spirit, nor that two of them or all three might coalesce and dissolve into one. In this case the modes of being would not be essential to the divine being. Because the threeness is grounded in the one essence of the revealed God; because in denying the threeness in the unity of God we should be referring at once to another God than the God revealed in Holy Scripture—for this very reason this threeness must be regarded as irremovable and the distinctiveness of the three modes of being must be regarded as ineffaceable. [361]

We have seen that Thomas Aquinas found he could retain the element of *incommunicabilitas* as well as *subsistere* in his concept of person, i.e., it proved to be serviceable to the concept of person in the doctrine of the Trinity. Nor is it any accident that *Conf. Aug. Art.* 1 included precisely these two elements in its definition: Person in the context of the doctrine of the Trinity means (*quod*) *proprie subsistit*[EN101]. The "*quod*"[EN102] in this definition must in fact be put in brackets. What *proprie subsistit*[EN103] is not the person as such but God in

EN 97 the essence of God with a certain mode of being
EN 98 the divine substance in a certain particular mode of subsisting
EN 99 the common divine essence and its own mode of subsisting
EN100 subsistence, mode of being
EN101 what subsists in its own what manner
EN102 what
EN103 subsists in its own manner

the three persons, God as thrice *proprie subsistens*[EN104]. It is worth noting that F. Diekamp (*Kath. Dogmatik*, Vol. I, 6th edn., 1930, 352 f.), who works with the *res subsistentes* of Thomas, comes to the conclusion that absolute subsistence belongs only to the divine substance as such, and only relative subsistence to the persons as such. But this relative *subsistere* of the persons is a *proprie subsistere*[EN105]. Similarly Calvin said that person means *subsistentia in Dei essentia quae ... proprietale incommunicabili distinguitur*[EN106] (*Instit.* I, 13, 6). In *Conf. Aug. Art.* I Melanchthon added in explanation: *Non pars aut qualitas in alio*[EN107], and in the *Loci: Non sustentata ab alio*[EN108]. Extending Melanchthon's explanation Quenstedt (*op. cit., th.* 12) strengthened the *incommunicabilis*[EN109] by paraphrasing: *per se ultimato et immediata subsistens*[EN110]. If one notes and stresses the fact that the distinctiveness in question can actually be denoted only by adverbs (*proprie*[EN111], etc.) or ablatives (*proprietaie*[EN112]) qualifying the verb *subsistere*, while the subject of this *subsistere*, and therefore of the *proprie subsistere* too, cannot strictly speaking be a *res*[EN113] or *substantia* different from the one essence of God but only this one essence of God itself, then the concept of "mode of being," strengthened and elucidated now by the adjective as "distinctive mode of being," will be the more clearly unpeeled as the core of what dogmatics has had to retain of the older concept of person. Certainly there is more to be said about the Father, Son and Spirit than is said in the formula "distinctive mode of being." We are dealing with God's modes of being, with God's threefold otherness. Calvin's definition is right when he says that *persona* means *natura divina cum hoc quod subest sua unicuique proprietas*[EN114] (*Instit.*, I, 13, 19). But from this and indeed from all the earlier definitions quoted we see that the "more" here—what Father, Son and Spirit are as "more" than "distinctive modes of being"—is the *natura divina*[EN115], the one undifferentiated divine essence with which Father, Son and Spirit are, of course, identical. If we now ask about the element that is non-identical, that distinguishes and is distinguished, the element that makes the Father the Father, the Son the Son and the Spirit the Spirit, the *quod subest sua unicuique proprietas*[EN116]—and we must obviously ask about this when we seek to investigate the threeness in the oneness—we shall have to be content with the less expressive formula, "distinctive mode of being." We also describe the one divine essence thereby, but we describe it thereby (and to be exact only thereby) as the one divine essence which is not just one but also one in three.

For this reason Father, Son and Spirit are not to be understood as three divine attributes, as three parts of the divine property, as three departments of the divine essence and operation. The threeness of the one God as we have met it in our analysis of the concept of revelation, the threeness of revealer, revelation and being revealed, the threeness of God's holiness, mercy and

---

[EN104] subsisiting in His own manner
[EN105] subsisting in a manner proper to each
[EN106] a subsistence in the essence of God which ... is distinguished by its own incommunicable character
[EN107] Not a part or a quality of something else
[EN108] not upheld by anything else
[EN109] incommunicable
[EN110] subsisting through itself both ultimately and immediately
[EN111] in its own manner
[EN112] with its own property
[EN113] entity
[EN114] the divine nature together with that which belongs to each one as its property
[EN115] divine nature
[EN116] that which belongs to each one as its property

love, the threeness of the God of Good Friday, Easter and Whitsunday, the   [362]
threeness of God the Creator, God the Reconciler and God the Redeemer—all
this can and should, as we shall soon show, draw our attention and serve as a
pointer to the problem of threeness in God. By separating the three elements,
we have not yet reached in these three elements as such the concept of the
three really distinctive modes of being in God. For whether it be a matter of
the inner property or the outer form of God's essence, all that is to be said can
and must finally be said in the same way of Father, Son and Spirit. No attribute,
no act of God is not in the same way the attribute or act of the Father, the Son
and the Spirit. The knowledge of God's revelation means, of course, the knowledge of specific and different qualities which cannot be reduced to a common
denominator and which will then make clear to us God's being as Father, Son
and Spirit. But because it is of the essence of the revealed God to have these
attributes, in His essence they, too, are indistinguishably one, and they cannot,
therefore, be distributed ontologically to Father, Son and Spirit. In the revelation attested in the Bible God always meets us, as we have seen, in varying
action, in one of His modes of being, or, more accurately, as distinguished or
characterised in one of His modes of being. But this relatively distinct revelation of the three modes of being does not imply a corresponding distinction
within themselves. On the contrary, we shall have to say that as surely as the
relatively different revelation of the three modes of being points to a corresponding difference in themselves, so surely it also and specifically points to
their unity in this distinction.

Thus we might envisage the essence of the Father by means of the concept of eternity, but
how could we do this without at once and in the very same way understanding the Son and
the Spirit in terms of the same concept? With Paul and Luther we can see in Christ the
revelation of God's righteousness, but obviously we then have to regard the Father and Spirit
as well in the same way. We can find in the Spirit the epitome of the divine life, but this
necessarily means that we understand the same life as the life of the Father and the Son. In
the story of the baptism of Jesus—I am here following Luther's exposition in *Von den letzten
Worten Davids*, 1543, W.A. 54, 59, 12—we shall call the One who appeared in the form of a
dove the Holy Spirit and not the Father or the Son, we shall call the voice that came from
heaven the voice of the Father and not the voice of the Son or the Spirit, and we shall call the
man baptised in the Jordan the incarnate Son and not the incarnate Father or the incarnate
Spirit; nevertheless, we shall not forget nor deny that everything, the voice from heaven, the
incarnate One, and the gift from above, are all the work of the one God, Father, Son and
Spirit. *Opera trinitatis ad extra sunt indivisa*[EN117].

The difference in ways of being, the *alius—alius—alius*[EN118], which is the
theme of our present enquiry, cannot have its basis here. But if not here,
where? The only possible answer which can be given, and which has in fact
been given from the very beginning, confirms us in thinking that we have

---

[EN117] The outward works of the Trinity are undivided
[EN118] one—another—another

69

[363]   done well to put in the centre of our whole investigation the concept of mode of being rather than that of person. This answer is that the distinguishable fact of the three divine modes of being is to be understood in terms of their distinctive relations and indeed their distinctive genetic relations to one another. Father, Son and Spirit are distinguished from one another by the fact that without inequality of essence or dignity, without increase or diminution of deity, they stand in dissimilar relations of origin to one another. If we have rejected the possibility of deriving the difference in the three modes of being from the material differences in the thought of God contained in the concept of revelation, because in the last resort there can be no question of any such differences, we can and must say now that formal distinctions in the three modes of being—that which makes them *modes* of being—can indeed be derived from the concept of revelation. These are the distinctions in their relation to one another. The Why of these distinctions can no more be explained, of course, than the Why of revelation. But it is possible to state and describe the That of revelation, as we have tried to do, and one cannot do this—as we could not—without encountering, in and with the material distinctions that are not our present concern, certain formal distinctions in the three modes of being which prove to be also irremovable distinctions as distinctions of the one essence of God the Lord.

Quite rightly reference has been made here first and foremost to the New Testament names of Father, Son and Spirit. If these three names are really in their threeness the one name of the one God, then it follows that in this one God there is primarily at least—let us put it cautiously, something like fatherhood and sonship, and therefore something like begetting and being begotten, and then a third thing common to both, which is not a being begotten, nor a proceeding merely from the begetter, but, to put it generally, a bringing forth which originates in concert in both begetter and begotten. But then, applying our ternary of revealer, revelation and being revealed, we can also say quite confidently that there is a source, an authorship, a ground of revelation, a revealer of himself just as distinct from revelation itself as revelation implies absolutely something new in relation to the mystery of the revealer which is set aside in revelation as such. As a second in distinction from the first there is thus revelation itself as the event of making manifest what was previously hidden. And as the result of the first two there is then a third, a being revealed, the reality which is the purpose of the revealer and therefore at the same time the point or goal of the revelation. More briefly, it is only because there is a veiling of God that there can be an unveiling, and only as there is a veiling and unveiling of God that there can be a self-impartation of God.

[364]   We might say further that the fact that God is the Creator is the presupposition of the fact that He can be the Reconciler and the fact that the Creator is the Reconciler is the ground of the fact that He can be the Redeemer. Or, the fact that God can be merciful to us in Christ is grounded in His holiness, and thus the love of God for us is grounded in His holiness and mercy. To clarify these relations of origin in the God of revelation Calvin was fond of the

terms *principium* (namely, *principium agendi*), *sapientia* (namely, *dispensatio in rebus agendi*), *virtus* (i.e., *efficacia actionis*[EN119]) (*Instit.* I, 13, 18, cf. *Cat. Genev.* 1545, in K. Müller, 118, 1. 25).

Now the real modes of being in God cannot be derived, of course, from the material distinctions in these or similar conceptual ternaries. For everything that is materially distinct here must be viewed as being even in its distinctness sublimated again in the unity of the divine essence. But they can be derived from the regularly recurring relations of the three concepts to one another as these occur most simply between the concepts of Father, Son and Spirit. The threeness in God's oneness is grounded in these relations. This threeness consists in the fact that in the essence or act in which God is God there is first a pure origin and then two different issues, the first of which is to be attributed solely to the origin and the second and different one to both the origin and also the first issue. According to Scripture God is manifest and is God in the very mode or way that He is in those relations to Himself. He brings forth Himself and in two distinctive ways He is brought forth by Himself. He possesses Himself as Father, i.e., pure Giver, as Son, i.e., Receiver and Giver, and as Spirit, i.e., pure Receiver. He is the beginning without which there is no middle and no end, the middle which can be only on the basis of the beginning and without which there is no end, and the end which is based wholly and utterly on the beginning. He is the speaker without whom there is no word or meaning, the word which is the word of the speaker and the bearer of his meaning, and the meaning which is the meaning of both the speaker and his word. But let us stay clear of the zone of *vestigia trinitatis*[EN120] on which we are already trespassing. The fact that the *alius—alius—alius* which can be illustrated by these other ternaries does not signify an *aliud—aliud—aliud*[EN121]; that the One and the Same can be this and that in the truly opposing determinations of these original relations without ceasing to be the One and the same; and that each of these relations as such can also be the One in whom these relations occur—for this there are no analogies. This is the unique divine trinity in the unique divine unity.

Our reference in what has just been said is to the concept which is known in dogmatic history as the doctrine of relations. It seems to have been familiar already to Tertullian: *Ita connexus Patris in Filio et Filii in Paracleto tres efficit cohaerentes, alterum ex altero*[EN122] (*Adv. Prax.*, 25). The Cappadocians (e.g., Gregory Naz., *Orat.* 29, 16) were the first to speak expressly of σχέσις, relation or connexion, as the element that constitutes the persons in God. In the West the doctrine was then plainly represented by Augustine. *His enim appellationibus* (Father, Son and Spirit) *hoc significatur quo ad se invicem referuntur*[EN123] (*Ep.*, 238, 2, 14) ...

[365]

[EN119] source ... the source of action, wisdom ... the structuring of action, power ... the effectiveness of action

[EN120] traces of the Trinity

[EN121] one thing—another thing—another thing

[EN122] In this way the connexion of the Father to the Son and the Son to the Paraclete makes the three coinhere, each out of the other

[EN123] For by these three terms ... that is signified by which they relate to each other *quae relative dicuntur ad invicem*[EN124] (*De trin.* VIII, *prooem.* 1). *Nonquisque eorum ad se ipsum, sed ad invicem atque ad alterutrum ita dicuntur*[EN125] (*ib.* V, 6). In the Middle Ages Anselm (*De proc. Spir.*, 2) coined the formula: *In divinis omnia sunt unum, ubi non obviat relationis oppositio*[EN126], and this was given the status of a dogma at the Council of Florence, 1441 (*Decr. pro Jacob.*, Denz. No. 703). In another passage Anselm stated it as follows: *Proprium est unius esse ex altro et proprium est alterius alterum esse ex illo*[EN127] (*Monol.*, 38, cf. also 61 and *Ep. de incarn.*, 3). Thomas Aquinas then introduced the concept of relation into his concept of person and defined the trinitarian *persona* as *relatio ut res subsistens in natura divina*[EN128] (*S. theol.* I, qu. 30, art. 1 c, cf. qu. 40, art. 1–2). Similarly Calvin's definition, which we now quote in full, is as follows: *personam voco subsistentiam in Dei essentia, quae ad alios relata, proprietate incommunicabili distinguitur*[EN129]. Luther very rightly expounded the whole doctrine of triunity in terms of the doctrine of relations: "The Father is my and thy God and Creator, who hath made thee and me, the selfsame work that thou and I are, the Son hath also made, and is as much thy and my God and Creator as the Father. Thus the Holy Ghost hath also made the same work that I and thou are, and is my and thy God and Creator as much as the Father and the Son. Yet there are not three Gods or Creators but one single God and Creator of the twain of us. Here by this faith I guard myself against the heresy of Arius and his like, that I divide not the single divine essence into three Gods or Creators, but in true Christian faith retain no more than the one God and Creator of all creatures. Again, if I now pass beyond and outside creation or the creature into the inward, incomprehensible essence of the divine nature, I find, as Scripture teacheth me (for reason is naught here), that the Father is a different person from the Son in the one undivided eternal Godhead. His distinction is that He is the Father and hath not divinity from the Son nor from any one. The Son is a distinct person from the Father in one and the same fatherly Godhead. His distinction is that He is the Son and hath divinity not from Himself nor from any one but only from the Father as eternally born of the Father. The Holy Ghost is a distinct person from the Father and the Son in one and the same Godhead. His distinction is that He is the Holy Ghost that proceedeth eternally from the Father and the Son together, and He hath Godhead neither from Himself nor from any one, but from both the Father and the Son together, and all this from eternity to eternity. With this faith I here guard myself against the heresy of Sabellius and his like, against Jews, Mahomet, and all that are wiser than God Himself, and mix not the persons into one person, but in true Christian faith retain three distinct persons in the one divine, eternal essence, all three of which, to us and creatures, are one God, Creator and Worker of all things" (*Von den letzten Worten Davids*, 1543, W.A. 54, 58, 4). In contrast, it is characteristic of the tritheistic weakness of Melanchthon's concept of person that, to the detriment also of the Lutheran orthodoxy that followed him, he did not at least incorporate the concept of relation in his definition but usually introduced it, if at all, only by way of later explanation.

The relations in God in virtue of which He is three in one essence are thus His fatherhood (*paternitas*) in virtue of which God the Father is the Father of the Son, His sonship (*filiatio*) in virtue of which God the Son is the Son of the Father, and His spirit-hood (*processio, spiratio*

[EN124] ... which are spoken in relation to each other

[EN125] None of them is called so [in relation] to himself, but to each other and to the third

[EN126] In the divine all are one, where the opposition of relationship does not stand in the way

[EN127] The particularity of the one is that he is out of the other, and the particularity of the other is that the other is out of him

[EN128] a relation in the manner of a subsistent entity in the divine nature

[EN129] I call a person a subsistence in the essence of God which, in relation to the others, is distinguished by an incommunicable character *passiva*EN130) in virtue of which God the Spirit is the Spirit of the Father and the Son. The fourth logically possible and actual relation, the active relation of the Father and the Son to the Spirit, cannot constitute a fourth hypostasis because there is no relative "opposition" between it and the first and second hypostases, because it is indeed already included in the first and second hypostases, because *spirare*EN131 is part of the full concept of the Father and the Son. *Spiratio convenit et personae Patris et personae Filii, utpote nullam habens oppositionem relationem nec ad paternitatem nec ad filiationem*EN132 (Thomas Aquinas, *S. theol.* I, qu. 30, art. 2c; cf. J. Pohle, *Lehrb. d. Dogmatik*, Vol. I, 1902, 329; B. Bartmann, *op. cit.*, 211). These three relations are the divine persons as such, explains Thomas (*paternitas est persona Patris, filiatio persona Filii, processio persona Spiritus sancti procedentis*EN133, *ib.*, art. 2, ad. 1). All modern Roman Catholic dogmatics agrees with him in this. The thing denoted by the concept person, explains M. J. Scheeben (*op. cit.*, p. 834), even though formally the term has no relative signification, is a subsisting relation or substance in a specific relation. "The divine persons in themselves are nothing but subsistent relations" (J. Pohle, *op. cit.*, p. 328). "The trinitarian persons do not have their own subject of inherence, but exist as *relationes subsistentes*EN134" (B. Bartmann, *op. cit.*, p. 211). A divine person is "an intradivine relationship in so far as it subsists for itself and is completely incommunicable" (F. Diekamp, *op. cit.*, p. 350). "The relations ... are ... that which makes the individual persons these persons" (J. Braun, *Handlexikon d. kath. Dogm.*, 1926, p. 228). In relation to all this both in Thomas' own explanation and more especially in those of his modern pupils we may well ask:

1. What has become of the definition of the persons as *res subsistentes in natura divina* (*S. theol.*, I, qu. 30, art. 1c)? Why are Roman Catholic dogmaticians silent about this? Why do they speak only of the reality of the relations as such? They are, of course, right; no other course is possible. The duplication (or quadruplication) of subject expressed in the *res* and *natura* must be abandoned as at least misleading.

2. If we hold Scheeben to his explanation that the name "person" in itself does not express relativity in God any more than in creatures, that formally it has no relative signification, and yet that relativity is the very thing that is to be expressed here, why should we cling to the concept of person which invariably obscures everything? "The terminology has been fixed by ecclesiastical and theological usage in such a way that it can no longer be discarded" (J. Pohle, *op. cit.*, p. 25).

The relevance of this argument is not apparent. It is obvious for one thing that the ancient concept of person, which is the only possible one here, has now become obsolete. It is also obvious that the only possible definition of the matter in question is not a definition of this ancient concept of person. Thus at the point where earlier dogmatics and even modern Roman Catholic dogmatics speak of persons we prefer to call the Father, Son and Spirit in God the three distinctive modes of being of the one God subsisting in their relationships one with another.

This, then, is the repetition in God, the *repetitio aeternitatis in aeternitate*, by which the unity of the revealed God is differentiated from everything else that may be called unity. We shall postpone our survey of the individual concepts

[366]

EN130 procession, passive spiration
EN131 spiration
EN132 Spiration pertains both to the person of the Father and to the person of the Son, inasmuch as it has no relation of opposition either to fatherhood or to sonship
EN133 fatherhood is the person of the Father, sonship is the person of the Son, and procession is the person of the Holy Spirit proceeding
EN134 subsistent relations

that have come to light here, especially *paternitas, filiatio* and *processio*[EN135], until they come up for discussion in their respective contexts. Our present task is to answer the general question of the trinity in unity, Augustine's: *quid tres?*

It is as well to realise that even when an answer has been given this question is still put again and again. There have been constant attempts to answer it. We, too, have now made such an attempt.

[367] We wished to give a relatively better answer than those which have been traditionally given in terms of the concept of person. But the fact that in the last analysis we could only group the familiar elements in the older concept of person (more intelligibly, we hope) around the concept of mode of being, may serve as a reminder that our answer cannot claim to be an absolutely better answer. The great central difficulties which have always beset the doctrine of the Trinity at this point apply to us too. We, too, are unable to say how an essence can produce itself and then be in a twofold way its own product. We, too, are unable to say how an essence's relation of origin can also be the essence itself and indeed how three such relations can be the essence and yet not be the same as each other but indissolubly distinct from one another. We, too, are unable to say how an essence's relation of origin can also be its permanent mode of being and, moreover, how the same essence, standing in two different and opposed relations of origin, can subsist simultaneously and with equal truth and reality in the two different corresponding modes of being. We, too, are unable to say how in this case 3 can really be 1 and 1 can really be 3. We, too, can only state that in this case it all has to be thus, and we can state it only in interpretation of the revelation attested in the Bible and with reference to this object. None of the terms used, whether it be essence or mode of being or relation of origin, whether it be the numeral 1 or the numeral 3, can adequately say what we ought to say and are trying to say in using it. If we pay attention only to what the terms as such can say in their immanent possibility of meaning; if we are unwilling or unable to accept the indication they are supposed to give, we shall only cause ourselves endless vexation. And who is not constantly faced by the question whether these terms are really an indication to him or whether, by clinging to their immanent possibility of meaning, he is not caused endless vexation? The axiom *non sermoni res, sed rei sermo subiectus est*[EN136], without adopting which we cannot really be theologians, is not really a self-evident axiom and never will be. The fact that this is so is obvious here too and here especially. The truth is that all the concepts which we have tried to use here have some value in relation to what we have to say, but that they then cease to have any value or their only value is that in their valuelessness, and with other valueless things of the same type, they point beyond themselves to the problem as it is set before us by Scripture. When we

---

[EN135] fatherhood, sonship, procession
[EN136] the subject matter is not subordinate to the language, but the language to the subject matter

74

have said what that is: Father, Son and Spirit, we must then go on to say that we have said nothing. *Tres nescio quid*[EN137] was the final answer that Anselm, too, found that he could and should give to Augustine's question. But the danger incurred here in relation to all concepts as such also arises in relation to the object. The inadequacy of all concepts not only implies the menacing proxim- [368] ity of a philosophical criticism based on the immanent possibilities of meaning of these concepts—this can be borne, because in the long run it is incompetent as such. What it also implies is the menacing proximity of theological error. We, too, are unable to avoid the fact that every step of ours in this field is exposed to danger, whether the threat comes from the tritheistic heresy or the modalist heresy, or whether there be on either side suspicion of the opposite error. We, too, are unable to take a middle course in such a way that every misunderstanding is ruled out and our orthodoxy is unequivocally assured. We, too, can in this respect return only a relatively satisfactory answer to Augustine's question. On all sides good care is thus taken to see that the *mysterium trinitatis*[EN138] remains a mystery. There can be no question of rationalising because rationalising is neither theologically nor philosophically possible here. That is to say, as philosophers we cannot give a full interpretation of the object with an apparatus of concepts already elucidated—for we always come up against the fact that from the standpoint of the object the decisive act of interpretation is an elucidation of the conceptual apparatus which is so radically ill-suited to this object. Again, as theologians we cannot really safeguard ourselves by means of this conceptual apparatus against the two opposing errors that threaten us here, for we always come up against the fact that in contrast to a theological language which uses this apparatus and is thus insecure, the truth creates the necessary safeguard for itself. Theology means rational wrestling with the mystery. But all rational wrestling with this mystery, the more serious it is, can lead only to its fresh and authentic interpretation and manifestation as a mystery. For this reason it is worth our while to engage in this rational wrestling with it. If we are not prepared for this we shall not even know what we are saying when we say that what is at issue here is God's mystery.

3. TRIUNITY

In the doctrine of the Trinity our concern is with unity in trinity and trinity in unity. We cannot advance beyond these two obviously one-sided and inadequate formulations. They are both one-sided and inadequate because a slight overemphasis on the unity is unavoidable in the first and a slight overemphasis on the trinity is unavoidable in the second. The term "triunity" is to be regarded as a conflation of the two formulae or rather as an indication of the

---

[EN137] Three I know not what
[EN138] mystery of the Trinity

conflation of the two to which we cannot attain and for which, then, we have no formula, but which we can know only as the incomprehensible truth of the object itself.

[369]   "Triunity," we say. The common German word for Trinity ("Dreifaltigkeit"), as Luther once said, is "right bad German." It has an "odd sound." Luther was obviously objecting to the tritheistic ring reminiscent of the fatal *triplicitas*. He suggested instead a "Gedritt" in God (*Sermon on LK.9²⁸ᶠ*, 1538, W.A. 6, 230). But "triunity" ("Dreieinigkeit") is to be preferred because better than *trinitas*[EN139] or *τρίας*[EN140], and certainly better than "Dreifaltigkeit" or even "Gedritt," it gives expression to both the decisive numerals, and its stress on the unity indicates that we are concerned here, not just about unity, but about the unity of a being one which is always also a becoming one. For this reason "Dreieinigkeit" is also to be preferred to "Dreieinheit."*

In practice, however, this concept of "triunity" can never be more than the dialectical union and distinction in the mutual relation between the two formulae that are one-sided and inadequate in themselves. We see on the one side how for those who hear and see revelation in the Bible the Father, Son and Spirit, or however we name the three elements in the biblical revelation, come together in the knowledge and concept of the one God. And we see on the other side how for them the source and goal of this knowledge and concept are never a sterile one but are rather the three, whatever we call them. In practice the concept of triunity is the movement of these two thoughts.

Ex uno omnia, per substantiae scilicet unitatem, et nihilominus custodiatur oikonomiae sacramentum, quae unitatem in trinitatem disponit, tres dirigens Patrem et Filium et Spiritum—tres autem non statu, sed gradu, nec substantia sed forma, nec potestate sed specie—unius autem substantiae et unius status et unius potestatis, quia unus Deus, ex quo et gradus isti et formae et species in nomine Patris et Filii et Spiritus Sancti deputantur[EN141] (Tertullian, *Adv. Prax.*, 2). Calvin often (e.g., *Instit.* I, 13, 17) referred to a saying of Gregory Nazianzus (*Orat.* 40, 41) which does in fact state very well this dialectic in the knowledge of the triune God: οὐ φθάνω τὸ ἕν νοῆσαι καὶ τοῖς τρισὶ περιλάμπωμαι· οὐ φθάνω τὰ τρία διελεῖν καὶ εἰς τὸ ἕν ἀναφέρομαι[EN142]. (*Non possum unum cogitare quin trium fulgore mox circumfundar: nec tria possum discernere quin subito ad unum referar*[EN143].) Similarly Gregory Naz. (*Orat.* 31, 14) developed the thought

---

EN139 trinity

EN140 triad

*   Editors' note. Since it is hardly possible to reproduce the nuance of *Dreieinigkeit* in recognisable English (cf. the "Three-in-Oneness" of the first edition), the term "triunity" is adopted here to render *Dreieinigkeit* rather than *Dreieinheit.*

EN141 All from one, namely, through the unity of substance, and yet the mystery of the economy is preserved, which distributes the unity into Trinity, ordering the three, Father and Son and Spirit – but three not in status but in degree, not in substance but in form, not in power but in type – being of one substance and one status and one power, because God is one, from whom these degrees and forms and types are numbered under the name of Father and Son and Holy Spirit

EN142 I do not succeed in contemplating the one without being illumined on all sides by the three; I do not succeed in grasping the three without being led back to the one

EN143 I am unable to think of the one without being quickly surrounded by the brilliance of the three; nor am I able to discern the three without being immediately brought back to to the one

that we can only think of God's act and will and essence as one, but then, remembering their distinct origins, we know three as the object of worship, even if we do not worship three alongside one another. The trinitarian dialectic is also very well presented in the "Preface on the All-Holiest Trinity" in the *Missale Romanum: Domine sancte, Pater omnipotens, aeterne Deus! Qui cum unigenito Filio tuo et Spiritu Sancto unus es Deus, unus es Dominus: non in unius singularitate personae, sed in unius trinitate substantiae. Quod enim de tua gloria, revelante te, credimus, hoc de Filio tuo, hoc de Spiritu sancto, sine differentia discretionis sentimus. Ut in confessione verae sempiternaeque Deitatis et in personis proprietas et in essentia unitas et in maiestate adoretur aequalitas*[EN144]. It should be noted that in the three-membered conclusion to this passage *maiestas*[EN145] counterbalances the *personae*[EN146] and *essentia*[EN147] in God, and *aequalitas*[EN148] (obviously equivalent to ὁμοουσία[EN149]) the proprietas and unitas, so that some effort is made to give a place of its own to the third thing to which the trinitarian dialectic points.

The triunity of God obviously implies, then, the unity of Father, Son and [370] Spirit among themselves. God's essence is indeed one, and even the different relations of origin do not entail separations. They rather imply—for where there is difference there is also fellowship—a definite participation of each mode of being in the other modes of being, and indeed, since the modes of being are in fact identical with the relations of origin, a complete participation of each mode of being in the other modes of being. Just as in revelation, according to the biblical witness, the one God may be known only in the Three and the Three only as the one God, so none of the Three may be known without the other Two but each of the Three only with the other Two.

It need not be specially proved that when the trinitarian distinction is in view in the Old Testament or the New the particular stress on one of God's modes of being never implies its separation from the others. What is always stated implicitly or explicitly—think of the express statements about the Father and the Son in John (e.g., Jn. 10$^{30,\ 38}$; 14$^{10,\ 11}$; 17^{11}) or the relation of Christ and the Spirit in Paul—is not, of course, the identity of the one mode of being with the others but the co-presence of the others in the one.

Since John of Damascus (*Ekdosis* I, 8 and 14) this insight has found expression in theology in the doctrine of the perichoresis (*circumincessio*, passing into one another) of the divine persons. This states that the divine modes of being mutually condition and permeate one another so completely that one is always in the other two and the other two in the one. Sometimes this has been grounded more in the unity of the divine essence and sometimes more in the relations of origin as such. Both approaches are right and both are ultimately saying the same thing. *Nec enim Pater absque Filio cognoscitur, nec sine Patre Filius invenitur. Relatio quippe ipsa vocabuli personalis personas separari vetat, quas etiam, dum non simul nominat,*

[EN144] Holy Lord, almighty Father, eternal God! Who with your only-begotten Son and Holy Spirit are one God: not in the singularity of one person, but in a Trinity of one substance. For what we believe of your glory, as you reveal it, the same we think of your Son and the Holy Spirit, without any difference of distinction. So that in the confession of the true and eternal Deity, the distinctness of persons as well as the unity of essence and the equality of majesty may be adored
[EN145] majesty
[EN146] persons
[EN147] essence
[EN148] equality
[EN149] consubstantiality

simul insinuat. Nemo autem audire potest unumquodque istorum nominum, in quo non intelligere cogatur et alterum[EN150] (*Conc. Tolet.* XI, Denz., No. 281). *Propter unitatem naturalem totus Pater in Filio et Spiritu sancto est, totus quoque Spiritus sanctus in Patre et Filio est. Nullus horum extra quemlibet ipsorum est*[EN151] (Fulgentius, *De fide ad Petr.*, 1). *Est et enim totus. Pater in Filio et communi Spiritu et Filius in Patre et eodem Spiritu et idem Spiritus in Patre et in Filio … Tanta igitur … aequalitate sese complectuntur et sunt in se invicem, ut eorum nullus alium excedere aut sine eo esse probetur*[EN152] (Anselm, *Monol.*, 59; cf. also Peter Lomb., *Sent.* I, *dist,* 19 E; Thomas Aquinas, *S. theol.* I, *qu.* 45, *art.* 5). On the basis of this doctrine the inner life of God would appear to be a kind of uninterrupted cycle of the three modes of being, and we are glad to be reminded of the inappropriateness of the figure resulting from the literal meaning of περιχώρησις [EN153] by the fact that instead of a temporal sequence the Latin Church adopted a spatial juxtaposition and thus preferred to speak in terms of *circuminsessio* (dwelling in one another, *immanentia, inexistentia*[EN154]) rather than *circumincessio*. In one way or the other this theologoumenon, which is not so far from the necessary biblical basis of genuine dogmatics as might at first sight appear, implies both a confirmation of the distinction in the modes of being, for none would be what it is (not even the Father) without its co-existence with the others, and also a relativisation of this distinction, for none exists as a special individual, but all three "in-exist" or exist only in concert as modes of being of the one God and Lord who posits Himself from eternity to eternity. Not unjustly, therefore, J. Pohle (*Lehrb. d. Dogm.*, Vol. I, 1902, 355) called the doctrine of perichoresis "the final sum of the two factors under

[371] discussion," namely, the doctrine of *unitas in trinitate*[EN155] and *trinitas in unitate*[EN156]. It must in fact be regarded as an important form of the dialectic needed to work out the concept of "triunity."

To the unity of Father, Son and Spirit among themselves corresponds their unity *ad extra*[EN157]. God's essence and work are not twofold but one. God's work is His essence in its relation to the reality which is distinct from Him and which is to be created or is created by Him. The work of God is the essence of God as the essence of Him who (N.B. in a free decision grounded in His essence but not constrained by His essence) is revealer, revelation and being revealed, or Creator, Reconciler and Redeemer. In this work of His, God is revealed to us. All we can know of God according to the witness of Scripture are His acts. All we can say of God, all the attributes we can assign to God. relate to these acts of His; not, then, to His essence as such. Though the work

---

[EN150] For the Father is not known apart from the Son, nor is the Son found without the Father. Indeed, the relation implied by the terms used for the persons forbids their separation, so that even when they are not named together, they are both implied. And no one is able to hear any one of these names without being obliged to understand the other

[EN151] On account of their natural oneness, the whole Father is in the Son and the Holy Spirit, also the whole of the Holy Spirit is in the Father and the Son. No one of them is outside of any of the others

[EN152] For the whole Father is in the Son and their common Spirit, and the Son in the Father and the same Spirit, and likewise the Spirit in the Father and the Son … And so great is … the equality in which they mutually embrace one another and are in one another, that no one of them may be shown to go beyond any other, or to exist without him

[EN153] perichoresis

[EN154] immanence, co-inherence

[EN155] unity in Trinity

[EN156] Trinity in unity

[EN157] outward

of God is the essence of God, it is necessary and important to distinguish His essence as such from His work, remembering that this work is grace, a free divine decision, and also remembering that we can know about God only because and to the extent that He gives Himself to us to be known. God's work is, of course, the work of the whole essence of God. God gives Himself entirely to man in His revelation, but not in such a way as to make Himself man's prisoner. He remains free in His working, in giving Himself.

This freedom of His is the basis of the distinction of the essence of God as such from His essence as the One who works and reveals Himself. On this freedom rests the incomprehensibility of God, the inadequacy of all knowledge of the revealed God. The triunity of God, too, is revealed to us only in God's work. This is why the triunity of God is incomprehensible to us. This is why all our knowledge of the triunity is inadequate. The comprehensibility with which it is presented to us, primarily in Scripture and secondarily in the Church doctrine of the Trinity, is a creaturely comprehensibility. It is absolutely and not just relatively different from the comprehensibility with which it exists for God Himself. It rests on the free grace of revelation alone that this comprehensibility in this absolute difference from its object is nevertheless not without truth. In this sense the triunity of God as we know it from God's work is truth. In a bridging of the gulf (from God's side) between divine and human comprehensibility it comes to pass that in the sphere and within the limits of human comprehensibility there is a true knowledge of God's essence generally and hence also of the triunity. In this sphere and within these limits revelation occurs. Otherwise how could it be revelation where this sphere is merely our sphere? How else could we perceive the triunity except in this sphere and within these limits? Only revelation as God's step towards us is, of course, the guarantee of its truth. As we cannot make the step across the abyss, [372] so we cannot be the guarantee. We can only let it be guaranteed for us. And we should not be surprised at the incomprehensibility in which it still remains for us as it becomes comprehensible to us. We should not confuse our comprehension and its allotted and appropriate truth with the truth of the triunity from which by God's grace it comes to our comprehension as this takes place in us with the appropriate and allotted truth. It is thus legitimate for us to differentiate the three modes of being of the one God on the basis of the revelation which takes place in the sphere and within the limits of human comprehensibility.

The revelation of God attested in Scripture forces us to make this differentiation. Scripture itself continually speaks in terms of these differentiations and it does so with great seriousness, i.e., in such a way that we are in no position to remove them without exegetical wresting. It shows us God in His work as revealer, revelation and being revealed, or as Creator, Reconciler and Redeemer, or as holiness, mercy and goodness. In these distinctions we can and should perceive the distinctions in the divine modes of being in the truth allotted and appropriate to us. The limit of our comprehension lies in the fact

79

that even as we comprehend these distinctions we do not comprehend the distinctions in the divine modes of being as such. These do not consist in distinctions in God's acts and attributes. If we were to assume this we should be assuming three gods or a tripartite essence of God. God's work would then be a remarkable combination of three divine truths or powers or even individuals. Hence we must believe already that even though the distinctions in God's work take place in the sphere and within the limits of our comprehensibility, here also and especially they do not signify the last word in the hidden essence of God, and the distinctions in God Himself cannot rest in these distinctions.

But why should they not draw our attention to the incomprehensible distinctions in God Himself, to the distinctions which rest on the various ways in which God posits Himself and is His own origin in the hiddenness of His Godhead? Why should not the comprehensible distinctions in God's revelation, provisional though they are, confront us with the problem of His incomprehensible and eternal distinctions? One must say at least that they can be regarded as fit and proper to give us this hint. There is an analogy—we recall our exposition of the doctrine of relations in this regard—between the terms Father, Son and Spirit along with the other formulations of this triad in revelation on the one side, and on the other side the three divine modes of being which consist in the different relations of origin and in which we have come to know the truly incomprehensible eternal distinctions in God. In these analogies, which are not present in the world like the alleged *vestigia trinitatis*[EN158]

[373] but which have been set up in the world by revelation, and by which (the mystery is not as it were abandoned and solved but rather denoted, and denoted precisely as a mystery, we have the truth of the triunity as it is assigned and appropriate to us. We shall not overestimate this truth. If we did, if we confused the analogy with the thing itself, if we equated the distinctions that are comprehensible to us with those that are not, in other words, if we thought we had comprehended the essence of God in comprehending His work, we should be plunged at once into the error of tritheism. But why should we on this account underestimate this truth? Even though we acknowledge the inaccessibility of the thing itself, why should we not accept it as a reference to the thing itself? *Abusus non tollit usum*[EN159]: why should we not use this reference as it is meant to be used as the creation and gift of revelation?

In the vocabulary of older dogmatics what falls to be said about this positive relation between Father, Son and Spirit in God's work and Father, Son and Spirit in God's essence is the doctrine of appropriations (attributions, assignments). By the specific assigning of a word or deed to this or that person of the Godhead, there should be brought to our awareness, as Leo the Great taught (*Serm.*, 76, 2), the truth of the triunity which is in fact undivided in its work and which still exists in three persons. *Ob hoc enim quaedam sive sub Patris, sive sub Filii, sive sub Spiritus sancti appellatione promuntur, ut confessio fidelium in trinitate non erret: quae cum sit inseparabilis, nunquam intelligeretur esse trinitas, si semper inseparabiliter diceretur. Bene*

[EN158] traces of the Trinity
[EN159] Misuse does not invalidate use

ergo ipsa difficultas loquendi cor nostrum ad intelligentiam trahit et per infirmitatem nostram coelestis doctrina nos adiuvat[EN160]. Augustine (*De doctr. chr.* I, 5) appropriated *unitas* to the Father, *aequalitas* to the Son and *connexio*[EN161] to the Spirit; Thomas Aquinas *potentia* to the Father, *sapientia* to the Son and *bonitas*[EN162] to the Spirit (*S. theol.* I, *qu.* 45, *art.* 6, *ad.* 2). Bonaventura (*Breviloq.* I, 6) has a wealth of appropriations which he partly took over from older sources and partly indicated himself: unity to the Father, truth to the Son and goodness to the Holy Ghost, or eternity to the Father, appearance (*species*) to the Son and event (*usus, fruitio*) to the Spirit, or principle to the Father, execution to the Son and goal to the Spirit, or omnipotence to the Father, omniscience to the Son and benevolence to the Spirit. A particularly typical biblical appropriation was found quite early in the ἐξ αὐτοῦ, δἰ αὐτοῦ, εἰς αὐτόν[EN163] of Rom. 11³⁶. We naturally have an appropriation before us when in Luther's Catechism the concepts of Father and creation. Son and redemption and Holy Ghost and sanctification are brought into the well-known close relation to one another, and in this regard it should be noted that whenever Luther comes to speak of the Trinity he never fails to refer to the real unity of what seem to be, and not just seem to be but actually are, threefold statements about God's work. Naturally we find another appropriation in the ternary which Calvin preferred, obviously borrowing from the great mediaeval tradition: *principium, sapientia, virtus*[EN164].

The clearest and most complete definition of the concept of appropriation is that given by Thomas Aquinas: *appropriare nihil est aliud quam commune trahere ad proprium ... non ... ex hoc quod magis uni personae quam alii conveniat ... sed ex hoc quod id quod est commune, maiorem habet similitudinem ad id quod est proprium personae unius quam cum proprio alterius*[EN165] (*De verit. qu.* 7, *art.* 3, cf. *S. theol.* I, *qu.* 39, *art.* 7–8). The rules to be noted in this definition are as follows according to Roman Catholic dogmaticians (cf., e.g., B. Bartmann, *Lehrb. d. Dogm.*, 7th edn., Vol. I, 1928. p. 215): [374]

1. The appropriation must not be arbitrary but must take place intelligibly. Not each and every triad, however significant in itself, is adapted even to denote truthfully the mystery of the triunity. There has to be a manifest kinship, similarity and analogy between the three things signifying and the three things signified, as there manifestly is between Father, Son and Spirit on the one hand and the three relations of origin on the other. If this is lacking the appropriation lacks significance.

2. The appropriation must not be exclusive. The appropriation of this or that quality or act of God to this or that mode of being must not be made a property of this mode of being or a distinction that is constitutive for it. What is appropriated belongs in fact to all the modes of being and the distinction between them cannot really be achieved by any appropriation, not even in the last analysis by the designations Father, Son and Spirit.

Evangelical dogmatics will have to add as a third and decisive rule that appropriations must not be invented freely. They are authentic when they are taken literally or materially or

---

[EN160] For this reason certain things are presented under the name Father or Son or Holy Spirit, so that the confession of believers in the Trinity should not go astray. For though it is not subject to division, it could never be understood to be Trinity if it were always spoken of inseparably. Therefore the very incapacity of speech serves the good by pulling our heart to understanding, and through our weakness, heavenly doctrine aids us

[EN161] unity, equality, connectivity

[EN162] might, wisdom, goodness

[EN163] of him, and through him, and to him

[EN164] source, wisdom, power

[EN165] to appropriate is nothing else than to apply that which is common to one in particular ... not ... because it is the case that it belongs more to one person than to another ... but because that which is common has a greater likeness to that which is proper to one person than to what is proper to another

both from Holy Scripture, when they are a rendering or interpretation of the appropriations found there. If they are this they will certainly not be arbitrary or exclusive either.

Our statement concerning the comprehensibility of Father, Son and Spirit in God's work obviously requires—we are now enquiring into the unity of the three modes of being *ad extra* too—a dialectical counterpart. It may always be seen already on the margin of what has been said thus far, but it must now be emphasised, that also and precisely in God's work, in God's entry into the sphere of the creature and therefore into the sphere and the limits of our comprehensibility, God is one both in His eternal truth and also in the truth assigned and appropriate to us. It would be pagan mythology to present the work of God in the form of a dramatic entry and exit of now one and now another of the divine persons, of the surging up and down of half or totally individualised powers or forms or ideas, of a shifting co-existence and competition of the three hypostases. Again it is impossible to draw the line plainly and generally between permitted and commanded appropriations and this forbidden mythology. The one may often bear a confusing resemblance to the other. But the line has been drawn; to the involution and convolution of the three modes of being in the essence of God there corresponds exactly their involution and convolution in His work. The fact that He is particularly manifest for us in this indissolubly and characteristically distinct act or attribute in this or that mode of being may not and must not mean that we have not to believe and worship God in the other modes of being even though they are temporarily hidden from us. Just as Scripture is to be read in context as the witness to God's revelation, just as, e.g., Good Friday, Easter and Pentecost can only say together what they have to say, so we must say that all God's work, as we [375] are to grasp it on the basis of His revelation, is one act which occurs simultaneously and in concert in all His three modes of being. From creation by way of revelation and reconciliation to the coming redemption it is always true that He who acts here is the Father and the Son and the Spirit. And it is true of all the perfections that are to be declared in relation to this work of God that they are as much the perfections of the Father as of the Son and the Spirit. *Per appropriationem*[EN166] this act or this attribute must now be given prominence in relation to this or that mode of being in order that this can be described as such. But only *per appropriationem* may this happen, and in no case, therefore, to the forgetting or denying of God's presence in all His modes of being, in His total being and act even over against us.

Materially, though not literally, the theological rule with respect to the Trinity: *opera trinitatis ad extra sunt indivisa*[EN167], is first found clearly in Augustine: *Sicut inseparabiles sunt, ita inseparabiliter operantur*[EN168] (*De trin.* I, 4). *Ad creaturam Pater et Filius et Spiritus sanctus unum*

[EN166] by appropriation
[EN167] the works of the Trinity toward the outside are undivided
[EN168] Just as they are inseparable in fact, so are they inseparable in their work

principium, sicut unus creator et unus dominus[EN169] (*ib.* V, 14). For: *Non potest operatio esse divina, ubi non solum aequalis est, verum etiam indiscreta natura*[EN170] (*C. Adrian.*, 15). In the dogma of the Roman Catholic Church this insight has found its most precise expression in the statement of the *Conc. Florent.*, 1441 (*Denz.* No. 704): *Pater et Filius et Spiritus sanctus non tria principia creaturae, sed unum principium*[EN171]. The emphasis with which Luther supported this truth may be recalled again at this point. We must say of it, no less than of the doctrine of the perichoresis, that it is to some extent a proof by way of example in relation to the opposing statements about the *unitas in trinitate* and the *trinitas in unitate*. With the doctrine of appropriations it constitutes the other form of the dialectical outworking of the concept of triunity.

4. THE MEANING OF THE DOCTRINE OF THE TRINITY

By the doctrine of the Trinity we understand the Church doctrine of the unity of God in the three modes of being of Father, Son and Holy Ghost, or of the threefold otherness of the one God in the three modes of being of Father, Son and Holy Ghost. All that had and has to be expounded here in detail could and can expound only the unity in trinity and the trinity in unity. This doctrine as such does not stand in the texts of the Old and New Testament witness to God's revelation. It did not arise out of the historical situations to which these texts belong. It is exegesis of these texts in the speech, and this also means in the light of the questions, of a later situation. It belongs to the Church. It is a theologoumenon. It is dogma. We have asked (§ 8, 2) about its root, i.e., the possibility on the basis of which it could be a dogma in a Church which sought to regulate its doctrine by the biblical witness. And we have seen that this possibility lies in the fact that in the Bible revelation means the self-unveiling, imparted to men, of the God who by nature cannot be unveiled to men. According to the biblical witness this matter is of such a nature that in the light of the three elements of God's veiling, unveiling and imparting we have cause to speak of the threefold otherness of the one God who has revealed Himself according to the witness of the Bible. The biblical witness to God's revelation sets us face to face with the possibility of interpreting the one statement that "God reveals Himself as the Lord" three times in different senses. This possibility is the biblical root of the doctrine of the Trinity. But in the Bible it remains on the level of possibility. We are now asking about the meaning of its actualisation. With what necessity and right did the Church formulate this dogma? It could do this. Did it have to do it? What insight was it expressing in the dogma and what reason have we, then, to take pains to understand it?

[376]

[EN169] With respect to creation the Father and Son and Holy Spirit are one source, just as they are one Creator and one Lord

[EN170] An act cannot be divided where the nature is not only equal, but even indivisible

[EN171] The Father and the Son and the Holy Spirit are not three sources of creation, but one source

§ 9. *The Triunity of God*

Now obviously we cannot discuss this question intelligently if the Church of earlier days which framed this theologoumenon and gave it the status of dogma has become so alien to us that we can view and evaluate it and its intentions only historically, i.e., in this case from outside, as strangers, not really thinking its thoughts with it.

This would be so, e.g., if we could not rise above the recollection that in the controversies before and after Nicaea a very considerable part was played by very non-theological antipathies in ecclesiastical and civil politics, in court relations, and in national and certainly economic matters as well; or if we could not rise above the recollection that the development of the dogma of the Trinity is unquestionably a chapter in the history of the philosophy of later antiquity, an offshoot of Stoic and Neo-Platonic Logos speculation; or if with the historical and systematic theologians of the school of A. Ritschl we could not rise above the recollection that the belief in revelation of the Christian world in which this dogma arose was shrouded beyond recognition in the mists of an ancient mystery religion nourished on Orientalisms of every possible kind, that it was embedded in a predominantly physical understanding of the revealed salvation, in a predominantly cosmic interest in the knowledge of revelation, in a predominantly sacramentally orientated piety with which we cannot really identify ourselves and the validity of which we shall perhaps have to call into serious question more from the standpoint of the Reformation than from that of the New Testament. If considerations of this kind, including perhaps a mere sense of reverence for a form sanctified by age, were to have the last word in regard to our participation in the rise of the dogma, what could this mean but that all these events, and the dogma as their result, and all later work attempted along the lines of the dogma, would be fundamentally alien to us? In relation to the decisive point of the dogma, namely, the Christian knowledge of God, we should then be faced by at least a deep suspicion if not an actual certainty that there is really nothing in it, that the only voice here is perhaps that of Byzantine politics, or Stoicism, or Neo-Platonism, or the ancient piety of the mysteries. And in this case any enquiry into the meaning of the doctrine of the Trinity could be pursued only with the aloofness of an astonished and disapproving spectator, and might just as well be abandoned.

[377]   We have to realise that if we adopt this attitude we are saying that the Church of earlier days lost, so to speak, its theme, that it need no longer concern us seriously in relation to what it was really intended to be, namely, the Church of Jesus Christ, and that its work does not have any relevance to us except perhaps as an object of contemplation from outside. If we evaluate it as we would evaluate a heresy or even an alien religion we are naturally in no position to ask seriously, i.e., sympathetically, about the meaning of its intention. But we have also to realise that this is a very daring and a very dangerous judgment. It is daring because in making it we are declaring that the Church of earlier days was basically a heresy or an alien religion—a judgment which is not indeed formally impossible, but which involves a heavy responsibility, especially when, as here, the issue is the line in dogmatic history along which, ever since the great and decisive battles of the 4th century, all the Church's significant theologians have unswervingly advanced, including the Reformers and their 17th century successors. And a judgment of this kind might well be dangerous because those in the Church who in this way want to see and understand

others only from outside must face the question whether on the contrary it is not perhaps they themselves who are outsiders as the adherents of a heresy or even an alien religion. It is surely more normal and safer to start at least with the assumption that the Church of the earlier period, and specifically the Church of this earlier period, is one and the same as the Church which we know and which we like to call the Church, so that it makes sense to ask seriously, i.e., sympathetically, what it intended by this dogma. The assumption that Jesus Christ did not altogether abandon His Church in this age, and that, notwithstanding all the things that might justly be alleged against it, it is still in place to listen to it as one listens to the Church—this assumption would always seem to have a very definite advantage over its opposite. In any case we certainly need very weighty reasons if we decide to drop, as it were, the Church of any period, adopting that attitude of contemplation and evaluation from outside and no longer listening seriously to its voice. Are the reasons really so compelling in relation to the early period of the Church when the doctrine of the Trinity arose?

In the dogmatic and theological history of every age, not excluding that of Protestantism, secular factors have played a part which tends to cover over all else. For all the gloating with which it was done, it was a good thing that the work of Pietism and the Enlightenment in Church History established so incontrovertibly the fact that even in such periods of supreme decision as that in which the dogma of the Trinity arose the history of the Church was anything but a history of heroes and saints. Yet in this case we should be just and perceptive and allow that not only the Church of Byzantium but also that of Wittenberg and Geneva, and finally the purest Church of any of the quiet in the land, have always and everywhere been, when examined at close range, centres of frailties and scandals of every kind, and that on the basis of the Reformation doctrine of justification at all events it is neither fitting nor worth while to play off the worldliness of the Church against the seriousness of the insights it has perhaps gained in spite of and in this worldliness. The same may be said about the indisputable connexion of the dogma with the philosophy of the age. By proving philosophical involvement we can reject the confessions and theology of any age and school, and we can do this the more effectively the less we see the beam in our own eye. For linguistically theologians have always depended on some philosophy and linguistically they always will. But instead of getting Pharisaically indignant about this and consigning whole periods to the limbo of a philosophy that is supposed to deny the Gospel—simply because our own philosophy is different—it is better to stick strictly to the one question what the theologians of the earlier period were really trying to say in the vocabulary of their philosophy. Caution is especially demanded when we insist on differences in the so-called piety of different periods and therefore claim that the piety out of which the dogma of the Trinity arose was completely different from our own piety with its sober focus, as they said some years ago, on "worldview and morality." What right have we to regard our own piety, even if its agreement with the Reformation and the New Testament seem ever so impeccable, as the only piety that is possible in the Church, and therefore to exalt it as a standard by which to measure the insights of past ages? Let us be sure of our own cause so far as we can. But antithetical rigidity especially in evaluating the subjective religion of others is something against which we can only issue a warning.

[378]

There seem to be no compelling reasons why we should so distrust the Church of the 4th century and its dogma that we abandon the question as to the meaning of this dogma.

On the other hand, if any one wishes to advance such reasons, we cannot rebut them with counter-arguments. There can be no contesting the formal possibility that any Church might be an apostate church which does not concern us and has nothing to say to us. If we do in fact deny this possibility, this is, as in all similar cases, a decision of faith, or, as we might say more cautiously, a decision which must regard itself as a decision of faith, which can have meaning only as a decision of faith, and for the justification of which we can only appeal in the last resort to the dogma itself and to Holy Scripture confronting both us and the dogma, asking whether the dogma, for all the undeniable and ineradicable limitation of its origin, does not express an insight, which a Church with an ear for Holy Scripture not only could reach but had to reach at a specific time; whether, by letting Scripture and the dogma speak for themselves, we can escape the conviction that divine truth is given human formulation here in a way in which it had to be formulated at some period, so that this formulation, once achieved, must never be lost or forgotten again; whether what took place here, while it was certainly exegesis and not infallible revelation, was not still the kind of exegesis that can be confidently described as not merely correct but also important. And if we answer this question in the affirmative, if we thus confess the possibility of regarding ourselves as in the same sphere as the Church of the past which perceived and confessed this [379] dogma as such, i.e., as being one and the same Church with it, if we thus enquire into the meaning of the doctrine of the Trinity, this does not imply a purely accidental personal decision. We should take into account the fact that even to this day this decision is that not merely of the Roman Catholic and Orthodox Churches but also basically of all the great Evangelical Churches as well.

None of them has actually revoked what took place when an express confirmation of the early symbols expressing the doctrine of the Trinity was made a constitutive part of the Reformation confessions in the 16th century. The liturgical recitation of the so-called Apostles' Creed, which is the practice in the Prussian and other territorial churches, repeats in its own fashion this significant event. And every baptism validly performed in our churches at least confronts us with the problem of the doctrine of the Trinity.

No one can say that he knows, and no one is competent to declare, that only pious reverence for a venerable landmark of Christianity has preserved some place for the doctrine of the Trinity in a more or less clear form even in the Evangelical Church as it is now ravaged by Modernism. This fact gives us the external right too, and indeed imposes upon us the task, of enquiring into its meaning at this point.

We should start with the fact that the rise of the doctrine of the Trinity, however varied the factors which contributed to it, was at least governed also by the need to clear up a question with which the Church saw itself confronted by Holy Scripture in the delivery of its message. Assuming that the Church is not only unfaithful by nature, as it has been, of course, in every age, but is also in some degree and sense faithful, so that in its proclamation it has tried to take up the witness of the Old and New Testaments, there can be no cause for surprise that it has come up against the question which found an answer in the doctrine of the Trinity. Nor can there be any cause for surprise that it came up against this particular question in such a relatively early period, nor need we be surprised at the violence of the conflicts into which it was plunged by this question and the inexorability with which it has adhered through the centuries to the broad line achieved at that time. The question which arose for it out of the commitment of its proclamation to Scripture, and which it answered in the doctrine of the Trinity, was in fact a basic and vital question of the first rank for Church preaching and therefore for Church theology too. We thus regard it as right and proper to put discussion of this question at the head of all dogmatics. This is a practical outworking of what many have said theoretically about its significance from the very earliest times.

But the question that is answered by the doctrine of the Trinity is a very specific question regarding the basic concept of the revelation of God or the basic fact of it as attested in Scripture.

Even if it be regarded as a mere offshoot of the Logos speculation of later antiquity one [380] must at all events concede that its occasion at least is the manifestation of Jesus Christ understood as the revelation of the Logos. It is trying to discuss the deity of this revealed, incarnate Logos. Its second theme, the concept of the Spirit, points in the same direction. And when it speaks of God the Father it is dealing with the point of origin and relation of these two, the Son and the Spirit.

The specific question about revelation which is answered by the doctrine of the Trinity is, however, the question who it is that reveals Himself, the question of the subject of revelation. One may sum up the meaning of the doctrine of the Trinity briefly and simply by saying that *God* is the One who reveals Himself. But if this meaning is to be fully perspicuous one must also reverse the emphasis and say that God is the One who *reveals* Himself. For the strictness and logic of the answer to the question about the subject of revelation consist in the fact that as we enquire into the interpretation of this answer we find ourselves referred back again to revelation itself. The Church doctrine of the Trinity is a self-enclosed circle. Its decisive and controlling concern is to say with exactitude and completeness that *God* is the Revealer. But how can it say this with exactitude and completeness unless it declares that none other than the *Revealer* is God? One might put this more simply by saying that the doctrine of the Trinity states that our God, namely, He who makes Himself ours in His revelation, is really God. And to the question, But who is God? there may then be given the no less simple answer, This God of ours. Is it not true that the main answer and the subsidiary answer are the simple but no less momentous presuppositions of all Christian thought and talk about God? The first and last criterion of Christian proclamation is whether it moves in the circle indicated

87

by these two answers. Christian theology can be only an exercise in this movement. The question of the subject of revelation and therefore of all God's dealings with man, which the Bible itself does not answer but poses in all its sharpness, calls indeed for an answer. Can we not understand the haste with which men felt called to answer it and the undoubtedly extraordinary zeal with which they set about this work? Was this not precisely because it was such a simple and yet such a central matter? And could the question be answered in any other way? Or is this problem not really set in the Bible? Could it be answered otherwise than it has been answered in the doctrine of the Trinity?

The problem which we think we see posed in the Bible and which points towards the Church doctrine of the Trinity consists in the fact that the being and speech and action and therefore the self-revealing of God are described there in the moments of His self-veiling or self-unveiling or self-impartation to men, that His characteristic attributes are holiness, mercy and love, that His [381] characteristic demonstrations are denoted in the New Testament by Good Friday, Easter and Pentecost, and that His name is correspondingly the name of Father, Son, and Holy Ghost. The Bible does not state expressly that the Father, Son and Holy Ghost are of equal essence and are thus in the same sense God Himself. Nor does it state expressly that thus and only thus, as Father, Son and Holy Ghost, God is God. These two express declarations, which go beyond the witness of the Bible, are the twofold content of the Church doctrine of the Trinity.

The doctrine of the Trinity means on the one side, as a rejection of Subordinationism, the express statement that the three moments do not mean a more and a less in God's being as God. The Father is not to be understood as the true God in distinction from the Son and the Spirit, and the Son and the Spirit are not, in distinction from the Father, favoured and glorified creatures, vital forces aroused and set in motion by God, and as such and in this sense revealers. But it is God who reveals Himself equally as the Father in His self-veiling and holiness, as the Son in His self-unveiling and mercy, and as the Spirit in His self-impartation and love. Father, Son and Spirit are the one, single, and equal God. The subject of revelation attested in the Bible, no matter what may be His being, speech and action, is the one Lord, not a demi-god, either descended or ascended. Communion with the One who reveals Himself there always and in all circumstances means for man that this God meets him as a Thou meets an I and unites with him as a Thou unites with an I. Not otherwise! Totally excluded is a communion with this God of the kind that we can have with creatures, namely, of such a kind that the Thou can be changed by an I into an It or He over which or whom the I gains control. Also and particularly as Son and Spirit, the One who reveals Himself according to the witness of Scripture does not become an It or He, but remains Thou. And in remaining Thou He remains the Lord. The subject of revelation is the subject that remains indissolubly subject. One cannot get behind this subject. It cannot become object. All Subordinationism rests on the intention of making the

4. *The Meaning of the Doctrine of the Trinity*

One who reveals Himself there the kind of subject we ourselves are, a creature whose Thouness has limits we can survey, grasp and master, which can be objectified, in face of which the I can assert itself. Note well that according to Subordinationist teaching even the Father, who is supposedly thought of as the Creator, is in fact dragged into the creaturely sphere. According to this view His relation to Son and Spirit is that of idea to manifestation. Standing in this comprehensible relation, He shows Himself to be an entity that can be projected and dominated by the I. Subordinationism finally means the denial of revelation, the drawing of divine subjectivity into human subjectivity, and by way of polytheism the isolation of man with himself in his own world in which there is finally no Thou and therefore no Lord. It was against this possibility that the Church was striking when it rejected Arianism and every form of Subordinationism. We ask whether it did well in this regard or not.

[382]

The doctrine of the Trinity means on the other side, as the rejection of Modalism, the express declaration that the three moments are not alien to God's being as God. The position is not that we have to seek the true God beyond these three moments in a higher being in which He is not Father, Son and Spirit. The revelation of God and therefore His being as Father, Son and Spirit is not an economy which is foreign to His essence and which is bounded as it were above and within, so that we have to ask about the hidden Fourth if we are really to ask about God. On the contrary, when we ask about God, we can only ask about the One who reveals Himself. The One who according to the witness of Scripture is and speaks and acts as Father, Son and Spirit, in self-veiling, self-unveiling and self-imparting, in holiness, mercy and love, this and no other is God. For man community with God means strictly and exclusively communion with the One who reveals Himself and who is subject, and indeed indissolubly subject, in His revelation. The indissolubility of His being as subject is guaranteed by the knowledge of the ultimate reality of the three modes of being in the essence of God above and behind which there is nothing higher. Totally excluded here is all communion that means evading His revelation or transcending the reality in which He shows and gives Himself. God is precisely the One He is in showing and giving Himself. If we hasten past the One who according to the biblical witness addresses us in threefold approach as a Thou we can only rush into the void. Modalism finally entails a denial of God. Our God and only our God, namely, the God who makes Himself ours in His revelation, is God. The relativising of this God which takes place in the doctrine of a real God beyond the revealed God implies a relativising, i.e., a denying, of the one true God. Here, too, there is no Thou, no Lord. Here, too, man clearly wants to get behind God, namely, behind God as He really shows and gives Himself, and therefore behind what He is, for the two are one and the same. Here, too, we have an objectifying of God. Here, too, the divine subjectivity is sucked up into the human subjectivity which enquires about a God that does not exist. Here too, but this time by way of mysticism, man finally finds himself alone with himself in his own world. This possibility, which

89

in its root and crown is the same as the first, is what the Church wanted to guard against when it rejected Sabellianism and every form of Modalism. And again we ask whether it did well in this regard or not.

[383] The doctrine of the Trinity tells us—this is the positive thing which it was defending on the polemical fronts—how far the One who reveals Himself according to the witness of Scripture can in fact be our *God* and how far He can in fact be *our* God. He can be our God because in all His modes of being He is equal to Himself, one and the same Lord. In terms of the doctrine of the Trinity knowledge of revelation as it may arise from the witness of Scripture means in all three moments of the event knowledge of the Lord as the One who meets us and unites Himself to us. And this Lord can be our God, He can meet us and unite Himself to us, because He is God in His three modes of being as Father, Son and Spirit, because creation, reconciliation and redemption, the whole being, speech and action in which He wills to be our God, have their basis and prototype in His own essence, in His own being as God. As Father, Son and Spirit God is, so to speak, ours in advance. Thus the doctrine of the Trinity tells us that the God who reveals Himself according to Scripture is both to be feared and also to be loved, to be feared because He can be God and to be loved because He can be our God. That He *is* these two things the doctrine of the Trinity as such cannot tell us. No dogma and no theology as such can. The doctrine of the Trinity as such is not the Word of God which might tell us. But if there is a ministry to this Word of God, a proclamation which can become the Word of God, and a ministry to this ministry, dogmatics as critical reflection on the proper content of proclamation, then the question as to the subject of revelation, to which the doctrine of the Trinity is an answer, must be the first step in this reflection. Scripture, in which the problem of the doctrine of the Trinity is posed, is always the measure and judge of the solution to this problem. It stands above the dogma of the Church and therefore above the critical reflection to which we let ourselves be led by the dogma of the Church. But all things considered we venture to think that, pending better instruction, this leading is an appropriate one.

GOD THE FATHER

The one God reveals Himself according to Scripture as the Creator, that is, as the Lord of our existence. As such He is God our Father because He is so antecedently in Himself as the Father of the Son.

1. GOD AS CREATOR

In the event which the Bible describes as revelation God deals with man as the Lord: not as a being of the kind and order to which man himself belongs and therefore not as a being over which man for his part might equally well be lord; nor yet as a being which exists and remains in and for itself in its own kind and order. These are the two errors or lies about God which are set aside by revelation. God deals with man as the Lord, i.e., as the authority which in distinction from all others is absolutely superior to man, but which, even in this absolute superiority, also concerns and claims man with the same absolute-ness. The fact that God reveals Himself, i.e., that He deals with man as Lord, is not equivalent to saying that He has and exercises power over man. Power is indeed the presupposition and means of lordship. We are speaking of lordship when one person brings himself to the awareness of another, an I to a Thou, as the bearer of power, when a superior will makes its power known. This is what takes place in the event that the Bible calls revelation. This is why the prevail-ing names for God are Yahweh in the Old Testament and Kyrios in the New.

But who is the Lord and therefore the God to whom the Bible is referring? As we have seen already, it is typical of the Bible in both the Old Testament and the New that its answer to this question does not point us primarily to a sphere beyond human history but rather to the very centre of this history.

The answer is that at the climax of the biblical witness Jesus of Nazareth is the Kyrios. He is the One who approaches man in absolute superiority. He is the self-revealing God. We shall return in the next section to this confession which characterises the whole form and content of the biblical testimony and which is decisive as the presupposition of the Christian Church.

Even in the New Testament, however, the answer that Jesus of Nazareth is the Lord is by no means self-evident. It never became this in the Church and it can never do so. Why not? If this Jesus of Nazareth was a true and real man, there is an asymmetrical element about the answer. At all events its symmetry has to be disclosed. In the first instance the New Testament ascribes the true and real deity expressed by the predicate Kyrios to One who is quite other than Jesus.

In the name Christ, which it gives to Jesus, it reminds us of the prophets, priests and kings of the Old Testament as authorised and sanctified men of Yahweh behind whom and above whom there stands the One who is primarily and properly authoritative and holy. It calls Jesus the Word or Son of God, the One who was sent into the world by God as the light and life of men. It understands the dignity of Jesus, the lordship of Jesus and the superiority of Jesus as basically different and subordinate compared to that of the Other who is properly called θεός [EN1]. In the so-called Synoptic Gospels this approach is especially prominent. It almost sounds like a false note, and is certainly an enigma, when even and precisely in these Gospels Jesus is called Kyrios. For what is Jesus here but a single pointer to the Lord whose kingdom (not His own) Jesus announces and declares by word and deed in a way that hardly distinguishes Him either formally or materially from John the Baptist, in relation to whom as the only One who is good (Mk. 10^{18}) Jesus associates Himself with His disciples in the address: Our Father!, whose will He very definitely differentiates from His own (Mk. 14^{36}), to whom He prays, as is repeatedly emphasised, and obedience to whom seems to be in the last resort the whole meaning of His calling and work. He is thus called the (ἅγιος) παῖς [EN2] of God like David and the Servant of the Lord of Isaiah 53 by what seems to be an ancient layer of the tradition, but one that was very highly regarded in the literature of the 2nd century, cf. Mt. 12^{18}; Ac. 3^{13,} 26; 4^{27,} 30. How could Jesus be more emphatically separated and distinguished from Him who is properly called God than by putting on His lips the doubly disconcerting: *Eloi, Eloi, lama sabachthani!* [EN3] (Mk. 15^{34})? The One who is properly called God in the Synoptics seems unquestionably to be the "Father in heaven" who constitutes the background of the event recorded and therefore, with incomparable significance, the basis of its meaning. Even in John there not only stands the much-noted "The Father is greater than I" (Jn. 14^{28}) but once again Jesus consistently portrays Himself as the emissary of the Father (the μόνος ἀληθινὸς θεός [EN4], Jn. 17^3) whose life is to do His will and speak His words and finish His work, whose triumph is simply to go to the Father, and through whom men come to the Father (Jn. 14^6). With regard to all the Gospels, the Fourth included, A. von Harnack was surely right when he said of Jesus: "Aim, power, insight, result, and stern compulsion—all come to Him from the Father. This is how it is in the Gospels; we cannot turn or twist it" (*Wesen d. Christentums*, 1906, p. 80). Similarly Paul is never tired of pointing to the Father, the "Father of Jesus Christ," who is side by side with Jesus and in some sense beyond Him and above Him. The greeting in nearly all his letters runs: Χάρις ὑμῖν καὶ εἰρήνη ἀπὸ θεοῦ πατρὸς ἡμῶν καὶ κυρίου Ἰησοῦ Χριστοῦ [EN5]. Does this imply that he is expressly calling "God our Father" the Father of our Lord Jesus Christ too? According to Eph. 1^{17}, where He is called ὁ θεὸς τοῦ κυρίου ἡμῶν Ἰησοῦ Χριστοῦ, ὁ πατὴρ πῆς δόξης [EN6] this might undoubtedly be the case. Or is it that the two, θεὸς πατήρ [EN7] and κύριος Ἰησοῦς Χριστός [EN8], as is assumed in the Vulgate and Luther's translation, are set alongside one another as the common source of grace and peace? What is beyond question is that the κύριος Ἰησοῦς Χριστός is separate from and subordinate to θεὸς πατήρ· Ἡμῖν

[EN1] God
[EN2] (holy) servant
[EN3] My God, my God, why have you forsaken me
[EN4] the only true God
[EN5] Grace to you and peace from God our Father and the Lord Jesus Christ
[EN6] the God of our Lord Jesus Christ, the Father of glory
[EN7] God the Father
[EN8] Lord Jesus Christ

εἷς θεὸς ὁ πατὴρ ... καὶ εἷς κύριος Ἰησοῦς Χριστός [EN9] (1 Cor. 8⁶); Ὑμεῖς δὲ Χριστοῦ, Χριστὸς δὲ θεοῦ [EN10] (1 Cor. 3²³); Ἀνδρὸς ἡ κεφαλὴ ὁ Χριστός ἐστιν ... κεφαλὴ δὲ τοῦ Χριστοῦ ὁ θεός [EN11] (1 Cor. 11³). Jesus Christ is κύριος εἰς δόξαν θεοῦ πατρός [EN12] (Phil.   [386] 2¹¹), He is the προσαγωγὴ πρὸς τὸν θεόν [EN13] (Eph. 2¹⁸). He will finally hand over the kingdom τῷ θεῷ καὶ πατρί [EN14] (1 Cor. 15²⁴). He is the εἰκὼν τοῦ θεοῦ [EN15] (2 Cor. 4⁴; Col. 1¹⁵). And so Hebrews calls Him the ἀπαύγασμα τῆς δόξης [EN16] (Heb. 1³), the πιστὸν ὄντα τῷ ποιήσαντι αὐτόν [EN17] (Heb. 3²), who offered Himself without spot to God (Heb. 9¹⁴), and it gives a depiction of His passion which is very reminiscent of the Synoptic portrayal: ὃς ἐν ταῖς ἡμέραις τῆς σαρκὸς αὐτοῦ, δεήσεις τε καὶ ἱκετηρίας πρὸς τὸν δυνάμενον σώζειν αὐτὸν ἐκ θανάτου μετὰ κραυγῆς ἰσχυρᾶς καὶ δακρύων προσενέγκας καὶ εἰσακουσθεὶς ἀπὸ τῆς εὐλαβείας, καίπερ ὢν υἱός ἔμαθεν ἀφ' ὧν ἔπαθεν τὴν ὑπακοήν [EN18] (Heb. 5⁷⁻⁸).

Looked at along these lines the lordship of Jesus as the Son of God is obviously only a manifestation, exercise and application of the lordship of God the Father. The essence of the deity ascribed to Jesus is to make clear and impart and give effect to who God the Father is, who God is in the true sense, and what He wills and does with man. It is to represent this God the Father.

Filius revelat agnitionem Patris per suam manifestationem [EN19] (Irenaeus, *C. o. h.* IV, 6, 3) ... *ut in suis verbis non tam se quam Patrem adspiciamus ... ut sic defixis oculis in Christum recta trahamur et rapiamur ad Patrem* [EN20] (Luther, *Comm. on Gal.* 1⁴, 1535, *W.A.* 40¹, 98, 25). We should "know that Christ is the proper epistle, the golden book wherein we read, and learn to see before our eyes the will of the Father" (*Two German Fast Sermons*, 1518, *W.A.* 1, 274, 41), "who is a mirror of the fatherly heart" (*Gr. Cat.*, 1529, *W.A.* 30¹, 192, 5). Along these lines A. von Harnack once formulated what was at the time a much disputed statement: "Not the Son but the Father alone belongs to the Gospel as Jesus proclaimed it"; more explicitly his meaning here is that Jesus' witness to His own person did not belong to the Gospel proclaimed by Him as one ingredient or proposition along with others but it belonged to it as an expression of the fact that He knew Himself to be the way to the Father.

If in answering the question about Him who in Scripture is called the Lord it is right to start with the confession: Jesus is Lord, it is also right to let ourselves be pointed first in the different and as it seems opposite direction, and thus to ask: What is the goal to which Jesus is the way? Whom or what does He reveal in so far as He reveals God the Father? What do we see in Him to the degree that

---

EN 9 But to us there is but one God, the Father ... and one Lord Jesus Christ
EN10 And you are Christ's; and Christ is God's
EN11 the head of every man is Christ ... and the head of Christ is God
EN12 Lord, to the glory of God the Father
EN13 access to God
EN14 to God, even the Father
EN15 image of God
EN16 the brightness of his glory
EN17 faithful to him who appointed him
EN18 In the days of his flesh, Jesus offered up prayers and supplications, with loud cries and tears, to him who was able to save him from death, and he was heard for his godly fear. Although he was a Son, he learned obedience through what he suffered
EN19 The Son reveals knowledge of the Father through his appearing
EN20 ... that in his words we should regard not so much Himself as the Father ... that thus, with our eyes focused on Christ, we should be taken and caught up directly to the Father

He is God's reflection and mirror? Who is the Father of our Lord Jesus Christ? The answer which the New Testament gives us here is a very different one from that which a natural and edifying but utterly arbitrary exposition of the word "father" might yield. What may be known as the manward will of the heavenly Father in what takes place through and to Jesus does not lie primarily in the direction of a genial affirmation, preservation and insurance of human existence but rather in that of a radical questioning and indeed abrogation of it.

Note that already in the Old Testament the term "father" is no less to be interpreted by "lord" than *vice versa* (Deut. 32⁶; Mal. 1⁶). That men are as such children of God, that God is a Father to them as such, is stated neither in the Old Testament nor the New. But according to the Old Testament Israel is chosen and called out of the multitude of nations to be the child of Yahweh. "Out of Egypt have I called my son" (Hos. 11¹). And by a "new birth," and so by a re-establishment of natural existence which is totally inconceivable to man and beyond its dissolution, man is set in this sonship according to the New Testament (Jn. 1¹²ᶠ·; 3³ᶠ·). "Every plant, which my heavenly Father bath not planted, shall be rooted up," is the inexorable law which applies here (Mt. 15¹³). It is in fact the suffering Servant of the Lord of Isaiah 53 who is rediscovered in Jesus (Ac. 8²⁶ᶠ·). In all four Gospels the story of Jesus' life is described as one which, strictly speaking, is from the very first a story of self-declaring and increasingly self-actualising death. Ἡμεῖς δὲ κηρύσσομεν Χριστὸν ἐσταυρωμένον ᴱᴺ²¹, writes Paul (1 Cor. 1²³), well aware that this is God's wisdom which is necessarily an offence to the Jews and foolishness to the Greeks. It is as the High-priest of the new covenant who is Himself the victim that the author of Hebrews understands Him. His obedience is an obedience of suffering (Heb. 5⁸), obedience μέχρι θανάτου, θανάτου δὲ σταυροῦ ᴱᴺ²² (Phil. 2⁸). For this reason God has highly exalted Him and given Him the name κύριος Ἰησοῦς Χριστός (Phil. 2⁹⁻¹¹). The Lamb that was slain is worthy to receive power and riches and wisdom and strength and honour and glory and praise (Rev. 5¹²). Ἐν τῇ ταπεινώσειή κείσις αὐτοῦ ἤρθη. This is why the continuation of His life is unthinkable: ὅτι αἴρεται ἀπὸ γῆς ἡ ζωὴ αὐτοῦ ᴱᴺ²³ (Ac. 8³³). He is the grain of wheat that must fall into the ground and die in order to bring forth much fruit (Jn. 12²⁴). Beyond the death of the man Jesus of Nazareth lies the place from which there falls on Him the light that makes Him the revelation of God the Father: ἐξ ἀναστάσεως νεκρῶν ᴱᴺ²⁴. He is instituted as the Son of God (Rom. 1⁴). God the Father acts on Him and through Him by raising Him from the dead (Gal. 1¹; 1 Cor. 6¹⁴; Rom. 4²⁴; 6⁴; Eph. 1²⁰). The believer calls Him who reveals Himself thus in Jesus Ἀββὰ ὁ πατήρ ᴱᴺ²⁵ (Gal. 4⁶; Rom. 8¹⁵). He who sees Jesus sees this Father (Jn.14⁷ᶠ·). The Jesus "who was delivered for our offences and was raised again for our justification" (Rom. 4²⁵) is the One to whom this applies. And since faith is faith in Jesus it is itself faith in the will and work of this Father. Being baptised into Christ is being baptised into His death, "being planted together in the likeness of his death" (Rom. 6³ᶠ·, cf. Phil. 3¹⁰), being crucified and dead with Him in His crucifixion (Gal. 5²⁴; Rom. 6⁶; Col. 3³; Eph. 4²²). Already in the Synoptics, then, following Jesus is identical with self-denial and taking up one's cross (Mk. 8³⁴) and one can save one's life only by losing it for Jesus' sake (Mk. 8³⁵). Beyond this strait gate lies absolutely everything the New Testament can say about καινότης ζωῆς ᴱᴺ²⁶ (Rom.

ᴱᴺ²¹ But we preach Christ crucified
ᴱᴺ²² unto death, even death on a cross
ᴱᴺ²³ In his humiliation justice was denied him … for his life is taken up from the earth
ᴱᴺ²⁴ by the resurrection from the dead
ᴱᴺ²⁵ Abba, Father
ᴱᴺ²⁶ newness of life

6⁴) in the baptised and believing. And the One who deals thus with men in Christ, who leads them along this way to this goal, is called by believers Father and "Father of the Lord Jesus Christ." He is the Father of the Son who was dead and is alive again, who was lost and is found (Lk. 15²⁹). *Μετανοεῖν*[EN27], to reverse one's thinking, to think afresh, to think through to God and His kingdom, really means in the New Testament too, and here especially, to consider the fact that we must die (Ps. 90¹², cf. Ps. 39⁵). Nor does it just mean this, but all else it might mean it can mean only if first and decisively it means this. Note that Thy name, Thy kingdom and Thy will are the objects of the first three petitions of the prayer directed to "our Father, which art in heaven" (Mt. 6⁹ᶠ·), and it is on these that the three which follow rest. In the context of the New Testament the Thy makes these petitions absolutely equivalent to the saying: "Teach us to reflect that we must die."

The One whom Jesus reveals as the Father is known absolutely on the death of man, at the end of his existence. His will enters the life of man, not identically with death, nor merely in the same way as death, but really with death, executing death on man, impressing the signs of death upon man. Only in the sharply drawn boundary line of the cross, which is to be drawn again and again, is His will revealed as the will to quicken, bless, and benefit. The life that His will creates will be a life that has passed through death, that is risen from death; it will be eternal life, truly a new birth. [388]

What is the bearing of all this on our question: Who is God the Father? As stated, this cannot mean that God the Father is identical with death, with the negation of human existence. Here rather death is vanquished in death and negation in negation. Resurrection is indeed the power of the cross and the gaining of life the power of the losing of life. But strictly and exclusively it is only as the power of the cross, of the losing of life, that there is resurrection here and the gaining of life. This implies at all events that God the Father is also not identical with what we know as our life or perhaps with its meaning and power, that His will stands over against our will to live, supreme, unbound, or rather in absolute control. Not only will it be impossible to establish what God the Father wills with us by the way of self-understanding, of analysis of our own existence. Rather it cannot be concealed from us that even to its deepest foundations and powers this existence of ours is set in radical crisis by the will of God, that as the will of God the Father is done upon it, it must become new. God the Father wills neither our life in itself nor our death in itself. He wills our life in order to lead it through death to eternal life. He wills death in order to lead our life through it to eternal life. He wills this transition of our life through death to eternal life. His kingdom is this new birth.

This is the reason for the remarkable relativising of the concepts of life and death which we find especially in Paul: 1 Cor. 3²²; Rom. 8³⁸; 14⁸; Phil. 1²⁰. Eternal life or resurrection life is undoubtedly for Paul the requickening of this life of ours—the requickening which is willed by God and is to be expected from God (1 Cor. 15⁵³; 2 Cor. 5⁴). But the requickening of this life of ours beyond the transition through death means that on this side of the gate it must lie on the scales with death and be jointly counterbalanced by the hope of faith.

[EN27] to repent

95

We sum all this up by saying that God the Father, whose will and work on men these are, is the Lord of our existence. He is this in the strict sense to the degree that He is the Lord over the life and death of man. All other lordship which is not to be seen on this frontier of death cannot be lordship over our existence. At the very most it can only be lordship in our existence. The lordship of a God identical with our will to live would be limited by the lordship of death. And the lordship of a God identical with death would be only the frontier of our ability to live. Neither would be lordship over our existence. For our existence is our will and ability to live in its limitation by death, not just our life [389] and not just its limitation by death. Not even then would it be real lordship. It would not be the bearer of a power which is really superior to us and which encounters us. The real Lord of our existence must be the Lord over both life and death. And this is precisely God the Father as we find Him attested in Scripture as the the One revealed in Jesus. But the Lord of existence is the Creator. For if God is the Lord of existence in the full sense of the term, this means that our existence is sustained by Him and by Him alone above the abyss of non-existence. It has no autonomous reality whether in its certainty as life or its imperilling by death. It is real in so far as He wills and posits it as real. It has an Author from whom as such it is absolutely distinct and to whom it is absolutely related, but not in such a way that it belongs essentially to this Author to have something really outside Himself, not in such a way that there is anything necessary for Him in this relation. It has an Author outside whom nothing is necessary, and who is not necessarily related to anything outside Himself. It has an Author who calls into existence and sustains in existence out of free goodness and according to His own free will and plan, in a free antithesis, determined only by Himself, to the nothing in which it might remain, but without anything being dependent on this. It has—this is what all these statements are describing—a Creator. And it is as the Creator that Jesus shows the Father to us. He also shows Him to us negatively: He whose will was done on Golgotha when in and with Jesus Christ the life of all of us was nailed to the cross and died in order that thereby and therein eternal life might be manifest—*He* is what the concept of Creator signifies.

Note how in Rom. 4^{17} the God of Abraham is called in one breath the ζωοποιῶν τοὺς νεκρούς[EN28] and the καλῶν τὰ μὴ ὄντα ὡς ὄντα[EN29].

By the name "father" we do, of course, denote the natural human author of our existence. But our natural human father is not our Creator. He is not the lord of our existence, not even the lord of our life, let alone our death. When Scripture calls God our Father it adopts an analogy only to transcend it at once.

Hence we must not measure by natural human fatherhood what it means that God is our

---

[EN28] quickening the dead
[EN29] calling those things which are not as though they were

Father (Is. 63^{16}). It is from God's fatherhood that our natural human fatherhood acquires any meaning and dignity it has. God is the Father ἐξ οὗ πᾶσα πατριὰ ἐν οὐρανοῖς καὶ ἐπὶ γῆς ὀνομάζεται (Eph. 3^{15}) [EN30].

God our Father means God our Creator (cf. for this Deut. 32^6 and Is. 64^7). And it should be clear by now that it is specifically in Christ, as the Father of Jesus Christ, that God is called our Creator. That God is our Creator is not a general truth that we can know in advance or acquire on our own; it is a truth of revelation. Only as that which we know elsewhere as the father–son relation is transcended by the Word of Christ the Crucified and Risen, only as it is interpreted by this Word, which means, in this case, only as it acquires from this Word a meaning which it cannot have of itself, only in this way may we see what creation means. But in this way we can see. The Father of Jesus Christ who according to the witness of Scripture is revealed in Jesus His Servant has the qualities of a Lord of our existence. The witness to Him leads us to the place where the miracle of creation can be seen. It bears witness to the holy God, the God who alone is God, the free God. It is this witness that we have to understand with the help of the basic statements of the doctrine of the Trinity. [390]

2. THE ETERNAL FATHER

The decisive statement by which the answer just given to the question: Who is God the Father? is elevated to the status of an element in the knowledge of the triune God along the lines of Church dogma, must be as follows: God as the Father of Jesus Christ can be our Father because even apart from the fact that He reveals Himself as such He already is the One He reveals Himself to be, namely, the Father of Jesus Christ, His Son, who as such is Himself God. God can be our Father because He is Father in Himself, because fatherhood is an eternal mode of being of the divine essence. In the One whose name, kingdom and will Jesus reveals, in distinctive differentiation from the One who reveals Him and yet also in distinctive fellowship with Him, we have to do with God Himself.

How is it that with the Church dogma we reach this understanding of the biblical witness to God the Father? The answer must simply be that we reach it as we accept the biblical witness and take it seriously to the degree that formally it absolutely conditions and binds the content of the revelation of the Father by its impartation in the person of the Revealer Jesus of Nazareth. Its content cannot be abstracted from this form. There can be no question here of distinguishing between content and form as though the content could be regarded as divine and necessary and the form as human and contingent, the former being the essence and the latter the historical manifestation of the

---

[EN30] from whom every family in heaven and in earth is named

revelation. The form here is essential to the content, i.e., God is unknown as our Father, as the Creator, to the degree that He is not made known by Jesus.

It is especially the Johannine tradition which expresses this exclusiveness with ever-renewed emphasis: Jn. 1[18]; 5[23, 37]; 6[46]; 8[19]; 14[6]; 17[25]; 1 Jn. 2[23] and 2 Jn. 9. Καθὼς γινώσκει με ὁ πατὴρ κἀγὼ γινώσκω τὸν πατέρα[EN31] (Jn. 10[15]) and therefore ὁ ἑωρακὼς ἐμὲ ἑώρακεν τὸν πατέρα[EN32] (Jn. 14[9]). But in the long run it is to be found with the same unmistakable clarity in the Synoptists too: Πάντα μοι παρεδόθη ἀπὸ τοῦ πατρός μου, καὶ [391] ουδεὶς ἐπιγινώσκει τὸν υἰὸν εἰ μὴ ὁ πατήρ, οὐδὲ τὸν πατέρα τις επιγινώσκει εἰ μὴ ὁ υἱὸς καὶ ᾧ ἐὰν βούληται ὁ υἱὸς ἀποκαλύψαι[EN33] (Mt. 11[27]).

If this exclusiveness is accepted and taken seriously, if that abstraction between form and content is thus seen to be forbidden, this rules out the possibility of regarding the first article of the Christian faith as an article of natural theology. Jesus' message about God the Father must not be taken to mean that Jesus expressed the well-known truth that the world must have and really has a Creator and was venturing to give this Creator the familiar human name of father. It must not be taken to mean that Jesus had in mind what all serious philosophy has called the first cause or supreme good, the *esse a se*[EN34] or *ens perfectissimum*[EN35], the universum, the ground and abyss of meaning, the unconditioned, the limit, the critical negation or origin, and that He consecrated it and gave it a Christian interpretation and baptised it by means of the name "father," which was not entirely unknown in the vocabulary of religion. In this regard we can only say that this entity, the supposed philosophical equivalent of the Creator God, has nothing whatever to do with Jesus' message about God the Father whether or not the term "father" be attached to it. Nor would it have anything to do with it even if the principle: Die and become! were related and perhaps identified with the transcendent origin and goal of the dialectic of losing life and gaining it. An idea projected with the claim that it is an idea of God is from the standpoint of the exclusiveness of the biblical testimonies an idol, not because it is an idea but because of its claim. Even the genuinely pure and for that very reason treacherously pure idea of God in a Plato cannot be excluded. If the exclusiveness is valid, Jesus did not proclaim the familiar Creator God and interpret Him by the unfamiliar name of Father. He revealed the unknown Father, His Father, and in so doing, and only in so doing, He told us for the first time that the Creator is, what He is and that He is as such our Father.

In interpreting the address "our Father" it is thus important that in Jn. 20[17] Jesus does not say: I go to our Father, but: ἀναβαίνω πρὸς τὸν πατέρα μου καὶ πατέρα ὑμῶν καὶ θεόν

[EN31] As the Father knows me and I know the Father
[EN32] he who has seen me has seen the Father
[EN33] All things have been delivered to me by my Father; and no one knows the Son except the Father, and no one knows the Father except the Son and any one to whom the Son chooses to reveal him
[EN34] being of itself
[EN35] most perfect being

μου καὶ θεὸν ὑμῶν EN36 It is not κατὰ φύσιν EN37 but κατὰ θεοῦ χάριν καὶ θέσει, ἀφάτῳ φιλανθρωπίᾳ EN38 through the Son and the Holy Ghost, that we have God as Father (Cyril of Jerus., *Cat.* 7. 7–8).

In relation to the knowledge of God the Father this implies that God is not just God the Father because He is the Creator and therefore our Father. He is so for this reason too, and this is the *opus ad extra* EN39 which is manifest in Jesus. But from the fact that in Jesus and Jesus alone He is manifest as the Creator and therefore as our Father it follows that He already is that which corresponds thereto antecedently and in Himself, namely, in His relation to the One through whom He is manifested, and therefore in His relation to Jesus. If it is true that we have to learn fatherhood from the will of God fulfilled on and by Jesus, and if it is also true that any abstraction of this will from the fact that it is fulfilled on and by Jesus is ruled out by the exclusiveness mentioned above, then we have to understand His fatherhood as that which applies previously to Jesus, and therefore as that which corresponds to a sonship in Jesus, irrespective of what it means for us. There is thus a fatherhood in God Himself whose truth does not first consist in the fact that He is the Creator and that we are His children by grace but already and primarily in the fact that a revelation of our new birth and therefore a revelation of creation, i.e., of His lordship over our existence, can take place. The possibility of this in God Himself is the Son of God who is identical with Jesus of Nazareth. In relation to Him and therefore as the Father of this Son God is antecedently Father in Himself. [392]

Faith in God the Father must be proclaimed in such a way that implicitly at once, and unconfused by recollection of other fatherhoods, faith in the only-begotten Son may be impressed upon the hearers. Τὸ γὰρ τοῦ πατρὸς ἄνομα ἅμα τῷ τῆς ὀνομασίας προσρήματι νοεῖν παρέχει καὶ τὸν υἱόν ... Εἰ γὰρ πατήρ, πάντως ὅτι πατὴρ υἱοῦ EN40 (Cyril of Jerus., *Cat.*, 7, 3–4). *Per prius paternitas dicitur in divinis secundum quod importatur respectus personae ad personam quam secundum quod importatur respectus Dei ad creaturam* EN41 (Thomas Aquinas, *S. theol.* I, qu. 33, art. 3c). God is Father *secundum relationem quam habet ad personam filii* EN42 (Polanus, *Syntagma theol. chr.*, 1609, III, 4, quoted from Heppe, *Dogm. d. ev.-ref. Kirche*, 1861, 92).

In relation to this original fatherhood of God the dogma of the Trinity speaks of the person or, as we should say, the mode of being of God the Father. It is not in this mode of being alone that God is God. He is so, too, in the possibility, or, as we must say, the possibilities in which He is revealed as the

---

EN36 I am ascending to my Father and your Father, to my God and your God
EN37 according to nature
EN38 according to the grace and plan of God, his ineffable love of humankind
EN39 outward work
EN40 For the name of the Father, in the speaking of the word, points to the Son .... For if he is Father, he is without doubt the Father of a Son
EN41 Fatherhood in the divine is spoken of sooner according to the relationship of one person to another than according to the relationship of God to the creature
EN42 according to the relation that he has to the person of the Son

§ 10. *God the Father*

One who acts upon us in the new birth. He is so, if there is not really to be an abstraction between revelation and its content, in the modes of being of the Son and the Holy Spirit as well. But precisely if this is so, the content of revelation, inasmuch as it is also the revelation of creation, of the divine lordship over our existence, refers us back to a corresponding inner possibility in God Himself which, in order, is to be understood as the first and original possibility presupposed in all others. In this first original possibility He is God the Father in the sense of the dogma of the Trinity: the eternal Father.

Πρὸ πάσης ὑποστάσεως καὶ πρὸ πάσης αἰσθήσεως, πρὸ χρόνων τε καὶ πρὸ πάντων τῶν αἰώνων τὸ πατρικὸν ἀξίωμα ἔχει ὁ θεός EN43 (Cyril of Jerus., *Cat.* 7, 5).

[393]
One should not say that the use of the name "Father" here is a transferred, improper and inadequate use. This could be said only if the standard of what is proper both here and generally were our language or the created reality to which our language is related. If the Creator is the standard of what is proper for the creature and therefore for our language too, then the very reverse must be said: Not merely the use of the name of father for the originating relationship in which one creature stands to another is improper, but in the last resort so is its use for the relation of God as Creator to the creature as we have read this off from the revelation of the new birth. God alone as He who He is by Himself, and therefore as the eternal Father of His eternal Son, is properly and adequately to be called Father. From the power and dignity of this only proper name of Father there flows by grace and for faith the improper—the really improper though certainly not on that account untrue—name of Father for God as the Creator, and from this again the naming of the intracreaturely originating relation, the thing that is called fatherhood in heaven and on earth (Eph. 3¹⁵). This, too, is to be regarded as a true but improper appellation dependent on the power and dignity of God's intratrinitarian name of Father.

Οὐ γὰρ ὁ θεὸς ἄνθρωπον μιμεῖται, ἀλλὰ μᾶλλον οἱ ἄνθρωποι διὰ τὸν θεόν, κυρίως καὶ μόνον ἀληθῶς ὄντα πατέρα τοῦ ἑαυτοῦ υἱοῦ, καὶ αὐτοὶ πατέρες ὀνομάσθησαν τῶν ἰδίων τέκνων EN44 (Athanasius, *Or. c. Ar.* I, 23).

God's trinitarian name of Father, God's eternal fatherhood, denotes the mode of being of God in which He is the Author of His other modes of being.

Fons ergo ipse et origo est totius divinitatis EN45 (*Conc. Tolet.* XI, 675, *Denz.* No. 275). In this mode of being the fathers describe Him as αὐτόθεος, ἄναρχος, ἀγέννητος, θεὸς ἐπί

EN43 Before every substance and before every perception, before time and before all ages, God possessed the quality of fatherhood

EN44 For God is not patterned after human beings, but rather, human beings are named fathers of their own children after God, who is pre-eminently and alone truly the Father of his own Son

EN45 He is the font and origin of the whole divinity

100

2. *The Eternal Father*

πάντων[EN46], as *a nullo originem habens, a se ipso existens, ingenitus innascibilis principium sine principio*[EN47].

It must be strictly noted that this origination, which is the incomparable model of the relation between Creator and creature, which itself in turn is the incomparable model of all intracreaturely originating relations, refers to the mutual relations of the divine modes of being and is not, then, to be taken to mean that there is between the Father on the one side and the Son and Holy Spirit on the other a relation of super- and subordination regarding their deity. The divine essence would not be the divine essence if in it there were superiority and inferiority and also, then, various quanta of deity. The Son and the Spirit are of one essence with the Father. In this unity of divine essence the Son is from the Father and the Spirit from the Father and the Son, while the Father is from Himself alone. That is to say, the intradivine possibility in virtue of which God can be manifest to us as the Creator and as our Father is not a self-grounded and self-reposing possibility. It rather presupposes a possibility of this kind and it presupposes an event in God in virtue of which it is posited as a possibility. It arises out of a self-grounded and self-reposing possibility in God. It is—and all this is to be regarded as an intradivine relation or move-ment, as *repetitio aeternitatis in aeternitate*[EN48]—the copy of an original, the issue from a source, the word of a knowledge and the decision of a will. This, the original, source, knowledge and will in God from which proceeds the second thing, the copy, issue, word and decision, in short, the fact that as the Creator and as our Father He can set Himself in relation to everything distinct from Him—this first thing in God Himself is the eternal Father in the sense of the doctrine of the Trinity. God is the eternal Father inasmuch as from eternity and in eternity He is the Father of the Son who from eternity and in eternity participates in the same essence with Him. In this relation and not in any other way God is God—the God who reveals Himself in the Son as the Creator and as our Father. From this insight arise two important conclusions especially with regard to this revelation of His through the Son.

[394]

1. From the eternity of the relation of the Father and the Son, in which that of the relation of both to the Holy Spirit is also contained, it necessarily follows first that not only God the Father is to be claimed as the Creator and as our Father, and that God the Father is not only to be claimed as the Creator and as our Father. We have said above that the use of the name Father for this relation and act of God *ad extra*[EN49] is a derived and improper use. Revelation in so far as it is the revelation of God the Creator and our Father, and in so far as this its content is not to be separated from its form as revelation in Jesus, leads us to the knowledge of God as the eternal Father. But in this very knowledge we

---

[EN46] God-in-himself, without origin, unbegotten, God over all
[EN47] having no origin, existing of himself, unbegotten, incapable of being born, source without a source
[EN48] repetition of eternity in eternity
[EN49] outward

cannot separate the Father from the Son and from the Holy Ghost. In this knowledge, then, there necessarily becomes plain to us the purely relative significance of the way of isolation on which we have reached this knowledge. It implies an "appropriation" (cf. § 9, 3) when by isolation we regard specifically God the Father as the Creator and as our Father and when we regard God the Father specifically as the Creator and as our Father. The triunity does not mean that three parts of God operate alongside one another in three different functions. *Opera trinitatis ad extra sunt indivisa*[EN50], as also the essence of God is a single and undivided essence and the *trinitas*[EN51] itself is an *individua trinitas*[EN52]. Thus not only the subject of the first article of the Creed is the Father Almighty, Creator of heaven and earth, but with Him, in the order and sense pertaining to each, the subjects of the second and third articles too. And again the subject of the first article is not only the Father Almighty, Creator of heaven and earth, but also, again in the appropriate order and sense, the subject of reconciliation like the subject of the second article and the subject of redemption like that of the third article. Not the Father alone, then, is God the [395] Creator, but also the Son and the Spirit with Him. And the Father is not only God the Creator, but with the Son and the Spirit He is also God the Reconciler and God the Redeemer. The very knowledge of the intratrinitarian particularity of the name of Father is thus a guarantee of the unity of God which would be endangered by regard for the particularity of God's revelation as the Creator and our Father if this were not guided by this apparently—but only apparently—very speculative intratrinitarian insight. Because God is the eternal Father as the Father of the Son, and with Him the origin of the Spirit, therefore the God who acts in reconciliation and redemption, and who reveals Himself as the Reconciler and Redeemer, cannot be a second and third God or a second and third part of God; He is and remains God *unus et individuus*[EN53] in His work as in His essence.

All theological favouritisms are thus forbidden: the one-sided belief in God the Father which was customary in the Enlightenment; the so-called Christocentrism which Pietism loved and still loves; and finally all the nonsense that is and can be perpetrated with isolated veneration of the Spirit. We cannot call God our Father apart from the Son and the Spirit, nor can we call the Son Saviour or the Spirit Comforter without also having the Father in view in both cases.

This insight safeguards the trinitarian dogma of the eternal Father, the Father of His only-begotten Son.

2. But from the same eternity of the relation between Father and Son, in which the eternity of the relation of both to the Holy Spirit is also expressed, it follows, secondly, that the necessary relativisation of the knowledge of reve-

---

[EN50] The outward works of the Trinity are undivided
[EN51] Trinity
[EN52] undivided Trinity
[EN53] one and undivided

lation which leads us to perception of this eternal relation cannot imply any disparagement or discrediting of this way of knowledge. The fact that the understanding especially of God the Father as the Creator, and of God the Creator as the Father, is an improper understanding because God is One in His work and essence, does not mean that it is an untrue and illegitimate understanding which we must abandon. "Improper" here can only mean that it is not an exhaustive understanding, that it is one-sided, that it needs to be supplemented, that we cannot and should not adopt it exclusively, that we cannot and should not proclaim its exclusive validity, that it must imply what is not actually contained in it as such. The appropriation which we make when we understand God the Father and creation too in this particularity is not just permitted; it is also commanded. And in all its relativity the knowledge based upon it is true knowledge. Without making this appropriation we could not even see that it is "only" an appropriation. It is on the way of knowledge founded upon it, and upon it alone, that we can reach the goal from which the relativity of the way as a way may be perceived. In fact the appropriation simply corresponds to the reality of the revelation attested to us in Scripture, and the [396] impropriety of the knowledge based on the appropriation corresponds to the reality of the faith which apprehends the revelation, which is not sight. The dogma of the Trinity, which earlier reminded us of the unity of God's essence and work, will not lead us beyond revelation and faith, but into revelation and faith, to their correct understanding. It is quite out of the question, therefore, that the appropriation of especially God the Father for creation, or of creation for the Father, should be merely a provisional view which can be transcended and which will dissolve and disappear in a higher gnosis of the one God. In no sense does God's unity mean the dissolution of His triunity. God reveals Himself as the One He is. The dogma of the Trinity says this too. Because the relation of Father, Son and Spirit includes within it the unity and distinction of the three modes of being, the very eternity of this relation tells us that God's work *ad extra* too is no less truly distinct in its unity than united in its distinction. In regard to the work of Father, Son and Spirit *ad extra* we earlier applied the stipulation that they all work in the order and sense appropriate to them. This means that the unity of their work is to be understood as the communion of the three modes of being along the lines of the doctrine of "perichoresis" (cf. § 9, 3), according to which all three, without forfeiture or mutual dissolution of independence, reciprocally interpenetrate each other and inexist in one another. The unity cannot be taken to mean, then, that the truth with reference to God's work *ad extra* entails an extinction of the independence of the three modes of being in a neutral, undifferentiated fourth, so that with Modalism no statement relating to this *opus ad extra* can be seriously made about a specific mode of being, and all statements relating to this *opus ad extra* can be made indiscriminately about any individual mode of being. We are simply emphasising here an integral part of our theme, namely, that the Father is not the Son and is not the Spirit. This remains true in the *opus ad extra*

103

too, so assuredly is it true from and to all eternity. Part of the distinction is the appropriation in which we equate the Creator with God the Father and God the Father with the Creator. It is only an appropriation to the degree that it does not also express the truth of perichoresis, of the intercommunity of Father, Son and Spirit in their essence and work. But it expresses the truth and imparts true knowledge to the degree that with the equation it touches upon and denotes the distinction which there is also in the *opus ad extra*, the order and sense in which God as the Triune is the subject of the *opus ad extra indivisum*[EN54]. It expresses the truth to the degree that with its specific emphasis on the Father or Creator it points to the affinity between the order of God's three modes of being on the one hand and that of the three sides of His work as Creator, Reconciler and Redeemer on the other. There is an affinity

[397] between the relation of the Father to the Son on the one hand and the relation of the Creator to the creature on the other. In both cases, though in a sense which differs *in toto coelo*, we are concerned with origination. In respect of this affinity it is not merely permitted but commanded that we ascribe creation as a *proprium*[EN55] to the Father and that we regard God the Father *peculiariter*[EN56] and specifically as the Creator. Conversely, the eternal truth of this distinction, which is valid for the *opus ad extra* too, yields the insight that certain statements about the work of the Son and the Spirit cannot be appropriated to the Father even though God the Father is no less the subject of reconciliation and redemption than the Son and the Spirit.

> One cannot say of God the Father that He was conceived and born, that He suffered, died and rose again. One also cannot say of Him that there had to be prayer for His coming and that He was to be poured out on all flesh. For one thing, all these statements stand in affinity to the relation of the Son or Spirit to the Father and not *vice versa*; their content thus applies *peculiariter* to the Son and Spirit and not the Father. Again, the statements in the second article especially relate to God the Son in so far as in His action as the Reconciler He assumed humanity and hence creatureliness. Applied to God the Father they would thus collide with His affinity to the essence and action of God as the Creator. It is true that in the incarnation of the Word the Creator became a creature. It is also true that the Holy Spirit for whom we pray is the *Creator Spiritus*[EN57]. Hence we neither can nor should deny a presence of the Father also in the Son who was born and suffered and died and in the Spirit who was poured out at Pentecost. But it would be just as improper to say that God the Father died as to say that Jesus of Nazareth or the Spirit of Pentecost created heaven and earth.

It is, of course, impossible to draw an absolutely unambiguous line between what is commanded and what is forbidden. One can only say that the doctrine of perichoresis, which admits of misuse in a one-sided emphasis on the involution of the three modes of being, also contains the further element which should be a warning against misuse, namely, the understanding of the involu-

---

[EN54] undivided outward work
[EN55] thing proper
[EN56] particularly
[EN57] Creator Spirit

tion as a convolution, the presupposition of the eternal independence of the three modes of being in their eternal communion. And in any case one can say very definitely that any systematising of the one-sidedness such as is found in part in ancient Modalism (e.g., in the form of Patripassianism) is absolutely forbidden, since it would mean the dissolution of the triunity in a neutral fourth. The eternity of the fatherhood of God does not mean only the eternity of the fellowship of the Father with the Son and the Spirit. It also protects the Father against fusion with the Son and the Spirit. We must not arrive at this fusion on the basis of the principle *opera trinitatis ad extra sunt indivisa.* It would not only be contrary to the dogma of the Trinity. It would also be incompatible with any serious acceptance of the biblical witness which makes the Father and the Son one in their distinction. It is thus right and necessary that for all our [398] awareness of the unity of the Father with the Son and the Spirit the knowledge of the Father as the Creator and our Father should always be a particular knowledge. Only when it is taken seriously in its particularity does it lead to that awareness, and the very awareness will lead us constantly to take it seriously in its particularity too.

[399]   § 11

GOD THE SON

The one God reveals Himself according to Scripture as the Reconciler, i.e., as the Lord in the midst of our enmity towards Him. As such He is the Son of God who has come to us or the Word of God that has been spoken to us, because He is so antecedently in Himself as the Son or Word of God the Father.

1. GOD AS RECONCILER

We return to the starting-point of the previous section where we began with the question: Who is the One whom Holy Scripture calls the Lord, who has dealings with man in revelation? and where we gave the answer that at the climax of the biblical witness it is stated (obviously with the intention of stating what is true and valid for the whole of the biblical witness, including the Old Testament) that Jesus of Nazareth is this Lord. We then followed first of all the line in the New Testament message in which, in apparent antithesis to the statement, Jesus of Nazareth is understood rather as the Servant of the Lord who proclaims and does the will of His heavenly Father. But we then saw how also and especially the revelation of the Father might appear primarily as its pure Mediator Jesus, and how it cannot be abstracted in any sense from this Mediator according to the biblical witness. What God reveals in Jesus and how He reveals it, namely, in Jesus, must not be separated from one another according to the New Testament, and on the assumption that this prohibition is to be taken seriously we have to regard the concept of God as the Father in His relation to this Mediator of His revelation as a mode of being which truly and definitively appertains to Him; we have to regard His fatherhood as an eternal one.

We now turn our attention again to the other line of biblical testimony which we touched on for a moment and then left again, namely, the line on which the emphasis lies, not on the distinction of Jesus from the Father, but, without denying this distinction, directly on His communion and even unity with the Father. To the statements about the relation of the Father to the Son to which we referred in the previous section there corresponds exactly a series of statements about the relation of the Son to the Father. The development of [400] the dogma of the Trinity began with these statements and *a priori* it is to be expected that we shall have to follow the dogma again and specifically at this point too if the unity of the Son with the Father attested in these statements,

106

and therefore the deity of Jesus Christ, is to be understood as definitive, authentic and essential.

In this regard we must refer already to the ascribing of the name of Kyrios to Jesus, even though this is, of course, wrapped in all manner of obscurity. Is apostolic usage adopting here the title of the divine world-ruler well-known in Hellenistic Egypt? Or the title given in Syria to the cultic god in contrast to his slaves, the adherents of the cult? Or the title of the emperor in the imperial religion of Rome? Be that as it may, in the light of its significance beyond the confines of contemporary Judaism the name immediately removes the One described thereby far from the sphere of other men to the side of "deity" in the more or less serious sense of the concept as this might arise in the religious world in question; it sets Him at the point where there should in every case be offered to Him that bending of the knee to which Paul refers in Phil. 2^{10}. Furthermore—and this clarifies the matter at once—in view of the close connexion between the early Church and the Palestinian and Hellenistic Synagogue it cannot possibly have happened unawares and unintentionally that this word was at any rate used as well to translate the Old Testament name of God Yahweh-Adonai, and was then applied to Jesus. We are pointed in the same direction by the practical meaning of the name Jesus as the name in which they prophesied, taught, preached, prayed and baptised, in which sins were forgiven, demons driven out, and other miracles were done, in which His followers were to gather, in which they were to receive one another, in which they were to believe, on which they were to call, in which they were to be upheld, for the sake of which they were to be hated and despised, to renounce all their earthly possessions and even perhaps to die, in which again they are washed, sanctified and justified (1 Cor. 6^{11}), and which is, so to speak, the place, the sphere, in which all they speak and do is to take place (Col. 3^{17}). The name of Yahweh has precisely the same comprehensive and pervasive meaning in the Old Testament (cf. § 8, 2); the name of Yahweh is simply Yahweh revealed to men. Who, then, is Jesus if His name has this significance? Is there really any need of the express declaration of Paul (Phil. 2^9) that God has given Him the name that is above every name?

As a second general phenomenon which points in the same direction—it is the merit of K. L. Schmidt (*RGG²*, Art. "*Jesus Christ*") to have brought this emphatically to our attention—we may cite the fact that the New Testament tradition has presented the revealing activity of Jesus as an inextricable interrelation of word and act and indeed of word and miracle. *Τὰ περὶ Ἰησοῦ τοῦ Ναζαρηνοῦ*[EN1], apart from the final events in His life which are crucial for the meaning and direction of the whole, may be summed up in the words: *ἐγένετο ἀνὴρ προφήτης δυνατὸς ἐν ἔργῳ καὶ λόγῳ*[EN2] (Lk. 24^{19}), or: *ἃ ἤρξατο ποιεῖν τε καὶ διδάσκειν*[EN3] (Ac. 1^1). But these and similar summary accounts, which often enough (e.g., Ac. 2^{22}; 10^{38}) seem to be acquainted only with Jesus the miracle-worker, simply formulate an impression which an impartial reading of, say, St. Mark's Gospel, cannot fail to leave, namely, that the teaching, which is, of course, presented here, is not meant to be understood apart from but only through the interpretation of the action which invariably accompanies it. It is a weakness of R. Bultmann's *Jesus* (1926) that he ignores this insistent demand of the texts and construes Jesus one-sidedly in terms of His sayings. The acts which invariably speak and are to be heard as well are miraculous acts. How they are connected with the central content of the words of Jesus may be seen from the story of the paralytic in Mk. 2^{1-12}, where to the horror of the scribes—who immediately speak of blasphemy and not unjustly from their standpoint—Jesus not only speaks of the forgiveness of sins but actually forgives sins and, to

[401]

[EN1] the things concerning Jesus of Nazareth
[EN2] he was a prophet mighty in deed and word
[EN3] which he began both to do and teach

show His authority for this act-word, cures the paralytic. God's act as it takes place visibly, the totality of a gracious act on man, emphasises that the word spoken is God's Word. This is the meaning of the miracles ascribed to Jesus (and expressly to His apostles too on the basis of the authority conferred on them by Jesus)—and it marks off these miracles, however we assess them materially, as at any rate something very distinctive amid the plethora of miracle stories in that whole period. Their distinctive feature, however, lies in their complete and indissoluble combination with the word of Jesus, a combination which distinguishes this word no less from mere prophesying than the miracles from mere thaumaturgy, a combination in which both word and deed in the same way give evidence of something above and beyond ethos ("history") and physis of a higher authority confronting the whole state of human and indeed cosmic reality. Who is the One who, obviously speaking representatively for this higher authority, can speak thus because He can act thus and act thus because He can speak thus?

It might be said of the further titles ascribed to Jesus in the New Testament, the titles of Messiah-Christ, Son of Man and Son of God, that in themselves they are ambiguous or even obscure. Thus in the ancient Orient Son of God was a widespread term simply for the king. But the context of New Testament Christology makes this title, too, eloquent in a distinctive way. He whom the Gospel wants to depict, so the Fourth Evangelist begins, the Word which became flesh, tabernacled among us, and was seen by us in His glory (Jn. 1¹⁴), this Word, unlike all other words, was not a created human word only relating to God and only speaking of God and about God. As Word it was spoken where God is, namely, ἐν ἀρχῇ, *in principio*[EN4] of all that is, πρὸς τὸν θεόν, belonging to God, therefore itself θεός God by nature (Jn. 1¹), identical with the Word through which—πάντα δι' αὐτοῦ ἐγένετο[EN5]—God called into being and existence everything that is (Jn. 1³). No more and no less than God Himself is there when this Word, οὗτος[EN6], i.e., Jesus, whose story the Gospel aims to tell, is there as light in the darkness which does not apprehend the light (Jn. 1². ⁴⁻⁵). The θεὸς ἦν ὁ λόγος[EN7] is then expressly repeated in Jn. 1¹⁸ (according to the correct reading): μονογενὴς θεὸς ὁ ὢν εἰς τὸν κόλπον τοῦ πατρός[EN8], He has revealed the invisible God. The same equation between the seen, heard and handled object of Christian proclamation and the ὃ ἦν ἀπ' ἀρχῆς[EN9] is also made in 1 Jn. 1¹. Similarly Paul says: θεὸς ἦν ἐν Χριστῷ καταλλάσσων[EN10] (2 Cor. 5¹⁹), and: ἐν αὐτῷ κατοικεῖ πᾶν τὸ πλήρωμα τῆς θεότητος σωματικῶς[EN11] (Col. 2⁹). The passage Heb. 1⁵ᶠ·, in which the majesty of the Son of God is established even above the angelic world, is noteworthy because in the words quoted from the Psalms even the distinction between θεός[EN12], which is perhaps still to be construed adjectivally and inexactly, and ὁ θεός[EN13] disappears, and the Son is expressly called ὁ θεός. Jesus can be styled ὁ μέγας θεός[EN14] (Tit. 2¹³), ἴσος τῷ θεῷ[EN15] (Jn. 5¹⁸; Phil. 2⁷), ἐν μορφῇ θεοῦ ὑπάρχων[EN16] (Phil. 2⁶), the ἴδιος υἱός[EN17] of His Father (Rom. 8³²), the υἱὸς τῆς

EN 4 in the beginning
EN 5 all things were made through him
EN 6 he
EN 7 the Word was God
EN 8 the only-begotten God, who, being in the bosom of the Father
EN 9 that which was from the beginning
EN10 God was in Christ reconciling
EN11 in him the whole fulness of deity dwells bodily
EN12 God
EN13 God Himself
EN14 the great God
EN15 equal with God
EN16 being in the form of God
EN17 very Son

ἀγάπης αὐτοῦ[EN18] (Col. 1¹³), the υἱὸς ὁ μονογενῆς[EN19] (Jn. 3¹⁶. ¹⁸; 1 Jn. 4⁹), ὁ ἐκ τοῦ οὐρανοῦ καταβάς[EN20] (Jn. 3¹³, ³¹). He can say of Himself: ἐγὼ καὶ ὁ πατὴρ ἕν ἐσμεν[EN21] (Jn. 10³⁰). He has come from the Father (Jn. 16²⁸). He has already worked hitherto, as His Father has worked (Jn. 5¹⁷). He has life in Himself, as His Father has life in Himself (Jn. 5²⁶). Whoever has seen Him has seen the Father (Jn. 14⁹). He can say with the Father: Before Abraham was, I am (Jn. 8⁵⁸). And He can say to the Father: Thou lovedst Me before the creation of the world (Jn. 17²⁴). For He had glory before the existence of the world (Jn. 17⁵). Ὁ θρόνος σου ὁ θεὸς εἰς τὸν αἰῶνα τοῦ αἰῶνος[EN22] is what Heb. 1⁸ has God say to His Son. He is the Alpha and Omega, the First and the Last, the ἀρχή[EN23] and the τέλος[EN24] (Rev. 22¹³, cf. 1⁸. 17), He who is and was and is to come ὁ παντοκράτωρ[EN25] (Rev. 1⁸), the same yesterday, to-day and for over (Heb. 13⁸). For this reason it may be said of Him, as the Prologue of John already emphasises, that through Him God made the aeons (Heb. 1²), that He is the Word of power by which He upholds all things (Heb. 1³), that in Him everything was made that is in heaven and on earth (Col. 1¹⁶; 1 Cor. 8⁶). He is πάντων κύριος[EN26] (Ac. 10³⁶). He can say of Himself: All things are delivered unto Me of My Father ... and therefore: Come unto Me, all ye that labour and are heavy-laden, and I will refresh you (Mt. 11²⁷⁻²⁸). Similarly the content of Peter's confession in Mt. 16¹⁶: "Thou art the Christ, the Son of the living God," occurs again later (Mt. 26⁶³ᶜ·) as the "blasphemy" which leads Jesus to the cross.

[402]

This is the second line of the New Testament tradition that is found alongside the first line which we emphasised in the previous section. What is now meant by "Jesus the Lord" is the deity of Jesus Christ.

The New Testament statement about the unity of the Son with the Father, i.e., the deity of Christ, cannot possibly be understood in terms of the presupposition that the original view and declaration of the New Testament witnesses was that a human being was either exalted as such to deity or appeared among us as the personification and symbol of a divine being.

The essential understanding is threatened already if one agrees with M. Dibelius (*RGG²* Art. "*Christologie*") in formulating the problem of New Testament Christology as the way in which "knowledge of the historical figure of Jesus was so quickly transformed into faith in a heavenly Son of God." The question is whether one can presuppose that knowledge of a historical figure came first and a transforming of this into faith in the heavenly Son of God came second, so that we have then to ask in terms of the history of thought how this came about. We see no possibility of this road ending anywhere but in a blind alley. If the question is put in this way there are in the main two modern historical attempts to explain the origin of the above formulation (cf. for a description of them K. L. Schmidt at the beginning and end of the article quoted, but already Schleiermacher, *Der. chr. Glaube*, § 22), and materially these correspond exactly and very remarkably with the two most important side-lines of

---

[EN18] son of his love
[EN19] the only-begotten Son
[EN20] who came down from heaven
[EN21] I and my Father are one
[EN22] Thy throne, O God, is for ever and ever
[EN23] beginning
[EN24] end
[EN25] the almighty
[EN26] Lord of all

christological thought which arose as early as the 2nd century and which were finally rejected by the Church.

First, the New Testament statement about Christ's deity can be taken individualistically as the apotheosis of a man, a great man, who as such, through the mystery of his personality and work, had such an effect on those around Him that there inevitably arose the impression and idea that He was a God. Such a man was Jesus of Nazareth, the author and preacher of a life-style unheard of in His own time and more or less in later times—a life-style of childlikeness, freedom, obedience, love and faithfulness even to death, so that He became the more or less willing or unwilling Founder of the Christian religion and the Christian Church. From the inspired and inspiring country Rabbi He was, and as whom His disciples originally respected Him, He rose in their eyes to the stature of an Elijah. From the political Messiah He originally was for them as well, He rose to the stature of the Son of David who as such could also be called the Son of God, of a heavenly being who attests His presence in visions even after death, who lives on in His "spirit," and is thus pre-existent, until, gaining in fervour in inverse ratio to its remoteness from the historical object, the claim transcends itself and equation between Jesus and God is no longer impossible. The idea now is that at

[403] some specific point, at His birth or baptism or transfiguration on the mount or resurrection from the dead, God appointed the man Jesus to this dignity and adopted Him as His Son. This could be a good symbol for what men themselves had done in the zeal of their Christ-enthusiasm. To the "eye of faith" a remarkable man who had once been known as such, and who strictly was always kept in view, was idealised upwards as God, as could happen and actually had happened to other heroes. This is Ebionite Christology, or Christology historically reconstructed along the lines of Ebionitism.

Secondly, the New Testament statement about Christ's deity could also be taken in just the opposite sense, collectively. In Him, the theory runs, we have the personification of a familiar idea or general truth, e.g., the truth of the communion of deity and humanity, or the truth of the creation of the world by God's word and wisdom, or the truth of redemption by the way of "Die and Become," or the truth of the juxtaposition of truth and goodness or forgiveness and claim. The fact that the manifestation of this idea was seen in Jesus of Nazareth was more or less accidental and indifferent, so indifferent that the concrete humanity of His earthly existence, or finally even its historical reality, could be queried. He was believed in as theophany or myth, as the embodiment of a general truth, as the familiar Son of Man of Daniel or the familiar pre-existent Logos or the familiar world-deliverer of whom all Hellenism thought it had some knowledge, or as an analogue of the divine hypostases taught by the Rabbis when they spoke of *Memra* (the Word), *Shechinah* (the glory) and *Metatron* (the supreme archangel of God). As and to the degree that the symbol of this idea was seen and venerated in Jesus of Nazareth, He was called Kyrios, Son of God, and finally, in full awareness of the implied dialectic, God Himself. The power of the Christ-enthusiasm which had both the ability and the need to make this equation was the power of the idea, the power of the concept of the condescending and self-manifesting God, which simply found in its connexion with Jesus of Nazareth its specific crystallisation, just as then and in other ages it has demonstrably found similar crystallisations. The general "eye of faith" had now also and specifically fallen on Him. But what was in view was the idea, not the Rabbi of Nazareth, who might be known or not known as such with no great gain or loss either way, whom there was at any rate a desire to know only for the sake of the idea. This is Docetic Christology, or Christology historically reconstructed along the lines of Docetism.

These two conceptions or explanations of the statement about the deity of Christ seem to be in greater self-contradiction than is actually the case. The former understands Jesus as the peak or a peak of history soaring into superhistory. The latter understands Him as the sucker of super-history reaching down into history. According to the former He is the supreme manifestation of human life, while according to the latter He is the most perfect symbol of divine presence. Obviously it should not be very hard to relate these two conceptions to one another dialectically or to reconcile them with each other. Common to both is the notion that strictly speaking the New Testament statement about Christ's deity is a form of expression that is meant very loosely and is to be interpreted accordingly.

As early as the 2nd century the Church rejected both Ebionitism and Docetism and in so doing it also ruled out in advance the corresponding modern explanation. And the New Testament statement about Christ's deity can in fact be understood only on the assumption that it has nothing whatever to do either with the apotheosis of a man or with the personification of an idea of God or divine idea. It avoids these alternatives. But this takes place, of course, on a line in which the plane on which the Ebionite and Docetic lines intersect is itself cut by another plane, and therefore in a third dimension, perpendicular to it and to the two lines. If one thinks persistently on this plane with its two dimensions one can never escape [404] the dialectic of history and super-history or super-history and history, the conception of a Christ-enthusiasm in which a heavenly essence arises out of a historical form or a historical form out of a heavenly essence. In this case one will persistently speak, not of the Christ of the New Testament, but of idealising and mythologising man, and of Jesus as the object of the thought of this man. But if so one is not speaking of God's revelation. The New Testament statement about Christ's deity makes sense only as witness to God's revelation. Any other exegesis is blatantly opposed to the opinion of the authors and in conflict with them. Ebionitism and Docetism are misunderstandings of a dialectic that is inevitably at work in the thought and utterance of the New Testament authors, for it is indisputable that men—because it has pleased God to assume humanity—are thinking and speaking here, and that the first plane with its two dimensions is the sphere in which they think and speak. (We shall return to the dialectic present in the New Testament itself in connexion with the doctrine of the incarnation of the Word.) Even on this plane, however, what they think and say has a different meaning from that it seems to have when seen from the standpoint of Ebionite and Docetic thinking. This other meaning is given by the fact that while the thought and utterance of the New Testament witnesses takes place on the first plane like all human thought, it is related to the second plane which falls upon it perpendicularly and which is identical with God's revelation. It is thus true that even in what the New Testament witnesses think and say one may plainly see and distinguish a kind of opposite movement. It is true that especially in the Synoptists we are presented on the whole with a christological thinking which finds *God* in Jesus and that especially in the Fourth Gospel we are presented on the whole with another christological thinking which finds God in *Jesus*. But the first does not mean that the Synoptists found God in a mere man, in the figure of a great man, in an impressive personality, in a hero. And the second does not mean that John found an idea, a general truth of an intellectual, moral or religious kind, personified specifically in Jesus. One will search the New Testament documents in vain for the fatal starting-point of Ebionite Christology, i.e., personality, or the fatal starting-point of Docetic Christology, i.e., idea. These can never be anything but an arbitrary construction behind the documents and in contradiction with them. The starting-point of Synoptic thought, which finds *God* in Jesus, is the fact, manifest to certain men, of the divine envoy as such. It is the unambiguous fact of the man who was among them teaching and healing, dying and rising again, as a reality which did not first have to be disclosed and interpreted and asserted, but which directly called to their lips the confession: Thou art the Christ, the Son of the living God (Mt. 16¹⁶), not as a synthetic but as an analytic statement. And the starting-point of Johannine thought, which finds God in *Jesus*, was the fact, manifest to certain men, of the divine mission, message and revelation which they found in Jesus, the enactment of "grace and truth," "resurrection and life," the actual event of their being fed with the bread of life (Jn. 6³⁵), their actual drinking of the living water (Jn.

4[10]). "We beheld—his glory." And this led again, though now in the reverse direction, as a synthetic and not as an analytic statement, to Peter's confession, which must be here: Κύριε, πρὸς τίνα ἀπελευσόμεθα; ῥήματα ζωῆς αἰωνίου ἔχεις καὶ ἡμεῖς πεπιστεύκαμεν καὶ ἐγνώκαμεν ὅτι σὺ εἶ ὁ ἅγιος τοῦ θεοῦ[EN27] (Jn. 6[68]). In the light of these real starting-points of New Testament thought, and already with these starting-points, the common goal, the statement about Christ's deity, is easy to understand. It was not that a historical figure had first to be changed into a heavenly being or a heavenly being into a historical figure, and that either way knowledge had to be transformed into faith. The New Testament witnesses tell us how their unbelief, not their knowledge, was changed into faith, and the opposed movement of their thought then takes place within faith. This has in fact nothing whatever to do with the dialectic of Ebionitism and Docetism. For what is meant by the first step on a way at whose end a man is equated with God, and what is meant by the first step on another way at whose end God is a man? Can this be the end of a way if it was not already its beginning? Can the decisive assertion in the corresponding statements, or the corresponding statement which is to the same effect in both instances, be understood as a result of thought won in ascending or descending reflection or interpretation? Can this assertion be anything but an explanation of the presupposition taken directly from the presupposition, a *petitio principii*, as a logician would unquestionably have to say here? The material point in the New Testament texts is that *God* is found in Jesus because in fact Jesus Himself cannot be found as any other than God. And God is found in *Jesus* because in fact He is not found anywhere else but in Jesus, yet He is in fact found in Him. This factual element at the start of the two ways of New Testament thought is revelation, the point of reference which lies in another dimension and which distinguishes this thinking from that of the Ebionites and Docetics and their modern successors. Against the background of this factual material which is simply there in the New Testament texts one may certainly advance the following considerations too. When the Ebionite and Docetic Christologies presuppose that at the end of ascending or descending reflection—reflection on the man Jesus as such and reflection on deity in special relation to the man Jesus—we simply have a small or even a big exaggeration with whose help the statement about Christ's deity arises or is explained, they ascribe to the thought of the biblical witnesses an achievement which the latter themselves would have regarded as the blasphemy of which Jesus was accused, but falsely so, according to their records. If Jesus had called Himself, or the primitive Church had called Him the Son of God in the sense presupposed by these two conceptions, then He and His Church would have been rightly expelled from the Old Testament community. For what could the idealising of a man or the mythologising of an idea be but characteristically the very thing that the Old Testament understood by the setting up and worship of an idol, of an unworthy and empty rival of Yahweh? Those who think, or hyperbolically allege that they think, that a man can really become God or that the real God could have a copy in a man have very little understanding of the word "God" in the Old Testament sense. If we can claim that the first generation of the witnesses of Jesus are in any degree true Israelites or Palestinian Jews; if we can be confident that they understand the difference between God and man, not as a quantitative one that could be easily bridged, but as a qualitative one, then we can describe it as an *a priori* impossibility that they should have thought in the way they would have to have thought if they understood the statement about Christ's deity along the lines of those two conceptions. If they could make this statement at all as Palestinian Jews; if they believed that they could not only reject the charge of blasphemy against Jesus as a frightful misunderstanding but also proclaim it as the end of the Old Testament, as the event in which Israel, by rejecting no more and no less than

[405]

EN27 Lord, to whom shall we go? You have the words of eternal life. And we have believed, and have come to know, that you are the Holy One of God

Yahweh Himself, finally renounced its own birthright, then on their lips the statement could not be the product of ascending or descending speculation but in its twofold movement it could be only the expression of an axiomatic presupposition, an explanatory statement about the absolute beginning of their thought which is posited in advance for their thought. The explanation of their statement that Jesus is Lord is to be sought only in the fact that for them He was the Lord, and was so in the same factual and self-evident and indisputable way as Yahweh was of old Israel's God. The utter embarrassment of a historical approach which on the one hand cannot conceal the fact that the statement "is already essentially present in the most ancient literary testimonies, the epistles of Paul," and yet on the other hand will not [406] take this presupposition into account, may be seen in the words of Johannes Weiss: "The fusion of hitherto unrelated conceptual elements at this centre presupposes a power of attraction which we cannot overestimate. How strong the indirect or direct effect of the personality of Jesus must have been on the souls of His followers if they were ready to believe this of Him and to die for this belief!" (*RGG¹*, Art. "*Christologie*," I). What is the meaning of "power of attraction, of indirect or direct effect," in this case, in relation to this effect? One may well ask whether apart from all else, the early Church did not perhaps have more sense of historical reality and possibility when it left it to heretics to wander to and fro along the beaten tracks of apotheosis and hypostasis Christology and thought it more natural to seek the meaning of the New Testament statement about Christ's deity in the corresponding factual presupposition as this is presented to us in the New Testament itself.

Jesus is Lord—this is how we think we must understand the New Testament statement in concert with the ancient Church—because He has it from God whom He calls His Father to be the Lord, because with this Father of His, as the Son of this Father, as "the eternal Father's only child," He *is* the Lord—an "is" which we deny if we are unable to affirm it with those who first uttered it, yet which cannot be deduced, or proved, or discussed, but can only be affirmed in an analytic proposition as the beginning of all thinking about it. In distinction from the assertion of the divinisation of a man or the humanisation of a divine idea, the statement about Christ's deity is to be understood in the sense that Christ reveals His Father. But this Father of His is God. He who reveals Him, then, reveals God. But who can reveal God except God Himself? Neither a man that has been raised up nor an idea that has come down can do it. These are both creatures. Now the Christ who reveals the Father is also a creature and His work is a creaturely work. But if He were only a creature He could not reveal God, for the creature certainly cannot take God's place and work in His place. If He reveals God, then irrespective of His creaturehood He Himself has to be God. And since this is a case of either/or. He has to be full and true God without reduction or limitation, without more or less. Any such restriction would not merely weaken His deity; it would deny it. To confess Him as the revelation of His Father is to confess Him as essentially equal in deity with this Father of His.

But what does it mean for us—for this must be our starting-point as well—to confess Jesus as the revelation of His Father and therefore as His true Son? If now we consider this and stress that Jesus as the Revealer of the Father and His will and work does not merely proclaim to us our Lord but in so doing is Himself our Lord, so that He also reveals Himself as the Son of the Father, then to

[407] the degree that what takes place here is an act of God this obviously signifies something very different from the activity of God the Creator which we understood as the epitome of the content of the revelation of the Father. Over and above the reality of God's lordship over our existence it implies God's lordship in the fact that He turns to us, that indeed He comes to us, that He speaks with us, that He wills to be heard by us and to arouse our response. It signifies the reality of an intercourse which He has established between God and us. God does not just will and work. In His revelation in Jesus Christ He discloses to us His will and work. He does not treat us as dust or clay, even though we are this as His creatures. He does not just subject us to His power as Creator or cause us to be controlled by His power as Creator so as to fulfil His purpose in us. He seeks us as those who can let themselves be found. He converses with us as those who are capable of hearing, understanding and obeying. He deals with us as the Creator, but as a person with persons, not as a power over things. "Your brother is the eternal good." And this is by no means obvious. It is miraculous, and this not merely nor primarily as a miracle of power, as the mystery in which the principle *finitum non capax infiniti*[EN28] is abrogated. Naturally this is true too. But the abrogation of this principle is not the real mystery of the revelation of the Son of God. The real mystery is the abrogation of the other and much more incisive principle: *homo peccator non capax verbi divini*[EN29]. God's power to establish intercourse with us is also called in question of course, but in the long run not decisively, by the fact that He is infinite and we are finite, that He is Lord of life and death and we live as those who are limited by death, that He is the Creator and we are those who have been called out of nothing into being and existence. God's ability is decisively called in question, however, by the fact that we are God's enemies. How do we know that? Certainly not of ourselves. Certainly not in and with the fact that we are aware of the problematic nature of our being and existence as men, of the conflict between the spiritual and the natural sides of our existence, or of the conflict between our theoretical ideals and our practical achievements, or of the antinomies generally in which the course of our thought and existence runs. The fact that we are God's enemies never follows from these intrinsically incontestable facts, and if we were to view it as only an expression of these familiar facts it could only be described as a misanthropic exaggeration. The insight that "I have sinned ... and am no more worthy to be called thy son" (Lk. 15[18f.]) is not an insight of abstract anthropology. Only the son who is already recalling his father's house knows that he is a lost son. We know that we are God's enemies first and solely from the fact that God has actually established that intercourse with us. But precisely on the assumption of the factuality of this event we can regard this event itself only as miraculous. The Word of God whose revelation is attested in Scripture tells man that he is a rebel who

---

EN28 the finite is not capable of the infinite
EN29 the human as sinner is not capable of the divine word

has wantonly abandoned the fellowship between himself as creature and God [408] as Creator and set himself in a place where this fellowship is impossible. It tells him that he wanted to be his own lord and therewith betrayed and delivered up himself to the sphere of God's wrath, the state of rejection by God, and therefore of being closed up against God. It tells him that contrary to its destiny by creation his existence is a contradiction against God, a contradiction which excludes listening to God. It thus tells him, strangely, that he cannot hear at all the Word of God which tells him this, and that he cannot hear it because he will not hear it, because his life-act is disobedience and therefore factually, in respect of the use he makes of his life, it is a refusal to listen to what God says to him. Indeed, this content of the Word of God spoken to man makes it quite inconceivable that man should even get to hear God's Word, that God should turn to him at all and address him. The fact that he is closed up to what God can say to him is simply an expression of the wrath of God resting upon him. If this wrath of God is serious—and God's Word will tell us no other than that it is really serious—then will it not consist primarily and decisively in the fact that God has turned away His face from us and therefore will not speak with us, that even objectively, then, there is for fallen man no Word of God at all? If we hear it nevertheless, and if this has the twofold implication that we can actually hear it and that we do actually get to hear it—and only on this presupposition shall we evaluate ourselves and our situation *vis-à-vis* God in this way and not another—then we cannot understand the Nevertheless of our hearing as a possibility which ("in some way") we still have left or which can still be fashioned by us. We could obviously do this only in flagrant absent-mindedness and forgetfulness of what we are told by God's Word about ourselves and our situation before God. This interpretation of the Nevertheless of our hearing would then mean quite simply that we have not yet heard at all or have already ceased to hear. If we have heard and heard again—if this self-understanding really relates to our hearing and not to the self abstracted from this hearing—then we can regard this possibility of our hearing as one which is given to us as a sheer miracle both subjectively and objectively, as the Nevertheless of grace which has on our side no complement or precondition.

Τὸ φρόνημα τῆς σαρκὸς ἔχθρα εἰς θεόν· τῷ γὰρ νόμῳ τοῦ θεοῦ οὐχ ὑποτάσσεται, οὐδὲ γὰρ δύναται[EN30] (Rom. 8⁷). Ἐχθροὶ ὄντες κατηλλάγημεν τῷ θεῷ[EN31] (Rom. 5¹⁰). Ἐν αὐτῷ ζωὴ ἦν, καὶ ἡ ζωὴ ἦν τὸ φῶς τῶν ἀνθρώπων καὶ τὸ φῶς ἐν τῇ σκοτίᾳ φαίνει, καὶ ἡ σκοτία αὐτὸ οὐ κατέλαβεν[EN32]. (Jn. 1⁴⁻⁵) Εἰς τὰ ἴδια ἦλθεν καὶ οἱ ἴδιοι αὐτὸν οὐ παρέλαβον[EN33] (Jn. 1¹¹). Ὃ οἴδαμεν λαλοῦμεν καὶ ὃ ἑωράκαμεν μαρτυροῦμεν, καὶ τὴν

[EN30] Because the carnal mind is enmity against God: for it is not subject to the law of God, neither indeed can be

[EN31] When we were enemies, we were reconciled to God

[EN32] In him was life, and the life was the light of men. The light shines in the darkness, and the darkness has not overcome it

[EN33] He came unto his own, and his own received him not

μαρτυρίαν ἡμῶν οὐ λαμβάνετε[EN34]. (Jn. 3¹¹). Ὁ ἑώρακεν καὶ ἤκουσεν, τοῦτο μαρτυρεῖ, καὶ τὴν μαρτυρίαν αὐτοῦ οὐδεὶς λαμβάνει[EN35] (Jn. 3³²).

[409] This is how there comes into being the self-understanding of the real hearer with respect to the possibility of his hearing. He regards himself as one who continually robs himself of this possibility. He can regard God alone as the One who gives him this possibility, and by whose gift it is a possibility.

We shall have to speak of the subjective side of this possibility, and therefore of the possibility that we can hear what God says to us, in the next section, the doctrine of God the Holy Spirit. The fact that God can first tell us anything, this primary inconceivability in view of His wrath on sinful man, is in God's revelation the work of the Son or Word of God. The work of the Son or Word is the presence and declaration of God which, in view of the fact that it takes place miraculously in and in spite of human darkness, we can only describe as revelation. The term reconciliation is another word for the same thing. To the extent that God's revelation as such accomplishes what only God can accomplish, namely, restoration of the fellowship of man with God which we had disrupted and indeed destroyed; to the extent that God in the fact of His revelation treats His enemies as His friends; to the extent that in the fact of revelation God's enemies already are actually His friends, revelation is itself reconciliation. Conversely reconciliation, the restoration of that fellowship, the mercy of God in wrath triumphant over wrath, can only have the form of the mystery which we describe as revelation.

Paul describes Christ as Him δι᾿ οὗ νῦν[EN36] (i.e., in Paul: in the presence of the *regnum gratiae*[EN37] denoted by revelation) τὴν καταλλαγὴν ἐλάβομεν[EN38] (Rom. 5¹¹). To God's good-pleasure to have His πλήρωμα[EN39] dwell in Him there corresponds His will δι᾿ αὐτοῦ ἀποκαταλλάξαι τὰ πάντα εἰς αὐτόν[EN40] (Col. 1²⁰). God was κόσμον καταλλάσσων[EN41] in Him, 2 Cor. 5¹⁹ says to the same effect. Hence the apostolic ministry is the διακονία τῆς καταλλαγῆς[EN42] (2 Cor. 5¹⁸) which comes to a head in the challenge καταλλάγητε τῷ θεῷ[EN43] (2 Cor. 5²⁰). Thus the concept of reconciliation coincides with that of revelation though not with that of redemption (ἀπολύτρωσις, σωτηρία)[EN44]. In the New Testament redemption is from the standpoint of revelation or reconciliation, the future consummating act of God which has still to come: νυνὶ δὲ ἀποκατήλλαξεν (ὑμᾶς) ἐν τῷ σώματι τῆς σαρκὸς αὐτοῦ[EN45] (Col. 1²²). Καταλλαγέντες σωθησόμεθα[EN46] (Rom. 5¹⁰). For the eschatological use of ἀπολύτρωσις[EN47] cf. Lk. 21¹⁸; Rom. 8²³; Eph. 4³⁰; Heb. 11³⁵, and for

---

[EN34] We speak that we do know, and testify that we have seen; and ye receive not our witness
[EN35] And what he hath seen and heard, that he testifieth; and no man receiveth his testimony
[EN36] by whom now
[EN37] kingdom of grace
[EN38] we have received atonement
[EN39] fullness
[EN40] by Him to reconcile all things unto Himself
[EN41] reconciling the world
[EN42] ministry of reconciliation
[EN43] be ye reconciled to God
[EN44] redemption, salvation
[EN45] yet now hath he reconciled (you) in the body of his flesh
[EN46] Being reconciled, we shall be saved
[EN47] redemption

the similar use of σωτηρία EN48 cf. 1 Thess. 5[8f.]; Rom. 13[11]; Phil. 1[19]; 2[12]; Heb. 1[14]; 9[28]. In distinction from this reconciliation is the act of God which is the basis of this prospect of the future, the act in Christ as the μεσίτης EN49 between God and man (1 Tim. 2[5]) or of the new covenant (Heb. 9[15]; 12[24]), the bearer and bringer of εἰρήνη EN50 as it is understood in Paul especially as the underlying purpose of God's gracious address to man (cf. the combination of χάρις EN51 and εἰρήνη EN52 in the greetings) and as it is explained as a divine act in Eph. 2[14–15].

The inconceivable element in revelation as such, in revelation as reconciliation which can be a reality only as it comes from God, is the fact of the Son of God who is the Lord in our midst, and therefore amid our enmity towards God. Because the love of God manifested in this fact cannot be identical with the love of God for the world which He willed to create and did create, for sin and death lie between this world and our world; because the love of God manifested in this fact is rather His love for the lost world of man who has become guilty before Him (Jn. 3[16]), for the world whose continuity with the original one is completely hidden from us, therefore we cannot confuse God's lordship in the one case with God's lordship in the other, or directly identify them, but in relation to the one (creation) we must speak of a first mode of God's being and in relation to the second (reconciliation) we must speak of a second mode of His being. For as we have to say that reconciliation or revelation is not creation or a continuation of creation but rather an inconceivably new work above and beyond creation, so we have also to say that the Son is not the Father but that here, in this work, the one God, though not without the Father, is the Son or Word of the Father.

[410]

It is hard to see how the distinction of the mode of being of the Son of God from that of the Father—and the same distinction must also be made from that of the Holy Spirit—can be denied without speculatively changing and weakening the seriousness of God's wrath against sin, of the opposition between original man and fallen man, of the world of creation and our world of sin and death, into a mere tension within a totality which is known to us and can be surveyed by us. On this assumption the inconceivability of revelation as a divine act of reconciliation will naturally be contested. It will be seen to follow as a second or third act in the same creation series which we can view as a totality, and God the Reconciler can easily be identified with God the Creator. Thus Schleiermacher regarded sin quantitatively as a mere lack, and he then logically viewed reconciliation ("redemption") as the crowning of creation, and, again consistently, he interpreted the Trinity modalistically, regarding the three modes of being as dissolved in the depths of God. A similar doctrine of the Trinity would also seem to lie behind the even more unfettered gnosis of E. Hirsch in respect of the synthesis of genesis and fall (*Schöpfung und Sünde*, 1932). It may also be said conversely that such disasters will inevitably happen in the doctrine of creation and reconciliation if the necessary safeguards are not provided by a sound doctrine of the Trinity.

EN48 salvation
EN49 mediator
EN50 peace
EN51 grace
EN52 peace

117

On the other hand we must also say that since the reference in God's revelation is to His lordship amid our enmity against Him, and therefore to the miracle of reconciliation, this work cannot be the work of a superman or demigod. The uniqueness of God's love for the world of fallen man, the power of reconciliation, will be underestimated if the true deity of the Reconciler is called in question. A superhuman or semi-divine event, an event which is not strictly miraculous but in the last resort self-evident, an event within the cosmos and therefore creaturely, does not correspond to the seriousness of the problem it is supposed to solve, nor to the character of omnipotent grace which the event that Holy Scripture describes as the event of reconciliation or revelation actually has. The character of omnipotent grace which this event has, and in the light of which the problem that it solves is of infinite seriousness, requires the acknowledgment that its subject is identical with God in the full sense of the word.

[411]   It is in this light, with reference to the reconciliation whose subject can be no less than God Himself if its power and the seriousness of the problem that it solves are to be perceived, if it is not to be regarded as a mere appearance of reconciliation, that the knowledge of the true deity of Christ has rightly been asserted and proclaimed from time immemorial. The so-called Homily of Clement (I, 1) begins with the declaration that we are to think of Jesus Christ ὡς περὶ θεοῦ [EN53] and forthwith it interprets this in the words: ὡς κριτοῦ ζώντων καὶ νεκρῶν [EN54].' One should not μικρὰ φρονεῖν περὶ τῆς σωτηρίας ἡμῶν [EN55]. To think meanly of Christ is to show at once that one has only a mean hope too. There is interrelation and necessary correspondence in the knowledge πόθεν ἐκλήθημεν καὶ ὑπὸ τίνος καὶ εἰς ὃν τόπον [EN56]. Similarly Gregory of Nyssa lays down that the benefactor can and must be known from his acts and the nature of one who does something must be disclosed by the event of his deed: Ἀφ' ὧν γὰρ εὖ πάσχομεν, ἀπὸ τούτων εὐεργέτην ἐπιγινώσκομεν, πρὸς γὰρ τὰ γινόμενα βλέποντες, διὰ τούτων τὴν τοῦ ἐνεργοῦντος ἀναλογιζόμεθα φύσιν [EN57]. Those who ascribe creatureliness to the Son and Spirit, and thus subject themselves to a creature, are not placing their hope in God and are deceiving themselves in thinking that they are put in a better position as Christians (*Or. cat.* 14 and 39). Luther constantly stressed this connexion too: *Vincere peccatum mundi, mortem, maledictionem et iram Dei* [EN58] are not the works of a *humana aut angelica potestas* but *mera opera divinae maiestatis. Qua re cum docemus homines per Christum iustificari, Christum esse victorem peccati, mortis et aeternae maledictionis, testificamur simul eum esse natura Deum* [EN59] (on Gal. 1³, 1535, W.A. 40¹, 81, 18; on Gal. 1⁴, *ib.*, p. 96, l. 15; on Gal. 3¹³, *ib.*, p. 441, l. 16, 25, 31) ... "for if sin is thus a big thing and its cleansing costeth so much that such a lofty person as Christ is here extolled must Himself set to and cleanse it Himself, what then in such great matters could avail our poor and helpless acts, for we are creatures, nay, sinful and wicked perishing creatures? that were

---

[EN53] as of God
[EN54] as the judge of the living and the dead
[EN55] think meanly of our salvation
[EN56] whence, by whom and whither we have been called
[EN57] For from those benefits which we receive, we know our benefactor, and in looking upon those things which happen, we gain a sense of the nature of the one who works on our behalf
[EN58] To vanquish the world's sin, death, damnation and wrath of God
[EN59] human or angelic power, but pure works of the divine majesty. For this reason, when we teach that human beings are justified through Christ, that Christ is the conqueror of sin, death and eternal damnation, we testify by that very act that he is God by nature

as if to undertake to set heaven and earth aflame with an extinguished firebrand. There must be here as great a payment for sin as God himself is who is injured by sin" (*Sermon on Heb.* 1[1f], 1522, *W.A.* 10[11], 161, 21). "Now God maketh none a king who is not God, for He will not let the reins out of His own hands, and will alone be lord over heaven and earth, death, hell, devil, and over all creatures. Since He then maketh Him a lord over all that is made, He must already be God" (*Sermon on Jn.* 3[1f.], 1526, *W.A.* 10[12], 296, 37). "For if the person who offered himself for us were not God, it would help and avail nothing before God that he was born of a virgin and likewise suffered a thousand deaths. But it bringeth blessing and victory over all sin and death that the seed of Abraham is also very God who giveth Himself for us" (*Sermon on Phil.* 2[5f.], 1525, *W.A.* 17[11], 236, 25). "We men are all sinners and lost. If then we are to be righteous and blessed, it must come about through Christ. But because we are righteous and blessed through Christ alone, He must be more than a pure and simple man. For man's hand and power can make no one righteous and blessed, God must do it Himself" (*Sermon on the Passion, How Christ was Buried, and on* Is. 53, *E.A.* 3, 276). The answer to *qu.* 17 of the *Heidelberg Catechism* is to the same effect: The Mediator must be true God "so that by virtue of His Godhead He might bear the burden of the wrath of God in His humanity, and acquire and restore to us righteousness and life."

Thus Jesus is Lord as the Son of God who has come to us or as the Word of God that has been spoken to us. We say here something which goes beyond the statement that God is the Creator or "our Father in heaven." Jesus reveals the God who is the Creator and "our Father in heaven." But as He does so, as that which is unheard of takes place, namely, that this God is revealed in Him, He reveals Himself to us, so assuredly does the fact of revelation signify a new thing *vis-à-vis* its content, so assuredly is reconciliation not to be understood as the completion of creation but as a miracle in and on the fallen world. We have seen in the previous section that in the context of the New Testament witness this new revelation of the Creator and our Father cannot be abstracted from the person of the Revealer. It was in the light of this unity of the content of revelation and the person of the Revealer that we then understood the original and proper sense of the fatherhood of God: He is Father because He is the Father of this His only-begotten Son. From the same unity we at once have the further result of the divine sonship of Jesus Christ. There is no abstract person of the Revealer, but the person of the Revealer is the person of Jesus Christ, who is subordinate to the Creator revealed by it, yet who is also indissolubly co-ordinate with Him, who is with Him; in this person the revelation is a reality. In other words, there is no Jesus *per se* who might then acquire also the predicate of a bearer of the revelation of his Father. Nor is there any revelation of the Father *per se* which might then be apprehended in Jesus in exemplary and pre-eminent fashion. Jesus *is* the revelation of the Father and the revelation of the Father *is* Jesus. And precisely in virtue of this "is" He is the Son or Word of the Father.

[412]

Our criticism of Ebionite and Docetic Christology has shown us that in the New Testament witness the person and thing really constitute this unity and that the thinking of the apostles about Jesus Christ, whether it began with the person or the thing, never took the form of a syllogism but always ended with the knowledge of Christ's deity because it had already begun there. In this respect, too, we can only dodge the unity of the content of revelation and the person of the Revealer if we evade the New Testament witness and disregard the prohibition and command set forth therein.

And now in the light of what has been said about creation and reconciliation we can add that the divine sonship of Jesus also results from the fact that creation (the content of His revelation of the Father) and reconciliation (the content of His self-revelation) are completely different from one another in their significance for us and yet are also completely related to one another in their origin. In trying to follow the tracks of Holy Scripture itself we have already been able to grasp the concept of the Creator only on the apparent detour *via* knowledge of God as the Lord of life and death, as the God of Good Friday and Easter. And in trying to grasp the concept of the Reconciler we have had to presuppose that there is a world created by God even though fallen and lost and that there is a man created by God even though actually [413] existing in enmity against Him. Only in the One who acts on us as the Reconciler through the cross and resurrection could we perceive the Creator, and only in the Creator who remains the Lord of our being in spite of our enmity can we perceive the Reconciler.

Τῷ γὰρ ἐξ ἀρχῆς τὴν ζωὴν δεδωκότι μόνῳ δυνατὸν ἦν καὶ πρέπον ἅμα καὶ ἀπολομένην ἀνακαλέσασθαι[EN60] (Gregory of Nyssa, *Or. cat.*, 8).

We must distinguish them, these two, and we must obviously distinguish them in such a way that we perceive and acknowledge the relation of subordination that is present here. We must say, then, that the Reconciler is not the Creator, and that as the Reconciler He follows the Creator, that He accomplishes, as it were, a second divine act—not an act which we can deduce from the first, whose sequence from the first we can survey and see to be necessary, but still a second act which for all its newness and inconceivability is related to the first. God reconciles us to Himself, comes to us, speaks with us—this follows on, and, we must also say, it follows from the fact that He is first the Creator. We can also say that it follows on and from the fact that He is "our Father in heaven." If He were not first the Creator and Father who is the Lord of our being, against whom we have sinned, whose wrath is thus upon us, but whose wrath is but the reverse side of His love as Creator and Father, how then could He be the Reconciler, the Peacemaker? To this order of creation and reconciliation there corresponds christologically the order of Father and Son or Father and Word. Jesus Christ as the Reconciler cannot precede the Creator, "our Father in heaven." He stands to Him in the irreversible relation of following on Him and from Him as the son follows on the father and from the father and the word follows on the speaker and from the speaker. But again this subordination and sequence cannot imply any distinction of being; it can only signify a distinction in the mode of being. For reconciliation is no more readily com-

---

[EN60] For only the one who has from the beginning given life is in a position to renew that life when it has been lost

prehensible and no less divine than creation. It is not as if reconciliation, unlike creation, could be made intelligible as a creaturely event. As creation is *creatio ex nihilo*EN61, so reconciliation is the raising of the dead. As we owe life to God the Creator, so we owe eternal life to God the Reconciler.

*Ipse est autem creator ejus, qui salvator ejus. Non ergo debemus sic laudare creatorem, ut cogamur, imo vere convincamur dicere superfluum salvatorem*EN62. (Augustine, *De nat. et grat.* 33, 39). *Creasti me, cum non essem, redemisti me cum perditus essem. Sed conditionis quidem meae et redemptionis causa sola fuit dilectio tua*EN63 (Anselm of Canterbury, *Medit.* 12). "This fleeting corruptible life in this world we have through God, who, as we confess in the first article of our Christian creed, is the almighty Creator of heaven and earth. But eternal incorruptible life we have through the passion and resurrection of our Lord Jesus Christ, who hath sat down at the right hand of God, as we confess in the second article of our Christian creed" (Luther, *Sermon on Mt.* 22³⁴ᶠ· *E.A.*, 5, 151). How could the second act be less great or miraculous than the first? One might argue the very opposite and see the greater miracle in the second, in reconciliation. Thus God is addressed as follows in the offertory of the Roman   [414]
Mass: *Deus, qui humanae substantiae dignitatem mirabiliter condidisti et mirabilius reformasti ... *EN64, and in the Kyrie-Tropus *"Cuncti potens": Plasmatis humani factor, lapsi reparator*EN65. But the dispute is pointless. *Intelligant redempti tui, non fuisse excellentius, quod initio factus est mundus, quam quod in fine saeculorum Pascha nostrum immolatus est Christus*EN66 (*Oratio* after the 9th prophecy in the vigil on Easter Eve).

Here genuine miracle stands side by side with genuine miracle. On neither side can there be any question of more or less miracle and therefore of more or less deity. In both cases we simply have an either/or. Here, then, sonship as well as fatherhood, in and with the super- and subordination expressed thereby, is to be understood as unrestrictedly true deity.

2. THE ETERNAL SON

Who is the Son of God? We have heard the provisional answer: Jesus Christ as the One who reveals the Father and the One who reconciles us to the Father is the Son of God. For as this One He reveals Himself to us as the Son who has come to us or God's Word that has been spoken to us. The dogma of the

---

EN61 creation from nothing

EN62 But he who is [humanity's] savior is himself its creator. Therefore we ought not so to praise the creator, that we are driven to say or rather convicted of saying that the savior is superfluous

EN63 You created me when I did not exist; you redeemed me when I was lost. Moreover, the sole cause of my being created and redeemed was your love

EN64 God, who wonderfully established the dignity of human nature and even more wonderfully has restored it ...

EN65 Maker of the human form, restorer of its fall

EN66 May those whom you have redeemed understand that it was not more excellent that the world was made in the beginning than that Christ was sacrificed as our Passover at the end of the ages

Trinity adds something new to this insight from Scripture's witness to revelation only to the extent that it adds the interpretation that Jesus Christ can reveal the Father and reconcile us to the Father because He reveals Himself as the One He is. He does not first become God's Son or Word in the event of revelation. On the contrary, the event of revelation has divine truth and reality because that which is proper to God is revealed in it, because Jesus Christ reveals Himself as the One He already was before, apart from this event, in Himself too. His sonship on the basis of which He can be the Revealer, the Mediator, the Reconciler, is not a mere contrivance of God behind which, in some higher essence of God which remains a mystery, there is no sonship or word-ness in God, but perhaps an inexpressible and speechless it-ness, a divine, a θεῖον EN67 with a different or unknown name. No, revelation has eternal content and eternal validity. Down to the very depths of deity, not as something penultimate but as the ultimate thing that is to be said about God, God is God the Son as He is God the Father. Jesus Christ, the Son of God, is God Himself as God His Father is God Himself.

How does this interpretation of the biblical witness to revelation arise? We can give here only the very simple but momentous answer that it arises because as a final word we accept the truth and validity of the equal and incomprehensible divinity of both the work of creation and also the work of reconciliation, and therefore the truth and validity of the unity of the Father and the Son as [415] the witness presents this to us as distinctive of the revelation attested by it. The Church dogma of Christ's deity as compared with the New Testament statement about Christ's deity says no other than that we have to accept the simple presupposition on which the New Testament statement rests, namely, that Jesus Christ is the Son because He is (not because He makes this impression on us, not because He does what we think is to be expected of a God, but because He is). With this presupposition all thinking about Jesus, which means at once all thinking about God, must begin and end. No reflection can try to prove this presupposition, no reflection can call this presupposition in question. All reflection can only start with it and return to it. The Church dogma of the deity of Christ arose out of this insight and it expresses this insight. For when it explicitly takes the deity of Christ to be eternal deity, when we say that the Son who has come to us or the Word that has been spoken to us is antecedently the Son or Word of God *per se*, we are simply saying in practice that the statement about Christ's deity is to be regarded as a basic and not a derivative statement. This is how the apostles understood it, the dogma says, and this is how we, too, must understand it if we are to understand the apostles. This is how we must understand the apostles and the statement, then, if our own understanding is not to be led astray from the understanding of the early Church which expressed and deposited this understanding in the dogma. Our own understanding as we have attempted it here has not so far led us astray

---

EN67 divinity

from the dogma of the early Church but has rather led us to it. Things might have been different. The dogma does not have divine dignity for us but only human pedagogic dignity. We might have turned our backs on it, but we have no cause to do so. As an expression of our own understanding of the New Testament too we can and we must say what the dogma says. We cannot understand the New Testament statement about Christ's deity in any different or better way than by studying it in harmony with the early Church, i.e., by directly comparing with it the dogma of the eternal deity of Christ. The dogma as such is not to be found in the biblical texts. The dogma is an interpretation. But we can convince ourselves that it is a good and relevant interpretation of these texts. We thus accept it. The deity of Christ is true, eternal deity. We see it in His work in revelation and reconciliation. But revelation and reconciliation do not create His deity. His deity creates revelation and reconciliation.

Κύριος ὢν κατὰ ἀλήθειαν, οὐκ ἐξ προκοπῆς τὸ κυριεύειν λαβών, ἀλλ᾽ ἐκ φύσεως τὸ τῆς κυριότητος ἔχων ἀξίωμα. Καὶ οὐ καταχρηστικῶς ὡς ἡμεῖς κύριος καλούμενος ἀλλὰ τῇ ἀληθείᾳ κύριος ὤν [EN68] (Cyril of Jerusalem, *Cat.* 0, 5).

Jesus Christ is the true and effective Revealer of God and Reconciler to God because God in His Son or Word does not posit and make known a mere something, however great or meaningful. He posits and makes known Himself [416] exactly as He posits and knows Himself from and to all eternity. He is the Son or Word of God for us because He is so antecedently in Himself.

It is one of the many optical illusions of Modernist Protestantism to have imagined that it should and could interpret and discredit this "antecedently in himself," i.e., the confession of Christ's true and eternal deity, as the exponent of an untheological metaphysical speculation by claiming that the Reformers adopted a very different position in this matter from that of the ancient and mediaeval Church. What is usually adduced from the actual statements of the Reformers in support of this thesis is, however, quite inadequate to prove that they ever dreamed of attacking or even altering in the slightest degree the dogma of the deity of Christ.

The main passage to call for consideration here is in the first edition of Melanchthon's *Loci* (1521). In the introduction to this oldest Evangelical dogmatics Melanchthon distinguishes among the *Loci theologici* [EN69] those which are *prorsus incomprehensibiles* [EN70] and those which according to the will of Christ must be *compertissimi* [EN71] to all Christian people. Of the first it must be said: *mysteria divinitatis rectius adoraverimus, quam vestigaverimus* [EN72]. For the latter involves great danger, and God has veiled His Son in flesh *ut a contemplatione maiestatis suae ad carnis adeoque fragilitatis nostrae contemplationem invitaret* [EN73]. Melanchthon is thus

---

[EN68] He is truly Lord, not having received lordship as a reward, but having the dignity of lordship by nature. And he is not called Lord improperly, as we are, but is Lord in truth
[EN69] theological topics
[EN70] utterly incomprehensible
[EN71] fully and certainly familiar
[EN72] we will have done better to adore the mysteries of the divinity than to investigate them
[EN73] that he might lead us from contemplation of his majesty rather to the contemplation of the flesh and on to our weakness

declaring that he sees no reason to spend too much time on the *loci supremi de Deo, de unitate, de trinitate Dei, de mysterio creationis, de modo incarnationis*[EN74]. The Scholastics had become fools in investigating these things and the *beneficia Christi*[EN75] had been obscured thereby. For the arguments (*e philosophia*[EN76], says the second edition, 1522) which they had presented had often been more worthy of a heretical than a Catholic dogma. The other *loci*[EN77], however, are vital: on the power of sin, the law, and grace. *Nam ex his proprie Christus cognoscitur, siquidem hoc est Christum cognoscere, beneficia eius cognoscere, non quod isti docent eius naturas, modos incarnationis contueri. Ni scias, in quem usum carnem induerit et cruci affixus sit Christus, quia proderit eius historiam novisse?*[EN78] As the physician must know more about plants than their nature, namely, their *vis nativa*[EN79], so Christ must be known as *salutare*[EN80] as this is made plain precisely in these other *loci* of which the Scholastics did not speak. We should follow Paul's example in Romans, where, as though foreseeing *disputationes frigidae et alienae a Christo*[EN81], he did not deal with the Trinity, the incarnation, or *creatio activa et passiva*[EN82], but with the law, sin and grace, i.e., with the *loci, qui Christum tibi commendent, qui conscientiam confirment, qui animum adversus satanam erigant*[EN83]. The Rationalists of the 18th and early 19th centuries (cf., e.g., J. J. Spalding, *Über die Nutzbarkeit des Predigtamtes*, 1772, 138 f.; K. G. Bretschneider, *Handbuch d. Dogmatik*, Vol. I, 4th edn., 1838, 553), and in recent times especially A. Ritschl (cf. *Rechtf. u. Versöhnung*[4], Vol. 3, 374, *Theologie und Metaphysik*, 1874, 60) and his followers (e.g., B. M. Rade, *Glaubenslehre*, Vol. 1, 1924, 53; H. Stephan, *Glaubenslehre*, 2nd edn., 1928, 166, 240), are the ones who thought they had much to rejoice about in this passage. But we must not conceal the fact that the passage does not really say what they are pleased to find in it. It reflects a passing mood but not a theological position which became historically significant even for Melanchthon. And even the mood was not directed against the content of the trinitarian dogma but against its importance in relation to other dogmas which lay nearer to Melanchthon's own heart. Moreover it was not occasioned by Melanchthon's own, perhaps critical, preoccupation with the dogma of the Trinity. It was occasioned on the one hand by his intensive preoccupation with the other dogmas under the influence and inspiration of Luther and on the other hand by his indignation at the unchurchly theoretical way in which the Scholastics, i.e., the theologians of the later Middle Ages with whom he was primarily acquainted, had dealt with the doctrine of the Trinity. It was a passing mood. Only the later emergence of antitrinitarians was needed to change it at once and to make room for the dogma of the Trinity in his *Loci* in spite of the passage quoted. The mood never achieved significance in the confessions or the theological work of the Reformation.

[417]

Friends of the Melanchthon passage might do better to appeal to Calvin if they knew him better. In 1537, during his first stay in Geneva, the theological and ecclesiastical adventurer

---

EN74 the highest topics concerning God, the divine unity, the Trinity, the mystery of creation, the manner of the incarnation
EN75 benefactions of Christ
EN76 from philosophy
EN77 topics
EN78 For it is from these that Christ is properly known, and indeed this is to know Christ: to know his benefactions and not what those [Scholastics] teach about pondering his natures [or] the modes of incarnation. If you did not know for what reason Christ put on flesh and was fixed to the cross, why would it benefit you to know his history?
EN79 natural force
EN80 salvific
EN81 debates both sterile and far from Christ
EN82 active and passive creation
EN83 topics to commend Christ to you, strengthen your conscience and fortify your soul against Satan

2. The Eternal Son

Petrus Caroli could publicly accuse Calvin of antitrinitarianism, and not without gaining a hearing even among serious people. The circumstances relating to the charge were as follows. The *Confession de la foy* of 1536 (in K. Müller, 111 f.), which was so authoritative at the beginning of the reformation in Geneva, though its contents are, of course, less characteristic of Calvin than of Farel, who was then the leader, has nothing at all to say about the doctrine of the Trinity either in its doctrine of God or its Christology. Furthermore the first draft of the *Institutio* of Calvin himself, which appeared rather earlier in the same year (*cap.* 2, *De fide*), does indeed give a very sound and respectful exposition of the doctrine of the Trinity, and shows that there is not a vestige of truth in Caroli's charge that Calvin avoided the terms *trinitas*[EN84] and *persona*[EN85], but it should still be noted that the author hardly has a burning interest in the matter. Even in his defence against Caroli in 1545 Calvin himself writes that true knowledge of Christ's deity consists in putting all our confidence and hope in Him and calling on His name. *Quae practica notitia certior haud dubie est qualibet otiosa speculatione. Illic enim pius animus Deum praesentissimum conspicit et paene attrectat, ubi se vivificari, illuminari, salvari, justificari et sanctificari sentit*[EN86] (*Adv. P. Caroli calumnias, C.R.* 7, 312 f.). Calvin also seems to have had at that time various objections to the authority and authenticity of the symbols of the early Church (*C.R.* 5, 337; 10², 84, 86; 7, 311 f.). And it is a fact that when Caroli demanded that he should subscribe to these symbols to prove his orthodoxy he strenuously refused to do so because of the "tyranny" of such a demand (*C.R.* 7, 315; 10², 120 f.). From both the theological and the human standpoint the whole controversy is most obscure. What does emerge from the passage quoted, and especially from the first edition of the *Institutio*, is that Calvin at that period, like Melanchthon sixteen years earlier, was preoccupied with other matters, these being, as in the case of Melanchthon, the problems of appropriating salvation rather than its objective presuppositions. In the case of Farel one might well ask whether he had not really lost sight of the latter and was thus well on the way which would lead to antitrinitarianism. like many of his contemporaries. But one cannot say this of Calvin even in relation to this period. For even at this early time he had the presuppositions more plainly in view than the Melanchthon of the 1521 statements had. With the lack of a true and distinctive doctrine of the Trinity which he had traced back to Arianism, Caroli, who seems to have been rather confused, was also accusing Calvin of attributing to Christ the Old Testament name of Jehovah. Calvin naturally meant this as an *elogium divinitatis*[EN87] (*C.R.* 7, 312; 10², 121; 9, 708). Again one cannot speak of anything but a churlish mood (strengthened by Caroli's arbitrary accusation) even in the Calvin of this period, nor was it directed against the objective presuppositions, but against their doctrinal formulation by the ancient Church. How far he was from drawing antitrinitarian deductions from this mood is unequivocally attested by the structure of the *Institutio* and also by his attitude in the Servetus case. [418]

The real issue in this whole matter is plain in Luther, to whom also appeal is usually made. It is Luther's insights that lay behind the statements of Melanchthon and indirectly behind those of Calvin too. From his perception that man's justification is in Christ alone and therefore by faith alone, Luther rightly concluded that all human theology can only be theology of revelation. As it is arbitrary and dangerous in the matter of justification to orientate oneself to a preconceived idea of the Law or one capriciously abstracted from the statements of Scripture; so it is arbitrary and dangerous in theology generally to start with a preconceived

---

[EN84] Trinity

[EN85] person

[EN86] This practical cognizance is doubtless more certain than any idle speculation. For the pious mind sees God as most truly present and almost touches him there where it feels itself enlivened, illumined, saved, justified and sanctified

[EN87] affirmation of divinity

§ 11. *God the Son*

idea of God or one capriciously abstracted from the statements of Scripture. The total theological question, like the question of justification in detail, can be answered only with reference to the God who reveals Himself in Christ. Already in 1519 Luther mentions a thought he was often to repeat: This is the *unicus et solus modus cognoscendi Deum*[EN88] (shamefully neglected by the *doctores Sententiarum*[EN89] with their *absolutae divinitatis speculationes*[EN90]), that *quicumque velit salubriter de Deo cogitare aut speculari, prorsus omnia postponat praeter humanitatem Christi*[EN91] (Letter to Spalatin, February 12, 1519, *W.A. Br.* I, 328 f.). About the same time we find him writing polemically: *Proinde, qui vult Deum cognoscere, schalam terrae infixam contueatur: cadit hic tota ratio hominum. Natura quidem docet, ut simus propensiores ad contemplanda magna quam abiecta. Hinc collige, quam inique, ne dicam impie, agant et speculantur, sua confisi industria, summa Trinitatis misteria: quo loco sedeant angeli, quid loquantur sancti. Cum tamen in carnem natus est Christus atque in carne mansurus sit. Vide autem, quid continget illis. Primo*[EN92]: "If they should poke their heads into heaven and look around in heaven they would find no one but Christ laid in the crib and in the woman's lap, and so they would fall down again and break their necks." *Et ii sunt scriptores super primum librum Sententiarum. Deinde adeo nihil consequuntur istis suis a speculationibus, ut neque sibi neque aliis prodesse aut consulere possunt*[EN93]. "Start here below, Thomas and Philip, and not up above" (*Schol. in libr. Gen. on Gen.* 28, *W.A.* 9, 406, 11). Even better known is the following passage: "For I have often said and say it again that when I am dead men should remember and guard against all teachers as ridden and led by the devil who in lofty positions begin to teach and preach about God nakedly and apart from Christ, as heretofore in high schools they have speculated and played with His works up above in heaven, what He is and thinks and does in Himself, etc. But if thou wilt fare securely and rightly teach or grasp God so that thou find grace and help with Him, then let not thyself be persuaded to seek Him elsewhere than in the Lord Christ, nor go round about and trouble thyself with other thoughts nor ask about any other work than how He hath sent Christ. Fix thine art and study on Christ, there let them also bide and hold. And where thine own thought and reason or anyone else leadeth or guideth thee otherwise, do but close thine eyes and say: I should and will know no other God save in my Lord Christ" (*Sermon on Jn.* 17³, 1528, *W.A.* 28, 100, 33; cf. also *Comm. on Gal.* 13, *1535, W.A.* 40¹, 75 f.; *W.A. Ti.* 6, 28). One should not fail to note that in so far as these statements of Luther are polemical in content they are not concerned with the doctrine of Christ's deity, and in so far as they are concerned with the doctrine of Christ's deity they are not polemical in content. What Luther wants—this is his point in this train of thought—is that deity in general and Christ's deity in particular should not be known along the path of autonomous speculation but along the path of knowledge of God's revelation, which means in practice along the path of knowledge of the *beneficia Christi* and therefore the *humanitas*

[EN88] the one and only way of knowing God

[EN89] teachers of the sentences

[EN90] speculations on pure divinity

[EN91] whoever wishes to think or reflect profitably on God should utterly disregard everything except the humanity of Christ

[EN92] Accordingly, let anyone who wants to know God have regard for the ladder fixed in the ground: here all human reason fails. For nature teaches that we are more eager to turn our attention to great than lowly things. Learn from this, how wickedly and – dare I say? – impiously they behave when they speculate, confident in their diligence, on the lofty mysteries of the Trinity: on where the angels are enthroned and what the saints say, when after all Christ was born in the flesh and will remain in the flesh. But look what happens to them. First

[EN93] And these are those who write on the first book of Sentences. And then they attain absolutely nothing from those speculations of theirs, so that they are able to profit or counsel neither themselves or others

Christi[EN94], i.e., His human reality as attested in Scripture, through which His benefits reach us. But Luther does want it to be known—and this must never be ignored or pushed into the background. More prudent than the Melanchthon of 1521, Luther does not fail to point out that in Jacob's dream we have angels both ascending and descending: *angeli ascendentes et descendentes: doctores precones verbi Dei*[EN95]. The path is first from below upwards, from the *natura humana Christi*[EN96] to *cognitio Dei*[EN97]. But it does really lead upwards and therefore it leads downwards again too. *Deinde cum* Χριστός *in sic humilibus formis cognitus est, tum ascenditur et videtur, quod est Deus. Et tunc cognoscitur quod Deus benigne, misericorditer despectat*[EN98] (*Sermon on Gen.* 28[12f.], 1520, W.A. 9, 494, 17 f.). Thus even knowledge of God's goodness depends again on the fact that the path leads from above downwards. "*Nos Christiani*[EN99] do not have enough about how a Creator is to be compared with a creature. *Sed docemus postea ex scriptura*[EN100] what God is in Himself ... *quid est deus in seipso?*[EN101] ... *quid*[EN102] is He in Himself where He hath His divine being by Himself? *Ibi Christiani: Is unicus dominus, rex et creator, per filium sic depinxit se, quod in deitate*[EN103] He is so ... *Non solum inspiciendus deus ab extra in operibus. Sed deus vult etiam, ut agnoscamus eum etiam ab intra*[EN104]. What is He inwardly?" (*Sermon on Jn.* 1[1f.], 1541, W.A. 49, 238, 5).

What is left of the whole appeal to the Reformation in this matter is in the last resort the mere fact that the burning problem of the Reformation was a different one from that of the 4th century, and that in the urgency of the conflict about their own problem the Reformers did and perhaps had to permit themselves sometimes to set the problem of the 4th century aside and put it in its proper place in a somewhat impatient gesture. But no one can seriously maintain that for them it did not occupy this place, or that they did not know it as the natural presupposition of their own problem, or that they did not recognise it again at the very latest in the controversy with their radical adversaries who were emerging at that time. Whether we explain it (with Stephan, *op. cit.*, p. 140) as a lack of theological consistency that they not only did not attack the doctrine of the early Church but in its proper place very solemnly affirmed it, or whether (with A. Ritschl, *Rechtfert. u. Versöhnung⁴*, Vol. 1, 145 f.) we see in this attitude the results of their ecclesiastico-political regard for the mediaeval *corpus christianum*[EN105], the fact as such is plain, and we are right to stick to it. The Reformers never dreamed of allowing Christology to be resolved or dissolved in a doctrine of the *beneficia Christi*. Can we not agree once and for all that it is one thing when Melanchthon says (*Loci*, 1535, C.R. 21, 366): *scriptura docet nos de filii divinitate non tantum speculative sed practice, hoc est iubet nos, ut Christum invocemus, ut confidamus Christo*[EN106], and quite another when, as Ritschl

---

EN 94 humanity of Christ
EN 95 angels ascending and descending: teachers and preachers of God's word
EN 96 human nature of Christ
EN 97 knowledge of God
EN 98 And so when Christ is known in these humble forms, then one may ascend and see that he is God. And then one knows that God looks down upon us kindly and mercifully
EN 99 We Christians
EN100 But afterwards we do teach from scripture
EN101 What is God in himself?
EN102 what
EN103 There the Christians [say]: This one Lord, King and Creator, has depicted himself through his Son as in his deity
EN104 It is not the case that God is to be perceived only in His outward works. God also wishes us to come to know Him from within
EN105 body of Christendom
EN106 scripture teaches us about the Son's divinity not so much speculatively as practically, that is, it commands us that we should call upon Christ and place our confidence in Christ

and his disciples desired, the *speculative* is simply eliminated or simply transformed into the *practice?*

But the objection that we have only an untheological speculation in the dogma of Christ's deity is materially nonsensical and untenable and in the long run it is bound to recoil on its authors.

J. J. Spalding, who was perhaps the first to try to use the Melanchthon passage in this way, is typical of everything that is usually said along these lines even to our own day when he argues: "Not what the Son of God is in Himself, in His nature which is impervious to our understanding, is part of our true Christianity, of the religious knowledge which is generally necessary and fruitful, but what He is for us, that for which He was given to us, what we should thank Him for, how we should receive and use Him in order to attain to the blessedness to which He would lead us. And how definitely we can dispense with all those hard words and even harder concepts!" (*op. cit.*, p. 142). "If there exists a clear divine declaration

[420]   that after my offences a conversion is again granted to me and access to my blessedness is still open; if in this declaration I am told that this is mediated and given to me in Jesus Christ, I do not see why this basis of my reassurance should not be sufficiently reliable for me. To regard such a generally declared assurance as inadequate, not to be ready to trust it with full confidence, until I myself first see how God could make this blessing possible, or whether He was even competent to forgive sins, would mean the assumption on my part of a kind of right of judgment on the holy laws of God's government that cannot possibly belong to me. He promises me forgiveness through Christ; more I do not need. What my Redeemer had to do and had to be in order to accomplish this is no part of my religion whether in respect of my virtue or of my peace of mind; I simply leave it to Him who has so clearly given me His word about my reacceptance. This declaration and assurance of the true God that He will forgive me is incomparably more necessary for me to know than the way in which He brings it about that He can forgive me; and it would be hard to find adequate grounds for making both equally essential and important in religious knowledge" (p. 144 f.). In short, knowledge of what the dogma says gives to Christians "not the slightest addition to their blessedness and their solace, but a correspondingly greater one to the futile burdening of their understanding" (p. 147). This line of argument, which is typical of Enlightenment theology (in the broadest sense of the term), completely fails to see that the point of the dogma is not at all to enrich or obscure simple and self-sufficient religious knowledge by an explanation of the possibility of its content which is as subtle as it is superfluous, but that the issue in this religious knowledge—whatever burdening of the understanding this may involve and irrespective of the sense in which it may belong to my religion, virtue and peace of mind—is the mystery of the Word of God, i.e., that the truth of what Christ is for us, the truth of His *beneficia*[EN107], is the truth of the event of the divine manifestation and not the truth of a generally declared reassurance detached from this event. That the true God has forgiven me—this and not merely that He will forgive me is after all the content of the religious knowledge at issue here—can be heard and understood as truth only in the mystery of the way of God out of His divine majesty and into my sin-shattered creatureliness. What connexion is there between the general truth that there is divine reconciliation (as truth that can be heard and understood apart from the mystery of this way) and the truth of the grace of God? The dogma of Christ's deity has to do with this truth, and therefore with the mystery of this way, and therefore with the distinction between the Whence and Whither of this way, and therefore with the distinction between the Son of God in Himself and for me. On the distinction between the "in Himself" and "for me" depends the acknowledgment of the freedom

---

[EN107] benefactions

and unindebtedness of God's grace, i.e., of the very thing that really makes it grace. It is this acknowledgment that is made in the Church dogma, whereas Enlightenment theology (in the broadest sense of the term) is obviously at war with it.

It is strange but true that the Church dogma of the true and eternal deity of Christ with its "antecedently in Himself" is the very thing that denies and prohibits an untheologically speculative understanding of the "for us." And the very man who thinks he must reject the Church dogma undoubtedly does this because he is in the grip of an untheologically speculative understanding of the "for us." This may be be shown in three respects.

1. If we will not listen to the fact that Christ is antecedently God in Himself in order that in this way and on this basis He may be our God, then we turn the [421] latter, His being God for us, into a necessary attribute of God. God's being is then essentially limited and conditioned as a being revealed, i.e., as a relation of God to man. Man is thus thought of as indispensable to God. But this destroys God's freedom in the act of revelation and reconciliation, i.e., it destroys the gracious character of this act. It is thus God's nature (*c'est son metier*EN108, Voltaire) to have to forgive us. And it is man's nature to have a God from whom he receives forgiveness. That and not the Church dogma which forbids this thought is untheological speculation.

2. If we will accept only the Son of God for us without remembering that He is antecedently the Son of God in Himself this certainly cannot be called the knowledge of faith—if, that is, the knowledge of faith is the knowledge of a divine act, of an unveiling of the veiled God, and therefore of a coming forth or a way of God; if the knowledge of faith is distinguished from other knowledge by the fact that it is knowledge of the mystery of the speech of God—the speech of God which arises out of a silence of God, which is truth as an actual event between a *terminus a quo* and a *terminus ad quem* and not otherwise. If we think we can understand the *beneficia Christi* apart from this event, then it is we, and not the Church dogma that reminds us of this event, who are engaged in untheological speculation.

3. If we want to restrict the task of theological reflection to an understanding of Christ in His revelation but only in His revelation in itself and as such, then what standard and criterion can there be for this understanding, this highly vaunted *beneficia Christi cognoscere*EN109? Obviously the criterion will have to be something man himself has brought. It may thus be, within the limit of our capability, either the evaluation of human greatness or the evaluation of the idea of God or a divine being. Since Christ is to be rated highly according to this humanly possible evaluation, we may to that extent, on the basis of our value judgment, call Him the Son of God. We are thus confronted again by the two christological types which we have learned to know as the Ebionite and the Docetic.

EN108 that's his job
EN109 knowing the benefactions of Christ

A. Ritschl—according to our classification his Christology, unlike that of the religious school which followed him, undoubtedly belongs to the Docetic type—has described as follows the process whereby there may be knowledge of Christ's deity on this presupposition: "If the grace and faithfulness and lordship over the world which are displayed both in Christ's mode of action and also in His bearing of suffering are the essential attributes of God that are decisive for the Christian religion, then in certain historical circumstances it was logical to establish the correct evaluation of the perfection of God's revelation through Christ in the predicate of His deity" (*Unterricht in d. chr. Rel.*, 1875, § 24; cf. *Rechtfertigung und Versöhnung*[4], Vol. 3, 370 f.).

[422] But all this interpreting, estimating and evaluating by a standard cocksurely imported and applied to Christ by the theologian—is not this real untheological speculation (even though in result and in its actual wording it does seem to bring us back again to the content of the Church dogma)? On the other hand, does not the Church dogma with its "antecedently in Himself" strike this standard out of our hands when it says to us that the knowledge of Christ's deity can only be the beginning and not the result of our thought?

Undoubtedly the dogma of Christ's deity snaps any correlation between the divine revelation and human faith. The cycle of religious psychology, the theory of two accessible elements of truth in a unity of tension, and all such well-meant inventions no matter what we call them, can never lead us to what this dogma is seeking to say. And if everything that cannot be grasped by these instruments is for that reason illegitimate metaphysics, then certainly this dogma is metaphysics of that kind. But on the basis of the three points made above we may simply turn the tables and say that the illegitimate metaphysics in which the Reformers obviously did not indulge consists in absolutising the correlation that we suppose we can attain and survey and understand, in regarding it as the reality in which God has as it were delivered Himself up to man and human thought and speech, instead of remembering that our being in this relation may always be pure illusion, and our thought within it and speech about it may always be pure ideology, if they are not grounded in God Himself and continually confirmed by God Himself. Because and to the extent that what the dogma states is true, that God's Word is the Word of God, for that reason and to that extent the correlation is also true. Its truth hangs as on a nail on the truth of which the dogma speaks. Similarly all the truth of our thinking and speaking about it hangs on knowledge of the truth of the dogma. Without this it is empty dreaming and chatter even though it has for a long time called itself a theology of revelation and faith. Just because Christ is the Son of God antecedently in Himself, there are two elements of truth in mutual tension (the elements of truth in Ebionite and Docetic thought) in which we recognise that He is God's Son for us and not *vice versa*. How could a theology which does not know the freedom of God's grace, which does not know the mystery of His way, which does not know the fear of God as the beginning of wisdom, how could such a theology come to call itself a theology of revelation and faith? How could it be knowledge of the *beneficia Christi*? Is not this defiant arrogance, all the worse because it pretends to be so humble? But there is no sense in scolding here. With particularly painful clarity we are faced here by the rift which divides the Evangelical Church. Those who are at loggerheads here can neither understand nor convince one another. They not only speak another language; they speak out of a different knowledge. They not only have a different theology; they also have a different faith. In the last resort we can only protest at this point as we can only protest against the assertions of Roman Catholic theology in other contexts. [423]

For dogmatic science the most important record of the Church dogma of the deity of Christ is the portion of the second article of the so-called *Symb. Nicaeno-Constantinopolitanum* which relates to this problem.

The *Symb. Nic. Const.* is a baptismal creed of the last third of the 4th century, perhaps the baptismal creed of the Church of Constantinople (or Jerusalem?), in which the decisive trinitarian decisions of the Council of Nicaea (325) were adopted and which according to a not wholly certain tradition is supposed to have achieved recognition at the Council of Constantinople in 381. It became an established part of the Eastern liturgy from 565 and of the Western from 1014. We say that it is for us the most important record of the dogma of the deity of Christ on the following grounds:

1. Of the three ancient creeds accepted by the Reformation Churches its definitions are at this point both the most trenchant and also the most succinct.

2. While simply repeating for the most part the ancient creed of Nicaea at this point, it offers us the definitive results of the patristic discussion of Christ's deity.

3. On account of its liturgical significance in the Eastern and Roman Catholic Churches, it is well adapted to remind us that over and above ecclesiastical divisions there was ecumenical consensus on the Christian confession, even though this was continually obscured.

4. It says unequivocally what Liberal Protestantism refuses to listen to, and for that very reason its validity must be recognised absolutely in an Evangelical dogmatics.

We shall conclude our consideration of the present problem with a short commentary on the relevant passage. It runs thus:

($\Pi\iota\sigma\tau\epsilon\acute{u}o\mu\epsilon\nu$ ...)

1. $\epsilon\grave{\iota}s\ \acute{\epsilon}\nu\alpha\ \kappa\acute{u}\rho\iota o\nu\ \mathrm{'I}\eta\sigma o\hat{u}\nu\ X\rho\iota\sigma\tau\acute{o}\nu$
2. $\tau\grave{o}\nu\ \upsilon\grave{\iota}\grave{o}\nu\ \tau o\hat{u}\ \theta\epsilon o\hat{u}\ \tau\grave{o}\nu\ \mu o\nu o\gamma\epsilon\nu\hat{\eta}$
3. $\tau\grave{o}\nu\ \acute{\epsilon}\kappa\ \tau o\hat{u}\ \pi\alpha\tau\rho\grave{o}s\ \gamma\epsilon\nu\nu\eta\theta\acute{\epsilon}\nu\tau\alpha\ \pi\rho\grave{o}\ \pi\acute{\alpha}\nu\tau\omega\nu\ \alpha\grave{\iota}\acute{\omega}\nu\omega\nu$
4. $\phi\hat{\omega}s\ \acute{\epsilon}\kappa\ \phi\omega\tau\acute{o}s,\ \theta\epsilon\grave{o}\nu\ \grave{\alpha}\lambda\eta\theta\iota\nu\grave{o}\nu\ \acute{\epsilon}\kappa\ \theta\epsilon o\hat{u}\ \grave{\alpha}\lambda\eta\theta\iota\nu o\hat{u},\ \gamma\epsilon\nu\nu\eta\theta\acute{\epsilon}\nu\tau\alpha\ o\grave{\upsilon}\ \pi o\iota\eta\theta\acute{\epsilon}\nu\tau\alpha$
5. $\acute{o}\mu o o\acute{u}\sigma\iota o\nu\ \tau\hat{\omega}\ \pi\alpha\tau\rho\acute{\iota}$
6. $\delta\iota'\ o\hat{\upsilon}\ \tau\grave{\alpha}\ \pi\acute{\alpha}\nu\tau\alpha\ \acute{\epsilon}\gamma\acute{\epsilon}\nu\epsilon\tau o$

(Text, *Denzinger*, No. 86)

(*Credo* ... EN110)

1. *in unum Dominum Jesum Christum*EN111
2. *filium Dei unigenitum*EN112
3. *et ex Patre natum ante omnia saecula*EN113
4. *Deum de Deo, lumen de lumine, Deum verum de Deo vero, genitum non factum*EN114
5. *consubstantialem Patri*EN115
6. *per quem omnia facta sunt*EN116

(Text, *Missale Romanum*)

EN110 I believe ...
EN111 in one Lord Jesus Christ
EN112 the only-begotten Son of God
EN113 and born from the Father before all ages
EN114 God of God, light of light, true God of true God, begotten not made
EN115 consubstantial with the Father
EN116 through whom all things were made

1. We believe in the one Lord Jesus Christ. The term "Lord" points in the first instance to the significance of Jesus Christ for us. In relation to us He is the Bearer of authority and power. He has a claim on us and control over us. He commands and rules. But He does not do so accidentally and provisionally, nor partially and restrictedly, like other lords. His lordship is not derivative nor grounded in a higher lordship. It is lordship in the final and definitive sense of the word. It is self-grounded lordship. This is the point of the "one" Lord. Its meaning is that the confession "Jesus Christ is Lord" is not just an analysis of the meaning of Jesus Christ for us as this is manifested to us in faith. It tells us that grounded in Himself, and apart from what He means for us, Jesus Christ is what He means for us, and that He can mean this for us because quite apart therefrom He is it antecedently in Himself.

[424]

> How could faith (as the apprehension of what Jesus Christ means for us) succeed in regarding itself as the justification of that confession? On the contrary, faith can regard itself as justified by the fact that prior to all apprehension of ours Jesus Christ is in Himself the very One as whom He gives Himself to be apprehended by us. *Christus quamquam sit coelestis et sempiternae conditor civitatis, non tamen eum, quoniam ab illo condita est, Deum credidit, sed ideo potius est condenda, quia credidit ... Roma Romulum amando esse Deum credidit, ista istum Deum esse credendo amavit*[EN117] (Augustine, *De. civ. Dei* XXII, 6, 1).

The phrase "the one" Lord relates Jesus Christ directly to the Father of whom the confession has said emphatically in the first article that He is the one God. If there can be no rivalry between the words "God" and "Lord" when they refer to the one being—to the one being in the same way as the statements about creation and reconciliation refer to the one work of this one being—then this phrase already makes the decisive point that Jesus Christ is Himself this being, that He is not just His legate or plenipotentiary, but that He is identical with Him. Because He is the one Lord, because He is the Lord in this strictest sense, His lordship for us, in His revelation, has no beginning and no end; it breaks in upon us with the unique and incomparable thrust of eternal truth and reality itself; it cannot be perceived or inferred from any standpoint whatever; knowledge of it begins with its acknowledgment. Only if He were another Lord, one of the lords within our world, could things be different. But He is this Lord, the "Lord of all lords" (Deut. 10^{17}; 1 Tim. 6^{15}). He has this significance for us because it corresponds to what His being is "antecedently in Himself."

2. We believe in Jesus Christ as the only-begotten Son of God. The term "Son" will be dealt with under point 4. The phrase "only begotten" first emphasises the oneness, which means the exclusiveness and uniqueness of the revelation and reconciliation enacted in Jesus Christ. To believe in Him as the Son of God is to know no other Son of God alongside Him, i.e., to know no other

---

[EN117] Although Christ is the founder of the heavenly and eternal city, still it did not believe him to be God because it was founded by him, but it is rather the case that it was founded because it believed ... Rome believed Romulus to be a god because it loved him; this city loved Christ because it believed that he is God

revelations which would be for us the revelation of God Himself, to know no other reconciliations in which we would be aware of being reconciled to God Himself. There are indeed other, immanent revelations and reconciliations accomplished within the created world; there are revelations of the spirit and revelations of nature. One man can reveal himself to another. And man can be reconciled to his destiny, even to death, and even—which is perhaps the greatest thing of all—to his fellow-man. But none of all this is the act of the Son of God. At any rate if a man believes in Jesus Christ as the Son of God, if God is revealed to him in Him and he is reconciled to God through Him, he will not see works of other sons of God in all those revelations and reconciliations. If they are to be authentic revelations and reconciliations, they can only be identical with *the* revelation and reconciliation through *the* Son of God. Jesus Christ will have to be recognised as living and acting in them. The one revelation and reconciliation will not be one among others. Yet this is not all that the confession is saying in the clause about the only-begotten Son of God.

[425]

If this were all it might still mean that the New Testament υἱὸς μονογενής EN118 should be interpreted by υἱὸς ἀγαπητός EN119, which also occurs in the New Testament. And this might mean that a being distinct from God was the object of God's special good-pleasure, favour, choice and adoption, that this being alone was called son by God and installed as God's son with the dignity and rights of sonship. And this would mean for us that he would have to be acknowledged and believed in by us as such. The exclusiveness of this belief, the so-called "absoluteness of Christianity," would then be the content of the confession. But if by μονογενής EN120 the confession is confessing the oneness and uniqueness of the revelation that took place in Jesus Christ, this is something very different from the absoluteness of Christianity. The confession is not saying that in faith, even in faith understood as a decision, we can and should choose one possibility among many others and label and claim it as absolute in distinction from the many others. How can this kind of exaltation of Jesus Christ attach itself to faith when the meaning of His exaltation by His heavenly Father is already quite different, when it is not an innovation but the confirmation of something original and intrinsic? The uniqueness of Jesus Christ as the Son of God, and therefore the uniqueness of the revelation and reconciliation enacted in Him, is not a predicate subsequently conferred on Him by God. It is to be understood as the content of an analytic, not a synthetic, statement. Μονογενής is not to be interpreted by ἀγαπητός EN121 but *vice versa: Non ideo μονογενής dicitur, quia ἀγαπητός sed ideo est ἀγαπητός quia μονογενής* EN122 (Quenstedt, *Theol. did. pol.*, 1685, I, *cap.* 9, *sect.* 1, *th.* 34).

The only-begotten Son is according to Jn. 1¹⁸ the one God. God Himself, God in Himself, is in the mode of being of the only-begotten of the Father. This is why this Only-begotten is the object of the Father's love and this is why He can be the object of our faith. Before all revelation and all faith, before it is

---

EN118 only-begotten Son
EN119 beloved Son
EN120 only-begotten
EN121 beloved
EN122 He is not called only-begotten because He is beloved, but rather is beloved because only-begotten

given to man to behold the glory of this Only-begotten (Jn. 1¹⁴), this glory is the glory of God Himself. And this is why it is "grace and truth" in its revelation. This is why its revelation has to be unique. The uniqueness of its revelation and of reconciliation corresponds to what God in His own being is antecedently in Himself: the Son of the Father, beside whom there can no more be a second Son of the Father than there can be a second God alongside the one God.

[426]   3. We believe in Jesus Christ as the begotten of the Father before all time. Our starting-point here, too, must be the fact that this is said of Jesus Christ as the Revealer of God and therefore of the God who acts on us and for us in time. Hence the statement about God as such does not stand abstractly as a second statement alongside a first statement about God as the Lord of our history. The statement about God as the Lord of our history is underscored by the statement that He is God as such and not a mere analogy of God, even the highest, in a sphere of reality distinct from God. He does not signify God Himself; He is God Himself. The phrase "before all time" does not, then, exclude time, whether the *illic et tunc*^EN123 of revelation as it is attested in Scripture or the *hic et nunc*^EN124 in which it is to become revelation for us. It does not exclude but includes time, concretely this time, the time of revelation. Hence it does not exclude history; it includes it. But the fact that time (the time of our time, the time and history of the sinful creature—and this is also the time and history of revelation) is included in a divine "before all time" is not something that we can take for granted. It is grace, mystery, a basis that we must recognise in the fear of God. Hence the statement about God as such, about God Himself, must be explicitly made even at the risk of the misunderstanding that we might be speaking without revelation and faith, that we might be speaking "non-historically," at the very point where everything depends on our speaking correctly about revelation and faith, about history. Even the statement about God as the Lord of our history is not as such immune from misunderstanding. In itself it might be construed as a statement of anthropological metaphysics. But it, too, can and must be construed only as an underscoring of the statement about God as such. Certainly the statement about the pre-existence of Jesus Christ is only an explication of the statement about His existence as the Revealer and the Reconciler, as the God who acts in us and for us in time. But just as truly the statement about His existence is only an explication of the statement about His pre-existence. This One, the Son of God who exists for us, is the Pre-existent. But only this One, the pre-existent Son of God, is the One who exists for us. The dogma of the incarnation of the Son of God will elucidate the first statement. The dogma of the deity of Christ which is our concern here emphasises the second.

The second article of the *Nic. Const.* distinguishes very clearly between these two circles of

---

EN123 there and then
EN124 here and now

knowledge. The dogma of the incarnation is not stated explicitly in the *Nic. Const.* but in the *Ephesinum* of 431 and the *Chalcedonense* of 451.

"Begotten of the Father before all time" means that He did not come into being in time as such, that He did not come into being in an event within the created world. That the Son of God becomes man and that He is known by other men in His humanity as the Son of God are events, even if absolutely distinctive events, in time, within the created world. But their distinction does not itself derive or come from time. Otherwise they would be only relatively distinctive events, of which there are others. Precisely because they have divine power, because the power of this world is here the power of the world to come, because the power of God's immanence is here the power of His transcendence, their subject must be understood as being before all time, as the eternal Subject, eternal as God Himself, Himself eternal as God. Jesus Christ does not first become God's Son when He is it for us. He becomes it from eternity; He becomes it as the eternal Son of the eternal Father.

[427]

"Before all time" should not be regarded, then, as a temporal definition. *Absque initio, semper ac sine fine: Pater generans, Filius nascens et Spiritus sanctus procedens*[EN125], says the *Conc. Lat.* IV, 1215, of God's three modes of being. On a passage often quoted in this context, namely, Ps. 2[7]: "Thou art my Son, this day have I begotten thee," Cyril of Jerusalem has the pertinent comment: Τὸ δὲ σήμερον, οὐ πρόσφατον, ἀλλ᾽ ἀΐδιον· τὸ σήμερον ἄχρονον, πρὸ πάντων τῶν αἰώνων[EN126] (*Cat.* 11, 5). *Vox "hodie" notat diem immutabilis aeternitatis*[EN127], is Quenstedt's paraphrase (*op. cit.*, th. 15), and in regard to its relation to time he then interprets the concept of the generation of the Son from the Father as follows (*th.* 28): *Haec generatio Filii Dei non fit derivatione aut transfusione, nec actione, quae incipiat aut desinat, sed fit indesinente emanatione, cui simile nihil habetur in rerum natura. Deus Pater enim filium suum ab aeterno genuit et semper gignit, nec unquam desinet gignere. Si enim generatio filii finem haberet, haberet etiam initium et sic aeterna non esset*[EN128]. Of this divine "antecedently" (which decides the temporal event that affects us to-day), we can and must say equally, then, that it takes place to-day, that it took place yesterday, and that it will take place tomorrow. *Nec tamen propterea generatio haec dici potest imperfecta et successiva. Actus namque generationis in Patre et Filio consideratur in opere perfectus, in operatione perpetuus*[EN129]. That is to say, the transcendence of the "antecedently" over all time cannot mean an emptying of the temporal event which is based on this "antecedently," for this is genuine and eternal transcendence. What is real in God must constantly become real precisely because it is real in God (not after the

---

[EN125] From the beginning, always and without end: the Father begetting, the Son being born, and the Holy Spirit proceeding
[EN126] And this "today" is not something new, but eternal: a timeless "today", before all ages
[EN127] The word "today" denotes the day of unchanging eternity
[EN128] This begetting of the Son of God does not occur through derivation or transfusion, or action which might have a beginning or a cessation, but happens through an unceasing emanation, to which there is no analogy in the natural world. For God the Father has begotten his Son from eternity, and always is begetting him; nor will he ever cease to beget him. For if the begetting of the Son were to have an end, it would also have a beginning, and so would not be eternal
[EN129] Nevertheless this begetting cannot be termed either incomplete or successive. For the act of begetting between the Father and the Son should be considered both complete as a work and perpetual in its working

manner of created being). But this becoming (because it is this becoming) rules out every need of this being for completion. Indeed, this becoming simply confirms the perfection of this being.

4. We believe in Jesus Christ as light of light, very God of very God, begotten, not made. In this clause we have the true and decisive trinitarian definition of Christ's deity. It states two things: First, that in God's work and essence we have to distinguish light and light, God and God, to distinguish them in the same way that in the created world we have to distinguish a source of light and a light that emanates from it, or a light that kindles and a light that is kindled, or father and son, or speaker and the word spoken. Then we have to understand this distinction as a distinction in God Himself. We have not to understand it as though there were God on the one side and a creature on the other, but in such a way that the one God is found equally on both sides. We shall try to understand the two series that are discernible here together, in their mutual relationship to one another.

[428] In the first instance the statements about distinction and unity in God are simply statements about revelation as the Church has found it attested in Holy Scripture. At this point, in this revelation, God is here and God is there, God is in this way and God is in that way, God is the Creator and God is the Reconciler, and yet He is one and the same God. We have here the concealed God and the revealed God, and yet the concealed God is no other than the revealed God and *vice versa*. In the first instance the dogma simply corresponds to the dialectic of revelation as such; it repeats the distinction and the unification. But according to the preceding clause it is now incontestable that with reference to the revelation that took place in Jesus Christ, in interpretation of the revelation as such, we have to say something that is more than the revelation. By revelation we have to say something that is beyond and above the revelation. We have to say that, as Christ is in revelation, so He is antecedently in Himself. Thus He is antecedently in Himself light of light, very God of very God, the begotton of God and not His creature. We have to take revelation with such utter seriousness that in it as God's act we must directly see God's being too.

To say that our concern is with the distinction and unity of two modes of being in God is to say already that while we can and must try to define this distinction and unity we cannot expect to grasp it in these definitions. We can and must think them out and express them. To try to avoid doing so is to try to evade knowledge of them. But it is with the biblical witness to God's revelation, as we have felt we must understand it, that knowledge of them is imposed on us as at least the task of dogmatics. We have good reason to recall that knowledge of God's Word can only be knowledge in faith. Decisively, then, it can only be acknowledgment, man's responsibility to the question which is set by this object. This responsibility cannot be discharged by grasping this object or seizing control of it. The object will always remain an object for what we think and say. What we think and say will never be commensurate with it; it will always be incommensurate (inadequate). Even though we reproduce the dogma or indeed the very statements of Holy Scripture it is only by God's grace and not intrinsically that the content of knowledge can be proper to what we think and say. Regarded immanently, what we think and say will always be in itself inadequate and broken thought and utterance.

(*a*) Relatively the least vulnerable of the three phrases in the clause is the middle one: "Very God of very God." The ἐκ denotes very briefly the distinction in modes of being: Very God grounded in and proceeding from very God—that is Jesus Christ. That is God only in this mode of being. The distinction of mode of being in which Jesus Christ is God consists, then, in the relation to another mode of being, a relation which the ἐκ[EN130] shows to be a grounding in or proceeding from. Conversely the unity of the two modes of being as *modes* of being of an absolutely identical *being* is denoted by the repetition of the noun θεός[EN131] along with the emphatic repetition of the adjective ἀληθινός[EN132]. [429]

In what became the official Latin text the crescendo: *Deum de Deo, lumen de lumine, Deum verum de Deo vero*[EN133], is obviously intentional. In his controversy with Caroli, Calvin called the passage a *battologia, a carmen magis cantillando aptum quam formula confessionis, in qua syllaba una redundare absurdum est*[EN134] (*Adv. P. Caroli calumnias, C.R.* 7, 315 f.). But it is better to think that the intensification of thought from lesser to greater definition is meant to be achieved as it were *in actu*[EN135].

The difficulty in even this very simple formula consists in the fact that as soon as we try to explain the ἐκ either as above or similarly, it unavoidably gives rise to the idea of two autonomous beings in a specific relation of dependence to one another, or, if this concept is avoided, it becomes meaningless, so that there is no longer any reference to a distinction in the *Deus verus*[EN136]. The truth signified actually lies beyond the words that signify it. *Deus verus* and *Deus verus* do not confront one another as autonomous beings but are twofold in one and the same autonomous being. This is what no language can render adequately; even the language of dogma can render it only very inadequately.

(*b*) In the first phrase "light of light" we have a lofty but all the more parlous attempt at illustration. In the first instance what is probably in view is the image of the sun and sunlight, of which the fathers were particularly fond. Jesus Christ as one mode of being in God is related to the first mode of being in which it is grounded and from which it proceeds, in the same manner as sunlight is to the sun.

[EN130] of, from, out of
[EN131] God
[EN132] true (very)
[EN133] God of God, light of light, true God of true God
[EN134] piece of stuttering, a song more suited to singing than to serve as a form of confession, in which repeating [even] one syllable is absurd
[EN135] in the act of speaking it
[EN136] true God

§ 11. *God the Son*

ὢν ἀπαύγασμα τῆς δόξης αὐτοῦ^{EN137} we read of the Son of God in Heb. 1³. *Cum radius ex sole porrigitur … sol erit in radio, quia solis est radius, nec separatur substantia sed extenditur. Ita de Spiritu Spiritus, et Deo Deus, ut lumen de lumine accensum*^{EN138} (Tertullian, *Apolog.* 21).

We can only rejoice in what is indeed the loftiness and beauty of the figure used in this phrase, and yet we have to confess not only that it presupposes the existence in time and space of that denoted by it but also that it is exposed to very different physical interpretations of which probably not one would say what is really being said here. We incur similar difficulties if we find in the *lumen de lumine*^{EN139} a light that kindles and a light that is kindled. In this metaphor the confession is certainly not trying to offer a *vestigium trinitatis*^{EN140} in the created world. It is not trying to make a statement about the hypostatic character and the *homoousia*^{EN141} of light in that twofold possibility of meaning. But just because, strictly speaking, it is unable to do this, the metaphor remains inadequate as a statement about Jesus Christ and the object plainly continues to transcend the word.

[430]   (*c*) The decisive phrase is naturally the third: "Begotten, not made."

In the negative part, which we take first, it tells us that as a mode of being in God Jesus Christ is certainly from God, yet He is not from God in the way that creatures from the highest angel to the smallest particle of sun-dust are from God, namely, by creation, i.e., in such a way that He had His existence, as an existence distinct from God, through the will and word of God. This can, of course, be said of the human nature of Christ, of His existence as a man in which, according to Scripture, He meets us as the Revealer of God and the Reconciler to God. But it cannot be said of Him who here assumes human nature, of Him who here exists as man ("for us men," as *Nic. Const.* says later) but does not allow His being and essence to be exhausted or imprisoned in His humanity, who is also in the full sense *not* man in this humanity, who is the Revealer and Reconciler in His humanity by virtue of that wherein He is not man. He who becomes man here to become the Revealer and Reconciler is not made. Otherwise revelation and reconciliation would be an event within creation and, since creation is the world of fallen man, they would be a futile event. Because the One who here became man is God, God in this mode of being, therefore, and not otherwise, His humanity is effective as revelation and reconciliation.

We now turn to the positive side of the phrase. Surprisingly enough it denotes the real becoming of Jesus Christ, His eternal becoming appropriate to Him as God, His relation of origin and dependence as God in His distinctive

---

^{EN137} being the brightness of his glory
^{EN138} When a ray shines forth from the sun … the sun will be in the ray, because the ray is the sun's, and the substance is not separated but extended. In the same way the Spirit is from Spirit and God from God, like light lit from light
^{EN139} light from light
^{EN140} trace of the Trinity
^{EN141} consubstantiality

138

mode of being. And it uses a figure of speech from the creaturely realm to do this. And, one might add, it uses the figure of speech which characterises this sphere as no other could. "Begotten," which means, in an eminent sense, that He has come into being as all living things in creation have come into being on the basis and presupposition of the divine Word of creation, that He has come into being in the context of sex and the nexus of the species, that He has come into being as the worm has come into being, that He has come into being as man comes into being, in the process in which creation and sin, in what is perhaps the most enigmatic way, are not interfused but opposed even as they exist together. We must not shut our eyes to this stumbling-block if we are to reach understanding here.

Thomas Aquinas thinks that what is properly expressed by the metaphor of generation is the *processio verbi*[EN142] (*S. Theol.* I, *qu.* 27, *art.* 2). On this point we must say that *generatio*[EN143] and the *processio verbi* are certainly to be regarded as terms for the same thing, yet not in such a way that one of the terms can be simply reduced to the other. *Processio verbi* may also be regarded as an important figure of speech but in its own way it is inadequate too. Both metaphors, that of the Son and that of the Word of God, point to an object with which they are not commensurate. But for that very reason each of them must be taken seriously, and neither should be abandoned with a reference to the other.

Obviously the natural character of the metaphor of begetting makes it clear [431] at the outset that in all that is said about Father and Son in description of the two modes of being in God we have a frail and contestable figure of speech. We denote God in this way but we do not grasp Him.

The early Church, which did not invent the metaphor but found it in Holy Scripture, where it is the most prominent figure of speech for this fact, was by no means unaware of its inadequacy and often stated this. *Est in hoc mysterio generationis vocabulum ab omnibus imperfectionibus generationis physicae adhaerentibus purgandum*[EN144] (Quenstedt, *op. cit., th.* 47). And already Cyril of Jerusalem demands expressly that not only the most patent physical sense of the term generation but also the sense of intellectual generation (e.g., in the teacher–pupil relation) and that of spiritual generation (as in believers when they become children of God) must be completely ruled out in this regard (*Cat.* 11, 9).

But what, then, does the metaphor mean?

In place of the categories of understanding which have been rightly rejected Quenstedt put a new one invented for the purpose when he spoke (*op. cit., th.* 47) of a *generatio hyperphysica, quae fit ab aeterno, sine omni temporis successione, materia et mutatione et in sola essentiae communicatione consistit*[EN145]. But Irenaeus had made the same point in a more illuminating way when he declared: *Si quis itaque nobis dixerit: Quomodo ergo Filius prolatus a Patre est? dicimus ei, quia prolationem istam, sive generationem, sive nuncupationem, sive adapertionem aut*

[EN142] procession of the Word
[EN143] begetting
[EN144] In this mystery the term "begetting" must be cleansed of all the imperfections associated with physical begetting
[EN145] a supernatural begetting, which is eternal and consists only in the communication of essence, involving neither matter, nor change of substance, nor any succession of time

quolibet quis nomine vocaverit generationem eius inenarrabilem exsistentem, nemo novit, non Valentinus, non Marcion, neque Saturninus, neque Basilides, neque angeli, neque archangeli, neque principes, neque potestates, nisi solus qui generavit Pater et qui natus est Filius[EN146] (*C.o.h.* II, 28, 6) and so had Cyril of Jerusalem when he declared that the Father begets the Son ὡς οἶδεν αὐτὸς μόνος[EN147]; the only possible thing we can say of this begetting is how it did not take place (*Cat.* 11, 11). Μὴ ἐπαισχυνθῆς ὁμολογῆσαι τὴν ἄγνοιαν, ἐπειδὴ μετ᾽ ἀγγέλων ἀγνοεῖς[EN148] (*ib.*, II, 12). Εἰπέ μοι πρῶτον, τίς ἐστιν ὁ γεννήσας, καὶ τότε μάνθανε ὃ ἐγέννησεν[EN149] (*ib.*, 11, 14). Taken strictly, even the concept of *communicatio essentiae*[EN150] says something which cannot be said without denying the unity of God's essence, and it becomes obscure or meaningless if it is not taken strictly. It does not carry us beyond the barrier which Quenstedt, too, had to admit in another passage (*op. cit.*, I, *cap.* 9, *sect.* 2, *qu.* 8, *font. sol.* 5): *Satis est, nos hic* τὸ ὄν *tenere, quod scriptura docet,* τὸ ποῖον *vero reservare isti statui, qui mera lux erit*[EN151].

In all its secularity and inadequacy, which we cannot possibly overlook, the figure of the Father and the Son says that a similar—not the same but a very different, an inconceivably and inexpressibly different—nevertheless a similar distinction and continuity exists to that between the person of a father and the person of a son in the created world, that there is a similar being of the first for the second and a similar being of the second from the first, that there is a similar twoness and oneness of the same being, between the mode of being in which God is revealed to us in Jesus Christ and the mode of being from which He is as He who is revealed to us in Jesus Christ. The very thing which, veiled in

[432] the puzzling co-existence of creation and sin, we know only as the begetting of a son by a father, though it is not grasped but only denoted in its true How by this figure, being just as unfathomable to us in its true How as is the being of God generally—this same thing is God's self-positing in which He is also and through Himself alone indissolubly distinct, the Father of Jesus Christ and Jesus Christ the Son of the Father. Even this most forceful figure can do no more, and does not seek to do more, than summon us to knowledge, not trying even for a moment to tie us to itself but at once directing our gaze beyond itself to the object to which, powerless though it is in itself, it can respond, leading us to the acknowledgment in which alone knowledge can consist here. All the associations which might be meaningfully suggested by the image are legitimate, and none is legitimate. Everything we might think of in this connexion, the fruitfulness of the Father, the love that does not let Him want to be alone, the dependence of the Son's existence on the Father, the love He owes

---

[EN146] And so if anyone should ask us, "How then is the Son begotten of the Father?" we answer him that no one knows the mode of this coming forth, or generation, or designating, or revealing, or by whatever name one wishes to call his indescribable begetting: neither Valentinus, nor Marcion, nor Saturninus, nor Basilides, nor angels, nor archangels, nor principalities, nor powers, but only the Father who has begotten and the Son who has been born

[EN147] in a way that he alone knows

[EN148] Do not be ashamed to confess your ignorance, since you share it with the angels

[EN149] First tell me who the begetter is, and then learn what he has begotten

[EN150] communication of essence

[EN151] Here it is enough to hold to the "that" which Scripture teaches; leave the "how" to that future state where all will be light

to the Father with His existence, the indestructible fellowship between the two which is not grounded in choice but in their two-sided existence—all this may be expressed and on all this we must be able to be silent again. The knowledge expressed in the metaphor is a non-knowing knowledge. It should regard itself as a knowing non-knowledge. Like every human word—though this is seldom so clear as here—it can only serve the Word which God Himself says about Himself. In this figure, which even in itself and as such denotes the deepest mystery of creaturely life, we can and should think of everything that can be meaningfully thought of in relation to the Father–Son relation in God, and we should then say: We are unprofitable servants, we have only thought and said in figures what we were under obligation to do, but we cannot claim that what we have thought and said is correct. Correctness belongs exclusively to that about which we have thought and spoken, not to what we have thought and spoken.

That the "begotten," along with the whole metaphor of father and son, says nothing, or does not say the truth, respecting God, does not in the least follow from all this. What it says is inappropriate, but it does say something and it says the truth. If we call what is said about Father and Son figurative, it should be remembered that this can apply only to our human speech as such but not to its object. It is not true, then, that the father–son relation is itself originally and properly a creaturely reality. It is not true that in some hidden depth of His essence God is something other than Father and Son. It is not true that these names are just freely chosen and in the last analysis meaningless symbols, symbols whose original and proper non-symbolical content lies in that creaturely reality. On the contrary, it is in God that the father–son relation, like all creaturely relations, has its original and proper reality. The mystery of begetting is originally and properly a divine and not a creaturely mystery. Perhaps one ought even to say that it is *the* divine mystery. [433]

The *generatio ipsa* is *in divinis propriissima et longe verior et perfectior quam ullius creaturae*[EN152] (Quenstedt, *op. cit., qu. 8, ekth. 5*).

But we know only the figure of this reality in its twofold inappropriateness as a creaturely figure and a sinful creaturely figure. We can speak of the truth only in untruth. We do not know what we are saying when we call God Father and Son. We can say it only in such a way that on our lips and in our concepts it is untruth. For us the truth we are expressing when we call God Father and Son is hidden and unsearchable.

The *modus generationis ipsae* is *in Deo longe alius quam in nobis estque nobis incognitus et ineffabilis*[EN153] (Quenstedt, *loc. cit.*).

[EN152] begetting itself is most proper to the divine and is far truer and more perfect than that of any creature

[EN153] mode of begetting itself is in God entirely other than ours and is for us unknowable and ineffable

Nevertheless, in naming God thus we are expressing the truth. His truth. In this sense the "begotten" says precisely what a confession of faith can and should say at the necessary distance from but also in the necessary relation to its object. It explains God's mode of being in Jesus Christ as a real "Thence" and "Thither," as the bringing forth from a source which is real in God Himself. Though we cannot, of course, perceive it, this is the proper and original Father–Son relation, the fatherhood and sonship of God. And we must add that the force as well as the clarity of the "begotten" does at least also lie in its opposition to the rejected "made." Begetting is less than creating inasmuch as the former denotes the bringing forth of creature from creature whereas the latter denotes the bringing forth of the creature by the Creator. Yet begetting is also more than creating inasmuch as—and here the closed circle of creature and creature as we see it in what we know as begetting is a figure—it denotes the bringing forth of God from God, whereas creating denotes only the bringing forth of the creature by God.

Quenstedt differentiates as follows: *Generatio est entis similis secundum substantiam ex substantia gignentis productio. Creatio est entis dissimilis secundum substantiam ex nihilo extra essentiam creantis productio*[EN154] (*op. cit., qu. 8, font. sol.* 16).

In the superiority of bringing forth from God in God over bringing forth by God, in the superiority of the freedom in which God posits His own reality over the freedom in which He posits a reality distinct from Himself, in the superiority of the love in which He is an object to Himself over the love in which the object is something that exists by His will in distinction from Himself—in this superiority lies the significance of the "begotten, not made."

[434]   This sheds light on a Scholastic thesis which is important here in helping to explain the purpose of the dogma. (J. Kuhn, *Kath. Dogmatik*, Vol. 2, 1857, 464 can even call it "the supreme dogmatic definition and the climax of the Nicene faith.") Following Athanasius (*Or. c. Ar.*, 2, 29), John of Damascus (*Ekdosis*, I, 8) distinguished begetting as God's ἔργον φύσεως[EN155] and creation as His ἔργον θελήσεως[EN156]. Thomas Aquinas (*S. theol.* I, qu. 41. art. 2), borrowing from Hilary (*Lib. de Synod, can.,* 24 f.), then explains that the begetting of the Son is certainly to be understood as an act of divine will, but only as the act of will in which *Deus vult se esse Deum*[EN157], as the act of will in which God, in freedom of course, wills Himself and in virtue of this will of His is Himself. In this sense, identically indeed with God's being Himself, the begetting of the Son is also an ἔργον θελήσεως for here θέλησις[EN158] and φύσις[EN159] are one and the same. But the begetting of the Son is not an act of the divine will to the degree that freedom to will this or that is expressed in the concept of will. God has this freedom in respect of creation—He is free to will it or not to will it—and creation is thus

---

[EN154] Begetting refers to the production of an entity of like substance out of the begetter's own substance. Creation refers to the production from nothing of an entity of unlike substance and outside of the creator's essence

[EN155] work of nature

[EN156] work of will

[EN157] God wills himself to be God

[EN158] will

[EN159] nature

an ἔργον θελήσεως. But He does not have this freedom in respect of His being God. God cannot not be God. Therefore—and this is the same thing—He cannot not be Father and cannot be without the Son. His freedom or aseity in respect of Himself consists in His freedom, not determined by anything but Himself, to be God, and that means to be the Father of the Son. A freedom to be able not to be this would be an abrogation of His freedom. Thus the begetting of the Son is an ἔργον φύσεως. It could not not happen just as God could not not be God, whereas creation is an ἔργον θελήσεως in the sense that it could also not happen and yet God would not on that account be any the less God. Quenstedt sums it up concisely: *Filius Dei est obiectum volitum et amatum ipsius voluntatis divinae, non tamen per illam productus*[EN160]. The Father begets the Son *volens*[EN161], but not *quia voluit*[EN162] (*op. cit., qu. 8, ofnt. sol.* 13). He does not beget Him *necessitate coactionis*[EN163], but *necessitate immutabilitatis*[EN164] (Hollaz, *Ex. Theol. acroam.*, 1706, I, 2, 37).

It is pertinent to add here for the sake of completeness a reminder which is absent from the *Nic. Const.* The figure of the Father and the Son to whose express interpretation the *Nic. Const.* confines itself is not the only one by which we should try to understand the concept of the deity of Christ. Alongside it there is both in the New Testament itself and also in the vocabulary of the early Church another one, namely, that Jesus Christ is the Word of God. By this figure He is again a second mode of being in God which is distinct from the first one but again one in essence with this, just as the word that someone speaks is distinct from him and yet as his word is not different in essence from what he is. We are saying the same thing when we say either "Son of God" or "Word of God"—*Verbum suum qui est Filius eius*[EN165] (Irenaeus, *C.o.h.* II, 30, 9). One may perhaps say that the first term is more to the point when we understand God's action in Jesus Christ materially as reconciliation and the second is more to the point when we understand the action formally as revelation. But in the first instance the statement about Christ's deity as the Word of God simply relates to God's action on us in Jesus Christ as attested in Scripture. Thus primarily and simply we understand by this figure too the *beneficia Christi*. In its truth and clarity the Word of God that is spoken to us, like the Son who intercedes with us for God and with God for us, is no other and no less than God Himself.

When God speaks, then *Nous*[EN166] and *Logos*[EN167] share equal truth and dignity. *Deus totus existens mens et totus existens logos, quod cogitatur, hoc et loquitur et quod loquitur, hoc et cogitat*[EN168] (Irenaeus, *C.o.h.* II, 13, 8 and 28, 5). *Non enim se ipsum integre perfecteque dixisset, si aliquid* [435]

[EN160] The Son of God is the willed and beloved object of God's own will in itself, but is not produced through that will
[EN161] willingly
[EN162] because he willed
[EN163] through necessity of compulsion
[EN164] through necessity of immutability
[EN165] his word, which is his Son
[EN166] mind
[EN167] word
[EN168] God is both wholly mind and wholly word: what he thinks, he speaks; and what he speaks, he thinks

minus aut amplius in eius Verbo quam in ipso[EN169] (Augustine, *De trin.* XV, 14). *Etenim non potest aliud quam quod es aut aliquid maius vel minus te esse in verbo, quo teipsum dicis, quoniam verbum tuum sic est verum quomodo tu es verax*[EN170] (Anselm of Canterbury, *Prosl.*, 23). "When Moses saith, 'In the beginning God made heaven and earth,' no person is yet specifically named or expressed. But as soon as he saith further, 'And God said, Let there be light,' he expresseth that there was a Word with God before light came into being. Now the same Word that God speaketh there could not be the thing that was created there, neither heaven nor earth, since God, just by speaking what He does, maketh heaven and earth with the light and all other creatures, so He hath done nothing more to create save His Word, therefore it must have been before all creatures. But if it was before, ere time and creatures began, it must be eternal and another and higher being than all creatures, whereupon it followeth that it is God" (Luther, *Sermon on Gen.* 1¹, 1527, *W.A.* 24, 29, 4).

Jesus Christ, the Word of God, meets us as no other than God, but in another way, in a different mode of being compared with God in so far as God speaks the Word, in so far as the Word goes forth from Him.

"But if God speaketh and the Word falleth, He is not alone nor can He personally be Himself the Word that He speaketh. Therefore, because the Word is also God, it must be another person. Thus the two persons are expressed: the Father who speaketh the Word and hath essence of Himself, the Son who is the Word and cometh from the Father and is eternally with Him" (Luther, *op. cit.*, l. 14, cf. *W.A.* 10¹, 183, 13).

The same revelation thus compels us to separate God and His Word and also to unite them.

"Who cannot here gather from these words of Moses how there must be two persons in the Godhead and yet but one Godhead? unless he wisheth to deny clear Scripture. Again, who is so acute as he may here contradict? He must allow the word to be something other than God its speaker, and must yet confess it was before all creatures and the creature was made thereby; so he must certainly allow it also to be God, for apart from the creatures there is naught but God. So he must also confess, there is but one God. And so this scripture compelleth and concludeth that these two persons are one complete God, and each is the one, true, perfect, natural God who hath created all things, and that the Speaker hath not His being from the Word but the Word its being from the Speaker, yet all eternally and in eternity apart from all creatures" (Luther, *Sermon on Jn.* 1¹ᶠ·, 1522, *W.A.* 10¹, 184, 6).

This distinction and unity in God which is inescapably presented to us in revelation itself is acknowledged and underlined by the dogma when it understands Jesus Christ, the Word of God, as the eternal Word. The Word of God in which He gives Himself to be known by us is none other than that in which He knows Himself. For this reason and in this way it is God's own Word, the Word of truth to us in His revelation. According to the preceding development in the history of the dogma, it is beyond question that whenever the *Nic. Const.*

[EN169] For he would not have expressed himself fully and completely, if there is anything more or less in his word than in himself

[EN170] For there cannot be anything other than what you are, nothing greater or less than you are, in the word by which you express yourself, because your word is as true as you yourself are truthful

spoke of the Son of God it always meant the Word of God too. The Word is the   [436]
one Lord. The Word is spoken by the Father before all time. The Word is light
of light, very God of very God. The Word is spoken by God, not made. Alongside the statement that Jesus Christ is the eternal Son of the eternal Father one
may thus put the statement that He is the eternal Word of the Father who
speaks from all eternity, or the eternal thought of the Father who thinks from
all eternity, the Word in which God thinks Himself or expresses Himself by
Himself.

> Jesus Christ is God's eternal *emanatio intelligibilis utpote verbi intelligibilis a dicente, quod manet in ipso*[EN171] (Thomas Aquinas, *S. theol.* I, qu. 27, art. 1).

As the Word which God thinks or speaks eternally by Himself and whose
content can thus be no other than God Himself, Jesus Christ as God's second
mode of being is God Himself.

Yet we must not disguise the fact that on our lips and in our concepts this
way of speaking is also inappropriate. We do not know what we are saying when
we call Jesus Christ the eternal Word of God. We know no word which, though
distinct from a speaker, still contains and reproduces the whole essence of the
speaker. We know no *Logos* with an adequate *Nous*-content and no *Nous* which
can be exhaustively expressed in a *Logos*. We know no thought or speech which
can transcend the antithesis of knowledge and being in triumphant synthesis.
In short, we know no true word. Neither do we know, then, the true word
about the true Word, God's Word. We must say once more what we said about
the father–son relation. For us who think and speak in the doubly veiled
sphere of creatureliness and sinfulness, the true word is strictly and exclusively
the eternal Word concealed in God, Jesus Christ Himself. It is not that our
creaturely thought and word has in relation to the creaturely reason which
produces the creaturely logos a metaphorical aptitude which justifies the claim
that we are thinking and speaking the truth when we call Jesus Christ the Word
of God. It requires revelation and faith, and the connected gracious event of
the incarnation of the eternal Word and the outpouring of the Holy Spirit, if
what we know as word is to be continually awakened and raised up to this
metaphorical aptitude, so that it may become the truth when we call Jesus
Christ the Word of God.

"Now must we open wide the heart and understanding, that we regard not such a word as a
man's petty and halting word, but as he is great that speaketh, so great must we consider his
word. 'Tis a word he speaketh in himself, and it abideth in him and is never sundered from
him. Therefore according to the apostle's thought we must so think as God speaketh with
Himself to Himself and leaveth a word about Himself in Himself, but the same word is no
mere wind or sound, but bringeth with it the whole essence of the divine nature, and as is
said earlier in the epistle about appearance and likeness, the divine nature is so depicted

---

[EN171] intelligible emanation, in the same way as an intelligible word which comes from a speaker
   remains in him

[437] that it is wholly present in the likeness and it becometh and is itself the likeness, and the clarity thus exceedeth the appearance and passes essentially into the appearance. Accordingly then God also speaketh His word about Himself that His whole godhead followeth the word and naturally abideth in the word and is essential. Lo, we see there whence the apostle hath his language that he calleth Christ an image of the divine being and an appearance of the divine honour, namely, from this text of Moses, who there teacheth that God speaketh a word about Himself which may not be other than an image that indicateth Him. For every word is a sign that signifieth somewhat. But here is that signified, naturally in sign or word, which is not in other signs; therefore he rightly calls it an essential image or sign of his nature" (Luther, *op. cit.*, 186, 9).

On account of the inadequacy of this figure of speech it is inadvisable to bring the concept of the deity of Christ under the denominator of the image of "word."

There seems to be at least a strong tendency in this direction in Thomas Aquinas, cf. *S. theol.* I, *qu.* 27, *art,* 2 and also *qu.* 34. Nor does this rest on any particularly high estimation of "word" as the epitome of revelation. Scripture or Church proclamation, but rather on his anthropology, i.e., on his high opinion of the process of knowledge as the *similitudo supremarum creaturarum*[EN172] (*qu.* 27, *art.* 1). In regard to this it must be said that an *emanatio verbi manentis in dicente*[EN173] is metaphorically apt, not because such a *similitudo*[EN174] is immanent in it, but because it is awakened and raised up to be a *similitudo*, a likeness, and therefore to metaphorical aptness, in the event of revelation and faith. The same may naturally be said in opposition to Augustine's doctrine of the *vestigium*[EN175] or the *imago trinitatis*[EN176] in the three powers of the soul, *memoria, intellectus* and *amor*[EN177]. There is no *analogia entis*[EN178] but only an *analogia fidei*[EN179]. But it is instructive to see how the preference which on the basis of his own theory Augustine, too, gives to the concept of word: *Eo quippe filius quo verbum*[EN180], is then reversed again: *et eo verbum quo filius*[EN181] (*De trin.* VII, 2). He is well aware, of course, that by "Son" something is said about Jesus Christ which cannot be said by "Word" and which must always be added in thought to what we know as word, namely, the continuity and oneness of essence between Speaker and Spoken. So he must combine the images: *Verbo quod genuit dicens est, non verbo, quod profertur et sonat et transit, sed .... Verbo aequali sibi quo semper et immutabiliter dicit seipsum*[EN182] (*ib.,* VII, 1). *Seipsum dicens genuit Verbum sibi aequale per omnia .... Et ideo Verbum hoc vere veritas est*[EN183] (*ib.,* XV, 14). And Thomas Aquinas, too, does not hesitate to admit that different *nomina* are needed to express the perfection of the divine origin of Christ: *Filius, splendor, imago, verbum. Non autem potuit unum nomen*

[EN172] likeness of the highest creatures
[EN173] emanation of a word that remains in the speaker
[EN174] likeness
[EN175] trace
[EN176] image of the Trinity
[EN177] memory, intellect, love
[EN178] analogy of being
[EN179] analogy of faith
[EN180] For he is the Son inasmuch as he is the Word
[EN181] and he is the Word inasmuch as he is the Son
[EN182] He is a speaker by virtue of the Word which he begat, not by a word which is spoken and sounds and passes away, but .... By the Word that is equal to himself, through which he always and unchangeably expresses himself
[EN183] As he expressed himself he begat the Word that is equal to him in every respect ... And for this reason this Word is absolute truth

inveniri, per quod omnia ista[EN184] (namely, everything that is meant to be denoted by one or other of these terms) *designarentur*[EN185] (*S. theol.* I, *qu.* 34, *art.* 2, *ad.* 3). F. Diekamp's *conclusio theologica* that "the begetting of the Son from the Father is an intellectual one" (*Kath. Dogm.*, Vol. I, 6th edn., 1930, 329 f.) must be described as an unwarranted systematisation even of the view of Thomas. Cf. in this respect the more cautious attitude of B. Bartmann, *Lehrb. d. Dogm.*, Vol. I, 4th edn., 1928, 198 f., especially the references to Thomas given on p. 200.

It is when we use all the metaphors, including that of the Word, with an awareness of their limitations that in respect of the event of revelation and faith we shall always be the more confident to speak the divine truth in our human untruth: *peccatores iusti*[EN186].

5. We believe in Jesus Christ as being "of one substance (or essence) with the Father." Historically the incorporation of this phrase into the original Nicaenum was a bold anticipation, dubious in many respects, but ultimately justifiable both historically and materially. [438]

Ecclesiastically, it was more than doubtful that Constantine I presumed to force this ὁμοούσιος[EN187] on the council of 325 and that the majority of the council allowed the imposition of this imperial theology in spite of their well-considered persuasion to the contrary. Morally one is bound to sympathise, not with the orthodox minority who were given the victory in this way, and even less with the middle party of Eusebius which apparently yielded for the sake of peace, but rather with the unfortunate Arius and his few followers who preferred deposition and exile to abandoning their resistance. (There was a similar scandal to the detriment of the Nicene faith at Milan in 355.) Furthermore the meaning and intention behind the triumph of the ὁμοούσιος was far from clear; before Nicaea, and for a long time afterwards, it was by no means obvious whether the concept of *homoousia* (a term already familiar to Valentinian Gnosticism according to Irenaeus, *C. o. h.* I, 5, 1) did not involve subscription to Sabellianism or even a form of tritheism. In the 3rd and 4th centuries there was good reason to be opposed to this term. In 269 it had even been explicitly rejected at a council in Antioch in justifiable self-defence against Paul of Sasnosata. And even the group of theologians who eventually won the victory for the doctrine of Christ's eternal deity, the so-called Neo-Nicenes. finally accepted it only upon a very precise interpretation, i.e., in the sense of equality of essence along with distinction of the persons. It was understandable that the making of a dogma out of the hitherto relatively little discussed ὁμοούσιος should become the standard in a battle for or against it which occupied the whole period between 325 and 381 and in which, by wide detours and with many setbacks, the Church had later to learn to understand what it had intended and decided in 325 *hominum confusione et Dei providentia*[EN188]. One may well ask whether the authoritative theologians at the time of the Council of Constantinople, the Cappadocians in particular, would themselves have devised this formula. Even the West, which was better able to resist Arianism, and which at certain points was the salvation of the Nicene faith, did not finally produce the ὁμοούσιος but accepted it as a *fait accompli*.

In fact one can understand and acknowledge this formula only after recognising quite fearlessly the problems of its origin. But in this way one can and must acknowledge it. One

---

[EN184] Son, glory, image, word. For one name could not be found by which all these things
[EN185] could be described
[EN186] sinners made just
[EN187] of one substance
[EN188] through the confusion of human beings and the providence of God

must do so historically, for with the ἀληθινὸν θεόν[EN189] and the γεννηθέντα οὐ ποιηθέντα[EN190], but less ambiguously than either of these for the thought of the time, it proved to be the formula by which the Arian contradiction was finally bound to be unmasked as such and broken. Hilary (*De Syn.*, c. 83) once wrote not without humour: *Homousia si cui displicet, placeat necesse est, quod ab Arianis sit negatum*[EN191]. One must also acknowledge it materially, for even if the Church had great difficulty in seeing what it meant by it, and was far from seeing this when it was made a dogma in 325, what it did positively mean by it is for us who come after expressed clearly enough in this formula along with the others in the symbol.

"Of one substance or essence," i.e., of identical essence, is the meaning of ὁμοούσιος or consubstantialis as a dogma.

This is how it was understood by Athanasius, who was virtually the leading man in the Church in this whole matter: ἀνάγκη γὰρ ... τὴν ταυτότητα πρὸς τὸν ἑαυτοῦ πατέρα σώζειν[EN192] (*De. decr. nic. syn.* 23), ἵνα μὴ μόνον ὅμοιον τὸν υἱόν, ἀλλὰ ταὐτόν τῇ

[439] ὁμοιώσει ἐκ τοῦ πατρὸς εἶναι σημαίνωσιν[EN193] (*ib.*, 20), ἔχων ἐκ τοῦ πατρὸς τὴν ταυτότητα[EN194] (*Or. c. Ar.* I, 22). etc. This is also how it was understood in the West by Augustine in a way that was decisive for all later development. "In one and the same essence" is how Luther and the authors of the Book of Concord translated the phrase.

"Of equal essence" is included in this sense, for if the Son is of one essence with the Father He is also of equal essence with Him. On the other hand "of equal essence" does not have to mean "of one essence"; it might be construed polytheistically.

The Neo-Nicenes, for whom the sense "equality of essence" was the dominant one, wished to draw attention thereby to the problem of the distinction and autonomy of the persons, which had received little emphasis in Athanasius. Polytheism thus became a constant threat to Eastern theology. On the other hand, it must be admitted that the idea of oneness of essence made Modalism a constant threat to Western theology. One must say, however, that it is plain enough from the total context in which alone ὁμοούσιος is intelligible that unity of essence is not to be thought of without equality of essence (which is implicitly expressed in the concept itself). In other words, the distinction of the modes of beings is not to be forgotten nor their autonomy surrendered. On the other hand when the opposite is missing there is no obvious safeguard against polytheism. On this ground we vote for Athanasius' ταυτότης[EN195] i.e., for the Augustinian and Western interpretation of the ὁμοούσιος.

"Of one essence" is first and obviously a safeguard against the Arian understanding of Jesus Christ as a "demi-god from below" or a superman who is indeed like God but, being only like Him, is ultimately and in the last resort different from Him. It underlines and accentuates the γεννηθέντα οὐ

[EN189] true God
[EN190] begotten not made
[EN191] If anyone does not like the phrase "of the same substance", he must like the fact that it was rejected by the Arians
[EN192] for it is necessary ... to retain [the notion] that he have identity with his Father
[EN193] so that they might show that the Son is not only like, but is the same in likeness with the Father
[EN194] having identity with the Father
[EN195] identity

ποιηθέντα. It places Jesus Christ on the side of the Creator in contrast to every creature, even the highest.

But "of one essence" is also secondly a safeguard against the idea, current from the days of Origen, that Jesus Christ is a "demi-god from above" on a lower stage and of lesser quantity within the Godhead itself. It underlines and accentuates the ἀληθινὸν θεόν.

"Of one essence" is thus directed against the two extremes which with reference to the situation in the 2nd century we called the Ebionite extreme on the one side and the Docetic on the other.

"Of one essence" is also thirdly a safeguard against the differentiation or multiplication of God's essence through the distinction in modes of being. That is, it is a safeguard against polytheism. If forces us really to understand the "persons" as modes of being, i.e., not as two subjects but as twice the same subject (in indissoluble twofoldness of course, as may be inferred from the context of the creed), as two who are two only in their mutual relations and not in themselves, not in their essence. Ὁμοούσιος τῷ πατρί[EN196] means "I and the Father are one"—I and the Father, for only in this distinction does the "one" apply—yet "one," for only in this unity is there the I and the Father.

Of this most famous and, technically considered, most central concept of [440] the dogma we may say what we have said of all the formulae in the preceding phrases. We do not even remotely grasp the object to which there is an attempt to respond in this concept. Precisely when we do not construe the concept of *homoousia* polytheistically nor modalistically, precisely when we interpret it with Athanasius and Augustine as identity of essence on the one side and when, taking up the concern of the Neo-Nicenes, we let it speak to us of two distinct but equal modes of being in the one essence on the other side, it is plainly referring to an essence of which we have no idea at all; it thus becomes a concept of the type philosophy usually calls "empty concepts." We have stated often enough that distinction in unity and unity in distinction is the point in all trinitarian theology. In relation to the concept of *homoousia*, which is trying to express both at the same time, it is thus as well to grant that in the last resort we are familiar only with unities without distinction or distinctions without unity. All images fail at this limit of our thought and speech: the image of Father and Son, that of Speaker and Word, that of light and light, and that of original and copy, which is a metaphor too. For in these we never have one essence in what are really two modes of being or else we never have two modes of being in what is really one essence. Either we have one essence in what are only apparently and transitorily two modes of being or we have two modes of being with two corresponding essences. It all depends on our interpretation of the metaphors, and they can all be interpreted in two ways. The one real essence in two real modes of being is God Himself and God alone. He Himself

---

[EN196] Of one substance with the Father

and alone is both Father and Son, Speaker and Word, light and light, original and copy. From Him the created, sinful creature receives the truth of its relationships by revelation. It must confess Him, not independently or arbitrarily, but by His revelation in faith, if it is to know its own truth. The concept of *homoousia* is not an attempt at independent, arbitrary, so-called natural knowledge of God. It seeks to serve the knowledge of God by His revelation in faith. We have not concealed the historical and material ambiguity of this particular concept. Hence we neither can nor would hide the fact that considered in itself it serves the knowledge of God very badly. For philosophers and philosophical theologians it has always been easy game. But it may be that very little depends on its immanent soundness or unsoundness. It may be that even in its obvious frailty it was the necessary standard which necessarily had to be set up in the 4th century and which even to-day, as often before, has still to be kept aloft against the new Arians, not as the standard of a foolhardy speculative intuition of the Church, but as the standard of an unheard-of encounter which has overtaken the Church in Holy Scripture. If this is so, of what avail is anything that might be said against it? Do we not have to be aware of all these

[441] objections, and yet still acknowledge it as the dogma which the Church, having once recognised, can never let go again? For in all its folly it is more true than all the wisdom which has voiced its opposition to it. We have no reason to take any other view of it. We are under no illusion as to the fact that we do not know what we are saying when we take this term upon our lips. But still less can we be under any illusion as to the fact that all the lines of our deliberations on the deity of Christ converge at the point where we must assent to the dogma that Jesus Christ is ὁμοούσιος τῷ πατρί, *consubstantialis Patri*.

It is fitting that we should again listen to Luther, who by means of the distinction and unity of original and copy has also made the decisive point that must be made concerning the concept of *homoousia*: "Thus in these words 'tis powerfully taught that Christ is one true God with the Father, equal to Him in all things, without distinction, except that He is from the Father and not the Father from Him, like as radiance is from the brightness of the divine essence and not the brightness of the divine essence from the radiance." "So too when he says that He is the image of His substance he likewise attesteth powerfully that Christ must be true and natural God and yet there are not on that account many gods but one God. 'Tis said it is a counterfeit when a picture is made exactly like that of which it is a picture. But it is a lack in all pictures that they have not nor are the same essence or nature as that of what is depicted, but are of another nature or essence. As when a painter, or carver, or stone-mason depicts a king or prince on a canvas, block, or stone as exact and like as ever he can, so that all eyes must say: Lo, that is this or that king, prince, or man, etc. This is naturally an image or counterfeit. But it is not the essence or nature of the king, prince, or man, etc. It is a poor picture, image, or figure of it, and hath another essence, for its nature or essence is stone, wood, canvas, or paper, and whoso seeth or graspeth it doth not see nor grasp the essence, nature, or substance of the man, and every one saith, 'Tis a wooden or stone or canvas likeness. But it is not the living, essential likeness of the men .... But here Christ is the image of the Father, so that He is the likeness of His divine essence, and not made of another nature, but is (if one may so speak) a divine image which is of God and hath divinity in itself or of itself, as a crucifix is called a wooden likeness of Christ, being made of wood. And all men and angels are also made in the image of God. But they are not images of His essence and nature, nor made or arisen out of His divine nature. Christ, however, hath arisen from eternity out of His divine nature and is His essential image, *substantialis imago, non artificialis out facta vel creata*[EN197], which hath His divine nature wholly in itself and also in it, not made nor fashioned of aught else, just as the divine essence is not made nor fashioned of aught else. For if He had not the entire Godhead of the Father in Himself and was not complete God, He could not be nor be called the likeness of His essence, for the Father would still have something wherein the Son was not equal nor like unto Him, so He would in the last resort be quite unlike and in no wise His image according to essence. For the divine essence is the most single of all, indivisible, it must be entirely where it is or not there at all" (Luther, *Die drei Symbola oder Bekenntnis des Glaubens Christi*, 1538, W.A. 50, 276, 30 and 277, 1. 19).

6. We believe in Jesus Christ "by whom all things were made."

We have here an almost literal quotation from Jn. 1[3], which says even more explicitly than the symbol itself: πάντα δι᾽ αὐτοῦ ἐγένετο καὶ χωρὶς αὐτοῦ ἐγένετο οὐδὲ ἓν ὃ γέγονεν[EN198]; cf. also Jn. 1[10]: ὁ κόσμος δι᾽ αὐτοῦ ἐγένετο[EN199], 1 Cor. 8[6]: δι᾽ οὗ τὰ πάντα[EN200], Col. 1[15f]: He is πρωτότοκος πάσης κτίσεως ὅτι ἐν αὐτῷ ἐκτίσθη τὰ πάντα ... τὰ πάντα δι᾽ αὐτοῦ καὶ εἰς αὐτὸν ἔκτισται[EN201], Heb. 1[2]: δι᾽ οὗ καὶ ἐποίησεν τοὺς αἰῶνας[EN202]. [442]

It may be asked whether within the context of the creed this statement is one of the definitions of Christ's deity or whether it is not rather a pronouncement on His work as the Mediator of creation and thus a transition to the succeeding phrases on the incarnation and the work of reconciliation. The syntactical form, however, seems to point in another direction. And even if it were a pronouncement of the latter type, the content at any rate would still have to be understood strictly in terms of trinitarian theology, and, thus understood, it means that the Son of God, too, has a share in the work which is ascribed in the first article of the creed to God the Father, the work of creation. Thus understood, it is an indirect but all the more expressive confirmation of the ὁμοούσιος and therewith of all the preceding phrases. If the Son has a share in

---

[EN197] substantial image, not constructed or made or created
[EN198] All things were made through him, and without him was not anything made that was made
[EN199] the world was made through him
[EN200] through whom are all things
[EN201] the first-born of all creation; for in him all things were created ... all things were created through him and for him
[EN202] through whom also he made the worlds

what was called the special work of the Father, if He works with the Father in the work of creation, then this means, at least in the sense of Athanasius and the theology which finally triumphed in the 4th century, that He is of one essence with Him. In order that all things might be made by Him, in order that He might be the Mediator of creation, He Himself had to be God by nature.

Rejection of the Arian view of Jn. 1³ and par. is not expressly voiced in the symbol. According to Arius the Son is itself the creaturely instrument of the divine Creator. This is completely ruled out by the ὁμοούσιος and γεννηθείς οὐ ποιηθείς EN203. Thus the present clause interprets the ὁμοούσιος only to the degree that its own interpretation is governed by the context of the symbol.

Here again we have to remember the principle: *opera trinitatis ad extra sunt indivisa* EN204. It implies at this point that an appropriation is involved when, as in the continuation in the creed, revelation and reconciliation are ascribed to the Son. This appropriation is right and necessary since it is grounded in revelation itself. But revelation cannot be understood correctly if we do not add that as this appropriation cannot exclude the Father from being also the subject of this event (to the degree that the Father is also present and at work with the Son in revelation and reconciliation), so it cannot exclude the Son being also the subject of the event to which the first article refers, that is, the subject of creation. We are following John 1 and Luther's expositions of Genesis 1 and John 1 (which we quoted earlier) when we offer the interpretation that Jesus Christ is the Word by which God created the world out of nothing. As this Word of the Father He is, in distinction from everything created by Him, equal to the Father, very God from all eternity.

[443] Where has God created the world? asks Augustine. In heaven? On earth? In the air? In the water? In the universe? But these are all themselves created. Has He created them out of a being He first took in hand for the purpose? But *unde tibi hoc quod tu non feceras, unde aliquid faceres? Quid enim est, nisi quia tu es? Ergo dixisti et facta sunt atque in verbo tuo fecisti ea* EN205 (*Conf.* XI, 5, 7). *Eo sempiterne dicuntur omnia* EN206 (*ib.*, XI, 7, 9). Thus: *Fecit omnia per verbum suum et verbum eius ipse Christus, in quo requiescunt angeli et omnes caelestes mundissimi spiritus in sancto silentio* EN207 (*De cat. rud.*, 17, 28). *Constat ... summam substantiam prius in se quasi dixisse cunctam creaturam quam eam secundum eandem et per eandem suam intimam locutionem conderet* EN208 (Anselm of Canterbury, *Monol.*, 11). *Cum ipse summus spiritus dicit se ipsum, dicit omnia, quae facta sunt .... Semper in ipso sunt, non quod sunt in se ipsis sed quod est idem ipse* EN209.

EN203 begotten not made
EN204 the outward works of the Trinity are undivided
EN205 where did you obtain that which you did not create, so that you might create something? For what exists other than by the fact that you exist? Therefore you spoke, and they were created, and you created them in your word
EN206 By it [the word] all things are spoken eternally
EN207 He made all things through his Word, and his Word is Christ (himself), in whom the angels and all the purest celestial spirits rest in holy silence
EN208 It is established ... that the highest substance in a way expressed in itself the whole creation before it established it in accordance with and through this, its same inmost speech
EN209 When the highest Spirit expresses himself, he expresses all things which have been made ... They are always in him, not as what they are in themselves, as what he himself is

(*ib.*, 34). In the same sense Thomas Aquinas gave an affirmative answer to the question: *Utrum in nomine verbi importetur respectus ad creaturam? Deus enim cognoscendo se, cognoscit omnem creaturam. Uno actu*[EN210] God knows Himself and all that is outside Him, and so His Word is not just the precise image of the Father but also the original of the world (*S. theol.* I, *qu.* 34, *art.* 3). Similarly Luther: *Filius enim in se habet exemplar non solum maiestatis divinae, sed etiam exemplar omnium rerum creatarum*[EN211] (*Comm. on Gen.* 1²⁰ᶜ, 1535f., *W.A.* 42, 37, 30). Even the bodily warmth with which a hen hatches her eggs is according to Luther *ex verbo divino, quia, si absque verbo esset, calor ille esset inutilis et inefficax*[EN212] (*on Gen.* 1²², *ib.*, p. 40, 1. 9). In contrast it is rather laboured and lacking in humour when K. Bretschneider (*Handb. d. Dogm.*, Vol. I, 4th edn., 1838, 659) assures us that we "must regard the whole idea of the creation of the world by the Son as one which does not belong to religion but to Johannine and Pauline theology," or when A. Ritschl, following in the footsteps of earlier rationalism here, thinks he should comment on the relevant New Testament passages as follows: "This combination takes us beyond the sphere of theology proper and has no direct and practical significance for religious belief in Jesus Christ" (*Unterricht in d. chr. Rel.*, 1875, § 24). In relation to the biblical references and their exposition in the early Church we certainly can and should utter a warning against the inference, which is not ruled out to full satisfaction in Augustine or even Anselm, that the creation of the world was as essential to God as the begetting of the Son, that it was not the result of a *nova voluntas*[EN213] (as Augustine says. *Conf.* XII, 15, 18), that the existence of the world was necessarily included in God's Word (as it might perhaps seem to be according to the statement adduced from Anselm), that the world is thus an essential predicate of God. Nevertheless, one cannot possibly suspect the thought itself of being an unnecessary theologoumenon.

The idea does not have merely the abstractly trinitarian significance of making it clear that the work and therefore the essence of the Father and the Son are one and the same. In so doing, it also illumines and explains once again who and what Jesus Christ is in His revelation: not a stranger whom we might encounter as a stranger, interpreting and choosing according to our own thought and evaluation; not even a semi-stranger whom we should judge according to a knowledge of the God that sent Him which we have derived from some other source. But "he came to his own possession" (Jn. 1¹¹), to the world, to us whom He Himself created, who are from the very first His own, and He theirs. The Word which we hear in revelation, the Word by which we are summoned to the unmerited and from our standpoint impossible fellowship of God with sinners—this Word is none other than the Word by which we who should hear it are called into being along with all the reality that is distinct from God, without which we would not be either sinners or righteous, without which we would not be at all. The One who in revelation calls us out of our enmity against Him to Himself, who calls us out of death into life, is the One who in so doing also makes Himself known as the One who previously called us

[444]

[EN210] Is there a relation to the creature is implied by the name "Word"? For in knowing himself God knows every creature. By a single act

[EN211] For the Son has in himself not only the exemplar of the divine majesty, but also the exemplar of all created things

[EN212] from the divine Word, because, if it were without the Word, that warmth would be useless and ineffective

[EN213] new act of will

out of nothing into existence, into existence as *pardoned sinners*, yet into *existence* as pardoned sinners. We cannot hear the Word of justification and sanctification without being reminded that it is through this Word, in no other way and from no other source, that we who are justified and sanctified by this Word even exist. This Word is the ground of our being beyond our being; whether we hear it or not, whether we obey it or not, it is in virtue of its superior existence that our existence is a reality. This Word came to us before we came or not, and as we come or not. Our coming or not coming is possible only because this Word is real. The same Jesus Christ through whom God unites us to Himself even while we are His enemies has already united us to Himself as those who belong to Him because He alone holds us over the abyss. And it is by this first union with Him, manifested to us in and by the second, by revelation, that the significance of the second for us is measured. To be sinners, as we are shown to be in the revelation of Jesus Christ, means that we have separated ourselves from the One without whom we would not be even in this separation and yet, separated from whom, we cannot be in any true or proper sense. To be sinners means that we have come to a place where our existence is absolutely inconceivable because at this place it can be only a plunge into nothing, where our existence can be understood only as an event of inconceivable kindness, or it cannot be understood at all. And to attain to grace, as we are again shown to have done in the revelation of Jesus Christ, means that notwithstanding our separation He without whom we would not be, and yet from whom we have separated ourselves, not only does not let us fall into the nothing from which He called us, but also, addressing and claiming us as sinners. He grants to us over and above existence no less a gift than Himself, fellowship and intercourse with Himself. What does this mean? It means that in His revelation Jesus Christ the Word of God does not need to get from some other source the authority to address and claim us; He already has it antecedently in Himself. It is not a question of whether we want to respond to Him or not. We are already responsible to Him and in different ways our whole being is response to Him. In relation to Him there is no possibility of appealing or withdrawing to some domain of our own where we were once alone and where He does not yet

[445] reach us or does so no longer, to a neutral human existence, as it were, where it is first up to us to place ourselves or not under the judgment and the grace that He declares to us, and from which we might comfortably come to an understanding with Him. In fact we do not know anything about our human existence except through the Word which declares to us judgment and grace. In declaring this, it tells us that it is itself the ground of our being as men; on this ground alone are we men, and not otherwise. It comes to us because it already applies to us even before it comes. It is the hand that already holds us even as it grasps us. It is the ruling act of the king who was already a king before and who has both the might and the right to perform this act. It encompasses us on every side (Ps. 139^5). It is the Word which has power, the Word of the Lord.

And it is the Word of the Lord because it is the Word of the Reconciler who is also the Creator.

In our investigation of the New Testament doctrine of the deity of Christ we ended with the tautology that for the men of the New Testament Jesus Christ is the Lord because He is the Lord. Though we cannot avoid this tautology we can now put it this way: He is for them God the Reconciler as He is God the Creator. His judgment and grace concern them as He concerns their existence. We should, of course, immediately reverse this and say also that He concerns their existence as He comes to them with His judgment and His grace. The point cannot be that in their existence, in their creaturely humanity, they had a previously given criterion by applying which they then accepted His judgment and His grace and thus believed in Him as the Lord and the Son of God. On the contrary, His judgment and His grace bar every exit or escape to a humanity which is already given and assured as such. They take away every private criterion and spoil every private judgment. These men have found themselves, their being, and also the possibility of their own judgment only at the place where His wrath and His kindness have reached them. But there they have in fact found themselves and their being and therewith the possibility of their own judgment. They are as men who are judged by Him, And as men who are judged by Him they now judge; they judge concerning Him. They thus judge concerning Him: He is the Son of God. In saying this they are saying that He is our Reconciler as He is our Creator. They might just as well abandon the judgment "We are" as the judgment that "He is God's Son." For them the two are inseparable, for their knowledge of themselves, their existence, their creatureliness and their Creator is not from another source than knowledge of their reconciliation. For them there can be no question of any gap between a known Creator God and Jesus Christ as a Redeemer and Saviour who perhaps stands in some relation to God. As they know their reconciliation through Jesus Christ, they know themselves, their existence, their creatureliness, the Creator. There is thus taken away from under their feet the ground on which they would have to stand to ask, to seek, and to discover whether Jesus Christ is the Lord and the Son of God. So they can only begin with this knowledge and this confession. One would have to abstract again between the Creator and the Reconciler; one would have to make two words again out of what is for the men of the New Testament one word, to be able to find Ebionite or Docetic Christology in the New Testament.

In this sense, then, the statement illumines and explains who and what Jesus Christ is in His revelation. It says of Him that in His revelation He has the immediate power of the Creator over men. But in acknowledging this we shall not limit His power as Creator to His revelation. [446]

Already in the 2nd century writers like to compare with the $\delta\iota$ $o\mathring{\upsilon}$ $\tau\grave{\alpha}$ $\pi\acute{\alpha}\nu\tau\alpha$ EN214 the insight that the Church is the first creature of God made before the sun and moon $\kappa\alpha\grave{\iota}$ $\delta\iota\grave{\alpha}$ $\tau\alpha\acute{\upsilon}\tau\eta\nu$ $\acute{o}$ $\kappa\acute{o}\sigma\mu o\varsigma$ $\kappa\alpha\tau\eta\rho\tau\acute{\iota}\sigma\theta\eta$ EN215 (Hermae Pastor, *Vis.* II, 4, I; Clem. Hom., 14. 1). And in the 20th century R. Seeberg has interpreted this biblical concept as follows: "If God created the world with the resolve that the Church should come into being in it, then the will of God—and this is Christ—was already at work in the creation and formation of the world ..." In so far as the natural world was to be "the theatre of a spiritual historical world, the divine will that there be a history which leads to the Church ... was already at work in such a way at the creative fashioning of the world that the natural possibility was provided for the existence and continuity of a spiritual world" (*Chr. Dogmatik*, Vol. I, 1924, 463 f.). Even if we

---

EN214 through whom all things
EN215 and for its sake the world was established

155

ignore the fact that the Church is hardly the same thing as a "spiritual historical world," we must still comment as follows. Certainly Jesus Christ as the One by whom all things were made is also the κεφαλὴ τοῦ σώματος, τῆς ἐκκλησίας[EN216] (Col. 1[18]). As the former He can be and is the latter. But it is not as the latter that He is the former. It is not as the Head of the Church, not first and only in revelation, that He is the One by whom God made all things. Certainly He is so powerful in His revelation because He is already the Creator. But He is not first the Creator in the fact that He is so powerful in His revelation, nor is He the Creator only on this ground. If we permit reversals here, if we are not content to find the Creator again in the revelation, if we at once take the further step of deducing creation as such from revelation and basing it on this, this is just as much an illegitimate speculation as the attempt, which we criticised earlier, to understand revelation as *creatio continuata*[EN217]. To attribute the Church or revelation directly to creation or the creative will of God as such is to forget or ignore the fact that the Church or revelation can be an event only as an answer to the sin of man, or it is to be forced to try to integrate the sin of man into creation. It is also to forget the free loving-kindness of God which gives this answer, or to make it a necessary member in a dialectical process. Then this speculative synthesis of God's works—in a way which is no less unavoidable in Seeberg than Schleiermacher—finds appropriate expression in the abrogation of the distinction of the divine persons, in a modalistic doctrine of the Trinity. Only thus can one say that the world was created for the sake of the Church or revelation, and that this purpose is the meaning of the participation of the Son of God in creation. These conclusions are the necessary price of such syntheses. If we do not want to pay the price—and we have good reason not to want to pay it—then we must refrain from the syntheses.

The truth of the recognition that Christ in His revelation has the power of the Creator depends on its being the acknowledgment of a fact and not an arbitrary combination. When the power is experienced there is nothing to combine. Creation and revelation are not truths which are to be held alongside one another and compared to one another and set in relation to one another. They are the one reality of Jesus Christ as the Revealer with the power of the Creator. And this power of the Creator cannot be regarded as one that is specifically related or restricted to revelation alone.

[447]   Augustine is thus right when he has it that the angels, too, were created by the Word, and so is Luther when he says that the broody hen was created by the Word.

Creation, then, means deity in its originality above and beyond all creatureliness. To come back to the theology of the Trinity, this is what the creed is saying with its δἰ οὗ τὰ πάντα. By the δἰ οὗ[EN218] it completely distinguishes the Son from the Father. By the τὰ παντα[EN219] it completely unites Him here too to the Father. It is thus the first and last word of the dogma. It is the first and last word on who and what Jesus Christ is "antecedently in Himself." It is also the first and last word in the account of the reality of revelation as this may be seen quite plainly in the mirror of the witness of Holy Scripture.

[EN216] the head of the body, the church
[EN217] continuation of creation
[EN218] through whom
[EN219] all things

§ 12

GOD THE HOLY SPIRIT

The one God reveals Himself according to Scripture as the Redeemer, i.e., as the Lord who sets us free. As such He is the Holy Spirit, by receiving whom we become the children of God, because, as the Spirit of the love of God the Father and the Son, He is so antecedently in Himself.

1. GOD AS REDEEMER

We begin a third time with the New Testament witness: Jesus is Lord. But this time we add the query: How do men come to say this? We are presupposing that they believe and therefore speak. They are to be taken seriously in what they say. They are to be nailed to it. In other words, they do not say it as the result of arbitrary reflection but in acknowledgment of a fact. They do not say it out of a desire to give the man an office or to give the office a man, but because the man has an office and discharges it. They say it as the beginning and not the end of their thinking about Him. They say it because He is the Lord. They do not say, then, that He is a demi-god from above or from below—the incarnation of a divine idea or a superman. They say that He is God. But on this presupposition we are inevitably confronted by the question: How do they come to say this? How do they reach this beginning of their thinking about Him? How does it happen that they believe the Father through the Son and the Son through the Father? How do these contents get into this vessel? How does this predicate, this faith, come to this subject, the subject man? How can anyone have this faith? Can men believe?—if faith means meeting the Lord who is God, meeting Him as the New Testament witnesses met Jesus, in hard objectivity, in the world which is the world of men, in which everything is problematical, in which everything must first be tested, in which nothing, when tested, will yield the result that it is identical with God, and yet also meeting Him in such a way that nothing is problematical, that nothing is to be found by the way of testing, but the encounter with Him is as such encounter with God. This is what revelation means in the New Testament. But in the New Testament does not the man to whom it happens also belong to revelation? And how can a thing like this happen to a man? Might it not be said that at this [449] point the whole concept of revelation is problematical if the presupposition is that faith in revelation consists in that absolutely unproblematical knowledge of God in Christ? It is not as if a new question requiring a new answer did not arise at this point for the New Testament.

In the New Testament too and especially the possibility of faith is not automatically given with the fact that Jesus is present as the revelation of the Father or as the One He is, as the Son or Word of God. In relation to Him man, too, is always, and for the first time properly, the one he is. How does he come to see and hear at this point? When the First Epistle of John begins with the declaration: We attest and proclaim to you ὃ ἀκηκόαμεν, ὃ ἑωράκαμεν τοῖς ὀφθαλμοῖς ἡμῶν, ὃ ἐθεασάμεθα καὶ αἱ χεῖρες ἡμῶν ἐψηλάφησαν[EN1] (1 Jn. 1¹ᶠ·), this is the indication of a reality whose possibility is by no means self-evident in the New Testament. Οὐχ ὅτι ἀφ᾽ ἑαυτῶν ἱκανοί ἐσμεν λογίσασθαί τι ὡς ἐξ ἑαυτῶν[EN2] (2 Cor. 3⁵). "He that hath ears to hear, let him hear," says the Synoptic Jesus with reference to His preaching (Mk. 4⁹). "Flesh and blood hath not revealed it unto thee," is His reply to Peter's confession (Mt. 16¹⁷). In face of the incarnate Word at the heart of revelation there seems to be a kind of delaying or questioning or limiting of revelation. Will revelation, this revelation, real revelation, reach its goal after all? Will it get at man? Will it become manifest to him? This does not seem to lie only with the good or bad will of man. For if this manifesting takes place, if there are ears to hear, this means: "Unto you it is given to know the mystery of the kingdom of God. Ἐκείνοις δὲ τοῖς ἔξω ἐν παραβολαῖς τὰ πάντα γίνεται[EN3]. Seeing they shall see, and not perceive; hearing they shall hear, and not understand, so that they shall not be converted, and it cannot be forgiven them" (Mk. 4¹¹⁻¹²). When the givenness is not present, it must be in virtue of a supreme material necessity.

Becoming manifest has to be something specific, a special act of the Father or the Son or both, that is added to the givenness of the revelation of the Father in the Son.

The Father must reveal it to man (Mt. 16¹⁷). The Father must draw him (Jn. 6⁴⁴). The Father must give it to him (Jn. 6⁶⁵). Man must be given to the Son by the Father (Jn. 10²⁹). He must hear and learn from the Father (Jn. 6⁴⁵). But it can also be said that the incarnate Word of God Himself gives to those who receive Him the ἐξουσία[EN4] to be the children of God and as such to believe in His name, so that as such they are what they are, not in virtue of their first and natural generation and birth, but in virtue of their second and divine generation and birth (Jn. 1¹²⁻¹³; 3³). There can also be reference to a stream of living water, clear as crystal, flowing forth from the throne of God and the Lamb (Rev. 22¹). This is the added element of becoming manifest in revelation. The riches of grace are not just present for us in Jesus Christ but: ἐπερίσσευσεν εἰς ἡμᾶς ἐν πάσῃ σοφίᾳ καὶ φρονήσει γνωρίσας ἡμῖν τὸ μυστήριον τοῦ θελήματος αὐτοῦ[EN5] (Eph. 1⁸· ⁹).

This special element in revelation is undoubtedly identical with what the New Testament usually calls the Holy Spirit as the subjective side in the event of revelation.

Jn. 20²² says of the disciples that Jesus breathed on them, saying: λάβετε πνεῦμα ἅγιον[EN6], and by this λαμβάνειν[EN7], in full material agreement with Ac. 2, they become

---

[EN1] which we have heard, which we have seen with our eyes, which we have looked upon, and our hands have handled
[EN2] Not that we are sufficient of ourselves to think any thing as of ourselves
[EN3] But unto them that are without, all these things are done in parables
[EN4] authority
[EN5] he hath abounded toward us in all wisdom and prudence; having made known unto us the mystery of his will
[EN6] receive the Holy Spirit
[EN7] receiving

what they are, His apostles, His envoys. The πνεῦμα EN8 is what makes alive (Jn. 6⁶³; 2 Cor. [450] 3⁶). "No man can say that Jesus is the Lord, but by the holy πνεῦμα" (1 Cor. 12³). Because we have received the πνεῦμα that is of God, we know for what they are the things that are freely given to us by God (1 Cor. 2¹³). Sealed with the holy promise you heard the word of truth, the gospel of your salvation, and you came to believe (Eph. 1¹³). God must give us the πνεῦμα of wisdom and revelation to know Himself (Eph. 1¹⁷). Except a man be born of water and the πνεῦμα he cannot enter into the kingdom of God (Jn. 3⁶). Εἰ δέ τις πνεῦμα Χπιστοῦ οὐκ ἔχει, οὗτος οὐκ ἔστιν αὐτοῦ EN9 (Rom. 8⁹). Therefore Ac. 19²ᶠ tells us that the most striking mark of those who have been baptised only in the name of John but not in the name of Jesus is that they know nothing of the Holy πνεῦμα.

Πνεῦμα θεοῦ or Χριστοῦ EN10 is a figure of speech, like υἱὸς θεοῦ EN11. According to Jn. 3⁸; Ac. 2² πνεῦμα means wind, which comes from one place and moves mysteriously to another. More precisely it is in 2 Thess. 2⁸; Jn. 20²² breath, which comes out of the mouth of a living creature and can reach another living creature, invisibly, without removing the spatial distance between them. This little and removable paradox becomes in the New Testament and already in the Old Testament a metaphor for the great and irremovable paradox of divine revelation. The fact that God gives His πνεῦμα to man or that man receives this πνεῦμα implies that God comes to man, that He discloses Himself to man and man to Himself, that He gives Himself to be experienced by man, that He awakens man to faith, that He enlightens him and equips him to be a prophet or apostle, that He creates for Himself a community of faith and proclamation to which He imparts salvation with His promise, in which He binds men to Himself and claims them for Himself, in short, in which He becomes theirs and makes them His. As this incomparable thing the πνεῦμα is τὸ πνεῦμα τὸ ἅγιον EN12. It is holy because only thus is it God's πνεῦμα, and because its purpose is the sanctification, i.e., the setting apart, the seizing, appropriating and distinguishing of the men who receive it, the distinguishing by which they become that which in and of themselves they neither are nor can be, men who belong to God, who are in real fellowship with Him, who live before God and with God. One may regard Gen. 2⁷ as the model for all the biblical use of references to the divine πνεῦμα. Here we are told that God breathed into man's face the breath of life and that in this way man became for the first time a living soul: *et inspiravit in faciem eius spiraculum vitae et factus est homo anima vivens* (Vulg.).

In both the Old Testament and the New the Spirit of God, the Holy Spirit, is very generally God Himself to the degree that in an incomprehensibly real way, without on this account being any the less God, He can be present to the creature, and in virtue of this presence of His effect the relation of the creature to Himself, and in virtue of this relation to Himself grant the creature life. The creature needs the Creator to be able to live. It thus needs the relation to Him. But it cannot create this relation. God creates it by His own presence in the creature and therefore as a relation of Himself to Himself. The Spirit of God is God in His freedom to be present to the creature, and therefore to create this relation, and therefore to be the life of the creature. And God's Spirit, the Holy Spirit, especially in revelation, is God Himself to the extent

---

EN 8 spirit
EN 9 if any man have not the Spirit of Christ, he is none of his
EN10 The Spirit of God or of Christ
EN11 Son of God
EN12 the Holy Spirit

that He can not only come to man but also be in man, and thus open up man and make him capable and ready for Himself, and thus achieve His revelation [451] in him. Man needs revelation, for he is certainly lost without it. He thus needs to have revelation become manifest to him, i.e., he himself needs to become open to revelation. But this is not a possibility of his own. It can only be God's own reality when it does happen, and therefore it can lie only in God's own possibility that it can happen. It is God's reality in that God Himself becomes present to man not just externally, not just from above, but also from within, from below, subjectively. It is thus reality in that He does not merely come to man but encounters Himself from man. God's freedom to be present in this way to man, and therefore to bring about this encounter, is the Spirit of God, the Holy Spirit in God's revelation.

The work of the Holy Ghost is *nos aptare Deo*[EN13] (Irenaeus, *C.o.h.* 111, 17, 2). He is the *doctor veritatis*[EN14] (Tertullian, *De praescr.*, 28). He is the *digitus Dei, per quem sanctificemur*[EN15] (Augustine, *De spir. et lit.* 16, 28). *Intelligo spiritum Dei, dum in cordibus nostris habitat, efficere, ut Christi virtutem sentiamus. Nam ut Christi beneficia mente concipiamus, hoc fit Spiritus sancti illuminatione: eius persuasione fit, ut cordibus nostris obsignentur. Denique, solus ipse dat illis in nobis locum. Regenerat nos, facitque ut simus novae creaturae. Proinde, quaecunque nobis offeruntur in Christo dona, ea Spiritus virtute recipimus*[EN16]. (Calvin, *Catech. Genev.*, 1545, in K. Müller, 125, 1. 16). He is the *applicator, illuminator, sanctificator*[EN17] (*Syn. pur. Theol.*, Leiden, 1624, *Disp.* 9, 21).

The Holy Spirit is not identical with Jesus Christ, with the Son or Word of God.

Even in the saying in 2 Cor. 3[17]: ὁ δὲ κύριος τὸ πνεῦμα [EN18], we do not have an identification of Jesus Christ with the Spirit but rather a statement that to the Spirit belongs the κυριότης [EN19], the deity of the Lord, to whom there is reference in v. 16. The continuation is that where this Spirit is, who is the Lord, who is God, there is liberty, namely, liberty from the veiling of the heart which had continually made the reading of Moses unprofitable in the worship of the Jews, liberty to see and to hear. Then according to v. 18 there is reflected in us—our face is uncovered—the glory of the Lord, and so we are changed into His image, from His glory to a glory of our own, namely, ἀπὸ κυρίου, πνεύματος, through the Lord who is the Spirit. We are forbidden not merely by usage elsewhere but also by the meaning and context of the passage itself to identify the Spirit with Jesus Christ even here. Other passages in which the Spirit is clearly mentioned (1 Cor. 12[4f.]; 2 Cor. 13[13]; 1 Pet. 1[2], etc.)

[EN13] to conform us to God
[EN14] doctor of truth
[EN15] the finger of God, through whom we can be sanctified
[EN16] As I understand it, the Spirit of God, insofar as he dwells in our hearts, enables us to experience the power of Christ. For whenever we give thought to Christ's benefits, this happens by the illumination of the Holy Spirit: it is by his persuasion that they are sealed in our hearts, and he alone gives them a place in us. He regenerates us and makes it possible for us to be new creatures. Furthermore, whatever gifts are given us in Christ we receive in the power of the Spirit
[EN17] enabler, illuminator, sanctifier
[EN18] the Spirit is Lord
[EN19] lordship

along with the Father and Christ, or (1 Cor. 6¹¹) with Christ alone, need only be recalled at this point.

In the context of the New Testament witness the non-identity between Christ and the Holy Spirit seems to be as necessarily grounded as possible. Thus we find the Holy Spirit only after the death and resurrection of Jesus Christ or in the form of knowledge of the crucified and risen Lord, i.e., on the assumption that objective revelation has been concluded and completed. We have seen already that Christ is the revelation of the Father in His passage through death to life. Those who believe in Him and confess Him believe in Him and confess Him as the exalted Lord. Thus the Spirit in whom they believe and confess and He who is the object of this faith and confession stand as it were on two different levels. What comes over or down to us from above, from the exalted Lord, is, therefore, the Spirit.   [452]

This "descent" of the Holy Ghost is a concept found especially in Acts (cf. Ac. 2²; 10⁴⁴; 11¹⁵). Thus the "Receive ye the Holy Ghost" in Jn. 20²² can only be a saying of the risen Christ. For the same reason the outpouring of the Holy Spirit is depicted in Ac. 2 as a work which is added to the completed *kerygma* of the life, death and resurrection of Jesus by Him of whom this *kerygma* speaks. For the same reason again John's Gospel has the distinctive doctrine, but one which is important for an understanding of the New Testament as a whole, that Jesus is, in distinction from John the Baptist, ὁ βαπτίζων ἐν πνεύματι ἁγίῳ EN20 (Jn. 1³³). Streams of living water are to flow from the body of him that believes in Him, says the difficult passage Jn. 7³⁸ᶠ, with the addition that Jesus was referring to the Spirit whom those that believe in Him should receive, and with the important explanation: οὔπω γὰρ ἦν πνεῦμα, ὅτι Ἰησοῦς οὐδέπω ἐδοξάσθη EN21. In Jn. 14¹⁶ the Spirit then appears as the (again future) gift of the Father to the disciples, the gift for which Jesus will ask the Father on their behalf. The Father will send Him in Jesus' name (Jn. 14²⁶). On the other hand in Jn. 15²⁶ Jesus Himself will send from the Father Him that proceedeth from the Father (ὁ παρὰ τοῦ πατρὸς ἐκπορεύεται). But to this end Jesus according to Jn. 16⁷ must first leave the disciples: συμφέρει ὑμῖν ἵνα ἐγὼ ἀπέλθω. ἐὰν γὰρ μὴ ἀπέλθω, ὁ παράκλητος οὐ μὴ ἔλθῃ πρὸς ὑμᾶς. ἐὰν δὲ πορευθῶ, πέμψω αὐτὸν πρὸς ὑμᾶς EN22. Finally Jn. 16¹³ is just speaking of His coming in a general way. What we find in Jn. 20²² is obviously the fulfilment of this repeated promise.

In spite of all this, it can hardly be the idea of the New Testament that chronologically it was only after Good Friday and Easter that there were men who received the Holy Ghost. If so, what could it mean that faith is in all seriousness ascribed to many disciples and non-disciples even before Good Friday and Easter? What would Jesus' reply to Peter's confession mean (Mt. 16¹⁷)? The story of the transfiguration in Mk. 9²ᶠ and par. shows that the Synoptists at least reckoned with the possibility that chronologically there might be anticipation of the conclusion and completion of revelation, that there might be revelations of the exalted Christ, even before His appearing. And one might well ask whether the miracles of Jesus are not all to be regarded as, so to speak, backward-striking rays of the glory of the risen Lord, whether ultimately the entire life of Jesus is not meant to be considered in this retrospective light. Even in John, where the chronological schematism seems to be more consciously and

---

EN20 he who baptises with the Holy Spirit
EN21 for the Holy Spirit was not yet (given) because Jesus was not yet glorified
EN22 it is to your advantage that I go away, for if I do not go away, the Counselor will not come to you; but if I go, I will send him to you

strictly applied, the temporal relationship between Him who lived as a man among the disciples and the exalted Christ, and hence also between the promised Spirit and the given Spirit, is undoubtedly more complicated than might appear at a first glance. How are we to understand Jn. 2^{11} if the future is not also thought of as already present here even as the future? Similarly Jn. 20^{22} and the story of Pentecost in Ac. 2 are surely to be understood as explicit and solemn testimony to an event which chronologically was not restricted either forwards or backwards to Pentecost.

[453] We must now add at once that while the Spirit is the element of revelation which is different from Christ as the exalted Lord, while He is revelation to the extent that it becomes an event on us and in us, nevertheless He is still to be regarded wholly and entirely as the Spirit of Christ, of the Son, of the Word of God. He is not to be regarded, then, as a revelation of independent content, as a new instruction, illumination and stimulation of man that goes beyond Christ, beyond the Word, but in every sense as the instruction, illumination and stimulation of man through the Word and for the Word.

It is true that the Holy Spirit is expressly called the Spirit of Christ only in relatively few passages (Gal. 4^6; Rom. 8^9; Phil. 1^{19}; 1 Pet. 1^{11}). Usually He is simply the Spirit of God, which in a whole of passages must be taken to mean the Spirit of the Father. But no incongruence can be shown between Christ and the Spirit. John's Gospel again reproduces the meaning of the New Testament as a whole when it has Jesus say of the Spirit: ἐκεῖνος μαρτυρήσει περὶ ἐμοῦ^{EN23} (Jn. 15^{26}), οὐ γὰρ λαλήσει ἀφ' ἑαυτοῦ ἀλλ' ὅσα ἀκούει λαλήσει καὶ τὰ ἐρχόμενα ἀναγγελεῖ ὑμῖν. ἐκεῖνος ἐμὲ δοξάσει, ὅτι ἐκ τοῦ ἐμοῦ λήμψεται καὶ ἀναγγελεῖ ὑμῖν^{EN24} (Jn.16$^{13f.}$).

The statements about the significance and work of the Holy Spirit in the event which is called revelation in the New Testament can be arranged in three groups.

1. The Spirit guarantees man what he cannot guarantee himself, his personal participation in revelation. The act of the Holy Ghost in revelation is the Yes to God's Word which is spoken by God Himself for us, yet not just to us, but also in us. This Yes spoken by God is the basis of the confidence with which a man may regard the revelation as applying to him. This Yes is the mystery of faith, the mystery of the knowledge of the Word of God, but also the mystery of the willing obedience that is well-pleasing to God. All these things, faith, knowledge and obedience, exist for man "in the Holy Spirit."

Ἐν τούτῳ γινώσκομεν ὅτι ἐν αὐτῷ μένομεν καὶ αὐτὸς ἐν ἡμῖν, ὅτι ἐκ τοῦ πνεύματος αὐτοῦ δέδωκεν ἡμῖν^{EN25} (1 Jn. 4^{13}). The specific Pauline view of the Holy Spirit demands special attention here. The Spirit dwells in us (Rom. 8$^{9.\ 11}$). He is thus the ἀπαρχή^{EN26} (Rom. 8^{23}) or ἀρραβών^{EN27} (2 Cor. 1^{22}; 5^5; Eph. 1^{14}). He is also the projected light of the

---

EN23 he will bear witness about me
EN24 for he will not speak on his own authority, but whatever he hears he will speak, and he will declare to you the things that are to come. He will glorify me, for he will take what is mine and declare it to you
EN25 By this we know that we abide in him and he in us, because he has given us of his own Spirit
EN26 first fruits
EN27 pledge

162

salvation assigned to us by God. To participate in the Holy Ghost is to have "tasted the good word of God and the powers of the world to come" (Heb. 6⁵ᶠ·). With Christ or the Word the Holy Spirit bears witness to our spirit that we are the children of God: αὐτὸ τὸ πνεῦμα συμμαρτυρεῖ τῷ πνεύματι ἡμῶν ᴱᴺ²⁸ (Rom. 8¹⁶). God reveals to us διὰ τοῦ πνεύματος ᴱᴺ²⁹ what He wills to reveal to us because the Spirit searches all things, even τὰ βάθη τοῦ θεοῦ ᴱᴺ³⁰, and because He, the Spirit, does this for us and in us (1 Cor. 2¹⁰). He helps our infirmities (συναντιλαμβάνεται); we do not know what proper prayer is, but He intercedes for us (ὑπερεντυγχάνει) with His groanings that cannot be uttered (ἀλαλήτοις) by us, and so, since quite apart from our weakness or strength, our ability or inability to pray, there takes place in us something that is according to God (κατὰ θεόν), God hears and answers our prayer (Rom. 8²⁶ᶠ·). Through the Holy Spirit the love of God (or love for God) is shed abroad in our hearts (Rom. 5⁵). In short, because and so far as a man receives the Holy Ghost, he is a temple of God (1 Cor. 3¹⁶; 6¹⁹; 2 Cor. 6¹⁶); because and so far as he has received the Holy Ghost, he may be told to his face that the Word is "nigh thee, even in thy mouth and in thy heart" (Rom. 10⁸). The very common Pauline formula ἐν πνεύματι ᴱᴺ³¹ describes man's thinking, acting and speaking as taking place in participation in God's revelation. It is an exact subjective correlate of ἐν Χριστῷ ᴱᴺ³², which denotes the same thing objectively.

2. The Spirit gives man instruction and guidance he cannot give himself. A [454] point that we should remember in what has been said already is made quite explicit here: the Spirit is not identical, and does not become identical, with ourselves.

When Paul uses the term πνεῦμα in his anthropology he is not saying that the Holy Spirit either wholly or partially, either originally or subsequently, is part of man's own essence. When used thus πνεῦμα denotes at best the place (beyond σῶμα ᴱᴺ³³ and ψυχή ᴱᴺ³⁴) where reception of the Holy Spirit can become a reality (1 Thess. 5²³).

He is absolutely other, superior. We can only note what His Yes is to the Word of God. We can only repeat this Yes of His. As our Teacher and Leader He is in us, but not as a power of which we might become lords. He remains Himself the Lord.

In the main the Johannine doctrine of the Paraclete is especially relevant here. The term reminds us of Paul's important concept of *paraclesis*ᴱᴺ³⁵. This word, for which there is no real equivalent, denotes the combination of the admonition and comfort which God causes His people to experience and which the apostle has, as it were, to accept and pass on (cf., e.g., 2 Cor. 1³ᶠ·). This is what Jesus portrays as the special work of the Holy Ghost according to John's Gospel. As the Paraclete the Spirit is the "spirit of truth" (Jn. 14¹⁷; 15²⁶; 16¹³). Ἐκεῖνος ὑμᾶς διδάξει πάντα καὶ ὑπομνήσει ὑμᾶς πάντα ἃ εἶπον ὑμῖν ἐγώ ᴱᴺ³⁶. (Jn.

ᴱᴺ²⁸ it is the Spirit himself bearing witness with our spirit
ᴱᴺ²⁹ through the Spirit
ᴱᴺ³⁰ the deep things of God
ᴱᴺ³¹ in the Spirit
ᴱᴺ³² in Christ
ᴱᴺ³³ body
ᴱᴺ³⁴ soul
ᴱᴺ³⁵ encouragement
ᴱᴺ³⁶ he will teach you all things, and bring to your remembrance all that I have said to you

14²⁶). Ὁδηγήσει ὑμᾶς εἰς τὴν ἀλήθειαν πᾶσαν EN37 (Jn. 16¹³). Also identical with the Paraclete and therefore with the Holy Ghost is what is called the *chrisma* in 1 Jn. (and also 2 Cor. 1²¹). 1 Jn. 2²⁰ says of this: Ἔχετε ἀπὸ τοῦ ἁγίου καὶ οἴδατε πάντες EN38. "Ye need not that any man should teach you: but as the same anointing teacheth you of all things, it is in truth, and is no lie" (2²⁷). Also pertinent here is the fact that Paul ascribes to the Spirit an ἄγειν EN39 and to believers an ἄγεσθαι EN40 by the Spirit (Gal. 5¹⁸; Rom. 8¹⁴), and we should compare here the very direct instructions in which this ἄγειν can take concrete shape, especially according to Acts, e.g., Ac. 8²⁹; 10¹⁹; 13²; 16⁶, etc.

Along these lines the Spirit is obviously not so much the reality in which God makes us sure of Him as the reality in which He makes Himself sure of us, in which He establishes and executes His claim to lordship over us by His immediate presence.

3. Exegetically most obscure but materially of crucial importance is the fact that the Spirit is the great and only possibility in virtue of which men can speak of Christ in such a way that what they say is witness and that God's revelation in Christ thus achieves new actuality through it. Has God's personal coming to us, in the twofold sense in which we have viewed it, any independent signification as a work of the Holy Spirit alongside the fact that by the Holy Spirit man can and should become a real speaker and proclaimer of real witness and therefore of the real Word of God? Does not the New Testament doctrine of the Holy Ghost point beyond all that the Spirit can mean for the believer in this personal relation with God to that which, in the power of the Spirit, ought [455] to happen in the believer and through the believer for God, i.e., in the service of God? Is not the relation between the Spirit and the Church, or the relation between the Spirit and the will of the Lord of the Church which is to be executed, the dominating factor which governs all the rest?

A Whitsun sermon cannot be an exposition of Ac. 2¹⁻¹⁴ if it does not see and show that the outpouring of the Holy Spirit to which this passage refers consists very concretely in the fact that cloven tongues are seen and that the disciples on whom these alight begin to speak in other tongues: καθὼς τὸ πνεῦμα ἐδίδου ἀποφθέγγεσθαι αὐτοῖς EN41. (Repetitions of this event are reported in Ac. 10⁴⁶ and 19⁶.)

The second effect of this Whitsun miracle then consists in the fact that γενομένης τῆς φωνῆς ταύτης EN42 the members present from every possible nation both near and far hear the disciples declare τὰ μεγαλεῖα τοῦ θεοῦ EN43 in their own tongues (Ac. 2⁷ᶠ·).

A Whitsun sermon which aims to be an exposition of Ac. 2¹ᶠ· will have to talk about this speaking of the disciples and this hearing by Parthians, Medes and Elamites, etc. The impact of the address of Peter which follows in Ac. 2¹⁴ᶠ·, in so far as this is not a presentation of the *kerygma* itself, also consists purely and simply in the fact that what has happened is declared to be a fulfilment of the prophecy of Joel about the outpouring of the Spirit on all flesh,

---

EN37 He will guide you into all the truth
EN38 But you have been anointed by the Holy One, and you all know
EN39 leading
EN40 being led
EN41 as the Spirit gave them utterance
EN42 at this sound
EN43 the mighty works of God

which will mean that men—both men and women is the surprisingly strong emphasis—will "prophesy." This is what is fulfilled at Pentecost. Over against the Lord Jesus, absolutely subordinate to Him but distinct from Him, there is another element in the reality of His revelation, an apostolate, men commissioned, authorised and empowered by Him to witness, men whose human word can be accepted by all kinds of people as proclamation of the "wonderful works of God." This is the doing of the Holy Ghost. The difficult exegetical question here is how this gift of "tongues" at Pentecost is related to the special gift of individual members of the Christian community to which Paul gives the same name in 1 Cor. 12 and 14, and which he takes very seriously and values highly, but in respect of which he has many reservations and even criticisms. We do not have to pursue this question in the present content. But there is no doubt that what Paul knew by this name did not have either for himself or, on his view, for the community, the same central significance as that which is recorded in Ac. 2. There is also no doubt that what gives the thing recorded there its central significance, the commissioning, authorising and equipping of the apostolate, is for him too—and for him too as the work of the Holy Ghost—the presupposition of his own activity and message. Πρὸς φωτισμὸν τῆς γνώσεως τῆς δόξης τοῦ θεοῦ ἐν προσώπῳ Χριστοῦ EN44 God caused it to shine in our hearts as at the first day of creation (2 Cor. 4⁶). "Ye shall receive the power of the Holy Ghost coming upon you, and ye shall be my witnesses," says the risen Lord to His disciples (Ac. 1⁸). We find the same combination of πνεῦμα and μαρτυρεῖν EN45 in Jn. 15²⁶: The Holy Spirit shall testify of Me to you, and you also shall bear witness. Another saying of Jesus is to the effect that in the hour of trial the disciples are not to be anxious about what they shall say on their own behalf; they are to say what is then given them to say. Οὐ γάρ ἐστε ὑμεῖς οἱ λαλοῦντες ἀλλὰ τὸ πνεῦμα τὸ ἅγιον EN46 (Mk. 13¹¹ and par., with the variation in Lk. 12¹² that the Holy Spirit διδάξει ὑμᾶς ... ἃ δεῖ εἰπεῖν EN47).

The Holy Spirit is the authorisation to speak about Christ; He is the equipment of the prophet and apostle; He is the summons to the Church to minister the Word. To the extent that everything in which this authorisation, equipment and summons consists—we discussed this under 1. and 2.—is directed to [456] this goal, to the extent that it cannot be a private affair but only the affair of the Church, or rather the Lord of the Church, if there are individuals to whom the Spirit guarantees that God's revelation comes to them, individuals whom the Spirit constrains—to that extent we shall have to call this third operation of the Spirit the decisive one. If we ask concerning the mind of the Spirit (τὸ φρόνημα τοῦ πνεύματος, Rom. 8²⁷), we must answer that it consists in the fact that He is the gift of speaking about the "wonderful works of God." But if we ask what it means to receive and possess this gift, we shall constantly have to read off the answer from the first two definitions of our concept.

In the thesis we have described the nature and work of the Holy Spirit in revelation by two expressions which carry allusions to biblical statements: He is "the Lord who sets us free" and "by receiving Him we become the children of God." We may claim that these two expressions are a summary of what we must

---

EN44 To give the light of the knowledge of the glory of God in the face of Christ
EN45 witness
EN46 For it is not you who speak, but the Holy Spirit
EN47 will teach you ... what you ought to say

infer from the witness of Holy Scripture to the nature of the Spirit as an element of God's revelation in Jesus Christ.

The word "freedom" implies first and formally that when Scripture speaks of the Holy Spirit as an element in revelation we are dealing with an ability or capacity or capability which is given to man as the addressee of revelation and which makes him a real recipient of revelation. The problem by which we found ourselves confronted was: How can man believe? How does *homo peccator*EN48 become *capax verbi divini*EN49? The New Testament answer is that it is the Holy Spirit who sets man free for this and for the ministry in which he is put therewith.

Christ has "set us free for freedom," we read in Gal. 5[1]. Here and everywhere the term is undoubtedly contrasted with the idea of the servitude overcome in Christ. Primarily—but only primarily—this servitude consists in bondage to a law of God which man has misunderstood and misused, a law to which man ascribes divine authority and which he makes every effort to observe, although in practice he does not recognise in it the voice of the God who commands and is far from letting it serve him as real revelation. But the nature and curse of this servitude lies deeper. Because man is bound in this way he is not able nor free to receive real revelation. The converse is also true: Because he is not free for real revelation, he is in bondage. At all events, although in appearance, but only in appearance, he believes in God and hearkens to Him and strives diligently to serve Him, he is in fact powerless in relation to the living God, i.e., powerless to know Him as He is and to obey Him as He desires. The freedom for which Christ sets us free cannot, then, consist merely in freedom from that servitude. It must also consist—and decisively so—in freedom from that powerlessness, in freedom for the real revelation of God. This is confirmed by a glance at the important passage Jn. 8[30-59]. The Jews think they are free as the people of Abraham (v. 33). Jesus contests this: "Whosoever committeth sin, is the servant of sin" (v. 34), and so not free. Why and to what extent? "If the Son therefore shall make you free, ye shall be free indeed" (v. 36). But [457] this is the very thing that is impossible. Their sin is that the Word of Jesus finds no place in them (οὐ χωρεῖ ἐν ὑμῖν, v. 37), that they cannot hear it (οὐ δύνασθε ἀκούειν, v. 43). "He that is of God heareth God's words; ye therefore hear them not, because ye are not of God" (v. 47). Hence the freedom for which the Son (v. 36) or the truth (v. 32) makes them free cannot possibly be the mere negation of false bondage (which is hardly mentioned in this passage). Understood thus, freedom would immediately serve as a "pretext to give free rein to the flesh" (Gal. 5[13]), as a "cloke of maliciousness" (1 Pet. 2[16]). Thus understood, it would obviously be nothing but a new unfreedom. The truly free are free rather as the servants of God (1 Pet. 2[16]). It is not impossible that the paradox of 1 Cor. 7[22] about the Christian slave who by his calling is the Lord's freedman, and the Christian freeman who by his calling is Christ's slave, also points in this direction in addition to its most obvious sense. Certainly the freedom which is there where the Lord, the Spirit, is (2 Cor. 3[17]) denotes exclusively the freedom to turn to the Lord, to God, in contrast to the Jews, from whom the face of God remains hidden even as and although they read the sacred texts. No less plainly the "law of liberty" referred to in Jas. 1[25]; 2[12] is the order which is directly contrasted, but positively so, with the law of the Jews, an order under which a man stands who is not just a hearer but also a doer—and in James this means, not a forgetful nor a merely reputed hearer, but a real hearer of the Word of God who is claimed in his life-act, in his existence. The man who is

---

EN48 human as sinner
EN49 capable of the divine word

capable of being a doer of the Word of this kind, i.e., a real hearer, is free in the New Testament sense of the term. The reference is not to any kind of freedom or any kind of ability. In accordance with the freedom of God Himself, His freedom to be Himself, what is at issue here is a man's freedom for God, for the "glorious liberty" of the children of God (Rom. 8²¹), the *analogia fidei*EN50 of the divine freedom which alone really deserves to be called freedom. This, then, is a formal summary of the work of the Spirit in God's revelation. His work consists in freedom, freedom to have a Lord, this Lord, God, as Lord.

On the other hand the concept of divine sonship declares materially that when Scripture speaks of the Holy Spirit as an element in revelation the reference is to a being of the man to whom this freedom or ability belongs. These men are what they can be. They can be what they are. It is thus that they are real recipients of revelation. It is thus that they can believe. We ask again how *homo peccator* can become *capax verbi divini*. The second answer, which comprehends the first, must now be that he does not first become this in order to be it; he is it, and in virtue of this being he becomes it. He is the child of God. As such he is free, he can believe. And he is God's child as he receives the Holy Ghost. One can and should also say conversely: He receives the Holy Ghost as he is God's child. At all events, in receiving the Holy Ghost he is what in himself and of himself he cannot be, one who belongs to God as a child to its father, one who knows God as a child knows its father, one for whom God is there as a father is there for his child. This is the second and material summary of the operations of the Holy Spirit in God's revelation.

Linking up with our formal definition of the matter, we first repeat that freedom for God is the freedom of the children of God (Rom. 8²¹). Obviously the New Testament concept of divine sonship cannot compete in any sense with that of the divine sonship of Jesus Christ. On the contrary, it is absolutely dependent on this. The fathers made the distinction that Jesus Christ is *Filius Dei natura*EN51 while believers are *filii Dei adoptione*EN52. They can be this *adoptione*EN53 because Jesus Christ is so *natura*EN54. Because the Reconciler was the Son of God reconciliation or revelation consists for its recipients in being sons of God in the irremovable distinction between the blessed and Him who blesses them. "A man can receive nothing, except it be given him from heaven" (Jn. 3²⁷). While this does not apply to the divine sonship of Jesus it does apply to the divine sonship of those who believe in Him. "By faith, in Christ Jesus, ye are the sons of God, because ye have been baptised into Christ, and have (as such) put on Christ" (Gal. 3²⁶ᶠ·). To be God's child, a man must be called to the κοινωνία τοῦ υἱοῦ αὐτοῦ Ἰησοῦ ΧριστοῦEN55 (1 Cor. 1⁹). He must be begotten "with the word of truth" (Jas. 1¹⁸), and when this happens it is the "good gift" which comes to him "from above" (Jas. 1¹⁷). The birth in virtue of which he is God's child is emphatically a "birth from above" (Jn. 3³) distinct from his natural birth and resting on the ἐξουσία which the Logos Himself must give him. Yet all this does not imply a limitation, but rather an underlining, of the constant indicatives in which the New Testament says of believers that they are

[458]

EN50 analogy of faith
EN51 Son of God by nature
EN52 children of God by adoption
EN53 by adoption
EN54 by nature
EN55 the fellowship of his Son Jesus Christ

(Rom. 8^{14}), we are (Rom. 8^{16}), we are called and are (1 Jn. 3^1), we are now (1 Jn. 3^2), you are (Gal. 4^6), and even you all are (Gal. 3^{26}) sons or children of God, and therefore not servants (Gal. 4^7), who are only for a time part of the household (Jn. 8^{35}), but heirs (Rom. 8^{17}; Gal. 4^7), not Ishmael but Isaac (Gal. 4$^{30f.}$), not "strangers and foreigners" but "fellow-citizens with the saints, and of the household of God" (Eph. 2^{19}). To be such a child of God and to receive the Holy Spirit is one and the same thing. The Holy Spirit is τὸ πνεῦμα τοῦ υἱοῦ^{EN56} (Gal. 4^6) and hence the πνεῦμα υἱοθεσίας^{EN57} (Rom. 8^{15}).

How does He show Himself to be such? In a decisive passage Paul mentions only one thing in which everything is obviously included for him. In the Holy Spirit, and therefore as children of God, we cry, κράζομεν· Ἀββά, ὁ πατήρ^{EN58} (Rom. 8^{15}; Gal. 4^6). Remarkably, and certainly not by accident, this is the same cry as the Gospel narrative (Mk. 14^{36}) puts on the lips of Jesus when He is at prayer in Gethsemane. So then, in this form, the Son of God is the prototype of the sonship of believers. The children of God have put on this Christ. This child, sinful man, can meet this Father, the holy God, as a child meets its father, only where the only-begotten Son of God has borne and borne away his sin. His reconciliation does not consist in his being placed with the Son of God. It consists in what the Son of God has done and suffered for us. But in his being placed with the Son of God reconciliation is achieved in him. Herein consists his participation in the atonement effected in Christ. This is what it means to have the Holy Spirit. To have the Holy Spirit is to be set with Christ in that transition from death to life. The form of a real recipient of God's revelation, the form which gives the law to his thought, will and speech, will always be the form of the death of Christ (Rom. 6^5; Phil. 3^{10}). And so his freedom, ability and capacity for God can be understood only as the power of the resurrection of Christ, not as an immanent freedom of his own, but as that which is conferred on him by God, which he can neither manipulate nor understand, which can only be understood as factual, and factual indeed only as the fact of God. In this fact God makes us sure of Him and makes Himself sure of us, and He teaches us what we are to say as His witnesses. All statements about the Holy Spirit, like all statements about the Son of God, can relate only to this divine fact. For us as in the New Testament itself, they are comprehensible or incomprehensible only in the light of it.

[459] The present exposition should be compared with Luther's remarks on Gal. 4$^{6f.}$ (*W.A.* 40^1, 579–97): He calls 'Abba Father' the cry of the Holy Ghost in our hearts amid the very severe, the total powerlessness and despair of this heart of ours at its radical sinfulness, at its doubting even of God's graciousness, at the devil's accusation: *Tu es peccator*^{EN59}, at the wrath of God who threatens us with eternal damnation, in the temptation in which there is no experience of the presence and help of Christ, where even Christ only seems to chide us, where we can only cling to the *nudum verbum*^{EN60}. Then that cry rings out, pierces the clouds, fills heaven and earth, rings out so loudly that the angels when they hear it think they have never heard ought at all before, in fact that God Himself hears nought else in the whole world but this sound. And yet *quantum ad sensum nostrum attinet*^{EN61} it is but a trifling sigh in which we do not hear at all this cry of the Spirit. What we experience is the temptation that what we hear are the voices of hell and what we see is the face of hell. If we were now to trust our experience we could only give up ourselves for lost. There and thus—though those who speak *speculative tantum*^{EN62} of the Holy Ghost like Papists and fanatics do not, of course

---

^{EN56} the Spirit of the Son
^{EN57} the Spirit of adoption
^{EN58} Abba, Father
^{EN59} You are a sinner
^{EN60} naked word
^{EN61} to the extent that it falls within our perception
^{EN62} only speculatively

understand this—Christ is almighty, regnant and triumphant in us. The word, nay that unassuming little sigh (*gemitulus*), that *affectus*[EN63], in which in spite of everything and with no basis in experience we can still say "Father," this word now becomes more eloquent than any Cicero or Vergil. Curiously enough, in this same passage (*op. cit.*, 586, 13) Luther strikes his strongest blow against the *pestilens error*[EN64] of Roman Catholic doctrine that there is in this life no true and impregnable assurance of the grace of God. When and where is there such assurance? Certainly not in relation to ourselves but in relation to the *promissio et veritas Dei, quae fallere non potest. Aversis oculis a lege, operibus, sensu et conscientia*[EN65] this assurance becomes an event as appropriation of the divine promise. The promise brings us this assurance in so far as it brings us the possibility of that cry "Abba Father" which in our mouth and heart is the smallest thing but before God is the greatest thing, the one thing, as the cry of His own Spirit in us. *Tum certo definitum est in coelo, quod non sit amplius servitus sed mera libertas, adoptio et filiatio. Quis parit eam? Iste gemitus*[EN66]. But this takes place as I accept God's promise. And as for my accepting God's promise, *hoc fit, cum isto gemitu clamo et respondeo corde filiali isti voci: Pater. Ibi tum conveniunt pater et filius*[EN67]. (593, 18). But: *quanta magnitudo et gloria huius doni sit, humana mens ne quidem concipere potest in hac vita, multo minus eloqui. Interim in aenigmate cernimus hoc, Habemus istum gemitulum et exiguam fidem, quae solo auditu et sono vocis promittentis Christi nititur. Ideo quoad sensum nostrum res ista centrum, in se autem maxima et infinita sphera est. Sic Christianus habet rem in se maximam et infinitam, in suo autem conspectu et sensu minimam et finitissimam. Ideo istam rem metiri debemus non humana ratione et sensu, sed alio circulo, scilicet promissione dei, Qui ut infinitus est, ita et promissio ipsius infinita est, utcunque interim in has angustias et, ut ita dicam, in verbum centrale inclusa sit. Videmus igitur iam centrum, olim videbimus etiam circumferentiam*[EN68]. (596, 16).

In what has been said we have stated already that according to the testimony of Scripture the Holy Spirit is no less and no other than God Himself, distinct from Him whom Jesus calls His Father, distinct also from Jesus Himself, yet no less than the Father, and no less than Jesus, God Himself, altogether God.

We again recall 2 Cor. 3[17]: ὁ κύριος τὸ πνεῦμα, the Lord is the Spirit. We also think of the well-known πνεῦμα ὁ θεός, God is Spirit (Jn. 4[24]). In both these verses the reverse, the Spirit is the Lord, the Spirit is God, while it is not actually in the passages, is not only permitted but commanded as an inference from what is said. The same equation is presupposed in Ac. 5[3f.] where Ananias is accused of having lied to the Holy Ghost and then immediately after we

[460]

[EN63] feeling

[EN64] noxious error

[EN65] promise and truth of God, which cannot deceive. When we turn our eyes from the law, works, experience and conscience

[EN66] Then it is firmly established in heaven that there is no longer servitude, but pure freedom, adoption and sonship. What accomplishes this? That cry

[EN67] this happens when I call out with that cry and respond in filial affection with this word: Father. There and then Father and Son come together

[EN68] How great and glorious this gift is, the human intellect cannot conceive – let alone describe – in this life. Here we perceive it as a mystery. We have this cry and a tiny measure of faith, which is supported only by the sound we hear of the voice of Christ, who gives the promise. And so this thing, which as far as our perception goes is the centre, is in itself a vast and infinite sphere. So the Christian has something that in itself is vast and infinite, but which in his sight and perception is miniscule and infinitely limited. Therefore we ought not to measure this thing according to human reason and perception, but with reference to a different circle, namely, God's promise. As he is infinite, so is his promise infinite, however much it is presently enclosed in these narrow limits and so to speak in the word at the centre. For as we now see the centre, so some day shall we see the circumference, too

169

read: οὐκ ἐψεύσω ἀνθρώποις ἀλλὰ τῷ θεῷ [EN69] Similarly in Mk. 3²⁸ᶠ.—however we may understand it—there could not possibly be a blasphemy against the Holy Ghost which makes man guilty of an unforgivable, eternal sin, if the Spirit were less or something other than God Himself.

That not only these and similar verses but the whole New Testament doctrine of the work of the Holy Spirit implies the deity of His essence can properly be contested only if one has first explained away the fact that with its Ἰησοῦς Κύριος [EN70] the New Testament community confessed its faith in Jesus Christ as faith in God Himself. If the Christ of the New Testament is a demigod from above or below, then naturally faith in Him becomes a human possibility. Then, extraordinary though the phenomenon may be, one can show how faith in Him has arisen on certain grounds and presuppositions which we ourselves can perceive and control. But in this case there is in fact no need for the deity of the Holy Spirit who creates this faith. On this view the name "Holy Spirit" may very well be a mere name for a particularly profound, serious and vital conviction of truth or experience of conscience, or one may equally well omit it altogether when describing the basis of faith according to the New Testament.

Along these lines one may, with Karl Holl, describe as follows the experience and reflection of those pagan contemporaries of the primitive community who became believers: "This concept of God advanced by Jesus (namely, the concept that God is first and basically the God who forgives and only on that ground the God who demands), which ran so sharply contrary to all natural religions feeling, had nevertheless a hidden, irresistible power. It penetrated more deeply than any other concept of God. For it spoke to the conscience. Was it not convincing that the man who was reaching upwards to God should take his standard, not from human respectability or heroism, but from the unconditioned, from God's own moral nature, from His goodness? But those who seriously attempted this involuntarily lost sight of the distinction between right and wrong, pure and impure. The solemn initiatory saying of the mysteries: 'Whoso hath lived well and righteously,' became a superficiality. In place of it the γνῶθι σεαυτόν [EN71] now acquired its full stringency .... From the depths of such introspection there then grew up an understanding of Jesus' concept of God. Was it not really the case that the God by whose gifts man lived always sustained man with forgiving loving-kindness? The only problem was that man had lost awareness of Him. And was not the God who sought the heart of man, and even knew how to win back the lost, greater and holier and mightier in this love than all the gods of high Olympus? Thus everything fell into place to yield coherent sense. If a man grasped it, he had the feeling of waking from a dream. The boldness, the utter novelty, or, as one might say to-day in an overworked slogan, the irrational element in the preaching of Jesus, would not have done it alone. What is only irrational has at most the limited and transitory attraction of the forcefully arbitrary. But here the irrational produced an illuminating sense. What was a stumbling-block to sound common sense commended itself to the thoughtful as the revelation as a deeper and convincing truth about God and man. This was the victorious element in Christianity" ("*Urchristentum und Religionsgeschichte,*" *Ges. Aufs. z. KGesch.*, Vol. 2, 1928, 18). This analysis of

[461]

EN69 you have not lied to men but to God
EN70 Lord Jesus
EN71 know thyself

1. *God as Redeemer*

Holl's, which purports to be exegesis of the New Testament, should be compared with Rom. 8¹⁶ᶠ·; Gal. 4⁶ᶠ· and Luther's exposition of these passages. One can hardly try to argue that in both cases the same thing is being said in different words. No, in Holl's analysis there is clearly substituted for the Holy Spirit man's own faculty of distinction and judgment. It is by means of this that Jesus' concept of God can "penetrate" like any other, though more deeply than any other. It is in virtue of this that man, waking as from a dream, can in profound introspection become aware of something he was not aware of before. It is in virtue of this that he can establish as illuminating and meaningful that which at first offended him. It is in virtue of this that he can in a word convince himself of the "truth about God and man" which is expressed in Jesus' concept of God. The measurement here is not by the infinite circle of the divine promise but altogether *humana ratione et sensu*EN72. The "victorious element in Christianity" consists here, not in the fact that Christ is powerful in the powerlessness of man, not in the centre with no visible or palpable periphery, but in the fact that Christ's (or Jesus') "concept of God" has an illuminating and "coherent sense" for man, or at least for "the thoughtful." The expression "Holy Spirit" does not need to be used here, and the doctrine of the deity of the Holy Spirit is certainly not advocated. Obviously the New Testament has to be read in this way here because even where it speaks of Christ it is construed as if it were referring to the bearer of a particular concept of God of which man was unaware but which he can properly grasp, the bearer of the deep and convincing truth that the relation of forgiveness and demand, contrary to sound common sense (i.e., superficial Greek self-knowledge), is the reverse of what it is usually taken to be.

If we may now presuppose that this is not a tenable exegesis of New Testament Christology, then the transformation of the New Testament doctrine of the Spirit into a doctrine of a very profound and very conscientious conviction of truth is also untenable. For if it is true that the men of the New Testament perceived the deity of Christ, not on the basis of their knowledge and choice, but on the basis of their being known and chosen (not as the result but as the beginning of their thinking about Him), then the faith, or the basis of the faith of these men, cannot be regarded as a faculty which was unfortunately hidden from themselves, nor can the rise of faith be understood formally as waking up from a dream or materially as a recollection of how things always were at root. In this case the category of faith does not have any place in the history of religion and conscience cannot be evoked to explain its possibility as δός μοι ποῦ στῶEN73. Faith, New Testament πίστις, is rather to be understood as a possibility which derives from a mode of being of God, from a mode of being which is in essential unity with Him who in the New Testament is described as Father and as Son.

In faith an "anointing" or "sealing" is presupposed which can have no resemblance to the creature "anointed" or "sealed" (Athanasius, *Ep. ad Serap.* I, 23; III, 3). If this presupposition, the Holy Spirit, were a creature, he could not mediate to us any μετουσία θεοῦEN74 . Ourselves creatures, we should then be dealing with a mere creature, and would remain remote

---

EN72 according to human reason and perception
EN73 a place on which to stand
EN74 participation in God

[462]   from the θεῖα φύσις [EN75] But if it is true that by the Holy Spirit we are made worthy of that μετουσία [EN76], would it not be mad to try to deny His deity? (*ib.*, 1, 24). One may certainly question the vocabulary used here. But can one on that account question whether this is correct exegesis of the New Testament doctrine of the Spirit in contrast to the Modernist Protestant theologian cited above? If we look back at the results of our analysis of the New Testament doctrine of the Spirit, i.e., at the predicates which we have ascribed to the Spirit and His work in revelation, what else can we say but that *Spiritus vox hic a creaturae notione plane submovenda est* [EN77]? (*Syn. pur. Theol.*, Leiden, 1624, *Disp.* 9, 2).

But this also means that the creature to whom the Holy Spirit is imparted in revelation by no means loses its nature and kind as a creature so as to become itself, as it were, the Holy Spirit. Even in receiving the Holy Ghost man remains man, the sinner sinner. Similarly in the outpouring of the Holy Ghost God remains God. The statements about the operations of the Holy Spirit are statements whose subject is God and not man, and in no circumstances can they be transformed into statements about man. They tell us about the relation of God to man, to his knowledge, will and emotion, to his experience active and passive, to his heart and conscience, to the whole of his psycho-physical existence, but they cannot be reversed and understood as statements about the existence of man. That God the Holy Spirit is the Redeemer who sets us free is a statement of the knowledge and praise of God. In virtue of this statement we ourselves are the redeemed, the liberated, the children of God in faith, in the faith we confess with this statement, i.e., in the act of God of which this statement speaks. This being of ours is thus enclosed in the act of God. Confessing this faith in the Holy Ghost, we cannot as it were look back and try to contemplate and establish abstractly this being of ours as God's redeemed and liberated children as it is enclosed in the act of God. We may, of course, be strong and sure in faith—that we are so is the act of God we are confessing, the work of the Holy Spirit—but we cannot try specifically to make ourselves strong and sure again by contemplating ourselves as the strong and the sure. To have the Holy Spirit is to let God rather than our having God be our confidence. It lies in the nature of God's revelation and reconciliation in time, it lies in the nature of the *regnum gratiae* [EN78], that having *God* and our *having* God are two very different things, and that our redemption is not a relation which we can survey in its totality, i.e., which we can understand in both its aspects, God's and our own. Paradoxically enough we can understand it only in its divine aspect, i.e., in faith we can understand it only as it is posited by God. Faith is understanding it as posited and indeed fulfilled and consummated by God, but not by us, not in such a way that we may see ourselves in the being which corresponds to this fulfilment and consummation by God, i.e., in our redemption or beatitude or

---

[EN75] divine nature
[EN76] participation
[EN77] here the word Spirit must clearly be distinguished from any idea of a creature
[EN78] realm of grace

eternal life. If we could also understand it thus, this would mean that all the [463] difficulty of faith would be behind us. It would no longer have to be a Nevertheless. It would no longer have to be obedience and venture. It would no longer have to be faith at all. It would be sight. For it is sight when we can survey and see in its totality how what is true from God's standpoint is also true from ours. This would be more than God's revelation and reconciliation in time. It would be our being with Him in eternity, in the *regnum gloriae*EN79. If we cannot erase this distinction, if we cannot anticipate what lies beyond revelation and faith, this means necessarily that in so far as redemption implies our own being in addition to God's act we can regard it only as future, i.e., as the redemption that comes to us from God. We have it in faith.

But to have it in faith means that we have it in promise. We believe that we are redeemed, set free, children of God, i.e., we accept as such the promise given us in the Word of God in Jesus Christ even as and although we do not understand it in the very least, or see it fulfilled and consummated in the very least, in relation to our present. We accept it because it speaks to us of an act of God on us even as and although we see only our own empty hands which we stretch out to God in the process. We believe our future being. We believe in an eternal life even in the midst of the valley of death. In this way, in this futurity, we have it. The assurance with which we know this having is the assurance of faith, and the assurance of faith means concretely the assurance of hope.

'Ελπιζομένων ὑπόστασις, πραγμάτων ἔλεγχος οὐ βλεπομένων EN80 (Heb. 11¹). Hence the concept of sonship, which is very important as we have seen, is often elucidated, especially in Paul, by the concept of an inheritance (κληρονομία) into which we have not yet entered but which is legally in prospect, and sure and certain as such (Rom. 8¹⁷; Gal. 3²⁹; 4⁷; Tit. 3⁷; also Jas. 2⁵). Hence Gal. 5⁵ says that in the Spirit we wait for the righteousness which is hoped for (and which precisely as such is present in Jesus Christ), ἐλπίδα δικαιοσύνης ἀπεκδεχόμεθα EN81. Hence again 2 Cor. 5 says that we walk in faith and not in sight. Hence Rom. 8²³f·, in a passage we can never consult too often, says that we, the same (note the twofold καὶ αὐτοί), who have the ἀπαρχὴ τοῦ πνεύματος EN82, groan with all creation in expectation of sonship to the degree that this is to be understood as the fulfilment and consummation of the promise, the ἀπολύτρωσις τοῦ σώματος. Τῇ γὰρ ἐλπίδι ἐσώθημεν· ἐλπὶς δὲ βλεπομένη οὐκ ἔστιν ἐλπίς· ὃ γὰρ βλέπει τις, τί καὶ ἐλπίζει; εἰ δὲ ὃ οὐ βλέπομεν ἐλπίζομεν, δι' ὑπομονῆς ἀπεκδεχόμεθα EN83. God has regenerated you. How? Through the resurrection of Jesus Christ from the dead. To what? To a living hope, namely, the inheritance incorruptible, undefiled, that fadeth not away, reserved in heaven for you (1 Pet. 1³f·). We are called and are God's children. We are this now ... but it has not yet appeared what we shall be. We know that when He shall appear we shall be like Him (1

EN79 realm of glory
EN80 the substance of things hoped for, the evidence of things not seen
EN81 we wait for the hope of righteousness
EN82 first fruits of the Spirit
EN83 the redemption of our bodies. For in this hope we were saved. Now hope that is seen is not hope. For who hopes for what he sees? But if we hope for what we do not see, we wait for it with patience

Jn. 3$^{1f.}$.). Your life (i.e., your salvation) is hid with Christ in God. When Christ, our life, appears, then you too will appear with Him in glory (Col. 3$^{3f.}$). Abraham is the father of all believers because he did not consider his own sterile body nor that of Sarah but gave God the glory in the certainty that what He promised He could do (Rom. 4$^{19f.}$). Thus the Holy Ghost Himself is called the πνεῦμα τῆς ἐπαγγελίας^{EN84} (Eph. 1^{13}) and His office in relation to us is our sealing εἰς ἡμέραν ἀπολυτρώσεως^{EN85} (Eph. 4^{30}, cf. 1^{14}).

[464]

In the New Testament sense everything that is to be said about the man who receives the Holy Spirit and is constrained and filled by the Holy Spirit is an eschatological statement. Eschatological does not mean in an inexact or unreal sense but in relation to the ἔσχατον^{EN86}, i.e., to that which from our standpoint and for our experience and thought has still to come, to the eternal reality of the divine fulfilment and consummation. It is precisely eschatological statements and these alone, i.e., statements which relate to this eternal reality, that can claim real and proper meaning as statements about temporal relations. For what can be more real and proper for man than truth in this particular relation?

The New Testament speaks eschatologically when it speaks of man's being called, reconciled, justified, sanctified and redeemed. In speaking thus it speaks really and properly. One has to realise that God is the measure of all that is real and proper, that eternity comes first and then time, and therefore the future comes first and then the present, just as the Creator undoubtedly comes first and then the creature. Those who realise this will not take offence here.

Only of God Himself, which means at this point the Holy Spirit and His work as such, can one speak non-eschatologically, i.e., without this reference to something other, beyond, and future. It might be said, of course, that even our talk about God Himself and His work is eschatological to the extent that all our thoughts and words as such cannot grasp this object but can only point beyond themselves to it. But that to which they point when we are speaking of God and His essence and work has itself no margin or border. It is not related to an ἔσχατον but is itself the ἔσχατον. This is what we cannot say of the man we know even and precisely in faith. The man we know does not live an eternal life. This is and remains the predicate of God, of the Holy Spirit.

The Holy Spirit is Lord over every creature but is not lorded over. He deifies but is not deified. He fills but is not filled. He causes to participate but does not participate. He sanctifies but is not sanctified (John Damasc., *Ekdos.* I, 8).

Of ourselves, however, we must say that God so gives Himself to us in His revelation that we are and remain and indeed only truly become rich in Him and poor in ourselves. Both become our experience: that we are rich in God and that then and only then we truly become poor in ourselves. But we do not have the divine and spiritual riches and the divine and spiritual poverty in our

---

EN84 Spirit of promise
EN85 for the day of redemption
EN86 end time

experience. What we have in our experience, what can be changed and extended and developed quantitatively and qualitatively in us, what moves up and down or perhaps forwards in a straight line or in spirals, what can be the theme of the anthropology, psychology or biography of the believer, is a human sign of the fact that God has given Himself to us by His revelation in faith, and as such it is certainly not to be treated lightly. It would be strange indeed if such signs were not in evidence at all. Yet it is still true that "the things which are seen are temporal, but the things which are not seen are eternal" (2 Cor. 4¹⁸). Man remains man, the man who can deceive himself and others; the sign remains a sign, which may fade again and disappear. But the Holy Spirit remains the Holy Spirit, wholly and utterly the Spirit of promise. Even and especially the child of God in the New Testament sense will never for a moment or in any regard cease to confess: "I believe that I cannot of my own reason or power believe in Jesus Christ my Lord or come to Him." God remains the Lord even and precisely when He Himself comes into our hearts as His own gift, even and precisely when He "fills" us. No other intercedes with Him on our behalf except Himself. No other intercedes with us on His behalf except again Himself. No one else speaks from us when He speaks through us except Himself. "In thy light we see light" (Ps. 36⁹). The deity of the Holy Spirit is thus demanded. The essentiality, the directness of the work of the Holy Spirit is demanded. We are not grasping at more but at less, and ultimately at nothing at all, if in addition to the guarantee which is identical with God Himself we think we must grasp at an unequivocal experience, at a guarantee of the guarantee so to speak, in order that we may then decide for certainty of faith, as though a certainty for which we must first decide could be the certainty of faith. "If I have but thee, I ask naught of heaven and earth," and further: "Though body and soul languish within me, yet thou, God, art the strength of my heart and my portion for ever" (Ps. 73²⁵ᶠ·) This is how we think and speak ἐν πνεύματι EN87. But if we grasp at another, at ourselves, if we seek strength and confirmation in ourselves, we simply show thereby that we are still far from thinking and speaking ἐν πνεύματι, or have long since ceased to do so. We can comprehend God in ourselves only as we comprehend ourselves in *God,* just as we can, of course, comprehend ourselves in God only as we comprehend *God* in ourselves. It is precisely ἐν πνεύματι that we shall be ready either way to turn from ourselves to God and to pray to Him, not to contemplate God and manipulate Him. But again only the man who seeks everything in God prays to Him. And yet again only the man who seeks nothing in himself seeks everything in God.

Μακρόθεν ἑστώς EN88, not daring to lift his eyes to heaven, the publican in the temple prays: "God be merciful to me, a sinner." And this man went down to his house justified (Lk. 18¹⁰ᶠ·). Did Jesus go into the ship to Simon or not? Did He fill his ship with blessing or not?

EN87 in the Spirit
EN88 Standing afar off

[465]

[466] But what did Simon say to this? "Depart from me, for I am a sinful man" (Lk. 5$^{1f.}$). "It should be understood that ... all that is not Christ is altogether unclean and damned with birth and all life, And no purity or holiness cometh into us or out of us, but over and above us and far beyond us, yea, above all our sense, wit and understanding, in Christ alone by faith 'tis found and attained" (Luther, *Sermon at Torgau*, 1533, *W.A.* 37, 57, 32). This is how a man thinks and speaks ἐν πνεύματι.

What we have to offer, to sacrifice to God in order to pray aright, is ourselves in this total lack of any claim.

We have to sacrifice "a broken spirit," "a broken and a contrite heart" (Ps. 51^{17}), a heart that knows it must be created by God in us as a new heart, a spirit that knows it must be created by God in us as a new spirit, and must be sought in prayer for this reason (Ps. 51^{10}).

Whether prayer is made aright and answered depends on this total lack of any claim.

Rom. 8 is unthinkable without Rom. 7 (including Rom. 7^{24}), and indeed without Rom. 7 understood, not as a glance back at the past, but as an assertion about the present and about the whole temporal future even and especially of the Christian. The *Veni Creator Spiritus*[EN89] is true and will be heard when it is persistent beseeching, when no present or perfect *venit*[EN90] stands behind it to spoil everything. That simple *venit* is the truth just because it is in God and from God.

The impregnable basis of faith, the assurance of faith by God's revelation, depends on whether this basis, not just at the beginning but in the middle and at the end too, is sought in God alone and not anywhere else, not in ourselves. Grace is the Holy Spirit received, but we ourselves are sinners. This is true. If we say anything else we do not know the deity of the Holy Spirit in God's revelation.

2. THE ETERNAL SPIRIT

The Holy Spirit does not first become the Holy Spirit, the Spirit of God, in the event of revelation. The event of revelation has clarity and reality on its subjective side because the Holy Spirit, the subjective element in this event, is of the essence of God Himself. What He is in revelation He is antecedently in Himself. And what He is antecedently in Himself He is in revelation. Within the deepest depths of deity, as the final thing to be said about Him, God is God the Spirit as He is God the Father and God the Son. The Spirit outpoured at Pentecost is the Lord, God Himself, just as the Father and just as Jesus Christ is the Lord, God Himself. Once more, if we are asked how this statement comes to be made, we can only answer that to make it no special dialectical effort is [467] required; we have only to allow the biblical statements to stand; we have only to accept their validity and take them seriously. According to these statements the

---

[EN89] Come Creator Spirit
[EN90] he comes/he has come

work of the Holy Spirit in revelation is a work which can be ascribed only to God and which is thus expressly ascribed to God. The dogma of the Holy Spirit to which we now turn adds nothing new to this. Here again the dogma does not invent anything. It simply finds what was and is more or less plainly hinted at in the New Testament even though it obviously was not and is not to be found there. The dogma itself, then, is not in Scripture; it is exegesis of Scripture. It does not speak of any other deity of the Holy Ghost than that in which He is revealed to us according to Scripture. It insists, however, that this deity is true, proper and eternal deity. The Spirit is holy in us because He is so antecedently in Himself.

The doctrine of the deity and autonomy of the Spirit's divine mode of being achieved general understanding and acknowledgment in the Church much later than the corresponding doctrine of the Son. One can see it intimated from the very beginning, of course, in the primitive threefold structure of the creed. But in the main the 2nd and 3rd century Fathers confined themselves to speaking of the operation and gifts of the Holy Spirit, and there was often approximation to, or at all events no clear exclusion of, the Subordinationist view that He is a creature or creaturely force on the one hand and the Modalist view that He is identical with the Son or Logos on the other. At that time the position which later prevailed in both respects was understood with relative clarity and lack of ambiguity only by Tertullian (in his work against Praxeas), perhaps not without some connexion to the high regard he had for the Spirit as a Montanist. Even the Nicene Creed, though it uses ὁμοούσιος EN91 of the Son, is content, like the older symbols, simply to mention the Holy Ghost as an object of faith without opposing Arianism at this point as well. It was again Athanasius (in his letter to Serapion opposing Macedonius of Constantinople) who saw the connexions and spoke the decisive word in this regard. Not without some hesitation the Neo-Nicenes and the Council of 381 followed him. The dogma found precise formulation, corresponding to the definitions of the Son in *Nic.-Const.*, only in the 5th century (*Symb. Quicunque vult*). But for the full development of the doctrine we shall have to look as late as the final reception of the *filioque* EN92 into the creed of the Western liturgy (1014) and the schism of the Eastern Church occasioned by the rejection of this addition.

It is deeply rooted in the matter itself that Christian knowledge about the Holy Spirit permeated the Church so slowly and with such difficulty. The fact that the Holy Spirit is the Lord, that He is wholly and utterly God, the divine Subject, in the same sense as the Father of Jesus Christ and in the same sense as Jesus Christ Himself, is without doubt the harder and more exacting demand, not just or chiefly for formal thought, but in face of man's ideas about himself also and precisely in relation to God. He himself, his presence at God's revelation, is indeed the issue in the problem of the Spirit within the concept of revelation. Even though man may accept the fact that the author of revelation, the Father, is fully God, and perhaps that the Revealer, the Son, is also fully God in order to be able to be God's Revealer, the question remains open whether God has said that man's own presence at revelation, the reality of his encounter with the Revealer, is not his own work but is again in the full sense

[468]

EN91 of one substance
EN92 and the Son

God's work. If the Spirit, the Mediator of revelation to the subject, were a creature or creaturely force, then it would be asserted and maintained that in virtue of his presence at revelation along with God and over against God, man, too, is in his own way the lord in revelation. For even in circumstances that are unfavourable to us our relation to creatures and creaturely forces is a reciprocal one, a co-operation of freedom and necessity, a relation between one pole and its opposite. Even Modalism in relation to the Spirit, the identification of the Spirit with Christ, would imply that man confronts revelation as an object. Even as it gains control over him, he can also gain control over it. Even as a recipient of the fulness of grace man could still regard his faith as an active instrument (cf. A. Ritschl, *Rechtf. u Vers.*[4], Vol. 1, 1900, 157). By the doctrine of the deity and autonomy of the Spirit's divine mode of being man is, as it were, challenged in his own house. It is now clear that his presence at revelation cannot be the presence of a partner or counterpart, that from this presence no claims or privileges can arise *vis-à-vis* God, that this presence can only be a factual, incomprehensible and miraculous presence, factual because God is there, as we have already said, not just objectively but also subjectively, not just from above but also from below, not just from without but also from within. The dogma of the Holy Spirit means recognition that in every respect man can be present at God's revelation only as a servant is present at his master's work, i.e., following, obeying, imitating and serving, and that this relation—as distinct from that of human servant and master—cannot be reversed in any way or at any point. This developed recognition of the unconditionality and irreversibility of the lordship of God in His revelation is what makes the dogma of the Holy Spirit difficult, difficult, of course, intellectually too, but difficult intellectually only because man does not want the very thing that it states to be true.

It is logical that this doctrine had to be the last stage in the development of the trinitarian dogma. It had to be reached before the doctrine of grace, which then became the distinctive theme of the Western Church, could become a problem, before the struggle and victory of Augustine over Pelagius could take place. The Reformation with its doctrine of justification by faith alone can also be understood only against the background of this specific dogma. Its true and total significance, of course, has never been understood in Catholicism (not even in Augustine), and only very partially even in post-Reformation Protestantism. Modernist Protestantism in its entirety has simply been a regression to pre-Nicene obscurities and ambiguities regarding the Spirit.

[469]   For a more precise exposition of the dogma we shall now turn here again to the Nicaeno-Constantinopolitan Creed.

2. The Eternal Spirit

(Πιστεύομεν ...)

1. εἰς τὸ πνεῦμα τὸ ἅγιον, τὸ κύριον

2. τὸ ζωοποιοῦν

3. τὸ ἐκ τοῦ πατρὸς ἐκπορευόμενον

4. τὸ σὺν πατρὶ καὶ υἱῷ συνπροσκυνούμενον καὶ συνδοξαζόμενον.

(Credo[EN93] ...)

1. in Spiritum sanctum Dominum[EN94]

2. et vivificantem[EN95]

3. qui ex Patre Filioque procedit[EN96]

4. qui cum Patre et Filio simul adoratur et conglorificatur[EN97].

1. We believe in the Holy Ghost, the Lord. The underlying Greek text uses κύριον[EN98] adjectivally here. This implies no limitation of the statement as we have it in the Latin *Dominus* and English "Lord." Like the Father and the Son, the Spirit is not *Dominus*, Lord, as one Lord side by side with two others. He is Lord in inseparable unity with the Father as Lord and the Son as Lord. Our first point, with a backward glance at the ἕνα κύριον[EN99] of the second article, is that the Holy Spirit, with the Father and the Son, is the bearer of the lordship of God which is not based on any higher lordship. With the Father and the Son He is the one sovereign divine Subject, the Subject who is not placed under the control or inspection of any other, who derives His being and existence from Himself. But the adjectival use of κύριος[EN100], along with a fact that we have not yet taken into account, and which is not evident in Latin (or German), namely that πνεῦμα[EN101] itself is a neuter, forces us to note at once the special way in which the Holy Spirit is all this. These two circumstances indicate that He is it all in a neutral way, neutral in the sense of distinct, i.e., distinct from the Father and the Son whose modes of being are reciprocal, but neuter also in the sense of related, i.e., related to the Father and the Son, whose reciprocity is not a being against, but a being to and from and with one another. This togetherness or communion of the Father and the Son is the Holy Spirit. The specific element in the divine mode of being of the Holy Spirit thus consists, paradoxically enough, in the fact that He is the common factor in the mode of being of God the Father and that of God the Son. He is what is common to them, not in so far as they are the one God, but in so far as they are the Father and the Son.

Spiritus sanctus commune aliquid est Patris et Filii[EN102] (Augustine, *De trin.* VI. 5, 7). He stands "in the middle between the Begotten and Unbegotten" (John of Damasc., *Ekdos.* I, 13).

EN 93 I believe
EN 94 in the Holy Spirit, the Lord
EN 95 the giver of life
EN 96 who proceeds from the Father and the Son
EN 97 who together with the Father and the Son is worshipped and glorified
EN 98 Lord
EN 99 one Lord
EN100 Lord
EN101 Spirit
EN102 The Holy Spirit is something common to the Father and the Son

Nomen Spiritus sancti non est alienum a Patre et Filio, quia uterque est et Spiritus et sanctus[EN103]
(Anselm of Canterbury, *Ep. de incarn.* 2).

Thus, even if the Father and the Son might be called "person" (in the modern sense of the term), the Holy Spirit could not possibly be regarded as the third "person." In a particularly clear way the Holy Spirit is what the Father and the Son also are. He is not a third spiritual Subject, a third I, a third Lord side by side with two others. He is a third mode of being of the one divine Subject or Lord.

[470]   In this regard it is worth noting that the Church has forbidden the portrayal of the Holy Ghost in human form (Bartmann, *Lehrb. d. Dogm.*[7], Vol. 1, 1928, 194).

He is the common element, or, better, the fellowship, the act of communion, of the Father and the Son. He is the act in which the Father is the Father of the Son or the Speaker of the Word and the Son is the Son of the Father or the Word of the Speaker.

He is *communio quaedam consubstantialis*[EN104] (Augustine, *De trin.* XV, 27, 50). He is the *vinculum pacis* (Eph. 4[3]), the *amor*, the *caritas*, the mutual *donum*[EN105] between the Father and the Son, as it has often been put in the train of Augustine. He is thus the love in which God (loves Himself, i.e., loves Himself as the Father and as the Son, and) as the Father loves the Son and as the Son loves the Father. *Si charitas qua Pater diligit Filium et Patrem diligit Filius, ineffabiliter communionem demonstrat amborum, quid convenientius quam ut ille dicatur charitas proprie, qui Spiritus est communis ambobus*[EN106]. (Augustine, *De trin.* XV, 19, 37). To this extent—the figurative nature of the expression does not need to be emphasised—He is the "result" of their common "breathing," *spiratio. Amborum sacrum spiramen, nexus amorque*[EN107], as we read in the Kyrie-Tropus "*Cuncti potens*" (L. Eisenhofer, *Handb. der kath. Liturgik*, Vol. 2, 1933, 89).

How far is this act to be understood as a special divine mode of being? It is obviously to be regarded as a *special* divine mode of being because this common being and work of the Father and the Son is a special and distinct mode of divine being as compared to that of the Father and the Son. It is obviously to be understood as a *divine* mode of being because in this act of His divine being as Father and Son, in this reciprocal love of His, God cannot be or do anything other or less than what is equal to Himself. There cannot be any higher principle from which and in which the Father and the Son must first find themselves together. They can find themselves together only in their own principle. But this principle is the breathing of the Holy Spirit or the Holy Spirit Himself. Again the work of this love is not the created world; it is the reciprocal love of

---

EN103 The name of the Holy Spirit is not foreign to the Father or the Son, because each is both spirit and holy

EN104 a kind of consubstantial communion

EN105 bond of peace, love, charity, gift

EN106 If the love with which the Father loves the Son and the Son the Father shows their ineffable communion, there is nothing more appropriate than that the Spirit common to both should be called love

EN107 The holy breath of both, their communion and their love

the Father and the Son. The work, then, must be what is equal to them, and this equal is the Holy Spirit.

Father and Son are *non participatione, sed essentia sua, neque dono superioris alicuius, sed suo proprio servantes unitatem Spiritus in vinculo pacis*[EN108] (Augustine, *De trin.* VI, 5, 7). *Nam ideo amor non est impar tibi aut Filio tuo, quia tantum amas te et illum et ille te et seipsum, quantus es tu et ille, nec est aliud a te et ab illo*[EN109]. (Anselm of Canterbury, *Prosl.* 23). *Si nulla umquam creatura, id est si nihil umquam aliud esset quam summus spiritus Pater et Filius: nihilominus seipsos et invicem Pater et Filius diligerent. Consequitur itaque hunc amorem non esse aliud quam quod est Pater et Filius, quod est summa essentia*[EN110] (*Monol.* 53).

Thus God—and to this degree He is God the Holy Spirit—is "antecedently in Himself" the act of communion, the act of impartation, love, gift. For this reason and in this way and on this basis He is so in His revelation. Not *vice versa!* We know Him thus in His revelation. But He is not this because He is it in His revelation; because He is it antecedently in Himself, He is it also in His revelation. [471]

He is in His revelation the *donator doni*[EN111] because in Himself, as the Spirit of the Father and the Son, He is the *donum donatoris*[EN112] (Augustine, *De trin.* V, 11). *Donum vere dicitur non ex eo tantum, quod donetur, sed ex proprietate, quam habuit ab aeterno. Unde et ab aeterno fuit donum. Sempiterne enim donum fuit, non quia daretur, sed quia processit a Patre et Filio … temporaliter autem donatum est*[EN113] (Peter Lombard, *Sent.* I, dist. 18 D). *Donum non dicitur ex eo quod actu datur, sed in quantum habet aptitudinem ut possit dari. Unde ab aeterno divina persona dicitur donum, licet ex tempore detur*[EN114] (Thomas Aquinas, *S. th.* I, qu. 38, art. 1 and 4.) *Amor habet rationem primi doni, per quod omnia dona gratuita donantur. Unde cum Spiritus sanctus procedat ut amor … procedit in ratione doni primi*[EN115] (ib., art. 2c).

The Holy Spirit, says the dogma with its τὸ κύριον [EN116], is the Lord who acts on us in revelation as the Redeemer, who really sets us free and really makes us the children of God, who really gives His Church the words to speak God's

---

[EN108] preserving the unity of the Spirit in the bond of peace not by participation, but in their essence; not by any gift of some higher being, but through their own self-giving

[EN109] For the love between you and your Son is not unequal, for you love yourself and him and he loves you and himself as much as you and he exist, and [the love] is not anything else but you and he

[EN110] If no creature, that is, if nothing other than the highest spirit, the Father and the Son, ever existed, the Father and the Son would still love themselves and each other. And so it follows that this love is nothing else than what the Father and the Son are, which is the highest being

[EN111] the giver of gifts

[EN112] gift of the giver

[EN113] He is rightly called gift not only on account of being given, but on account of the property which he has possessed from eternity. Therefore, from eternity he was gift. And he was eternally gift not because he was to be given, but because he proceeded from the Father and the Son … but he has been given within time

[EN114] he is not called gift on account of the event of his being given, but insofar as he has an aptitude for being given. For this reason this divine person is called gift from eternity, although he is given in time

[EN115] Love has the form of a first gift, through which all gifts are freely given. For this reason since the Spirit proceeds as love … He proceeds in the form of the first gift

[EN116] the Lord

181

Word, because in this work of His on us He simply does in time what He does eternally in God, because this mode of being of His in revelation is also a mode of being of the hidden essence of God, so that it really is the hidden essence of God Himself, and therefore the Lord in the most unrestricted sense of the term, who, in all His inscrutability, is revealed in revelation in this respect too.

2. We believe in the Holy Ghost, the giver of life. This statement, too, teaches the deity of the Holy Spirit. Like the *per quem omnia facta sunt*[EN117] of the second article, it does so by referring to the fact that the Holy Spirit is with the Father (and the Son) the subject of creation. He is not just the Redeemer, so surely does redemption stand in indissoluble correlation with reconciliation, so surely does reconciliation reach its consummation in redemption. He is thus the Reconciler too, with the Son, and as the Spirit of the Son. And just as in reconciliation, and as its presupposition, God the Father is revealed through the Son, i.e., God the Creator, and the work of creation is shown to have happened through the same Word who became incarnate in Jesus Christ, so now the Holy Spirit is revealed as the One who in His own way co-operates in creation too.

In the first instance the ζωοποιοῦν[EN118], which reminds us of two New Testament verses Jn. 6[63]; 2 Cor. 3[6] that have been quoted already, is certainly to be understood soteriologically. But behind these passages there is again a reminiscence of the significance which the Old Testament assigns to *ruach* and *neshamah*[EN119] for the *regnum naturae*[EN120], of Gen. 2[7], where Adam, though he is not himself a πνεῦμα ζωοποιοῦν[EN121] as Christ the second Adam is said to be in 1 Cor. 15[45], is still a "living soul" through the "living breath" of God. And this leads us at once to the "Spirit" who according to Gen. 1[2] hovered ("brooded") over the "ocean" of creation when it was as yet without form and neither filled nor fashioned by any life, to the Spirit through whom the "host of heaven" is made according to Ps. 33[6], who is in all flesh according to Gen. 7[15], and who is in every place to which man might go according to Ps. 139[7], to that "breath" in every creature which according to Ps. 150[6] puts it under obligation to praise the Lord because according to Ps. 104[29f.] it is His, the Lord's breath, by which the creature is created and without which it would inevitably vanish away at once.

[472]

Already at the beginning of the section we have given thought to this general meaning of the term "spirit." In order it is the primary meaning. But epistemologically it can only be secondary. For as it is only through revelation (and therefore through the Spirit in the soteriological sense of the term) that we see that we and all that is in general the creation of God are, the same applies in particular to our creation by the Word and Spirit (now in the primary and general sense of the term). This general meaning "spirit," the significance of the Spirit as the Creator Spirit, consists, however, in the fact that creation in its own existence as distinct from God's existence is not only there

---

[EN117] through whom all things were made
[EN118] giver of life
[EN119] spirit and breath
[EN120] realm of nature
[EN121] life-giving spirit

according to the will of the Father effected by the Word but in and of itself it is and remains capable of this existence of its own, as it must always be sustained objectively too in its existence by the Word of God. The Holy Spirit is the Creator God with the Father and the Son in so far as God as Creator creates life as well as existence. From this standpoint we cannot avoid speaking of a presence and operation of the Holy Spirit which is presupposed in revelation, which is first and general, and which is related to the created existence of man and the world as such. This can as little be the object of a general and independent knowledge preceding revelation as can the *per quem omnia facta sunt*EN122 of the second article or the dogma of creation generally. It cannot, then, be the theme of a natural theology. It can be known and confessed only on the basis of revelation and in faith. But on the basis of revelation and of faith it must be confessed, already as a necessary consequence of the deity of the Holy Spirit, already in the light of the principle *opera trinitatis ad extra sunt indivisa*EN123, but also on account of its significant content.

Ἡ δὲ τοῦ ἁγίου πνεύματος μεγαλωσύνη ἀδιάλυτος, ἀπέραντος καὶ πανταχοῦ καὶ διὰ πάντων καὶ ἐν πᾶσιν ἀεί ἐστιν. πληροῦσα μὲν τὸν κόσμον καὶ συνέχουσα κατὰ τὴν θεότητα, ἀχώρητος δὲ κατὰ τὴν δύναμιν, καὶ μετροῦσα μέν, οὐ μετρωμένη δέEN124 (Didymus of Alexandria, *De trin.* II, 6, 2). *Spiritui sancto … attribuitur quod dominando gubernet et vivificet quae sunt creata a Patre per Filium*EN125. He is the *bonitas*EN126, and so the goal, and so the *primum movens*EN127 of creation (Thomas Aquinas, *S. theol.* I, qu. 45, art. 6, ad. 2). Therefore in the *Offertorium* of the vigil before Pentecost, with a clear reminiscence that the Holy Ghost in baptism is also the Holy Ghost in creation, the Roman Church prays according to Ps. 104³⁰: *Emitte Spiritum tuum et creabuntur et renovabis faciem terrae*EN128. And in the Introit for Whitsunday: *Spiritus Domini replevit orbem terrarum, allelujah: et hoc quod continet omnia scientiam habet vocis*EN129. And in the familiar Whitsuntide hymn:

> *Veni Creator Spiritus,*
> *mentes tuorum visita,*
> *imple superna gratia,*
> *quae tu creasti pectora.* EN130

[473]

And in the *Oratio* for the Ember Day (Saturday) in Whitsun week: *Mentibus nostris … spiritum sanctum infunde cuius et sapientia conditi sumus et providentia gubernamur*EN131. Luther, too, can

---

EN122 through whom all things were made
EN123 the outward works of the Trinity are undivided
EN124 The greatness of the Holy Spirit is indestructible and unbounded, being everywhere and through all things and in all things, filling the universe and encompassing the Godhead, unlimited in power, measuring all things and not itself subject to measure
EN125 To the Holy Spirit … is assigned that mode of lordship whereby he governs and gives life to what has been created by the Father through the Son
EN126 goodness
EN127 prime mover
EN128 Give forth your Spirit, and they will be created, and you will renew the face of the earth
EN129 The Spirit of the Lord has filled the whole world. Hallelujah! And that which contains all things has the power of speech
EN130 Come Creator Spirit, call upon the minds of your creatures, fill with the highest grace the hearts which you have created.
EN131 Into our minds … pour the Holy Spirit by whose wisdom we were made and by whose providence we are governed

speak of a duplex *Spiritus quem Deus donat hominibus: animans et sanctificans*[EN132]. Thus all *homines ingeniosi, prudentes eruditi, fortes, magnanimi*[EN133] are impelled by the *Spiritus animans. Soli autem christiani ac pii habent Spiritum sanctum sanctificantem*[EN134] (*W.A. Ti.*, 5, 367, 12). And Calvin in his general definition of the three modes of being of God could even describe the Holy Ghost as God's *virtus per omnia quidem diffusa, quae tamen perpetuo in ipso resideat*[EN135] (*Cat. Genev.*, 1545, in K. Müller, 118, l. 28). He interpreted Gen. 1^2 as follows: Both the existence of things, created first as chaos (*inordinata moles, massa indisposita*[EN136]), and also their nature or form (*pulcher ac distinctus ordo*[EN137]), in order not merely to be created but also to be, to persist, needed an *arcana Dei inspiratio*, a *vigor*[EN138] imparted to them by God (*Comm. on Gen.* 1^2, 1544, *C.R.* 23, 16). And Calvin regarded the thought which follows as an important expression of the doctrine of the deity of the Holy Spirit: *ille enim est, qui ubique diffusus omnia sustinet, vegetat et vivificat in coelo et in terra. Iam hoc ipso creaturarum numero eximitur, quod nullis circumscribitur finibus; sed suum in omnia vigorem transfundendo essentiam vitam et motionem illis inspirare, id vero plane divinum est*[EN139] (*Instit.* I, 13, 14). Again J. Gerhard teaches: *Quemadmodum in prima creatione Spiritus sanctus aquas fovendo iisque incubando fuit efficax, ita in rerum creatarum conservatione idem cum Patre et Filio efficaciter agit*[EN140]; in spring-time *qua cuncta revirescere et frondescere incipiunt, postquam per hiemem fuerunt emortua*[EN141], but also in the coming into being of each new individual in which its species is renewed (*Loci*, 1610, L. III, 10, 132). And Paul Gerhardt in the Whitsun hymn "Enter then thy gates":

> In thine own hands Thou bearest
> The whole wide world, O Lord,
> The hearts of men Thou turnest
> By thine own will and word.
> Thy grace, then, O vouchsafe us

3. We believe in the Holy Ghost, who proceedeth from the Father and the Son.

This clause corresponds to the *genitum non factum*[EN142] of the second article. It is meant in the first instance as a negation: the Holy Spirit is not a creature. No creature can be said to have proceeded from God, i.e., to be an emanation of the divine essence. The creation of the world and man is not a procession or emanation from God. It is the establishing of a reality distinct from God with an essence of its own and not the divine essence. What proceeds from God can

---

[EN132] twofold Spirit whom God gives to human beings: animating and sanctifying

[EN133] clever, prudent, learned, strong, generous people

[EN134] animating Spirit. But only Christians and pious folk have the sanctifying Holy Spirit

[EN135] power diffused through all things, but which abides eternally in himself

[EN136] disordered lump, unstructured mass

[EN137] proper and distinct order

[EN138] secret inspiration from God

[EN139] For he is the one who, diffused everywhere, sustains, animates and gives life to all things in heaven and on earth. To begin, he is not included in the number of creatures because he is not bounded by any limits; but transfusing his power into all things and breathing into them being, life and motion: this is indeed clearly divine

[EN140] In the same way that at the beginning of creation the Holy Spirit was effective in warming and incubating the waters, so in the conservation of created things he acts effectively with the Father and the Son

[EN141] when all things begin to revive and leaf out after they had died off through the winter

[EN142] begotten not made

only be God once again. And since the essence of God cannot be divisible, what proceeds from God—and this is how the dogma describes the Holy Ghost—cannot go out from Him; it cannot, then, be an emanation in the common sense of the term but only a mode of being of the one essence of God which intrinsically remains and is the same. In this case, obviously, the procession is not from the one essence of God as such but from another mode of being or other modes of being of this essence. Primarily, then, the clause is a description of the Holy Spirit, not now with reference to the *opus ad extra*EN143 common to the three modes of being, but with reference to His reality as a divine mode of being, i.e., to His reality in His relation to the other divine modes of being. This reality is of a kind that marks it out as being of divine essence with the Father and the Son. This is the first point made by the *qui procedit*EN144. [474]

> *Processionis vox accipienda est ... juxta actionem Dei ad intra ... id est qua ita agit Deus in essentia sua, ut reflexus in seipsum, divinae essentiae communione relationem realem constituat*EN145 (*Syn. Theol. pur.* Leiden, 1624, Disp., 9, 10).

The second point is that the Holy Spirit is differentiated from the Son or Word of God. The work of the Holy Spirit in revelation is different from that of the Son or Word of God. Though never separated from it, and to be distinguished only *per appropriationem*EN146, it is still not to be confused with it. If we are to refrain from going beyond revelation, we shall interrelate the objective element of the Word in revelation and the subjective element of the Spirit, only in the essence of God but not as modes of His being. We shall acknowledge that the Holy Ghost, both in revelation and also antecedently in Himself, is not just God, but in God independently, like the Father and the Son. Again there is no special and second revelation of the Spirit alongside that of the Son. There are not, then, two Sons or Words of God. In the one revelation, however, the Son or Word represents the element of God's appropriation to man and the Spirit the element of God's appropriation by man. But by analogy, if our thinking is not to leave the soil of revelation, a distinction must be acknowledged in the reality of what the Son and the Spirit are antecedently in themselves. Secondly, then, the *qui procedit* means that the divine mode of being of the Spirit is to be differentiated from that of the Son, which is denoted by *genitus*EN147, and implicitly, therefore, from that of the Father as well.

It is an isolated oddity that the *Pastor Hermae* (*Sim.* V, 5, 2; 6, 5f.; IX, 1) calls the Holy Ghost the Son of God. In the dogma itself the need to distinguish the Spirit not merely from the

---

EN143 outward work
EN144 who proceeds
EN145 The term 'procession' is to be understood ... as referring to an activity internal to God ...
     that is, the way God acts in his being so that, turned back on himself, he establishes a real
     relationship through the sharing of the divine essence
EN146 by appropriation
EN147 begotten

creature but also from the Son or Word of God follows logically from the *unigenitus*[EN148] of the second article. Both distinctions are included in the saying of Gregory of Nazianzus: ὃ καθ᾽ ὅσον μὲν ἐκεῖθεν ἐκπορεύεται, οὐ κτίσμα. καθ᾽ ὅσον δὲ οὐ γεννητόν, οὐχ υἱός[EN149] (*Or.*, 31, 8), and also in the statement of the *Quicunque vult: Spiritus sanctus a Patre et Filio, non factus nec creatus nec genitus, sed procedens*[EN150].

But what does the term "procession," ἐκπόρευσις, mean here? It is neither chance nor carelessness that this term is one which in itself might well be applied to the origin of the Son from the Father, so that it does not specifically [475] denote the distinctiveness of the origin of the Holy Spirit, but strictly and properly says only that alongside the begetting of the Son or speaking of the Word the Holy Spirit has His own and "in some way" different "procession" in God. The peculiarity of this procession as compared with the first one might be denoted by the term "breathing," *spiratio*, though in the strict sense it could only be "denoted" thereby. For what is the difference between breathing and begetting if in the same unconditional way both are meant to denote the eternal genesis of an eternal mode of being of God? Would not any conceivable or expressible distinction entail a denial once again either of the deity or of the autonomy of the divine mode of being of the Holy Spirit? The difficulty which confronts us here is in fact insurmountable.

Distinguere inter illam generationem et hanc processionem nescio, non valeo, non sufficio[EN151]. (Augustine, *C. Maxim.* II, 14, 1). John of Damascus made a similar declaration (*Ekdos.* I, 8), and it was often repeated later. *Quo modo a generatione differat, explicabit nullus*[EN152]. (M. Leydecker, *De veritate rel. reform.*, 1688, 28, quoted from H. Heppe, *Dogm. der. ev. ref. Kirche*, 1861, 94); often with the warning: *istud discrimen tutius ignoratur quam inquiritur*[EN153] (so F. Turrettini, *Inst. Theol. el.* I, 1679, L. III, qu. 30, 3). And for good reason the Church has never defined the more precise meaning of the *processio*[EN154].

The feeling one involuntarily has here, that the difficulty which faces us at this point might have a significance that is more than accidental, and that goes beyond this particular question, is correct. Why are we unable to express the distinction between the begetting of the Son and the breathing of the Spirit even though—assuming again that our thinking is not leaving the soil of revelation but we are regarding the revealed God as the eternal God—we are forced to maintain it? The moment we measure what for the sake of definition we call the *spiratio Spiritus*[EN155] by what we call the *generatio Filii*[EN156], some-

---

[EN148] only-begotten
[EN149] insofar as he proceeds from God, he is not a creature; insofar as he is not begotten, he is not the Son
[EN150] The Holy Spirit is not made or created or begotten, but is proceeding from the Father and the Son
[EN151] I do not know how to distinguish begetting on the one hand from procession on the other: I lack the strength, I lack the power
[EN152] How it differs from begetting, no one can explain
[EN153] it is safer to remain in ignorance of this distinction than to investigate it
[EN154] procession
[EN155] breathing of the Spirit
[EN156] begetting of the Son

2. *The Eternal Spirit*

thing we established plainly in our discussion of that *generatio*^{EN157} obviously takes on clarity and force, namely, that the *generatio* or *loquutio*^{EN158}, too, is just an attempt to express what man cannot essentially express, what his language is unable to achieve. How is the Son of God begotten? How is His Word spoken? We do not know, either when we are speaking of the eternal reality or when we are speaking of the temporal reality which can be denoted by these metaphors, for both are only metaphors. Our knowledge can be only an acknowledgment of the fact. This is why we are now in difficulties when, in order to learn what *spiratio* is, we try to compare it to *generatio*.

Augustine (*loc. cit.*) gave a reason for his definite nescio. It was as follows: ... *quia et illa* (*generatio*) *et ista* (*processio*) *est ineffabilis*^{EN159}. In next to the last chapter of his work on the Trinity (*De trin.* XV, 27, 50) he did, of course, return to the question, and he now seems able to give, at least by indication, a positive answer. Using his well-known doctrine of the *imago trinitatis*^{EN160} in the human soul he proposes for consideration the possibility that the genesis of the Spirit might be related to that of the Son in the same way as will or love is to knowledge in the soul. The will proceeds from knowledge without being an image of knowledge (*voluntatem de cogitatione procedere—nemo enim vult, quod omnino quid vel quale sit nescit—non tamen esse cogitationis imaginem*^{EN161}). Similarly the Spirit from the Son! This suggestion was taken up and greatly expanded by Thomas Aquinas (*S. theol.* I, qu. 27, art. 3 and 4). The procession of the Holy Spirit is the *processio secundum rationem voluntatis*^{EN162} which is distinguished from the *processio secundum rationem intellectus*^{EN163} by the fact that it proceeds from this and is related to this, presupposing it. *Ideo quod procedit in divinis per modum amoris, non procedit ut genitum, vel ut filius, sed magis procedit ut spiritus*^{EN164} (*art.* 4c). Modern Roman Catholic dogmatics (cf., e.g., F. Diekamp, *Kath. Dogm.*⁶, Vol. I, 1930, 345 f.) seems to regard this explanation as a real answer to the question and so it does not make any further use of Augustine's *nescio*^{EN165}. On the other hand one should not forget that in relation to the suggestion, Augustine, unlike Thomas, did not fail to point out that the light which is thrown on the question by the *imago trinitatis* which we ourselves are, is always opposed by the *infirmitas*^{EN166} which our *iniquitas*^{EN167} has caused and only God can heal, so that he preferred to close his book *precatione quam disputatione*^{EN168}. We for our part were unable to accept the entire theory of the *imago trinitatis* and we are thus forced to say that we cannot regard the question about the Spirit as answered by it. As we have seen, the understanding of *generatio* as knowledge or of the Son as the Word of God, while it is true and significant, is an inadequate understanding, whose real import is hidden from us when we think we understand, or really do so to the best of our ability. Hence the related explanation of the Holy

[476]

---

^{EN157} begetting
^{EN158} speaking
^{EN159} ... because both the former (begetting) and the latter (procession) are ineffable
^{EN160} image of the Trinity
^{EN161} the will proceeds from knowledge – for no one wills that [about] which he does not know what or of what kind it is – but is not the image of knowledge
^{EN162} procession according to the structure of the will
^{EN163} procession according to the structure of knowing
^{EN164} Therefore what in the divine proceeds in the form of love does not proceed as begotten, like the Son, but rather proceeds as Spirit
^{EN165} I do not know
^{EN166} weakness
^{EN167} sinfulness
^{EN168} with prayer rather than argument

Ghost as the will which proceeds from knowledge cannot help us at all except by furnishing another and rather arbitrary analogy. It is better that the impossibility of making a distinction, which Augustine conceded in the first saying, should, remind us, if we have forgotten, that the *processio* of the Spirit and the Son may indeed be denoted but cannot be comprehended.

This means no more and no less than that we cannot establish the How of the divine processions and therefore of the divine modes of being. We cannot define the Father, the Son, and the Holy Ghost, i.e., we cannot delimit them the one from the other. We can only state that in revelation three who delimit themselves from one another are present, and if in our thinking we are not to go beyond revelation we must accept the fact that these three who delimit themselves from one another are antecedently a reality in God Himself. We can state the fact of the divine processions and modes of being. But all our attempts to state the How of this delimitation will prove to be impossible. In our hands even terms suggested to us by Holy Scripture will prove to be incapable of grasping what they are supposed to grasp. What has to be said will obviously be said definitively and exclusively by God Himself, by the three in the one God who delimit themselves from one another in revelation. Nor can there be any repetition of this by us, not even the repetition in which we are aware of our own inability, in which we are constantly referred to the truth of God beyond the totally questionable truth of our own thoughts and words. The *ignoramus*[EN169] which we must confess in relation to the distinction that [477] we have to maintain between begetting and breathing is thus the *ignoramus* which we must confess in relation to the whole doctrine of the Trinity, i.e., in relation to the mystery of revelation, in relation to the mystery of God in general. If we could define this distinction we could define the Son and the Spirit and then we could define the Father as well, and therewith God Himself. For God Himself is the Father, the Son, and the Spirit. Only if these were not God could we achieve a definition here, the kind of definition that is more than description of the fact that God Himself is there in His revelation. But what is there in God's revelation is the Father, the Son, and the Spirit. Hence there could be a successful definition of these three only on the assumption that the Father, the Son, and the Spirit are not God. Therefore for the sake of what the doctrine of the Trinity must state, namely, that the Father, the Son, and the Spirit are God, no more must be said at this point and no definition must result here. This is the general significance of the *qui procedit* in trinitarian theology.

Τίς οὖν ἡ ἐκπόρευσις; Εἰπὲ σὺ τὴν ἀγεννησίαν τοῦ πατρός, κἀγὼ τὴν γέννησιν τοῦ υἱοῦ φυσιολογήσω καὶ τὴν ἐκπόρευσιν τοῦ πνεύματος, καὶ παραπληκτίσωμεν ἄμφω εἰς θεοῦ μυστήρια παρακύπτοντες[EN170] (Gregory of Nazianzus, *Or.*, 31, 8).

[EN169] ignorance
[EN170] What then is the procession? You speak of the unbegottenness of the Father, and I will discuss the begetting of the Son and the procession of the Spirit, and we will both go mad prying into the mysteries of God

2. *The Eternal Spirit*

But according to the Latin text of the creed, which we follow here, the procession of the Holy Ghost is His procession from the Father and the Son (*ex Patre Filioque*).

The main point to be noted here is that the creed, which has ἐκ τοῦ πατρός EN171 in the original, is not involved in the dispute that, arose on this matter. It follows Jn. 15²⁶ in saving "from the Father," but without saying: "and not from the Son." It could not say this, for at the time, even among Greek theologians, there was no opposition to the material content of the addition. Thus, no less unconditionally than the addition, Epiphanius would say: πατὴρ ἦν ἀεί, καὶ τὸ πνεῦμα ἐκ πατρὸς καὶ υἱοῦ πνέει EN172 (*Ancoratus*, 75), or Ephraem: The Father is the Begetter, the Son the Begotten from the bosom of the Father, the Holy Ghost He that proceedeth from the Father and the Son (*Hymnus de defunctis et trinitate*, 11), and as late as the 5th century Cyril of Alexandria: τὸ πνεῦμα τὸ ἅγιον ... πρόεισι δὲ καὶ ἐκ πατρὸς καὶ υἱοῦ EN173 (*Thes. de trin.*, 34). Again the creed could not exclude the *Filioque* because it is hard to see against what heresy the exclusion could have been directed. The opponents at whom the clause is aimed are again the Macedonians, who denied the deity of the Holy Spirit, but who affirmed His procession from the Son too, although in an Arian sense, i.e., as the procession of a creature from a creature. By ruling out the ἐκ τοῦ υἱοῦ EN174 the creed would have conceded, in glaring contradiction to its second article, that ἐκ τοῦ υἱοῦ implies less than ἐκ τοῦ πατρός. Yet in this dispute with the Pneumatomachi the creed had also not to teach the *Filioque* explicitly. With a backward glance at the γεννηθέντα ἐκ τοῦ πατρός EN175 of the second article, it wanted to make the origin of the Spirit parallel to that of the Son as regards consubstantiality with the Father. This could be achieved by the ἐκ τοῦ πατρός but by this alone (for the opponents were confessing the ἐκ τοῦ υἱοῦ in their Arian fashion). We may conclude, then, that there was no necessary reason—the factual reason adduced is not a necessary one—why the *Filioque* should not have been in the original creed. [478]

The fact that the *Nic. Const* did not have for many centuries a sacrosanct character in the West, and even then not to the degree that this was very soon accorded to it in the East, provided the formal possibility for the acceptance of the *Filioque* first of all into the liturgical use of the creed (beginning, as far as is known, in the early 6th century in Spain), while the fact that in the West the trinitarian doctrine of Augustine increasingly established itself as an expression of the common insight served as the positive reason. Approval of this practice by the Roman Curia had to wait a full five centuries. Almost at the very time when a quarrel arose between Frankish and Greek monks in Jerusalem (808) over the singing of the *Filioque* in the Mass, and when Pope Leo III defended the legitimacy of the disputed addition, the same Pope at a synod in Rome (810) disapproved of its insertion into the creed, and he had expressed a wish to Charlemagne (809), who championed the *Filioque* at the Synod of Aachen, that its use should be discontinued in the royal chapel. The general trend of thought in the West was still against it. But as the opposition of the Eastern Church to the doctrine enshrined in the addition became clearer, i.e., as the material negation which is not in the creed, and cannot be explained by it, came to light, the *Filioque* found official endorsement. The creed which became an acknowledged part of the Roman Mass in 1014 contained it. It thus became a dogma of the Western Church. Yet even in negotiations for union in later centuries the popes (cf. expressly Benedict XIV in the Bull *Etsi pastoralis*, 1742) did

---

EN171 from the Father
EN172 the Father has always been, and the Spirit is breathed forth by the Father and the Son
EN173 the Holy Spirit ... goes forth from the Father and the Son
EN174 from the Son
EN175 begotten of the Father

not insist that what was for the Greeks an addition to the liturgical text should be treated as a *conditio sine qua non*[EN176] for the ending of the schism but only that the truth stated in the addition should be confessed. The Reformation in its trinitarian theology was also strongly enough orientated to Augustine to accept quite naturally and without further ado the general Western confession, so that implicitly or explicitly the expression became an integral part of the Evangelical confessional writings. Some in the older Protestant theology (e.g., J. Cocceius, *S. theol.* 1662, 12, 8) might occasionally judge that it had been a mistake for the Roman Church to alter the creed when Leo III had solemnly endorsed it in its ancient form—the business is not in fact a shining testimonial to the Roman Catholic theory of the certainty of the Church's teaching authority as concentrated in the hands of the pope. It might be declared (so Quenstedt, *Theol. did pol.*, 1685, I, *c.* 9, *sect.* 2, *qu.* 12, *object. dial.* 16) that in this matter the orthodox decision belongs *non ad fidem simplicem, sed ad peritiam theologicam*[EN177], so that what matters is that it should not be flatly rejected by anybody. Even more generously it could be explicitly stated (so F. Turrettini, *Inst. theol. el.*, I, 1679, L. III, *qu.* 31, 6) that the Greek view of the matter was not to be regarded as a heresy but the Western view was simply to be regarded as better. Both Lutheran and Reformed, however, were almost completely unanimous that materially we should accept this decision even though it was reached in so unusual a way, apart from either council or pope.

In this whole affair the battle has really been fought sharply and seriously only by the Eastern Church, while the Western Church has on the whole confined itself to the defensive. (Cf. in this regard the formula of the *Conc. Lugd.* II, 1274, *Denz.* No. 460: *Damnamus et reprobamus qui negare praesumpserint, aeternaliter Spiritum Sanctum ex Patre et Filio procedere*[EN178].) In this regard it should also be noted that strictly speaking sharp feelings and statements are found in the East only from the time of Photius (9th century), whose real interest in the schism was very different, and always primarily in the form of indignation at the unlawful and unloving way in which the West acted when it changed the creed. (Cf. in this regard the

[479] moving complaints of A. St. Chomjakow in *Östl. Christentum. Dokumente*, edited by H. Ehrenberg, Vol. 1, 156 f.) As for the significance of the conflict at any rate in modern Russian orthodoxy, we find on the one side—even if he is not to be taken too seriously—L. P. Karsavin, who somewhat obscurely makes the *Filioque* responsible for the doctrine of the immaculate conception and the papal infallibility, for Kantianism, for the belief in progress, and for many other evils in Western culture (*Östl. Christentum*. Vol. 2, 356 f.), and on the other side we find the Archimandrite Sylvester of Kiev, who at the time of the negotiations for union between the Orthodox and the Old Catholics was prepared to agree on historico-dogmatic grounds that the *Filioque*, in any possible sense, can be said only with regard to the *opus trinitatis ad extra*[EN179], but not the inner life of God (*Answer to the Note on the Holy Spirit contained in the Old Catholic Scheme*, 1875), and then the incomparably saner V. Bolotow of St. Petersburg, who did indeed take the view that the Augustinian *Filioque* was a private opinion which had been wrongly given the status of dogma, but who still regarded Sylvester's thesis as quite untenable, pointing out that there is no negation of the *Filioque* in the creed, and finally concluding that the whole question had not been the cause of division and could not constitute an *impedimentum dirimens*[EN180] to intercommunion between the Orthodox and Old Catholics ("*Thesen über das Filioque,*" *Revue intern, de théol.*, 1898, 681 f.). This final standpoint may be regarded as the prevailing view in Eastern Orthodoxy to-day.

[EN176] necessary condition
[EN177] not to simple faith, but to theological experience
[EN178] We condemn and reject those who presume to deny that the Holy Spirit proceeds eternally from the Father and the Son
[EN179] outward work of the Trinity
[EN180] church-dividing impediment

2. *The Eternal Spirit*

We have reasons for following the Western tradition as regards the *Filioque*, and since the East–West schism is now a fact and this is one of the issues—whether rightly or wrongly is another question—there is cause to give some account of the matter.

Fundamentally what has brought us to this side is no less than the whole thrust of our attempted understanding of the doctrine of the Holy Spirit and the Trinity generally. Even supporters of the Eastern view do not contest the fact that in the *opus ad extra*, and therefore in revelation (and then retrospectively in creation), the Holy Spirit is to be understood as the Spirit of both the Father and the Son. But we have consistently followed the rule, which we regard as basic, that statements about the divine modes of being antecedently in themselves cannot be different in content from those that are to be made about their reality in revelation. All our statements concerning what is called the immanent Trinity have been reached simply as confirmations or underlinings or, materially, as the indispensable premises of the economic Trinity. They neither could nor would say anything other than that we must abide by the distinction and unity of the modes of being in God as they encounter us according to the witness of Scripture in the reality of God in His revelation. The reality of God in His revelation cannot be bracketed by an "only," as though somewhere behind His revelation there stood another reality of God; the reality of God which encounters us in His revelation is His reality in all the depths of eternity. This is why we have to take it so seriously precisely in His revelation. In connexion with the specific doctrine of the Holy Spirit this means that He is the Spirit of both the Father and the Son not just in His work *ad extra*[EN181] and upon us, but that to all eternity—no limit or reservation is possible here—He is none other than the Spirit of both the Father and the Son. "And the Son" means that not merely for us, but in God Himself, there is no possibility of an opening and readiness and capacity for God in man—for this is the work of the Holy Ghost in revelation—unless it comes from Him, the Father, who has revealed Himself in His Word, in Jesus Christ, and also, and no less necessarily, from Him who is His Word, from His Son, from Jesus Christ, who reveals the Father. Jesus Christ as the Giver of the Holy Spirit is not without the Father from whom He, Jesus Christ, is. But the Father as the Giver of the Holy Spirit is also not without Jesus Christ to whom He Himself is the Father. The Eastern doctrine does not contest the fact that this is so in revelation. But it does not read off from revelation its statements about the being of God "antecedently in Himself." It does not stand by the order of the divine modes of being which by its own admission is valid in the sphere of revelation. It goes beyond revelation to achieve a very different picture of God "antecedently in Himself." We must object already at this point quite apart from the results. What gives us the right to take passages like Jn. 15²⁶, which speak of the procession of the Spirit from the Father, and isolate them from the many

---

[EN181] outward

others which equally plainly call Him the Spirit of the Son? Is it not much more natural to understand opposing statements like this as mutually complementary, as is freely done in the reality of revelation, and then to acknowledge the reality disclosed thereby as valid to all eternity, as the way it is in the essence of God Himself? For us the Eastern rejection of the *Filioque* is already suspect from the formal standpoint because it is patently a speculation which interprets individual verses of the Bible in isolation, because it bears no relation to the reality of God in revelation and for faith.

This formal defect, however, takes on at once material significance. The *Filioque* expresses recognition of the communion between the Father and the Son. The Holy Spirit is the love which is the essence of the relation between these two modes of being of God. And recognition of this communion is no other than recognition of the basis and confirmation of the communion between God and man as a divine, eternal truth, created in revelation by the Holy Spirit. The intradivine two-sided fellowship of the Spirit, which proceeds from the Father and the Son, is the basis of the fact that there is in revelation a fellowship in which not only is God there for man but in very truth—this is the *donum Spiritus sancti*[EN182]—man is also there for God. Conversely, in this fellowship in revelation which is created between God and man by the Holy Spirit there may be discerned the fellowship in God Himself, the eternal love of God: discerned as the mystery, surpassing all understanding, of the possibility of this reality of revelation; discerned as the one God in the mode of being of the Holy Spirit.

[481]   *Missio haec temporalis (Spiritus sancti) praesupponit aeternum illum Spiritus sancti (aeque a Filio atque Patre) processum estque eius declaratio et manifestatio*[EN183] (Quenstedt, *Theol. did. pol.*, 1685, I, *cap.* 9. *sect.* 2, qu. 12, *beb.* 3).

This whole insight and outlook is lost when the immanent *Filioque* is denied. If the Spirit is also the Spirit of the Son only in revelation and for faith, if He is only the Spirit of the Father in eternity, i.e., in His true and original reality, then the fellowship of the Spirit between God and man is without objective ground or content. Even though revealed and believed, it is a purely temporal truth with no eternal basis, so to speak, in itself. No matter, then, what we may have to say about the communion between God and man, it does not have in this case a guarantee in the communion between God the Father and God the Son as the eternal content of its temporal reality. Does not this mean an emptying of revelation?

It would be even worse if the denial of the *Filioque* were not restricted to the immanent Trinity but were also applied to the interpretation of revelation itself, if, then, the Holy Spirit were to be one-sidedly and exaggeratedly regarded as the Spirit of the Father even in His *opus ad extra.* We must be very

---

EN182 gift of the Holy Spirit
EN183 This temporal sending (of the Holy Spirit) presupposes the eternal procession of the Holy Spirit (equally from the Son and the Father) and is its declaration and manifestation

careful here, for this is theoretically contested. Yet we cannot avoid asking whether, if that denial, the exclusive *ex Patre* is to obtain as an eternal truth, it is not inevitable that the relation of God to man will be understood decisively from the standpoint of Creator and creature, and that it will thus acquire a more or less developed naturalistic and unethical character, so that the Mediator of revelation, the Son or Word, will be set aside as the basis and origin of the relation, and it will take on the nature of a direct and immediate relation, a mystical union with the *principium et fons Deitatis*[EN184].

The distinctively unrestrained manner of thought and utterance of the Russian theologians and religious philosophers as it is presented to us in Ehrenberg's documents, obliterating the frontiers of philosophy and theology, of reason and revelation, of Scripture, tradition and direct illumination, of spirit and nature, of *pistis* and *sophia*[EN185] (but also the distinction between the economic Trinity and the immanent Trinity), may not have anything to do with the omission of the *Filioque*, but even if not, one would still have to speak of a remarkable coincidence between this omission and these characteristics, which could be very readily understood as the results or the necessary parallels of this omission.

But be that as it may, in the Eastern view of the relation between the divine modes of being we cannot recognise their reality as we believe we know it from the divine revelation according to the witness of Scripture.

We do not recognise it even in the version in which it does indeed rule out the ἐκ τοῦ υἱοῦ but is prepared to accept a διὰ τοῦ υἱοῦ[EN186] as a possible interpretation of the ἐκ τοῦ πατρός. For even this διὰ τοῦ υἱοῦ does not lead, and according to the intent of Eastern theology it is not meant to lead, to that on which everything seems to us to depend, namely, to the thought of the full consubstantial fellowship between Father and Son as the essence of the Spirit, corresponding as a prototype to the fellowship between God as Father and man as His child the creation of which is the work of the Holy Spirit in revelation.

[482]

Διὰ τοῦ υἱοῦ, *per filium*, has on its side the usage of most of the Greek and Latin Fathers before the schism. Neither can it be contested that in so far as the Son Himself is the Son of the Father the procession of the Spirit from the Son may be finally traced back to the Father. The Latin Fathers never disputed this. Augustine himself declared unequivocally: *principaliter*[EN187] the Spirit proceeds from the Father, and the Son has it from the Father, *ut et de illo procedat Spiritus sanctus*[EN188] (*De trin.* XV, 26, 47; cf. 17, 29; *In Joann. tract.*, 99, 8). But Eastern teaching after the schism, and even the older Eastern teaching in so far as it was later construed in a schismatic sense, says more than this. It takes ἐκ τοῦ πατρός in the sense of ἐκ μόνου τοῦ πατρός[EN189] and hence it does not see in διὰ τοῦ υἱοῦ a direct procession of the Spirit from the Son on the presupposition of the begetting of the Son, but sees in it

---

[EN184] source and fount of Deity
[EN185] faith and wisdom
[EN186] through the Son
[EN187] originally
[EN188] so that the Holy Spirit also proceeds from him
[EN189] from the Father only

rather a continuation or extension or prolongation of the procession of the Spirit from the Father. It found classical expression in the metaphor of the three torches in Gregory of Nyssa, the second of which was lit from the first and the third from the second (*De Spir.*, s. 3). It is also expressed (according to Bolotow, *op. cit.*, p. 692) in another comparison, that of the Father to the mouth, the Son to the word, and the Spirit to the breath that gives sound to the word: to the degree that the breath is breathed out for the sake of the word, to the degree that the pronouncing of the word inevitably entails the breathing, the word is the logical prius of the breathing and to that degree διὰ τοῦ υἱοῦ is valid. But to the degree that the word does not produce the breath, the breath coming from the mouth and not the word, ἐκ τοῦ πατρός is true but not ἐκ τοῦ υἱοῦ. According to a saying of Athanasius (*Ad Serap.* I, 20) which is often quoted, the secondary derivation of the Spirit is not an ἐκπορεύεσθαι[EN190] but an ἐκλάμπειν παρὰ τοῦ λόγου τοῦ ἐκ πατρός[EN191]. According to this view of the διὰ τοῦ υἱοῦ begetting and breathing are thus presented "as a straight-line movement in which the second proceeds from the first" (M. J. Scheeben, *Handbuch der kath. Dogmatik*, new impr., 1925, Vol. I, 820). The Son is a mediating principle, the Father alone being αἰτία or principle in the strict sense of the word.

Though in itself διὰ τοῦ υἱοῦ goes without saying, it must obviously be rejected if interpreted in the above sense. And in opposition to this interpretation the adherence of the West to ἐκ τοῦ υἱοῦ seems both logical and necessary. Where διὰ τοῦ υἱοῦ is taken in such a way that it does in fact rule out a true derivation of the Spirit from the Son as well, this means that there is no *relatio originis*[EN192] between Son and Spirit, and that only improperly can the Spirit be called the Spirit of the Son, i.e., not in the way that the Son is called the Son of the Father. Furthermore, if the Son is not also the true origin the Spirit, the Father and the Son do not have all things in common, the one being the origin of the Spirit in a primary sense and the other only in a secondary sense. Even the unity of God the Father is called in question if implicitly He is not already the origin of the Spirit as the Father of the Son, the origin of the Spirit from Him being a second function along with His fatherhood. Finally and above all, the Spirit on this view loses His mediating position between the Father and the Son and the Father and the Son lose their mutual connexion in the Spirit.

[483]   Possibly an unsubdued remnant of Origenist Subordinationism may be regarded as one of the sources of error in the Eastern conception. But above all it is the unity of the Trinity which we must see to be endangered at every point by the denial of the *Filioque*. We have seen elsewhere that tritheism was always the special danger in Eastern theology and we cannot escape the impression that when the Trinity is constructed in such a way that the *Filioque* is denied the *trinitas in unitate*[EN193] is very perilously overemphasised as compared with the *unitas in trinitate*[EN194]. It was for the sake of the *unitas*[EN195] that the *Filioque* forced itself on Augustine and then carried the West. Our decisive reason for adhering to this view is to be found in the fact that only in this *unitas*, and not in the strange juxtaposition of Father and Son with respect to the Spirit which may be seen in the Eastern doctrine, do we have anything corresponding to the work of the Holy Spirit in revelation. If the rule holds good that God in His eternity is none other than the One who discloses Himself to us in His revelation, then in the one case as in the other the Holy Spirit is the Spirit of the love of the Father and the Son, and so *procedens ex Patre Filioque*[EN196].

[EN190] proceeding
[EN191] shining forth from the Word which is from the Father
[EN192] relation of origin
[EN193] Trinity in unity
[EN194] unity in Trinity
[EN195] unity
[EN196] proceeding from the Father and the Son

2. *The Eternal Spirit*

In accordance with what has been said, the positive meaning of the Western version of the dogma may be summarised as follows.

As God is in Himself Father from all eternity, He begets Himself as the Son from all eternity. As He is the Son from all eternity, He is begotten of Himself as the Father from all eternity. In this eternal begetting of Himself and being begotten of Himself, He posits Himself a third time as the Holy Spirit, i.e., as the love which unites Him in Himself. As He is the Father who begets the Son He brings forth the Spirit of love, for as He begets the Son, God already negates in Himself, from eternity, in His absolute simplicity, all loneliness, self-containment, or self-isolation. Also and precisely in Himself, from eternity, in His absolute simplicity, God is orientated to the Other, does not will to be without the Other, will have Himself only as He has Himself with the Other and indeed in the Other. He is the Father of the Son in such a way that with the Son He brings forth the Spirit, love, and is in Himself the Spirit, love. It is not, of course, to satisfy a law of love, nor because love is a reality even God must obey, that He must be the Father of the Son. The Son is the first in God and the Spirit is the second in God, that is, as God is the Father of the Son, and, as Father, begets the Son, He also brings forth the Spirit and therefore the negation of isolation, the law and the reality of love. Love is God, the supreme law and ultimate reality, because God is love and not *vice versa*. And God is love, love proceeds from Him as His love, as the Spirit He Himself is, because He posits Himself as the Father and therefore posits Himself as the Son. In the Son of His love, i.e., in the Son in and with whom He brings forth Himself as love, He then brings forth in the *opus ad extra* too, in creation, the creaturely reality which is distinct from Himself, and in revelation the reconciliation and peace of the creature that has fallen away from Him. The love which meets us in reconciliation, and then retrospectively in creation, is real love, supreme law and ultimate reality, because God is antecedently love in Himself: not just a supreme principle of the relation of separateness and fellowship, but love which even in fellowship wills and affirms and seeks and finds the other or Other in its distinction, and then in separateness wills and affirms and seeks and finds fellowship with it. Because God is antecedently love in Himself, love is and holds good as the reality of God in the work of reconciliation and in the work of creation. But He is love antecedently in Himself as He posits Himself as the Father of the Son. This is the explanation and proof of the *qui procedit ex Patre*[EN197].

[484]

But just because we explain and prove it thus, we must now continue that similarly, as God is the Son who comes forth from the Father, He brings forth the Spirit, He brings forth love. In this mode of being, too, He negates loneliness in His absolute simplicity; He is orientated to the Other; He does not will to be without the Other out of whom He is. How else could He be the Son but as the Son of the Father? How could He be less the origin of love in being the

---

[EN197] who proceeds from the Father

195

Son than in being the Father? Distinct as Father and Son, God is one in the fact that His distinction is that of the Father and the Son, so that it is not the kind of distinction which might also arise in a supreme principle of separateness and fellowship, a loveless distinction, but the distinction which affirms fellowship in separateness and separateness in fellowship. How, then, can the breathing of the Spirit belong less essentially, less properly and originally, to the Son than to the Father? In relation to the *opus ad extra* we must also ask: If it is true that God reveals Himself to us through His only-begotten Son, if it is also true that God's only-begotten Son is no less and no other than God the Father, if it is true again that God's revelation is also the revelation of His love, if revelation would not be revelation without the outpouring and impartation of the Spirit through whom man becomes the child of God, can it be that this Spirit is not directly the Spirit of the Son as well? Is it only indirectly, only derivatively, that the Son is here the Giver of the Spirit, of the revelation of love? But if He is this immediately and directly, how can this be if He is not so in reality, in the reality of God antecedently in Himself? If here, and already in creation when seen from here, love is God's reality in the Son and through the Son, we have no reason and no warrant to think beyond that which is valid here. It is also the love of the Son antecedently in Himself, in eternity. As the Son of the Father He, too, is thus *spirator Spiritus*[EN198]. He is this, of course, as the Son of the Father. To that extent the *per Filium*[EN199] is true. But here *per Filium* cannot mean *per causam instrumentalem*[EN200]. This Son of this Father is and has all that His Father is and has. He is and has it as the Son. But He is and has it. Thus He, too, is *spirator Spiritus*. He, too, has the possibility of being this. This is how we explain and prove the *qui procedit ex Patre Filioque*[EN201].

[485]   At this point it might be asked whether, to correspond with the procession of the Father from the Son, there should not also be asserted a procession of the Son from the Father and the Spirit. In favour of this one might on the one side argue exegetically that in more than one respect the work of the Holy Spirit in revelation is presented as a work of creating or begetting. In particular one might adduce the birth of the Spirit (Jn. 3[5f.]) which is a condition of seeing and entering the kingdom of God. If, one might ask, the children of God are born of the Spirit, might we not say something of the same regarding the Son of God too? And in fact is not something of the same said about the Son of God in revelation? In the story of the baptism of Jesus in the Jordan (Mk. 1[9f.] and par.), is not His divine sonship shown to be established by the Spirit alighting upon Him? Does not Rom. 1[3] also say that Jesus Christ was instituted the Son of God with power κατὰ πνεῦμα ἁγιωσύνης ἐξ ἀναστάσεως νεκρῶν[EN202]? And what are we to say especially about Lk. 1[35], where the angel's prophecy of the impending conception of the Virgin Mary contains the words: πνεῦμα ἅγιον ἐπελεύσεται ἐπὶ σέ, καὶ δύναμις ὑψίστου ἐπισκιάσει σοι, διὸ καὶ τὸ γεννώμενον ἅγιον

[EN198] breather of the Spirit
[EN199] through the Son
[EN200] through an instrumental cause
[EN201] who proceeds from the Father and the Son
[EN202] according to the spirit of holiness, by the resurrection from the dead

2. The Eternal Spirit

κληθήσεται υἱὸς θεοῦ[EN203] or Mt. 1 18, which says of Mary: εὑρέθη ἐν γαστρὶ ἔχουσα ἐκ πνεύματος ἁγίου[EN204], or Mt. 1 20, where we read: τὸ γὰρ ἐν αὐτῇ γεννηθὲν ἐκ πνεύματός ἐστιν ἁγίου[EN205]? If we apply at this point our rule that material dogmatic statements about the immanent Trinity can and must be taken from definitions of the modes of being of God in revelation, are we not compelled to accept a relationship of origin between the Spirit and Son which is neither begetting nor breathing but a third thing? And one might also wish to add that the circle of mutual relations in which God is one in three modes of being is only then closed and complete, and that already for this reason one should postulate an origin of the Son from both the Father and the Spirit.

This second, systematic argument may be dismissed at once. If the circle or *perichoresis* between the three modes of being of God had really to be a circle of mutual origins, and if it had to be complete as such, then an origin of the Father from the Son and from the Spirit would also have to be discovered. But the *perichoresis*, though it is complete and mutual, is not one of origins as such, but a *perichoresis* of the modes of being as modes of being of the one God. It is a further description of the *homoousia*[EN206] of Father, Son, and Spirit, but has nothing to do with begetting and breathing as such, and therefore needs no supplementation in this direction, so that the postulate cannot be said to have, formally, a legitimate basis.

It is more difficult to meet the first, exegetical objection. To do this we must note throughout that the work of the Holy Spirit in relation to the Son in revelation, to which all the passages refer, is not of such a kind that it can be described as commensurable with the eternal begetting of the Son by the Father or the eternal breathing of the Spirit by the Father and the Son. so that another eternal relation of origin can and should be read off from it. What the commensurability lacks is as follows. The begetting and breathing are a bringing forth from the essence of the Father, or of the Father and the Son, but not from another essence. But the bringing forth of the Holy Spirit described in the passages quoted is always a bringing forth from some other essence whose existence is presupposed. This may be seen very clearly in Jn. 3. Birth of the Spirit is a new birth, a regeneration, and the man to be born of the Spirit as a child of God is already there when this happens. He, this man, is born of the Spirit as a child of God. But one obviously cannot say that the child of God this man becomes is created or begotten by the Spirit. The child of God is what it is in fellowship with Jesus Christ, the eternal Son of God. The same applies to the story of the baptism in the Jordan, which is undoubtedly to be viewed as a parallel to the story of the Virgin Birth. It is this man Jesus of Nazareth, not the Son of God, who becomes the Son of God by the descent of the Spirit. Again the installation of Jesus Christ as the Son of God by the Holy Spirit in Rom. 1 is [486] expressly related to the resurrection. The ὁρισμός[EN207] is the exaltation and revelation of Him who was crucified and who died to the glory of the Son of God. It denotes the participation of the One hitherto called Jesus Christ according to His humanity, in the majesty of the eternal Son. This Son of God as such does not derive His being from this ὁρισμός, nor from the Holy Spirit. But the One called Jesus Christ according to His humanity derives it from the Holy Spirit that He should be the Son of God. The situation is much the same in the references to the Virgin Birth which also call for consideration here. The incarnation of the Word of God from Mary cannot consist in the fact that here and now the Son of God comes into being for the first time. It consists in the fact that here and now the Son of God takes to

---

[EN203] the Holy Ghost shall come upon thee, and the power of the Highest shall overshadow thee: therefore also that holy thing which shall be born of thee shall be called the Son of God
[EN204] she was found with child of the Holy Ghost
[EN205] for that which is conceived in her is of the Holy Ghost
[EN206] consubstantiality
[EN207] declaration

Himself that other which already exists in Mary, namely, flesh, humanity, human nature, being as man. Furthermore the dogma of the Virgin Birth does not in any sense imply that the Holy Spirit is the father of the man Jesus and thus becomes, in the incarnation of the Son of God, the Father of the Son of God as well, It tells us that the man Jesus has no father (just as He has no mother as the Son of God). What is ascribed to the Holy Spirit in the birth of Christ is the assumption of human existence in the Virgin Mary into unity with God in the mode of being of the Logos. That this is possible, that this other, this being as man, this flesh, is there for God, for fellowship and even unity with God, that flesh can be the Word when the Word becomes flesh, is the work of the Holy Spirit in the birth of Christ. This work of the Spirit is prototypal of the work of the Spirit in the coming into being of the children of God; in the same way, not directly but indirectly, *per adoptionem*[EN208], in faith in Christ, we become that which we are not by nature, namely, children of God. On the other hand, this work of the Spirit is not ectypal of a work of the Spirit on the Son of God Himself. What the Son "owes" to the Spirit in revelation is His being as man, the possibility of the flesh existing for Him, so that He, the Word, can become flesh. How could one derive from this that He owes His eternal sonship to the Spirit? He is the eternal Son of the essence of the eternal Father which is also His own, not by the assumption of another essence. Therefore what we may infer from these passages as regards understanding of the eternal Trinity has nothing whatever to do with an origin in God. It is rather a confirmation of what has been said already, namely, that as the Holy Spirit in revelation unites God and man. Creator and creature, the Holy One and sinners, so that they become Father and child, in the same way He is in Himself the communion, the love, which unites the Father to the Son and the Son to the Father.

With this explanation and proof, however, we have already said the final thing that has always been said, and must necessarily be said, in explanation of the Western view, namely, that the *ex Patre Filioque*[EN209] denotes, not a twofold, but rather a common origin of the Spirit from the Father and the Son. The fact that the Father is the Father and the Son the Son, that the former begets and the latter is begotten, is not common to them; in this respect they are different divine modes of being. But the fact that between them and from them, as God's third mode of being, is the Spirit, love—this they have in common. This third mode of being cannot result from the former alone, or the latter alone, or co-operation of the two, but only from their one being as God the Father and God the Son, who are not two "persons" either in themselves or [487] in co-operation, but two modes of being of the one being of God. Thus the one Godness of the Father and Son is, or the Father and the Son in their one Godness are, the origin of the Spirit. What is between them, what unites them, is, then, no mere relation. It is not exhausted in the truth of their being alongside and with one another. As an independent divine mode of being over against them, it is the active mutual orientation and interpenetration of love, because these two, the Father and the Son, are of one essence, and indeed of divine essence, because God's fatherhood and sonship as such must be related to one another in this active mutual orientation and interpenetration. That the Father and the Son are the one God is the reason why they are not just

---

[EN208] by adoption
[EN209] from the Father and the Son

united but are united in the Spirit in love; it is the reason, then, why God is love and love is God.

Tertius enim est Spiritus a Deo et Filio[EN210] (Tertullian, *Ad Prax.*, 8). In revelation it is true, says Augustine, that *Spiritus et Dei est qui dedit, et noster qui accepimus*[EN211]; it is true that the Spirit of God can also be called the spirit of Elijah, or the spirit of Moses, or the spirit of a man. This wonderful truth has its basis in God Himself in the fact that Father and Son (even if the Son from the Father and the Father *principaliter*[EN212]) are the *principium*[EN213] of the Holy Ghost: *Non dua principia, sed sicut Pater et Filius unus deus et ad creaturam relative unus creator et unus dominus, sic relative ad Spiritum sanctum unum principium.*[EN214] (*De trin.* XV, 14, 15). This unity of origin of the Spirit was given the status of a dogma at the *Conc. Lugd.* II, 1274: *Non tanquam ex duobus principiis, sed tanquam ex uno principio, non duabus spirationibus, sed unica spiratione procedit*[EN215] (*Denz.* No. 460). And the *Conc. Florent.* in 1439, adopting Augustine's exposition of the *per Filium* quoted earlier, added: *Quoniam omnia quae Patris sunt, Pater ipse unigenito Filio suo gignendo dedit praeter esse Patrem, hoc ipsum quod Spiritus sanctus procedit ex Filio, ipse Filius a Patre aeternaliter habet a quo etiam aeternaliter genitus est*[EN216]. In this sense, it was held, the *Filioque* was added to the creed *veritatis declarandae gratia et imminente necessitate*[EN217] (*Denz.* No. 691).

4. We believe in the Holy Ghost "who with the Father and the Son together is worshipped and glorified." This final clause of the creed to call for consideration here again defines the deity of the Holy Spirit. To some extent it links up with the first one. This said that as the Father and as the Son is the one Lord, so, too, is the Spirit. Now we read that as the one Lord is to be worshipped and glorified as Father and as Son, so He is also as Spirit. Note that the Latin text, by adding *simul*[EN218], rules out the tritheistic appearance which would not have been avoided by a mere *cum*[EN219] and is perhaps not altogether avoided by the Greek compounds. "With" here does not mean "alongside"—the divine modes of being are not alongside one another—but "together with" or "in and with," yet again not in such a way that the Spirit is a mere attribute or relation of the Father and the Son, but in such a way that one might equally well say of the Father or the Son or both that they are to be worshipped and glorified together with the Holy Ghost. The meaning, then, is "like" the Father and the Son.

[EN210] For the Spirit is a third from God and the Son
[EN211] that the Spirit is both God's who has given him and ours who have received him
[EN212] originally
[EN213] source
[EN214] They are not two sources, but just as the Father and the Son are one God and, relative to creation, one Creator and one Lord, so relative to the Holy Spirit they are one source
[EN215] He does not proceed from two sources, but from one source; nor from two breathings, but from a single breathing
[EN216] Because all things which are the Father's—excepting his identity as a father—the Father himself has given to the only-begotten Son in begetting him, this too: that the Holy Spirit proceeds from the Son, the Son himself has from the Father eternally, by whom he is also eternally begotten
[EN217] for the purpose of declaring the truth and by imminent necessity
[EN218] together with
[EN219] with

§ 12. *God the Holy Spirit*

One may compare the *Gloria Patri et Filio et Spiritui sancto*[EN220] in the Roman Mass or the Evangelical liturgy, or Luther's hymn to the Trinity:

> "We believe in Holy Ghost,
> God with Father and the Son ..."

or the third stanza of M. Rinckart's "Now thank we all our God":

> "All praise and thanks to God,
> The Father now be given.
> The Son and Him who reigns
> With them in highest heaven ... "

What is obviously stressed here is the deity of the Spirit as it must now be established from the human standpoint. One might ask why the emphasis should be made in a phrase with a liturgical character as it were? Why does it not say, who with the Father and the Son is to be believed in or to be loved? Whatever the historical explanation may be, we must say at least that the reference does in fact carry with it a twofold safeguard in this particular form. By being denoted as object of worship (*proskynesis*) and glorification the $\pi\nu\epsilon\hat{\nu}\mu\alpha$, which is, abstractly considered, neuter, is brought into relation to the personality of God as this is denoted by the terms $\pi\alpha\tau\acute{\eta}\rho$[EN221] and $\upsilon\acute{\iota}\acute{o}\varsigma$[EN222]. Not intrinsically—the same applies to the Father and the Son as well—but by identity with the one God, the Spirit, too, is not a neuter, an It, but a He, the great, original, incomparable He, over whom man has no power but who has all power over man. And by being denoted object of worship and glorification the Spirit, who in revelation is the Spirit of God and man (*Spiritus Dei et noster*), the consummation of the fellowship between God and man, is again very emphatically withdrawn from man's sphere. He dwells in us and there is a being of man in the Spirit, but this must not leave us even for a moment under any illusion as to the fact that the qualitative and not just quantitative distinction between God and man is not abrogated even or especially in revelation, but that it is rather established in revelation, this distinction being the presupposition of fellowship between God and man. The Holy Spirit, in distinction from all created spirits, is the Spirit who is and remains and always becomes anew transcendent over man even when immanent in him. Worship and glorification mean approach to Him on the presupposition and in observance of distance from Him, not just any distance, not the cold mathematical distance of the finite from the infinite, but the distance of man as creature from God as Creator, of man as sinner from God as Judge, of man as pardoned from God as the One who is freely and causelessly merciful. Hence *proskynesis*, glory to God in the highest! Nowhere is there more obvious danger of confusing the subject

---

[EN220] Glory be to the Father and to the Son and to the Holy Spirit
[EN221] Father
[EN222] Son

and object of faith or love than in relation to this third mode of God's being in revelation. But all such confusion is ruled out by the clause: "Who with the Father and the Son together is worshipped and glorified." This gift, the *donum Spiritus sancti*, refuses to be abstracted from its Giver. But the Giver is God. We can have the gift only when and as we have God. At this point we may simply refer again to the significance of this particular clause for the whole doctrine of the operations of the Spirit, and especially for the whole doctrine of faith. One would think a blind man would have to see here that if man's presence at God's revelation, the *Deus in nobis*[EN223], is to be stated with real content, it can be understood only from the standpoint of the divine Subject, of the Subject who cannot be set aside as such. Even and especially the doctrine of the *gratia Spiritus sancti applicatrix*[EN224] cannot lead to an independent anthropology. Justification and sanctification are acts of this divine Subject precisely as this Subject makes Himself ours. He makes Himself ours as the *Spiritus sanctus, qui cum Patre et Filio simul adoratur et conglorificatur*[EN225]. Thus and not otherwise He becomes our salvation. We have had this clause constantly before us in all that has had to be said about the appropriation of grace and salvation in our discussions thus far, and we shall have to keep it before us in the future. Hence we hardly need to give it special emphasis again at this juncture.

[489]

One can hardly conclude an exposition of God's triunity in any better way than Augustine did at the end of his work on this subject (*De trin.* XV, 28, 51). There he declares again in simple terms that he believes in God the Father, Son and Holy Spirit because God has revealed Himself thus in Scripture. The "Truth" would not have expressed itself in this way *nisi trinitas esses. Ad hanc regulam fidei dirigens intentionem meam, quantum potui, quantum me posse dedisti, quaesivi te, et desideravi intellectu videre quod credidi et multum disputavi et laboravi*[EN226]. And now he finds himself constrained to pray: *Libera me, Deus, a multiloquio quod patior intus in anima mea, misera in conspectu tuo et confugiente ad misericordiam tuam*[EN227]. He knows how hazardous is not just what he says but also what he thinks. Hence he prays that he may not grow hard or sleepy in what he has said or thought in what is only man's much-speaking. He realises that only God Himself can be the consummation of what man thinks and speaks about Him. R. Seeberg (*Lehrb. d. Dogmengesch.*, Vol. 2, 1923, 163) concludes from these words of Augustine that at the end he was worried about the "fulness of visions." Now that might very well be. There are theologies whose authors have no need to be worried at the end, since for good reasons the "fulness of visions" has been spared them. Augustine was not in this happy position. He had run the risk and the "fulness of visions" had in fact come upon him. When this risk is run, one may come to grief. And a theologian who runs the risk

---

[EN223] God in us

[EN224] enabling grace of the Holy Spirit

[EN225] the Holy Spirit, who together with the Father and the Son is worshipped and glorified

[EN226] unless you were the Trinity. Directing my understanding to this rule of faith, as much as I have been able, as much as you have made me able, I have sought you, and I have desired to see in my understanding what I have believed, and to this end I have engaged in much debate and effort

[EN227] Free me, God, from the wordiness which afflicts me in my soul and which, wretched in your sight, flees to your mercy

may not only come to grief himself but also bring destruction on others. This explains Augustine's final prayer and also the closing words of the book: *Dominus Deus une, Deus Trinitas, quaecumque dixi in his libris de tuo, agnoscant et tui: si qua de meo, et tu ignosce, et tui. Amen* [EN228].

[EN228] My one Lord God, Triune God, whatever of yours I have written in these books, may those who are yours acknowledge; if [there is] anything of mine, may both you and yours take no notice [of it]. Amen

INDEX OF SCRIPTURE REFERENCES

INDEX OF SUBJECTS

human beings
  consciousness of   43, 47, 48, 51
  Holy Spirit received by   172
  as pardoned sinners   154
  Trinity in soul of   42–3
  triunity of   40

Idealism   33
incarnation   134–5
inheritance   173

Jesus Christ
  antecedently God in Himself   129–30
  baptism of   19, 69, 196–7
  as begotten, not made   136, 138–42,
    195
  crucifixion of   24–5
  deity of   109–13, 119, 122–3, 126,
    128–31, 136, 143, 155
  divine sonship of   91–3, 119–20, 132–4,
    167, 173
  as Eternal Son   121–56
  freedom by   166–7
  God incarnated as   134–5
  God revealing self in   25–6, 113–15
  God's relation to   101–2, 141
  Holy Spirit and proclamation/speaking
    of   164–5
  Holy Spirit differentiated from   185
  Holy Spirit's relation to   102–4
  humanity of   138
  Jews rejecting   24
  as Kyrios   91–2, 107
  as light of light   136–8
  lordship of   92–3, 113, 119, 132
  as Mediator   106, 151
  name of   107
  as one substance/essence with
    Father   147–51, 153
  power of God in   156
  as Reconciler   104, 123, 134, 138, 155
  reconciliation through   133–4
  as Revealer   97, 113, 119–20, 122–3,
    134, 138, 140, 156, 177
  revelation through   133–4
  titles of   108
  for us   132
  as very God of very God   136, 137
  by whom all things were made   151–6
  as Word of God   143–5, 187
  Word of God revealed through   28

justification   154
  deity of Jesus Christ and   126
  by faith alone   125–6, 178
  Reformation and   178
  revelation and   125–6

knowledge
  of God through self-revealing   7–8
  non-knowing   141
  of unity of God   59–60
Kyrios   91–2, 107

language
  revelation and   44–6, 50
  vestigia trinitatis and   50
legend   32
Liberal Protestantism   131
Linguistic problem   50
Lord's Prayer   24
love   195–6, 199

metaphysics   130
Modalism   89, 105, 177, 178
Modalist Monarchism   58
Modernist Protestantism   9, 16, 86,
    123, 172
modes of being   66–71, 74, 77,
    79–80, 82, 101, 117, 136, 180,
    188, 197
monotheism   56–7, 59
mystery
  Trinity as   9, 75
  of Word of God   128
mysticism   28
myth   32–5

natural theology   8
Neo-Platonism   84
Neo-Protestant theology   64
Nicaeno-Constantinopolitan Creed   178,
    189–90
Nicene Creed   177

pantheism   8
Patripassianism   105
Pentecost   36, 37, 53, 88
perichoresis   77–8, 103–4, 197
Pietism   28, 85, 102
pneumatology   17
Pneumatomachi   58
polytheism   8

Trinity (*Cont'd*)
  "personality" in 64–5
  "person" in 56, 58, 61–7, 73–4, 180
  in religion 47
  revelation and 15–18, 37, 65, 87–8
  Roman Catholic doctrine of 65
  roots of doctrine of 9–38, 40, 47, 53–4
  speaking about 45–6
  Subordinationism rejected by doctrine
    of 88–9
  tritheism and 64, 66
  in unity 59–75
  unity in 53–9, 78–9
  unity of God and 56–7
  vestigium trinitatis 38–52
tritheism 64, 66, 82, 199
triunity 72, 75–90
  defining 75–6
  doctrine of appropriations and 80–2
  of God 8, 20, 48, 53, 77, 103, 201
  of man 40
  modes of being and 77
  revelation and 8, 20

vestigium trinitatis 38–52, 71, 80
  in culture 41
  in history 41–2, 48
  in nature 41
  in religion 42
Virgin Birth 197–8
vital forces 58
vocation 35
volition 43

Whitsunday 69
Word of God
  Church proclamation and 10
  as epitome of revelation 146
  forms of 10
  Holy Scripture and 10
  Holy Spirit differentiated from 185
  Jesus Christ as 143–5, 187
  Jesus Christ revealing 28
  as light of light 145
  mystery of 128
  revelation and 10, 153–4
  as very God of very God 145

INDEX OF NAMES

Made in the USA
San Bernardino, CA
29 May 2020